Studying Congregations

Studying Congregations

A NEW HANDBOOK

EDITED BY NANCY T. AMMERMAN, JACKSON W. CARROLL, CARL S. DUDLEY, AND WILLIAM McKINNEY

AUTHORS: NANCY T. AMMERMAN, JACKSON W. CARROLL, CARL S. DUDLEY, NANCY L. EIESLAND, WILLIAM McKINNEY, ROBERT L. SCHREITER, SCOTT L. THUMMA, AND R. STEPHEN WARNER

Abingdon Press
Nashville

STUDYING CONGREGATIONS

Copyright © 1998 by Abingdon Press

This book is printed on acid-free paper.

Library of Congress Cataloging-in-Publication Data

Studying congregations : a new handbook / edited by Nancy T. Ammerman . . . [et al.].
    p.   cm.
    Includes bibliographical references and index.
    ISBN 0-687-00651-1 (pbk. : alk. paper)
    1. Parishes—United States.   2. Church management—United States.   3. Sociology, Christian—United States.   I. Ammerman, Nancy Tatom, 1950–   .
BV700.S78   1998
250—dc21   98-18487
                                                                                                            CIP

ISBN 13: 978-0-687-00651-9

11 12 13 14 15—20 19 18

MANUFACTURED IN THE UNITED STATES OF AMERICA

Contents

Introduction

AN INVITATION TO CONGREGATIONAL STUDY

This book begins with the assertion that congregations are important. For most people in the United States, in fact, congregations are at the heart of individual and collective religious history. Any student who is curious about how ordinary people experience their religion would do well to begin his or her exploration in the gathered communities that have formed the bedrock of American religion.[1]

Indeed, it is difficult to tell the story of this country's history without reference to the voluntary coming together of the Puritans of the Massachusetts Bay Colony, the Baptists of Rhode Island, the Anglicans of Virginia, the Quakers of Pennsylvania, the Roman Catholics of Maryland, the Methodists and Disciples of the frontier, the Mormons and their long trek toward religious liberty in Utah, newly freed Blacks forming independent denominations and congregations after the Civil War, and Catholic parishes rising in the burgeoning cities of the nineteenth century.

The story of the congregation is not simply an American story, however. The impulse to congregate is present in virtually all the world's living religious traditions. In other times and places, people have gathered in other ways, including state-supported regional cathedrals; set-apart monasteries; national organizations for missions, publishing, and other special purposes; as well as around the hearth for home-based private devotionals. But the fact that most religious participation in this country is voluntary, not legally obligatory; collective, not individualized; and popular, not the preserve of an elite, has meant that American people of faith have tended to organize themselves into congregations.

The congregational form—local, voluntary, lay-led, religious assemblies—is an ancient and hallowed norm in the Baptist, Jewish, and Congregational traditions, but over the history of the United States and for various reasons, it has been adopted into the polity of other traditions. Indeed, a pattern of de facto congregationalism, the unofficial yet persistent adoption of congregational forms, is increasingly prevalent, even in traditions such as the Presbyterian, Methodist, and Episcopal, where it is not the official norm.[2] Even the U.S. Roman Catholic church has seen its geographic parish system altered by the assertion of lay people's right to attend the (Catholic) church of their choice.[3] Non-Christian groups newer to the United States have also adopted congregational forms—founding membership-based, legally incorporated, nonprofit organizations that employ religious professionals—to meet their needs in this country.[4] Indeed, it is very likely that the freedom to worship with like-minded others offered by American norms of congregational practice is one of the reasons for the comparatively robust presence of institutional religion in the United States today.

Congregations are, we believe, essential to the religious health of the United States and central to the religious well-being of a very large portion of this country's population. *The Yearbook of American and Canadian Churches* reports some 350,000 local communities of faith in the United States alone, with almost 135 million members and an average weekly attendance in excess of 65 million adults. More individuals belong to congregations than to any other voluntary association, and they provide as much financial support for the work of their religious communities as is given to all other philanthropic causes combined.

Congregations influence in varied ways both the individuals who belong to them and the communities in which they are present.[5] They have rightly been described as generators of "social capital." They provide critical opportunities for gathering, communities of friendship and mutual support, spaces in which people can give voice to their discontents, and organizations through which they can mobilize for action. By the very presence of their buildings, their steeples and stained glass, they call people beyond themselves. Through educational programs, congregations not only transmit knowledge of the faith tradition and its meaning for contemporary life but also transmit values that promote community solidarity and continuity. Historically, congregations have socialized youth and newcomers, sustained people in need, and provided various rites of passage that mark significant life transitions: birth, adolescence, marriage, and death. They have often supported community values and institutions, but at times they have also challenged those values and institutions in an effort to reform or transform them in light of the congregation's convictions. Thus congregations have significance not only for the individuals who belong to them but also for the society beyond their membership. They contribute to the sustenance and uplifting of their communities and play an irreplaceable role in the moral education of children and adult members.

Beyond the numbers, the history, and their community contributions, congregations are also important for their purely religious significance. Few, if any, religious traditions see gathering as irrelevant, but some have especially emphasized the importance of the community as the place where God is worshiped and Scripture read and taught, as signs of God's presence in the world. Christian historian Martin Marty asserts, "While efforts to establish an essential form of communal life for Christians everywhere may be futile and may limit imagination, *something like* the local assembly will remain fundamental.... [Congregations] will take on varied colorings in different times or cultures, but in every case they serve to perpetuate embodiment, which is essential in the whole church."[6] Those who care about religious people and religious traditions would do well to understand these lively gatherings called congregations.

Still, not all that congregations do is unambiguously praiseworthy. They can hurt the people in them and cause harm to the social fabric of their communities. Whether we approach them out of scholarly curiosity or out of concern for their religious thriving, it is important to acknowledge their weaknesses, as well as their strengths. For instance, congregations can often contribute as much to divisions within society as to their healing. The voluntary nature of congregations, the extent to which a congregation is composed of people who have chosen to be together, lends itself to social exclusiveness. Birds of a feather flock together. Thus we get congregations of the well-to-do and congregations of the poor, congregations of Irish and of Germans, those of English speakers and those of Korean speakers, and, most notorious of all, those of Whites and those of Blacks, reinforcing the mutual suspicions and prejudice and the already high walls between racial communities. For that reason, theologians have often found the congregational principle itself to be ethically suspect. Yet it is deeply embedded in American ways of life. Accordingly, the

American landscape today is dotted with congregations of Swedish Lutherans, Korean Presbyterians, Puerto Rican Pentecostals, Polish Catholics, Sephardic Jews, Thai Buddhists, and Indo-Pakistani Muslims, to name only a few. Establishing a congregation's unique balance between gathering with one's own and remaining connected to a larger, more diverse community is at the heart of what it means to congregate. It is also a dilemma that can easily lead to unhealthy exclusion and conflict.

This book attempts to take congregations seriously. We celebrate the importance of congregations to religious life, and we remain aware of the dangers and pain that are present in any human gathering, religious or otherwise. We invite the reader to think carefully about the nature of congregational life and to enter into the fascinating world of traditions and texts, stories and social hours, committees and ministries that are formed as people of all faiths gather into enduring local communities called congregations.

An Invitation to Whom?

This book is an invitation to engage in a systematic look at congregational life. As such, it is directed to a number of audiences. It is an invitation, for instance, to scholars—historians, sociologists, anthropologists, and others—to think of congregations as places where religious life can be studied, where human efforts at giving order and meaning to life can be understood, and where the practices of human community can be examined. For such people, this book will be read alongside other books that provide the methodological rigor necessary in each discipline and the theoretical nuance that will place these findings in broader disciplinary frames of interpretation.

This book is also an invitation to theologians. What happens in congregations is theological. People of faith, gathered in congregations, work every day to make sense of their lives and to devise ways of relating to the divine powers that lie within and beyond them.

That work deserves to be taken into account in the thinking of theologians whose primary community is the academy. Theologians who come to the study of congregations will do so with their own methods and disciplines, but by taking seriously the everyday work of congregations, their work can be enhanced.

Most importantly, perhaps, this is also an invitation to people who inhabit and lead congregations to take their own habitat seriously. Many who read this book will be looking for immediate help with a specific effort, including seminary students who have been assigned to study a congregation, doctor of ministry students who need to think about how to design an effective project, pastors who have just come to a new congregation, leaders of immigrant religious groups trying to understand religious life in the United States, and consultants and denominational leaders called in to resolve a conflict. This book is an invitation to move beyond checklists and formulas, beyond the technical fixes to a deeper understanding of the dynamic life that animates each individual congregation. It is to you who work with and care about congregations that this book is most directly addressed.

This is also an invitation to all those who engage in the study of congregations to do so with great humility and care.[7] Our object of study is, after all, a human community filled with people whose lives must be treated with respect. What is said to a researcher in confidence must be protected, even when that researcher is a fellow member of the congregation. In addition, what has been kept private so as to allow the community to get along must be handled with utmost care when it becomes public knowledge in the course of a congregational inquiry. Some private knowledge needs to be made public in order for healing to occur—one thinks especially of patterns of abuse, sexual and otherwise—but no one should assume that even such a healthy alteration in a congregation's pattern of life does not have consequences. Indeed, the very act of asking questions, of systematically observing, will change the congregation's life—even when there are no skeletons to be exposed. Every congregation ought to have a fully informed opportunity to give its consent to the study process.

More even than giving their consent to be studied, congregations ought to have the opportunity to participate as partners in the study. Congregations can help to formulate the questions to be addressed and identify the best sources of information. They can also offer ways of interpreting that information that might never occur to an outsider or an academic. Those "native categories" will often challenge the interpretive schemes scholars of all sorts bring to the study of a congregation. Just when you think you have a congregation pegged, they manage to elude your efforts at definition. No student of a congregation can ever presume to have captured its essence. That essence is constantly changing, and the wise student will find ways to work alongside those she or he is studying, offering interpretations and definitions with humility in the face of the complex reality that is a congregation.[8]

One of the most critical reasons for working collaboratively to study a congregation is that such study is likely to be part of a process of change, change about which the congregation should be intentional. As we have already noted, the very act of engaging in study will produce change. No one should embark on such a study assuming otherwise. But often congregations undertake a study as a prelude to *seeking* some sort of change. Most likely, change is sought because the congregation has reached some sort of turning point: new growth has challenged old patterns, a bequest has presented the congregation with unexpected opportunities, old programming seems suddenly stale, or a leaky roof appears as the harbinger of more repair to come. Clearly, leading a congregation toward change is best accomplished when everyone takes seriously and appreciatively the need for a disciplined understanding of the present reality of the congregation. It is important to begin with a clear picture of where you are. But that understanding is best achieved when the congregation and its leaders are working in concert to discover what they need to know in order to move ahead.

Such a study conducted in partnership can reveal the strengths on which the congregation can build, the symbols that can inspire new initiatives, and the stories that can be reclaimed for new purposes—as well as the ideas, activities, and processes that may stand in the way of change. Precisely because a good congregational study will reveal both strengths and weaknesses, the commitment to engage in such a study implies a commitment to address the patterns and habits it reveals. When you discover strengths and resources, they can be enhanced. When you discover failings, they can be addressed. The commitment to study the congregation should also be a commitment to engage its possible futures, and both those commitments are best made with as broad a consensus as possible.

An Invitation to What?

This book is an invitation to disciplined study of the congregation. In the broadest sense, everyone does research, of course. That is, everyone gathers information, tests it against experience, and responds to the information gathered in a way that seems appropriate. In the congregation, religious leaders gather impressions and insights from the people with whom they talk and the materials they read, from their observations of group activities, and from observing patterns of participation and community trends. Members are constantly studying the congregation, whether they are casually recognizing the building or reflecting on intimate experiences of personal care or communal celebration. We cannot escape the constant experience of gathering and sorting out information as a basis for acting.

But there come times when this routine information processing is inadequate. In such times, we become self-conscious and disciplined in the ways we gather information, test the information against experience, and determine how we will act. This book addresses these occasions.

The study we call for is disciplined in the ways information is both gathered and interpreted. Throughout the book, and especially in the chapter on methods, we invite you to gather information in systematic ways that will take you beyond intuitive awareness or haphazard investigation. While acknowledging that congregational leaders and members daily learn by highly informal means much of value about their congregation, this book strongly advocates that you pay careful attention to what you need to know, who can best give you that information, and what activities most need careful observation. We invite you to think about whose stories are represented and whose are missing in what you are hearing, to work more diligently at how you watch and listen to what goes on around you, and to undertake disciplined efforts at taking notes and keeping records. As you plan your congregational study, pay careful attention to the hints and cautions contained in the chapter on methods at the end of this book. Keep in mind throughout your study that seeing your congregation in new ways will require that you systematically seek new places from which to observe.

Engaging in a disciplined congregational study will require, for instance, a balance and sense of proportion often absent from the spontaneous self-descriptions of congregations. The extreme actions of a congregation's severest critics and most enthusiastic promoters, and especially the colorful language such people are wont to use, are far more noticeable and memorable than the regular patterns of behavior and moderate opinions of the majority of members. Small groups with strong views can, of course, be powerfully influential in a congregation. A carefully conducted study, however, can give less vocal members their legitimate voice.

A disciplined congregational study should also look for the structures or patterns that lie beneath multiple, seemingly unrelated, issues. Even when it is not troubled but rather is facing the happy prospect of having to choose among several opportunities for program and service, a congregation can benefit from a systematic review of its past successes and failures, illumination of its values, and mapping of

the styles of behavior that hold it together. It is patterns and regularities discovered through disciplined study that make such insight possible.

A disciplined congregational study must keep open the possibility that it will reveal what a congregation does not want to see. For example, an analysis of the social class or racial/ethnic profile of congregational members, when compared with that of the local community, may reveal that patterns of bonding are along class or racial lines, contradicting the members' professions of inclusiveness. An analysis of decision-making patterns may reveal considerable frustration with the essentially authoritarian and top-down style of the religious professional or key lay officials. Although such revelations may be painful, seeing the patterns enables the congregation to deal with them in a constructive fashion.

Finally, remember that a disciplined study also has a public character. Informal, intuitive, and usually unsystematic ways of finding out about a congregation are almost always private and personal exercises. At most these exercises are collections of individual responses, perhaps most typically gleaned at an informal gathering around the kitchen table. By contrast, congregational studies open the quest for congregational self-understanding to corporate participation. Because such studies are regulated by an established order of inquiry, a discipline for gathering information, and a set of rules for organizing and interpreting evidence, any interested member can review the data and audit the process by which conclusions were drawn and judgments rendered. Thus, through disciplined study, your congregation has access to a procedure conducted in broad daylight; whatever such study reveals is the shared property of the community itself.

The methods and resources we suggest in the following pages provide, therefore, a more disciplined and thorough process of accomplishing, at turning points in your congregation's life, what may be done naturally but more casually in other circumstances. The data you gather, interpret, and reflect upon provide the basis for affirming old or determining new directions of your congregation's ministry and mission.

Comparing Notes

Whenever people take the time for a disciplined look at their own activities, there is an irresistible urge to compare. How is our congregation like others? How is it unique? Does everyone have this problem? Fortunately, such comparison is now much more possible. Studying congregations is no longer the novel activity it was in an earlier era. When the predecessor to this book, the *Handbook for Congregational Studies,* was published in 1987, its authors were part of a larger movement calling for scholars and religious leaders alike to give greater attention to congregations. At that time, historians could write religious history, theologians write systematic theology, and seminary professors train ministers with little attention to the work of actual congregations. Even national denominational organizations could carry on the "work of the church" with mainly national and international goals in mind. Since the *Handbook* was published there has been a major change in the attention given to congregations by both scholarly and religious communities.

Congregations have certainly been rediscovered by American religious bodies at the national and regional levels. Religious leaders have increasingly directed their efforts toward local ministries and supporting the efforts of local congregations. There has also been tremendous growth among independent organizations that serve congregations through programs of research, education, consulting, and publication. Some are independent, ecumenical, nonprofit organizations, sometimes associated with an individual leader, such as the Alban Institute (founded by Loren Mead and now directed by James Wind), the Yokefellow Institute (Lyle Schaller), National Evangelistic Association (Herb Miller), and the Center for Parish Development (Paul and Inagrace Dietterich). Others are affiliated with universities or theological schools, such as the Cushwa Center for American Catholicism at Notre Dame, the Cohen Center for Modern Jewish Studies at Brandeis, the Ormond Center at Duke, the Ratner Center at Jewish Theological Seminary, the Institute for Church Growth at Fuller Theological Seminary, and Hartford Seminary's Center for Social and Religious Research. Still others, such as the Willow Creek Association, are networks of church leaders drawn together around a prominent congregation's model for ministry, while groups such as the Leadership Network provide high-tech pooling of resources among local congregational leaders. It is clear that local congregations have attracted the attention of all sorts of groups eager to study them and supply their needs.

In addition, there is now a burgeoning research literature on congregations. The Lilly Endowment, an Indianapolis-based family foundation, has been an important factor in bringing congregations to the attention of scholars and the public. It has supported several large-scale research projects that have led to publication of books such as the multi-volume collections, *The American Catholic Parish,* edited by Jay P. Dolan,[9] and *American Congregations,* edited by James P. Wind and James M. Lewis.[10] Early social scientific studies of individual congregations, such as Melvin Williams's *Community in a Black Pentecostal Church*[11] and Samuel Heilman's *Synagogue Life,*[12] have been joined by Nancy Ammerman's *Bible Believers,*[13] Stephen Warner's *New Wine in Old Wineskins,*[14] Lynn Davidman's *Tradition in a Rootless World,*[15] and a variety of others. These books have provided readers with a window on the heretofore private life of Baptist fundamentalist, evangelical Presbyterian, African American Pentecostal, and Orthodox Jewish congregations. Congregations have also received attention from journalists in the 1990s with the publication of *Upon This Rock* by Samuel Freedman,[16] *And They Shall Be My People* by Paul Wilkes,[17] and *Congregation* by Gary Dorsey.[18] This is only a tiny sampling of the work that has been and is being done by scholars and others who have discovered how much can be learned about religious life by paying attention to congregations.

Readers of this book are strongly encouraged to seek out these and other studies of congregations, looking for information about both groups apparently like their own and those clearly different. Such books and articles can offer methodological hints and insights that come through comparison. To get you started in that process, this book will introduce you to a number of congregations about which you may want to learn more. Examples from their histories will be offered as we seek to put flesh and bones on various ideas about congregational life. Among those you will encounter:

- *St. Paul Community Baptist Church* is an African American church in East New York (Brooklyn). Its pastor, Johnny Ray Youngblood, has helped this growing and activist congregation to address the vast human needs of its community. Their story is told in full in *Upon This Rock.*

- *Mendocino Presbyterian Church* is on the other side of the country and, being in a trendy California small town, dramatically different in racial and economic composition from St. Paul. Its transformation in the 1970s from a staid, moderate Presbyterian congregation to a booming evangelical community is described in full in *New Wine in Old Wineskins.*

- Another small town, Dacula, Georgia, is home to *First United Methodist Church, Dacula* (formerly Hinton Memorial United Methodist). This church is in the midst of a transition from traditional rural ways to programs that will meet the needs of the growing population of Atlanta suburbanites that now surrounds it. This story is told in Nancy Eiesland's *A Particular Place.*[19]

- The clash of rural and urban cultures is also present in the congregation called *Zion Holiness Church,* described by Melvin Williams in *Community in a Black Pentecostal Church.* The group of struggling African American city dwellers he describes had created a lively center of religious activity.

- *First Congregational Church,* Windsor, Connecticut, on the other hand, is old, historic, and affluent but still struggling with how to respond to God and to the needs of its community in the 1990s. This is the congregation from which Gary Dorsey wrote *Congregation.*

- You will encounter several congregations that are the subject of Nancy Ammerman's *Congregation and Community.*[20] Among them are *Good Shepherd Lutheran* in Oak Park, a suburb of Chicago. This mid size ELCA congregation was near death a decade ago but found ways to recruit and minister to the mobile young professionals in its community. *Grace Baptist Church* in Anderson, Indiana, is a large evangelical congregation full of blue-collar workers who have survived (with their church's help) the economic downturns in their community. *First Congregational* in Long Beach, California, is a historic downtown church that continues to play a visible, activist, public role in that large city.

In sidebars and in various illustrations, these congregations (among others) will provide a backdrop for what we will have to say, as well as points of comparison for you as you study your own congregation.

Perspectives for Studying Congregations

This book invites you to new ways of seeing a congregation. In addition to the tasks of gathering information to which we will direct you, you are also invited to try a variety of ways of looking at that information. We call these ways "frames" or "lenses" to suggest that they offer you a perspective, a vision, and a particular highlighting and marking off of what you see.[21] Congregations are real and particular human institutions; the frames are deliberately abstracted and generalized intellectual tools intended to facilitate understanding.

Our frames are intended to help the reader see congregations clearly despite habits of mind that often obscure them. They are intended to reorient thinking in ways that we hope will be fruitful. Framing, however, may cause discomfort, for the frames call for new perspectives on the realities they circumscribe. They invite the onlooker to adopt a new stance toward what is only too familiar. In the ecological frame, we look at the congregation as a naturalist would, seeing, for example, an animal swimming in a tide pool, wary of the other animals, navigating among and consuming various plants. In the cultural frame, we are anthropologists, looking at the congregation as an alien tribe with strange customs we need to comprehend. In the resources frame, we can imagine ourselves as corporate managers eager to put investments to better use. In the process frame, we are physicians, diagnosing the health and illnesses of the patient congregation, monitoring the metabolism, and sensing the blockages.

These are clearly not the only frames through which one could view a congregation. A number of other perspectives can be imagined. One might very profitably, for instance, adopt a gender frame, looking for the ways in which congregational life is systematically structured around the roles and relationships of women and men. Indeed, one cannot fully understand what happens in congregational life without paying attention to voices of both women and men, without looking for the ways in which congregations both empower and oppress women. The sorts of questions about power and inclusion that have been raised by feminist theorists are important ingredients in studying congregations.[22] For that reason, we have attempted to raise these issues throughout our discussion, integrating a gender perspective with each of the other lenses.

The frames we have developed here offer, then, four relatively comprehensive approaches to the understanding of what happens in congregations. At the same time, you should remember that each frame is partial. While each offers a complete picture to be viewed and assessed, one picture does not constitute the gallery necessary for displaying the complex reality of the congregation. As you experiment with one way of looking, always remember that another frame will offer you another equally important picture.

Although using the frames will require effort and discipline, we also want to suggest at the outset that the exercise calls for a playful attitude. Many years ago the historian Richard Hofstadter defined the intellectual as one who treated ideas with a combination of playfulness and piety. We recommend that attitude here: playfulness in imagination, piety in action.

The Ecological Frame

To use an ecological frame is to see the congregation as an organism in an environment in which there are many other organisms that together make up the social and religious world. In the terms used in the earlier *Handbook for Congregational Studies*, it is to see the congregation in relation to its social context, including all the various social, political, religious, and economic forces operative in that setting. Put another way, this frame allows us to see congregations as "open systems," implying systemic interaction both within congregations and between congregations and their environment. A congregation can affect its environment as the congregation engages in outreach activity, for instance, but it is also shaped by the people and resources and other institutions in that environment. Although your context does not determine your congregation's commitments, it does provide the setting within which you must make decisions.

The ecology with which you are concerned may begin with the particular neighborhood in which you are located, but it will also extend outward to include the larger region from which you likely draw members and participants, as well as the economic and political institutions that create the jobs and build the roads that bring people to your doorstep (or take them away). In addition, congregations are part of even larger ecologies of religious institutions—denominations, networks, and ecumenical coalitions—that define and shape local mission and identity. Indeed, events in every corner of our global village can have an impact on local congregational life. Refugees and immigrants arrive, wars and famines continue, stock markets rise and fall, and laws affecting religious liberty come and go. Each of these headline events may also affect the resources, needs, and sense of mission present in a given congregation.

The Culture Frame

A culture frame asks you to imagine the congregation you are studying as a group that has invented ways of being together that are uniquely its own. Even if much of what the congregation's members do has been borrowed from the larger culture, their very being together over time has given them a distinct identity. The older *Handbook* noted that congregations have a history and a character that make them who they are, that give them identity. In this book, we will approach the task of discovering that identity through the lens of culture.

Culture includes all the things a group does together—its rituals, its ways of training newcomers, its work, and its play. It also includes artifacts. Everything from buildings to bulletins, from sacred objects to the most mundane tools, helps identify a particular congregation's habits and places of being. Finally, culture includes the accounts it gives of itself—its stories and heroes, its symbols and myths, its jargon, and its jokes. To look at a congregation engaging in its unique rituals, showing off the things with which it has surrounded itself, and telling the tales of the group is to use a cultural frame for understanding its life together.

The Resources Frame

To view a congregation through a resources frame is to ask what it has the potential "cap-ital" to accomplish. This sort of accounting is a new aspect of congregational study being introduced with this book. It was not included in the older *Handbook* and has rarely been addressed systematically. The "capital" to which you will give attention from this vantage point may be the congregation's members, its money, its buildings, its reputational and spiritual energies, its connections in the community, and even its history. These are the raw materials of congregational life. Some of them are hard and countable, such as money, people, and buildings; other resources are soft and elusive, such as shared experiences of hard times together or the strength of faith and commitment of the congregation.

Resources are not clearly fixed, even once they have been counted, rather they are potential that is released by decisions and commitments of the members. Even the most solid assets of buildings and bank accounts must be allocated by permission of those who keep the keys, based on perceptions of the purposes to which the assets will be put. Imagining the vast number and variety of resources alongside a realistic assessment of limits is the primary task of congregational studies done through a resources frame.

The Process Frame

A newly arrived minister may propose an open congregational meeting to debate some controversial issue in the congregation. "No," she may be told by a longtime lay leader. "That's not the way we fight in this church. Our way is to let things settle out and resolve themselves slowly." "Our way" is a characteristic of that congregation's process. It is not a formal set of rules, although such rules may also be part of a congregation's process, rather it is just as often inferred from observations and from what knowledgeable insiders take to be the norms for action.

The process frame calls attention to the underlying flow and dynamics of a congregation that knit together its common life and shape its morale and climate. Process perspectives ask how leadership is exercised and shared, how decisions are made, how communication occurs, and how conflicts are managed and problems are solved. Process is evident in the agreements congregations make to maintain the coherence of the body and to nurture its growth. Congregations have their own dynamics of power and patterns of relationship, often like family systems of interdependence. And they operate on assumptions about authority and power that come both from the larger cultures in which they are located and from their own traditions. To address these assumptions about how work gets done is to look at the congregation through a process frame.

Congregational Studies as Practical Theology

This book begins its exploration of congregational studies by inviting people who come to this task out of concern for the well-being of a particular congregation to place their concern and their work in a theological context. Thinking in disciplined ways about congregational life is one of the core tasks of religious leaders, and that can be, we believe, fundamentally a theological task. One of the exciting developments in the field of practical theology today is its rediscovery of the importance of faithful, accurate description of the way things are. Don Browning, for instance, in his book *A Fundamental Practical Theology,* suggests that the first task of practical theology is to ask, How do we understand this concrete situation in which we must act? He argues that this task of description is, in fact, a theological task. If we believe that God is active *in* the world, not just an afterthought brought in to explain what goes on in the world, then describing what is happening in the world is theological work.[23] The descriptive task has, then, both a normative and a critical dimension. As you learn more deeply about who you are, you can engage in more critical theological inquiry into the nature of God's activity in the world and your own role in it.

Asking and answering theological questions is, of course, an expected skill of religious leaders. The skill called for here is not, however, the ability to remember the correct responses to ordination exam questions. Those engaged in congregational study must learn to ask both what a group says about its faith in God and what its actions say for it. How do group members treat each other? Who is in and who is out? How are boundaries drawn and maintained? How do they treat outsiders? How do they make decisions? What objects and events get special care? When do they reprimand their children, and when do they reward them? How do they worship? And what stories do they relish telling? Students of congregations must remember that talking is action, too. What people say and how they say it express their understanding of God. Accordingly, our chapter on theology will invite you to look at the narratives, practices, and texts that embody both the implicit and the explicit theology of the congregation. Throughout your study—not just at the end—you can be engaged in the theological work of discernment and visioning, of prayer and worship, of repentance, and of celebration.

Congregational Studies and Congregational Leadership

Whatever the presenting issue that moves a congregation toward disciplined study of its life together, the notion of framing and reframing is almost always useful, both for what it teaches along the way and for its ability to open up possible new directions. As you engage in the disciplined study of your congregation, you will undoubtedly be asking, "So what?" and "Where do we go from here?"

Samuel Freedman provides a wonderful illustration of the consequences of what we are calling framing and reframing in his book *Upon This Rock.*[24] Called at age twenty-six to be senior pastor of a congregation that his mentor called "one of God's Alcatrazes," Johnny Ray Youngblood demonstrates the value of viewing a situation from multiple perspectives. As

Freedman tells the story, in the first days of his ministry at St. Paul, Youngblood employed what this book is calling a *process* frame. As he sought to discover how things got done at St. Paul, he ended up in severe conflict (over finances) with one of the church's longtime trustees, and the trustee left the church (to the relief of many in the congregation). With his assistant, Sarah Plowden, Youngblood then turned to the church's *resources*. As they analyzed the church's income and expenditures, they discovered an overpayment of utility bills. They were then able to use the extra money for painting, electrical work, and hallway signs that read "FIND BURIED TREASURE IN YOUR BIBLE." Meanwhile, everything Youngblood did in those early years took keen account of St. Paul's *ecological* context: a community with great needs in one of Brooklyn's poorest neighborhoods with multiple institutions presumably (but rarely) serving its needs. In addition, he skillfully guided the congregation in developing new rituals and folkways (such as dressing down for Easter) and in constructing a new material environment they could call their own. In short, he helped them to invent a new *culture*. Freedman writes:

> Reverend Youngblood was at war with tradition—if not with the proud history of the black church, then certainly with the customs passed unquestioningly from generation to generation. He announced the battle in myriad ways—reading the Emancipation Proclamation from the pulpit, telling critics he shed "two tears in a bucket" for their concerns, and most of all repeating one favored parable. A little girl sees her mother cutting the wings off a chicken she is about to roast. When the little girl asks why, the mother says, "Because that's the way my momma always did it." So the girl asks her grandmother, who answers, "Because that's the way *my* momma always did it." Finally the girl asks her great-grandmother, who says, "Because my pan was too small."[25]

Freedmen's account illustrates very powerfully the art of leadership in a setting that is full of problems. But the power of the example is not in a minister's use of technical tools for ministry. The larger story is in the young minister's link between solving problems and leading his congregation. In Youngblood's war, as in most struggles for genuine change, it is when the young pastor was most frustrated and confused that a breakthrough became possible. As he sat in his car one afternoon and stared at the church building with all of its problems, "the word popped into his mind: *formaldehyde.* This building was a corpse stinking of formaldehyde. He saw only three choices for Saint Paul: expand, move, or lose him.... 'Lord,' Reverend Youngblood said aloud in the car, 'I believe You sent me here. But You got to show me. Can anything happen here? I can't stay if nothing can happen.'" According to Freedman, Youngblood received his response later that afternoon from the book of Ezekiel. His ministry at St. Paul was transformed as Youngblood again reframed his understanding of his call. Like the prophet, Youngblood would use his captivity as a source of strength. What had been a corpse stinking of formaldehyde became "dry bones" from which new life might emerge.

Leadership, then, is not a set of traits that a "good leader" must have but an activity that can be exercised by various people in the congregation. As an *activity,* leadership involves (1) helping the congregation gain a realistic understanding of its particular situation and circumstances; (2) assisting members to develop a vision of their corporate life that is faithful to their best understanding of God and God's purposes for the congregation in this time and place; and (3) helping members embody that vision in the congregation's corporate life. This book will close with a chapter that offers a more thorough look at the tasks of leadership. As the case of the Reverend Youngblood illustrates, leadership begins with asking questions and gathering information. It requires the ability to adopt a variety of perspectives on the congregational realities one observes. It also requires faithfulness and imagination.

Getting Started

Gaining new perspectives on congregational life—both to understand its present reality and to envision its possible future—requires the disciplined study to which this book is an invitation. We are well aware that religious leaders may turn to a book like this one for practical help with day-to-day problems. One management specialist notes, "Managers are not confronted with problems that are independent of each other, but with dynamic systems of changing problems that interact with each other." He calls such situations "messes." "Problems are abstractions extracted from messes by analysis," he continues. "Managers do not solve problems: they manage messes."[26]

We suspect that for many readers the success or failure of this book will lie in the help it provides in dealing with messes in congregations they know best. But bringing some insight to a mess requires the disciplined work that will be described in the chapters that follow. In addition, we urge religious leaders to think about the process of studying congregations as an ongoing activity, done in good times as well as bad. Some messes can be avoided when leaders have the sorts of deep understanding that come from careful examination of congregations when they are at their best.

While you may already have an idea about which frame will best help you, we strongly urge you to try out each of the perspectives we describe. We also urge you to keep one finger at least metaphorically in the methods chapter while you read. As you think about new ways of seeing your situation, you can also begin to think about how you might gather the information that would help you gain that perspective. In addition, keep another metaphorical finger in the theology chapter, recognizing that all the work you will do calls for attention to what you are learning about God and God's activity in your place.

We also urge you to begin thinking now about a few key aspects of your study. First, you will need to *clarify and limit the task at hand.* This is easier said than done. On some occasions when the need for congregational study arises, it is difficult to be entirely clear about what the precise problem is. Some situations are simply "messes." Likewise, a smoothly running system rarely flags the most

sensible point of entry for study. Nevertheless, identifying what you most want to understand may mean that you concentrate more on how decisions are made than on how children are educated, for instance. Begin with the best statement you can make about what your questions are and continually come back to that statement as you learn more throughout the study.

Second, you can begin now to think about what information you need and why. As you read subsequent chapters, make notes about what sorts of information you will need to address the questions that bring you to this study. Why do we want this information? and What will we do with it? are important questions to be considered as one is deciding what information will be gathered in the study process.

Third, you should begin immediately to think about who will be involved in the study process. There is no set rule about this. In some cases, it will be the clergy and lay leaders of the congregation who will take the initiative not only in calling for the study but in carrying it out. Two guidelines are important. First, the group undertaking the study needs authorization by the congregation's governing body to do so. Without such authorization, it will be difficult to secure the needed information; equally as important, it is unlikely that the results of the study will be taken seriously. Second, and somewhat related, it is important to build ownership across the congregation for the study. When possible, the study group should include representatives from various formal and informal interest groups within the congregation, and the congregation should be kept informed of the progress of the study and especially of the results. It is to such a study group or team that the methods and techniques of the following chapters are primarily directed.

There are times, however, when outside assistance is important. One such situation is when a conflict has escalated to the point that no person within the congregation is trusted to represent adequately the concerns of all groups that have an interest in the outcome.

Outside assistance is also desirable when the study needed is more complex than congregational leaders are able to manage, through lack of either needed expertise or time. There are those who believe that outside assistance is generally advisable, not only because of the difficulty of the task of congregational study, but also because of the ability of an outsider to see things congregational members cannot see because of their very familiarity with the situation.[27] We recognize the merits of this view while believing that it is also possible, and sometimes necessary, for a congregation to engage in a self-study.

Finally, it is never too early to think about how you will use the information you gather to address the issue(s) that the congregation is facing. There are many studies that have gathered dust upon completion because of inadequate attention to how they would be used. If you begin with as clear a focus as you can muster, are intentional about what information you gather, and involve key decision makers in the process from the beginning, you stand a better chance of both gaining the insight you need and putting that insight to use. From the time the congregation recognizes it has reached a turning point in its life through every step of its efforts to better understand itself to the moment it makes an informed response to the congregation's situation, both leaders and members need to see themselves as a team working together toward the future.

For troubled congregations, then, the task of congregational study offers the hope of clarity, intelligibility, and improvements in the many vexing difficulties in congregational life. For strong congregations full of energy and hope, congregational study will help identify directions for even greater mission and service. And for all kinds of congregations, the guidelines recounted here offer an order that makes it possible for a whole community—because it has entered into a common agreement on how to proceed—to participate in the enrichment and deepening of its self-understanding. It is on the basis of such self-understanding that congregations can become the faithful communities their own highest ideals call them to be.

About the Authors

This book is the product of an informal coalition of scholars and researchers who share an interest in congregations. Known as the Project Team for Congregational Studies, the eleven team members meet a few times each year for discussion of common projects and for mutual professional support. Its members, in various combinations, have written numerous books on congregations and sponsored national conferences and institutes on congregational studies. Current membership includes Nancy T. Ammerman, Jackson W. Carroll, Carl S. Dudley, Nancy L. Eiesland, Ardith S. Hayes, Lawrence Mamiya, William McKinney, Robert Schreiter, R. Stephen Warner, Jack Wertheimer, and Barbara G. Wheeler. The specific writing and editorial work of the various members on this book is noted throughout, but those whose names do not appear on chapters have nevertheless contributed in immeasurable ways to the shaping of the ideas and frameworks of this volume. We struggled together with its contents for nearly four years.

Former team colleagues whose contributions over the years are also reflected in this book include Rebecca Chopp, William Hamilton Holway, James F. Hopewell, Mary C. Mattis, and Loren B. Mead. We also acknowledge the contributions of C. Kirk Hadaway, Speed B. Leas, Mary C. Mattis, and Wade Clark Roof, much of whose work on the earlier *Handbook* is still reflected here. Over the years the team has enlisted help from a wide variety of people in critiquing its work. We note with appreciation the contribution of many people to the team's evolving thinking about congregations: David Kelsey, G. Douglass Lewis, James Lewis, David Leege, David Roozen, Allison Stokes, Katie Day, James P. Wind, and Barbara Brown Zikmund. Participants in various institutes convened by the team have helped test materials presented in this book, and we thank the several dozen people who have helped us in this way, especially those participating in a Hartford Seminary-sponsored gathering in 1996. Among those who offered especially helpful and detailed responses to our first draft of this book were Sandra Boyd and Sarah Polster. Our various home institutions have provided time and support for which we are grateful: Auburn Seminary, Catholic Theological Union in Chicago, Duke University, Emory University, Hartford Seminary, Jewish Theological Seminary, Pacific School of Religion, and the University of Illinois at Chicago. In particular, the work of Mary Jane Ross at Hartford Seminary's Center for Social and Religious Research has been invaluable. Finally, the original *Handbook* was supported by a grant from Trinity Grants Board of Trinity Church in New York City. This volume was made possible by a grant from the Lilly Endowment, which has generously supported the team throughout its life. We especially acknowledge the collegial support of Craig Dykstra and James Wind in this effort.

This collection of people, then, brings to the task of studying congregations a variety of religious and disciplinary perspectives. Many of us are social scientists, trained in the methods and approaches of sociology and history. Others of us are theologians and teachers of the arts of ministry. Some of us teach in colleges and universities, while the majority of us teach and hold administrative positions in seminaries. Most of us are Protestants, but the current Congregational Studies Team includes one Catholic and one Jewish member. Some of us actively work with congregations, providing advice and consultation, although many of us spend more time with our "research hats" on. We bring all of these perspectives to this book, shaping its mix of academic and practical advice, its theological and research agendas. What we all share in common is a commitment to the well-being of congregations. We study them because we think they matter. This book is our invitation to you to join us in that task.

NOTES

1. The extent to which historians have written American religious history *without* attention to congregations is quite remarkable. The histories provided in the two volumes edited by James P. Wind and James W. Lewis, *American Congregations* (Chicago: University of Chicago Press, 1994), are a major contribution toward closing that gap.

2. R. Stephen Warner, "The Place of the Congregation in the Contemporary American Religious Configuration," in *American Congregations*, 2: 54-99.

3. Elfriede Wedam and R. Stephen Warner, "Sacred Space on Tuesday: A Study of the Institutionalization of Charisma," in *"I Come Away Stronger": How Small Groups Are Shaping American Religion*, ed. Robert Wuthnow (Grand Rapids, Mich.: Eerdmans, 1994), 148-78.

4. On immigrant religion in the United States, see Frederick Denny, *Islam and the Muslim Community* (San Francisco: Harper & Row, 1987), Yvonne Yazbeck Haddad and Adair T. Lummis, *Islamic Values in the United States: A Comparative Study* (New York: Oxford University Press, 1987); Tedsuden Kashima, *Buddhism in America: The Social Organization of an Ethnic Religious Institution* (Westport, Conn.: Greenwood Press, 1977); Paul David Numrich, *Old Wisdom in the New World: Americanization in Immigrant Theravada Buddhist Temples* (Knoxville: University of Tennessee Press, 1995); and R. Stephen Warner, "The Place of the Congregation in the Contemporary American Religious Configuration."

5. For a fuller discussion of the contributions of congregations to their communities, see Nancy Tatom Ammerman, *Congregation and Community* (New Brunswick, N.J.: Rutgers University Press, 1997).

6. Martin E. Marty, *The Public Church* (New York: Crossroad, 1981), 45.

7. James P. Wind has written helpfully about this humble and collaborative approach to congregational studies in "Congregational Studies: A Progress Report," *Congregations* 22, no. 6 (November-December 1996): 14-16.

8. Samuel Freedman has written about his own particular journey as a white Jewish male in the African American world of St. Paul Community Baptist Church. His reflections can be found in "Crossing the Border," *CommonQuest* (Spring 1996): 12-21. Gary Dorsey's reflections on his time with First Church, Windsor, are a major theme in his 1995 book *Congregation: The Journey Back to Church* (New York: Viking, 1995). What he fails to note, however, are the effects of his presence and of his writing about them on the congregation itself. The process of studying a congregation always has effects on both the student and the subject of study.

9. Jay P. Dolan, ed., *The American Catholic Parish: A History from 1850 to the Present*, 2 vols. (New York: Paulist, 1987).

10. Wind and Lewis, eds. *American Congregations*.

11. Melvin D. Williams, *Community in a Black Pentecostal Church* (Pittsburgh: University of Pittsburgh Press, 1974).

12. Samuel Heilman, *Synagogue Life* (Chicago: University of Chicago Press, 1973).

13. Nancy T. Ammerman, *Bible Believers: Fundamentalists in the Modern World* (New Brunswick, N.J.: Rutgers University Press, 1987).

14. R. Stephen Warner, *New Wine in Old Wineskins* (Berkeley: University of California Press, 1988).

15. Lynn Davidman, *Tradition in a Rootless World* (Berkeley: University of California Press, 1991).

16. Samuel G. Freedman, *Upon This Rock: The Miracles of a Black Church* (New York: HarperCollins, 1993).

17. Paul Wilkes, *And They Shall Be My People: An American Rabbi and His Congregation* (New York: Atlantic Monthly Press, 1994).

18. Gary Dorsey, *Congregation: The Journey Back to Church* (New York: Viking, 1995).

19. Nancy L. Eiesland, *A Particular Place: Exurbanization and Religious Response in a Southern Town* (New Brunswick, N.J.: Rutgers University Press, 1998).

20. Ammerman, *Congregation and Community*.

21. The concept of framing was introduced to the Project Team for Congregational Studies by the work of Lee Bolman and Terrence Deal, in *Reframing Organizations: Artistry, Choice, and Leadership* (San Francisco: Jossey-Bass, 1991). See especially pp. 15-16. Although there is a good deal of similarity between the particular frames we have formulated and the frames Bolman and Deal describe, we have attempted to suggest ways of viewing congregations that are somewhat different from their more generic organizational studies frames.

22. Two helpful recent studies that put gender at the center of analysis are Joanna Bowen Gillespie, *Women Speak of God, Congregations and Change* (Valley Forge, Pa.: Trinity Press International, 1995); and Sally B. Purvis, *The Stained Glass Ceiling: Churches and Their Women Pastors* (Louisville: Westminster/John Knox, 1995).

23. Donald S. Browning, *A Fundamental Practical Theology* (Minneapolis: Fortress, 1991).

24. The following account is summarized from chapter 3 of Freedman's book, *Upon This Rock: The Miracles of a Black Church*.

25. Freedman, *Upon This Rock*, 96.

26. Russell Ackoff, "The Future of Operational Research Is Past," *Journal of Operational Research Society* 30, no. 2 (1979): 90-100, cited in Donald A. Schön, *The Reflective Practitioner* (New York: Basic Books, 1982).

27. This is the position taken by Loren B. Mead, "Seeking Significant Intervention," in *Building Effective Ministry*, ed. Carl S. Dudley (San Francisco: Harper & Row, 1983), 155-59. See also in the same volume, Lyle E. Schaller, "A Practitioner's Perspective," 160-74.

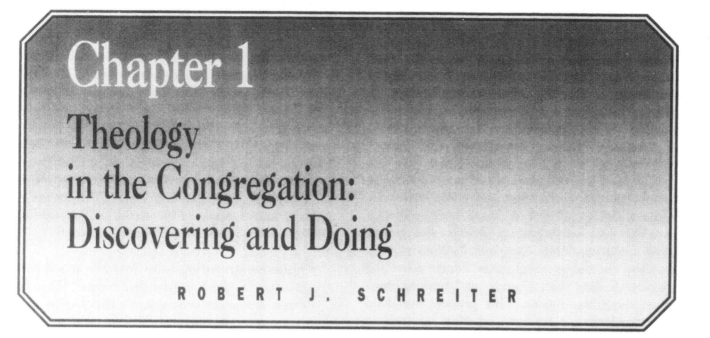

Chapter 1
Theology in the Congregation: Discovering and Doing

ROBERT J. SCHREITER

Introduction: Theology in the Congregation

There are many reasons for studying congregations. This chapter starts you on the path of congregational studies by examining one of the fundamental reasons for undertaking such a task at all. What makes congregations the special places they are is that they are focused on God, in whom they live, move, and have their being. Their members congregate to remember how God has acted in the history of the world and in their own lives. They congregate to discern what is happening to them and to the world today, and to listen for where God is leading them. Theology is an expression of the relation between God and such congregations of faithful, seeking people.

A thousand years ago Anselm gave theology its classical definition: Theology is faith seeking understanding. "Understanding" happens on many levels in the congregation. First, understanding involves grasping more clearly what our experience of God tells us about who God is and what God has done for us. Our knowledge of God is always indirect, and the quest for God is often circuitous and obscure. Yet if Augustine was correct, there is a restlessness in our hearts that can be eased only by coming to dwell in God. It is this experience of God that moves us not only to try to understand, but also to worship.

Second, if we believe God is not simply there, but is also active in the world, then experiencing God also reveals something about ourselves and our world. To be a congregation is also to engage in a quest to see our world in a special way from the perspective of God who has created that world and sustains it. "Understanding" is therefore about coming to terms with the world in which we live and what happens to us in that world. All the things that make up our lives—the hopes and the heartbreaks, the triumphs and the tragedies, the experiences of just getting by, and the moments of real transcendence—these are all the stuff of theological reflection as we try to understand those experiences from God's perspective as well as our own.

Finally, faith seeking understanding is also about action. The knowledge of God we seek is not simply information about God. It is a knowledge that grows out of a relationship with God that cannot but change us—challenging us to examine how we live our lives, drawing us into transformation, calling us to be prophets, and creating a deeper faithfulness.

Faith seeking understanding, then, is about all these things: discernment, worship, making sense of our lives, and transformative action. Seen in this light, theology is more than an added value that a congregation might seek when everything else is in place. It is really at the heart of the life of the congregation. It helps clarify why a congregation has come together in the first place, why it stays together through good times and bad, and how it responds to the challenges that come its way.

The fundamental purpose of your congregational study is to discover and grasp better the understandings of faith at work in a congregation. As your congregation clarifies and grasps those understandings, they can then serve as a platform for doing many other things: affirming identity, dealing with change, and making decisions about the future. This process can help your congregation understand what it wants to pass on to the next generation and what it wants to tell new members. Study can help your congregation choose the most appropriate response to the things happening to it. And the study process can help your congregation articulate better what kind of leadership it needs or how best to allocate resources. How your congregation understands itself and how it decides to move forward is informed by how it sees God at work.

Why Do Theology in a Congregation?

Why take up the task of developing a theology for your congregation? The mere mention of the word "theology" evokes for some people flights of abstraction that venture far from the life of the congregation. For those who have had theological education, theology may recall the travails of seminary or university classrooms. In some congregations theology itself may be suspect as something that will lead people away from the Bible or the Holy Spirit into dangerous or frivolous human constructions.

In a world where people seek meaning, however, that meaning has to be made explicit—and that is one way of talking about theology. When a congregation wants to transmit its values, it needs to talk theology. And when congregations are faced with major decisions, they usually want to make those decisions on more than economic or utilitarian or pragmatic grounds; they

want the decision to be informed by their faith.

In our approach to congregational studies, we will explore the rationale and use of theology for two related purposes. First, theology is important as you locate and deepen the identity of the congregation; second, theology can help your congregation to deal with change.

First, and most frequently, a congregation takes up the task of doing theology because it seeks a better sense of its identity. That desire can grow out of many different interests:

- Your congregation may want to track the journey in faith it has undergone. This is often the case when such theologies are developed to prepare for an anniversary celebration or a new building dedication. In the words of the African American hymn "We've Come This Far by Faith," you may ask: Just how far is that? And what have we come through?

- It may also be that your congregation has decided to undertake a program of spiritual renewal and needs a benchmark from which it will work. Here the questions are: Just who are we? What do we want to become?

- It may be time for your congregation to rewrite a mission statement or call new leaders for the congregation. If the mission or vision statement is to be grounded in the life of the congregation, the statement must seek to engage the reality of its life, lest it become vacuous and therefore useless. (You will further explore vision statements and leadership in chapter 6.)

- Your congregation may have a sense that it is drifting or losing members and that it needs a clearer sense of its own identity. Doing theology will help give it a distinctive edge as it discovers its defining moments from the past and discerns whether those moments engage well the challenges of today.

Any of these concerns may prompt an interest in developing a theology. Identity is an issue seldom raised until it has become somehow problematic. When a congregation's identity is challenged or under threat, then speaking of it becomes of paramount importance.

Second, theology becomes important especially when a congregation is faced with major change and important decisions about its future. In such a situation, it must have a keener understanding of itself in order to negotiate the changes before it. Changes frequently involve conflict, further prompting the need for theological clarity. No matter what the challenge confronting the congregation, its theological stance must be made explicit and accessible so as not to be superseded by pragmatic or utilitarian strategies.[1] Some examples:

- Your congregation needs to make a decision about relocating to another area. Most members have moved away from the neighborhood of the sanctuary and now must travel a great distance. Or the need to relocate may have to do with building a new house of worship to meet the needs of an expanding membership.

- Your congregation has grown so large that it has lost the face-to-face quality that was important to those who were there at the founding. Should it split into two congregations?

- Your congregation has become so small that it must consider merging with another congregation or disbanding altogether.

- Challenges often come from changes in the general environment in which the congregation finds itself. How will your congregation respond to plant closings, immigrants coming into the area, or pending legislation that does not reflect cherished religious values in the congregation?[2] In many instances, the congregation has very little control over the changes as such. A formerly small town congregation now finds itself in the midst of an exurban sprawl. To whom shall it address itself, and how?[3]

Any response a congregation makes must be more than pragmatic or expedient if the congregation hopes to be faithful in its discipleship and consistent with the religious tradition it represents. Doing theology in the midst of such change helps a congregation find itself and employ its theological resources to respond.

The study of theology in congregations, then, should be seen as more than a luxury a congregation cannot afford or as icing on the congregational-study cake. Theology can go to the heart of why this congregation has come together in the first place and where it finds itself now. Theology can be the springboard for spiritual renewal and revitalization of a congregation. And theology can help congregations meet change not only in a way more faithful to their traditions and aspirations, but proactively and prophetically if that is God's call to them.

An Invitation to Practical Theology

In recent years a new way of doing theology, called practical theology, has emerged. Practical theology is tied closely to the lives of congregations and individuals. Rather than moving from faith to life (theory to practice), it moves from life to faith and then back to life (practice to theory to practice). Practical theology begins, therefore, by describing the situation of the congregation and then correlates that situation with the faith and the beliefs of the congregation. From there, practical theology moves back to the life of the congregation to a refocused practice. This is different from the more familiar way of doing theology wherein one starts with faith and beliefs and then tries to reshape a congregation's practices to those outside standards. Practical theology as it is now being understood places high priority both on the facts of the situation in which a congregation finds itself and on the experience of the congregation. These facts and experience are not just the stuff to be shaped and formed by belief, but are active partners in discerning the meaning and place of those beliefs in the world in which the congregation lives. In other words, describing the situation is part of theological reflection itself, not just a prelude to it.

Congregational study as described in this book is an exercise in this new practical theology. The frames through which the congregation and its environment are observed, to which you will be introduced in the subsequent chapters, are not preludes to taking up the questions of theology, but are integral to that process. This is the case for two reasons. First, as has just been pointed out, description of the environment is not something extrinsic to the theological process, but is deeply part of it. Theology does not exist in the abstract; it is always rooted in a context. Knowledge of the context is part of the theology itself. Second, how we read the environment and the practices and beliefs of a congregation is never a neutral process. It is always laden with values, orientations, and understandings that the observer has accumulated over the years. The point practical theology is making is that theology does not begin when a congregation turns to its explicit beliefs. It has already begun from the moment it begins to describe where it is located and what it has been.

In the discussion of practical theology in recent years, a number of models have been proposed for how the task might best be undertaken. Two of the most helpful explorations of practical theology have been written by Thomas H. Groome[4] and Don S. Browning.[5] Each outlines a series of steps (five "moves" for Groome and four "movements" for Browning). Although the steps may not always happen in sequence, they do provide a valuable conceptual guide to the work the practical theologian is undertaking.

For both Groome and Browning, the first step in the practical theological process is describing the situation in which the congregation finds itself. The purpose of the descriptive and analytic frames provided in the following chapters of this book is to help congregations to make this initial theological move, intentionally grounding their theological work in their current setting and its challenges. Groome calls this "naming the present praxis,"[6] and Browning calls it "descriptive theology." In this move, a congregation tries to describe what it is now doing—its own congregational culture and what members say about who they are, the way decisions are made, their use of resources, and the like. You will want to give special attention to the specific areas of congregational life that gave rise to your study, seeking to understand both the implicit and the explicit theology contained in them (about which more will be said in a moment). Just what is happening here? And what does it say about us and what we really believe?[7]

The second step in doing practical theology involves moving beyond this descriptive work. It involves examining the stories, creeds, doctrines, and scriptures that are the historic resources of your faith tradition. Writing from within the Christian tradition, Groome calls this "making accessible the Christian story and vision." Each congregation needs to retell the stories that capture its tradition's vision of God and of humanity, of sin and deliverance, and of the nature and destiny of the world. Ideas and images that have been passed down through the ages need to be made accessible for each group of faithful people. Here you are looking especially for parallels to your current situation and instances in the tradition that illumine and challenge that situation.[8]

Practical theology differs from much traditional theological work in the third move it makes. Rather than simply using historical sources as a measuring rod against which to critique the current situation, practical theology calls for a conversation between the two. Yes, the ideas and narratives of the tradition should call your current practices into account. But the things you are discovering about God can also bring about new theological understanding. How does the congregation's story illumine and give a fresh perspective on the biblical story or other stories from the congregation's heritage? And how do those stories illumine or challenge the congregation's story about itself? This is what Groome calls a "dialectical hermeneutic," that is, a situation in which two sets of stories interpret each other and offer each other new insights and perspectives.

For both Groome and Browning, the final move in doing practical theology is action, a renewed practice of the faith, what Browning calls "strategic practical theology." Having listened to the conversation between your own congregational story and the rich resources of your tradition, it is time to imagine and plan for the next chapter. It is time to take concrete action, to seek change in yourselves and your world. Encounter with scripture and the heritage of faith can be transformational. Describing your own situation in theological terms can be transformational, as well. Out of the conversation between the two, a renewed vision is possible.

The whole task of studying a congregation, then, can be seen as an exercise in practical theology. Although it uses tools drawn from many other sources (as the following chapters make clear), the end result is not intended to be only a demographic, sociological, or financial profile. It is, rather, a picture of a living community of faith that struggles to be faithful to its understanding of God and God's purposes for the congregation and for the world. That is why understanding the study of your congregation as a theological undertaking helps keep your efforts in focus.

The Roles of Imagination and Memory

Doing theology is about thinking, but it must also be understood that it is fueled principally by imagination and memory. Although you will certainly want to include reading, writing, and study of theological texts as part of your practical theological work, you should also include music, art, stories, and other exercises in imagination. Psychologists (in the United States, at least) have said that over 90 percent of all people think eidetically, that is, in images. Images, and the connective strands that turn them into metaphors and narratives, play an important role in organizing our knowledge. It is the arresting images that capture our atten-

tion, as the advertising media have long known. To think of practical theologies being done in images is not to capitulate to the moguls of Madison Avenue, but to recognize a basic aspect of the human condition. Images and narratives help us remember and recall quickly an important idea. Because of their multivalent character, images and narratives can carry many—even contradictory—ideas at the same time. For example, to Christians the waters of baptism carry both the meanings of death and life; fire evokes images of the Holy Spirit and of hell.

Your theological work may, for instance, draw together diverse aspects of a congregation's life into a single image or phrase that gives a congregation a quick grasp of itself. Take, for example, the Reverend Johnny Ray Youngblood's St. Paul Community Baptist Church, which proclaimed itself "a church unusual," with the motto "child-centered, adult-run, elder-ruled."[9] "A church unusual" could confront the problems of its decaying environment in East New York, taking what appeared to others to be great risks and succeeding. St. Paul's focused especially on the needs of children, because their environment in so many ways militated against their advancement and growth. The motto emphasized that adults were not absent at St. Paul's as they were in so many other parts of children's lives. And the motto further pointed to the small core of wise men (elders) who are the church's leadership.

But, you may ask, what is theological about such an identifying image? Would not a social analysis, without theology, yield the same thing? If all St. Paul's did was to forge such slogans or mottoes after an analysis of its environment, the congregation could be said to have no theological identity. But what gave it theological identity was the way the Reverend Youngblood opened up these themes time and again in his sermons, in meetings of the elders and other groups at St. Paul's, and when suggesting programs that would promote the life of the community. In all these instances, he found in the biblical stories the story of this "church unusual." Thus, for one Easter Sunday sermon, Youngblood chose the story of the raising of Lazarus, an unusual choice of text even for "a church unusual". In that sermon he explored the plight of the Black male in a poor community, bound and tied by poverty and racism and seemingly incapable of escaping his fate. By underlining at once the need for different patterns of child rearing and adult support, he was able to illumine what resurrection would mean for the Black male, as well as the deeper meaning of the Resurrection as new life. Similarly, the housing construction project he spearheaded became known as the Nehemiah project, placing the rebuilding of East New York within the story of Nehemiah's rebuilding Jerusalem.

Some traditions, it should be noted, lend themselves to theological work that includes visual images, but others (such as Judaism, Islam, and the Reformed tradition in Christianity) discourage or forbid representations of God or even human figures in houses of worship. This may make it difficult for a congregation to think in images, because its religious experience is more aural than visual. The cadences and text of hymns and the presence of stories, however, can easily compensate for any shortfall here. In such cases, it is better to emphasize stories over images.

An image becomes a theological image, in fact, when the narratives to which it is related are brought into contact with the narratives and images of a congregation's scriptures and history. The theological image then throws new light on the question: Where is God active (or absent) in this time and place? Why is our story so much like stories we find in the Bible? How do the endings of those stories suggest our story will turn out, especially with regard to God's action? Because identity is so often articulated in stories or narratives in communities (we talk about ourselves in stories more often than through concepts), the answer to the question about the activity (or absence) of God often comes out in a story.

Many congregations do this kind of theological work almost instinctively. It is reflected often in the names given to houses of worship, like Grace Evangelical Lutheran Church or Temple Beth El. The great narratives of the Bible become ways of situating the narratives of the congregation's life. The Exodus story, for example, has often become a symbol of liberation, a way of asserting subjecthood for many oppressed peoples.[10] And the story of the suffering and death of Christ has for centuries provided a framework for suffering Christians to make sense of their own pain.

In addition, memories of the history of your own denominational tradition may be part of your practical theological work. An example of this among Mormons is the story of the great trek west from Nauvoo, Illinois, to Salt Lake City. Pictures and stories of pioneers and beehives remind Mormons of this defining moment in their history. They bespeak endurance in the midst of hardship, the bitter memory of persecution, and the power of a utopian vision to forge a community. Such experiences have been an important part of Mormon identity. But as the Church of Latter Day Saints expands worldwide, many Mormons wonder if an important part of their identity will be lost as more and more Mormon converts do not have ancestors who were part of the great Western trek.

Memory is the basis of any identity that is more than ephemeral. One of the strengths of congregations is their ability to endure over time, even with changes of leadership and membership. The remarkable odyssey of Mendocino Presbyterian Church, as recounted by Stephen Warner, is a monument to that.[11] (You can read more about Mendocino in the next chapter.) Even their shift from a liberal to a more conservative evangelical stance encompassed a past and a memory. Memory is not only important for a representation of an individual congregation to itself, memory of the religious tradition of which it is a part is important as well. If the congregation can only connect itself to stories of itself, then a narcissistic loop begins to form that will not give that congregation, in the long run, either a satisfying identity or an ability to negotiate change within its environment.

The importance of remembering the tradition will be weighed differently across congregations. Certainly Judaism and Islam keep memory central to the traditions and practices of the faith. In societies where modernization has hit strongly, on the other hand, memory often has to survive in the face of what some sociologists call detraditionalization, in which tradition loses its normative force for the shaping of identity.[12] In these situations, memory is often lost or preserved only in unrelated segments. Identities then are constantly being constructed anew, often through acts of consumption (bearing out Feuerbach's old adage "You are what you eat"). The construction of identity out of a range of possible choices is seen as one of the tasks of the individual in such a modern society. Congregations operating in the United States and in similar societies, particularly if they are in the mainstream of the culture, often must struggle to maintain any sense of their specific religious tradition. Jews find their children assimilating into Gentile culture, and denominational differences in Protestant Christianity become more and more blurred. One of the questions to be asked when constructing a theology in a congregation is: How much of a role does an ongoing memory of our religious tradition play in our identity as a congregation today?

James Hopewell, a pioneer in congregational studies, emphasized both memory and imagination for developing a congregation's theology. His book *Congregation* remains one of the best resources for looking at the roles these two aspects of thinking play in developing a congregation's self-understanding.[13] As you undertake a congregational study that is informed by practical theology, be ready to stretch your mind in new directions.

Who Does Theology in the Congregation?

If doing theology is to be part of your congregational study, it is important to think about different roles that will be exercised. Four deserve attention here.

The first is that of the formal and informal leaders of the congregation, both members and clergy. Those whose skill, longevity, and influence put them at the heart of your congregation's life will have a special role in the theological work you do. They typically have the best overview of the congregation, although they may not agree among themselves just what that overview is and how it is to be interpreted. Leaders often embody the memory of the congregation, and they will be essential both in providing a description of practices and environment, and in correlating the congregation's story with scripture and heritage. As you articulate new images and tell old stories about God's activity among you, congregational leaders will be essential interpreters.

The second role is that of the entire congregation itself. Members certainly provide the grist for the theological mill, with their stories of suffering and hope, of being perplexed and receiving insight. They may provide a healthy counterbalance to the leaders' view of the congregation's past and present. If you are intentional about providing opportunities for a broad segment of the congregation to participate, members can contribute diverse voices, offer the insight of an arresting image, or suggest the scriptural passage that best illumines the situation. It is the congregation as a whole, after all, that must finally understand and practice the insights of your practical theological work. The ideas and stories and images must be tangible to members of the congregation. The theology you develop must be able to illumine members' own experience and connect them to the great stories of their tradition. They must be able to recognize their own stories and resonate with the connections being made. That will happen most easily when the whole congregation is kept involved in your practical theological work.

Those with some professional theological training, often the minister but also others in the congregation and beyond, play the third role. Their task is to help identify and articulate the themes that will be the source and stuff of theological reflection. Stories about struggles to understand why bad things happen must be identified as stories of suffering.

Stories about reconciliation need to be identified as such and lifted up. The other part of their task is to provide a longer memory of religious experience in the past. In other words, theologically trained participants can connect the stories of the congregation with the stories of the Bible and the religious tradition. Years of confusion in the congregation, for example, might be linked to the years of the Hebrews wandering in the desert. Recall the Reverend Youngblood's use of the Lazarus story mentioned above. The image of Lazarus, bound and entombed and freed by Jesus, offered a powerful image of liberation.

Those with professional theological training may also serve as a link to the experience of other communities today. In some of the heavily Hispanic Roman Catholic dioceses in Texas, the base community model of church has been imported from Latin America and modified for local use. This gives, among other things, a new sense of belonging to people who were otherwise marginalized in an Anglo-dominated church. The theologically trained leaders, then, can remind the congregation that they are not the whole of those who believe in God, that they are part of something larger—of the Christian church or of Judaism or of the House of Islam.

There is always a danger that theologically trained leaders will dominate the process of doing theology. But as a resource about religious experience past and present, and as pathfinders for the process of theology in the congregation, such leaders can be a valuable asset.

Finally, there is a role for outsiders, often embodied in the consultant for a self-study process. Consultants or other figures who stand outside the congregation are sometimes able to spot things the other participants cannot or do not want to see. Although they do not know the congregation as well as long-time members, such outsiders may offer important perspectives through experience with other congregations. Depending on the nature of the congregation's polity, such connection to the outside may be of utmost theological importance, because it represents a theology of communion between congregations.

Doing practical theology, then, will involve insiders and outsiders, leaders and members, as well as the congregation's theologically trained staff and members. As you enter a time of congregational study, you will need to plan for how this theological work will be tended. You may want to establish an ongoing study group or occasional congregational gatherings or to focus on theological dynamics as you tend to other work—or all of the above.

An important task of leadership in a congregational study is coordinating the theological process. This involves, first, assuring that all voices are allowed into the conversation and have an opportunity to be heard. Orchestrating this can be difficult, but nonetheless it is absolutely necessary. Coordination also involves keeping the theological questions before the congregation at each stage of the process. Every part of the descriptive process is laden with values, ideas, and options that have theological import. Description is part of the theological process, not just a prelude to it.

Theology in the congregation, as you will see, is both process and product. Practical theology is both the stories told and the participatory theological reflection they engender in the congregation; both are needed to strengthen members' solidarity with one another and to deepen their religious commitment. Because of this, reflecting theologically can grow into an ongoing practice. In the many meetings of different groups at St. Paul's, for instance, the Reverend Youngblood frequently began with moments of prayer and theological reflection. Developing the agenda for a meeting also provided an opportunity to think about the theological direction of the congregation.

What Do Practical Theologians Look For?

Explicit and Implicit Theologies

When practical theologians do their work, they must begin by remembering that theology is expressed in the life of a congregation in a host of different ways. As you begin the task of describing the world of your congregation, it is important to distinguish between the explicit or official theologies and the implicit or unofficial theologies a congregation might have. The explicit theologies are generally easy to find. They are present in the official doctrines, creeds, and confessions a congregation subscribes to. The liturgies conducted, the sermons preached, and the hymns chosen for worship all reflect the theology that guides the congregation's life and represent its understanding of God. A mission statement often enshrines that theology in a very straightforward way. A congregation's religious heritage or denominational tradition carries much of the explicit theology it holds and to which it aspires.

Implicit theologies are theologies or fragments of theologies that inform the congregation's life but are not necessarily acknowledged or overtly expressed. They may be only half-formed and only present in certain sectors of a congregation. They may be present in a variety of places and activities in the congregation: in the stories a congregation tells about itself, in styles of leadership, and in the many ways it chooses to arrange its life. Implicit theologies sometimes manifest themselves in how the budget is allocated and who has power in the congregation. They almost certainly vary among the different groups, social and spiritual, that form under the auspices of the congregation.

Implicit theologies are frequently at odds with the explicit, official theologies a congregation may espouse. For example, a Christian congregation with a strong Reformed heritage may hold to a doctrine of the utter depravity of humankind, professing human beings' inability to help themselves. Yet the same congregation may sponsor a host of self-help programs, reflecting an implicit theology of optimism about the human condition. In such a case, the implicit theology prevailing in the surrounding culture overtakes the explicit theology of a denomination.

The implicit theologies in a congregation are sometimes harder to name than the explicit theologies, but they are crucial for under-

standing any congregation's life. These implicit theologies may often guide the congregation more surely than does its mission statement. They may reflect, too, truths about the congregation no one wants to hear. For example, in a congregation in a changing neighborhood, an implicit emphasis on ethnicity and ethnic belonging may harbor a theology meant to exclude newcomers, flying in the face of any explicit, official theology of inclusiveness. The implicit theologies often lie at the base of internal conflicts in a congregation, and making them explicit is an important part of resolving those conflicts.

Surfacing implicit theologies is an important part of congregational study because they often direct the life of a congregation in ways unbeknownst to the members themselves. As you use each of the frames set forth in the next several chapters of this book, ask about the theological meaning of what you see. Does the culture of your congregation, for example, suggest a different picture of who the congregation thinks God is from what it explicitly confesses in its worship? Does your congregation's allocation of resources give a different picture of theological priorities than its mission statement? Do your congregation's processes bespeak a different picture of power, authority, and service than its official account of itself? Does the ecology in which your congregation lives make some of its explicit theological ideals impossible to attain? Making these theologies explicit makes the picture of the congregation more complex and sometimes more uncomfortable. But surfacing implicit theologies is necessary if the study of the congregation is to be thorough.

Theologies do not begin, then, when a congregation sets out to create them. They are already operative in the congregation before such conscious activity is undertaken, although they are likely to be in somewhat inchoate form. Bringing those implicit theologies to awareness is the beginning of a good picture of the congregation's composite theology. This picture might best be imagined as a mosaic, made up of little bits of marble fashioned together. Like a mosaic, if each fragment of theology is looked at from too near a distance, the composite picture may not be entirely evident. Viewing the mosaic from too far away may blur the tiles' individual distinctiveness. The viewer needs to gain the proper perspective to see the design. So too with implicit theologies.

Multiple Theological Perspectives

It is important to emphasize that you will not likely find a single, coherent theology binding a congregation together. There will indeed be fragments, and the picture they create may not easily emerge. You will more likely uncover a variety of theologies, developed in diverse ways and to different extents. These theologies are also likely to differ based on differences in the experiences of members and groups within the congregation. People standing in different social locations within the congregation will understand and act in different ways. Among the differences to which you should be alert:

- Differences between congregational leaders and other members. Pastors, for example, may not have the long history with your congregation that many of the members do. Pastors have also been formed by previous experiences with other congregations and by theological education. Pastors and other leaders in the congregation may also have their sights set on how they wish to change the congregation rather than seeing it as it is.

- Generational differences. As in other parts of life, the formative experiences of each generation, especially those public events that happened as each generation was coming of age, will likely be evident in the generations' theological stance as well. Roman Catholics speak of pre- and post-Vatican II mentalities. Jews whose lives were touched directly by the Holocaust will experience things differently from a younger generation, which knows the experience only through stories. The experience of being an immigrant or a refugee will have a profound influence on the gen-

eration that lived through the experience but may have very different effects on their children, who do not remember or were born after the experience and who want to identify with their new country. Generations are never uniform in their thinking, but identifying public experiences at the time of each generation's coming of age (for example, the Great Depression, World War II, Vietnam, the OPEC oil embargo) often provides a unique window into the thinking of that generation's members. Thus, those who came of age during the depression of the 1930s will frequently remain concerned about scarcity, but those who came of age in the 1960s are more likely to assume abundance.

- Roles and experiences within the congregation. People serving as elders or in the vestry may develop a kind of "official" history of your congregation, for instance. Others whose involvement has been with certain organizations, such as the youth group or the mission society, will come to theology with distinct perspectives. When someone is seen primarily as the matriarch of the congregation, the newcomer, the pastor's child, or the best voice in the choir, that person's role will lead him or her to adopt different perspectives.

- Motivations for joining or staying in the congregation. These motivations yield implicit theology as well. For example, First Church of Windsor (about which Gary Dorsey writes[14]) is a classic New England parish with roots back into the seventeenth century. Alongside its history as the principal church of a New England town, the congregation experiences the eclecticism of much of today's American Christianity. Some people are members because their family has belonged for generations. Others join because of the distinguished age of the congregation, which reaches back three centuries. Still others come for the aesthetics of the worship service or the way the holidays are celebrated. Others are on a personal spiritual quest and have joined because that search is tolerated or encouraged in the congregation. And still others come because their friends are members or they like the minister. Each of these motivations (and there are more than those listed here) imply a theology about how to experience faith and how to encounter God.

• Congregation and denomination. A congregation's relation to any larger body may be the subject of practical theological work and the source of different implicit theologies. A small Baptist congregation may feel little need for denominational identity, whereas a United Methodist congregation down the street may be struggling to revive its sense of connection with the denomination. Roman Catholic ecclesiology is such that one can never think of the church as the congregation alone, but nondenominational congregations may have no theology of a church beyond their local gathering. Sometimes it is discovered that ethnic variations on a common tradition—quite common among Lutherans—highlight theological differences in what might be an untheological way. Different ways of relating to denominational tradition are part of the implicit theology present in most congregations.

• Congregation and parish. Congregations come in great varieties. They may be small, intentional communities with clear rules for membership. Or they may be large, territorial entities that bring together a highly diverse social group—as is the case with many urban and suburban Roman Catholic parishes whose members' only common denominator is geography. Or the congregation may be a community church and the only Protestant church in town and, therefore, the gathering place for people who might not otherwise readily congregate. Each of these kinds of congregations will contain a different mix of implicit theologies—many ideas and practices held in common in the intentional communities, a great diversity in parishes and community churches.

Each of these six perspectives, then, gives us a place from which to view the mosaic of a congregation's theologies. Each perspective can be used as the basis for questions about differences within the congregation. All these differences are a part of the unique picture of your congregation's theological practices, but they can also be the source of misunderstanding and conflict. Surfacing them will require a relationship of trust and confidentiality, along with opportunities to talk in a safe and accepting environment. Appreciating the strengths these differences can bring to a congregation's life will also require skilled interpretive leadership.

Narratives, Practices, and Texts

There are many ways to discover the theologies of a congregation. Perhaps one of the most useful approaches would be to see how theology appears in the narratives, practices, and texts of a community.

Narratives are the stories that shape and transmit the memories of a congregation. Practical theologians will listen for the stories people tell most readily about themselves. To whom do they compare their heroic figures? What events stand out? A good way to get into the narratives of a congregation is to read together the time line they have constructed (for constructing a time line, see chapter 7 in this book). Reading the time line with different people in the congregation will evoke the stories most central to its self-understanding. If the congregation is a historic "First Church," its stories may be heavily laden with references to the beginnings or to a distant past. In that instance, the congregation's theology may be one of earthly and heavenly citizenship, emphasizing responsibility for the security and the harmony of the community. If the congregation had to overcome great adversities (fire in the sanctuary, scandals, economic reversals), a theology of suffering and redemption may come to the fore.

Besides the time line, stories of significant leaders and members should be listened for. Congregational histories are often divided into eras corresponding to the tenure of the ministers or pastors. Significant donors, prominent families, and long-serving staff members all provide focuses for stories. Many recent books on individual congregations use this method, telling stories about key individuals, in their own narration. Reading histories of your congregation, especially in the company of a long-time member, will elicit these stories of heroes and servants.

Groome's practical theological method especially emphasizes the importance of narrative or story as a way the congregation expresses its identity. So much of memory is stored in narratives about what happened when the congregation began or crucial moments in its past. Stories change over time, but the stories that are returned to over and over again represent core elements of a congregation's identity. As has already been pointed out, when these stories are set down alongside those of the Bible or of the rabbis, the resonances between the two can create a theological connection. Sometimes the connections are clear. For example, the Exodus narrative is used by communities of oppressed people, or congregations ask which rabbi in the Hasidic tales sounds most like ours? Other possibilities abound. It should be noted that sometimes the lore invoked is not that of the Bible or rabbinical tradition (or the lives of the saints). Sometimes the correlation is with secular history and narratives, such as the story of Puritan beginnings in the northeastern United States (a "city on the hill") or later myths of American civil religion.

If narratives are the stories that shape our memory, *practices* are the pathways that shape our lives. Practices take us from the memories of the past and steer us through the uncertainties of the present. There are four areas of practice you should attend to, especially when trying to decipher the theologies of your congregation.

- The congregation's physical space. What is most prominent in the complex of buildings the congregation uses, or which part of the congregation's only building seems to be the center of its life? In many Roman Catholic parishes, for instance, the school buildings are more prominent than the church building, reflecting the commitment to parochial education. Were the buildings built by this congregation or acquired from another one? What does the sanctuary say about the theology of the congregation? Where are the pulpit and (for Christians) the altar or communion table? What does the social hall or fellowship center say about what the congregation values most dearly? Who controls each of the spaces? And who, both within and from outside the congregation, gets to use the spaces?

Questions about space are taken up in more detail in the chapters on culture and ecology, but remember that use and arrangement of space rests on implicit and explicit theological assumptions. Gothic architecture, for instance, may favor feelings of transcendence, whereas more horizontal architecture may emphasize the importance of immanence. Large amounts of space allocated for child care may support an implicit theology that sees the purpose of the congregation as the socialization of the young or contradict a theology that says religion is basically for adults. Even fences, windows, and parking lots tell a theological story.

- Patterns of worship and patterns of gathering. Even in highly liturgical traditions with set lectionary readings and other liturgical prescriptions, there are many local variants that should be noted. In a study of Roman Catholic parishes done some years ago, the assembled congregants' joining hands during the recitation of the Lord's Prayer and the exchange of peace were deemed by the participants to be the highlight of the service. This would point to a theology of community, in contrast to official Roman Catholic liturgical theology, which holds that the eucharistic prayer is the high point of the service.[15] If the tradition of the congregation is not strongly liturgical, the structure and dynamics of the worship service provide an important window into the congregation's own theology. Both what is done and how it is done are clues to the implicit theology at work there. Look especially at points where local practices might seem to be at odds with denominational traditions and ask why that might be.

Similarly, other kinds of gathering may be even more revelatory: social events, meetings of associations or clubs, and the conduct of the business of the congregation. Even within the strictures of a denomination, there is still a range of variation that will give clues about what the congregation sees as important and how it views its relation to God and the surrounding world. The chapters on congregational culture and processes in this book will be helpful as you attempt to describe the theologies at work in such gatherings.

- Special occasions. What events draw especially large numbers of participants? Are there events that are important that one would not have surmised from other data? What kinds of events is this congregation likely to celebrate with other congregations in its vicinity? What does this say about its theology? Are these largely civic holidays (Thanksgiving, Independence Day)? On the other hand, does the congregation have a sense of separateness about its special occasions? What are the annual special events beyond worship? The Strawberry Festival? The Soup Supper? A fiesta? What is the implicit "sacred calendar" for this congregation?

- Outreach. Where does the congregation extend its outreach—locally, nationally, and internationally? Is it helping settle Russian Jews or refugees from Central America? What reasons does the congregation give for its choice of projects? How does this congregation enact its expectations for God's presence in the world?

By attending to the regular routines and assumptions of a congregation's life in these four areas, you can begin to outline its implic-

it theological identity. Does the congregation see its physical space as a haven in a hostile world or a resource to be shared with the larger civic community? Is the annual covered dish dinner the most engaging event? Is food a central symbol for this congregation? Are the *quinceañeras* more important than Ash Wednesday? The theology that emerges out of practices might be described as a theology for the journey through life: We find out about the most important way stations and what we can expect from the world around us. Most especially we can see in practices what role the congregation as church, temple, or masjid is expected to play.

Finally, *texts* are what we say about ourselves. Texts often contain our explicit theologies, providing the anchors for identity. For example, passages on justification in the letter to the Romans are key for Lutherans, and Matthew's Great Commission is central for a mission-minded evangelical congregation. Texts embody the values and ideals we profess. But they also include implicit theologies in the sense that they may support particular practices or illumine some narratives in the congregation. Texts are always embedded in particular communities, taking on special meanings because of how they are used and interpreted there. They often represent more of that to which we aspire than what we may have achieved. But beyond the sacred texts of a congregation, there are three sets of texts that deserve your special attention when looking for the theologies operating in a congregation:

- First are the mission or vision statements the congregation may have produced. Chapter 6 of this book, on leadership, gives a closer look at these. Though sometimes general or vague to the point of meaninglessness, mission or vision statements can be the product of good practical theological work and always offer a window onto the aspirations of the congregation.

- The second set of texts you should examine are the educational curricula, both for children and adults. You should also try to find out just how these curricular materials are actually used. Are they the only ones available from the denomination? How are they supplemented? If the adult program is more free-form, what kinds of topics are returned to over and over again? What kinds of programs do members of the congregation want to see provided? What kinds of programs are tolerated but not actually sponsored by the congregation's leadership?

• Promotional materials and slogans are important texts as well. Is your congregation the "a church unusual," like St. Paul's? Or is it the "Saint Anthony Parish Family" (even though it has thousands of members)? Is it "open and affirming" for gays and lesbians? Or "your friendly downtown church"? What do your announcement boards say, both inside and outside the sanctuary? Does the congregation have any promotional literature? What makes its way into the bulletin each week?

Texts, along with practices and narratives, are places to begin the practical theological work of understanding the faith present in a congregation. Your task is to observe how the congregation patterns its life, how it tells its stories, and what its texts say (and do not say). You always want to be looking for what those pieces of congregational life say about the mosaic that is being created.

The Theological Content in Congregational Life

What theological questions should you ask as you reflect on narratives, practices, and texts? Here are some suggestions:

• About God. Is God distant or close by? What aspects of God (love, justice, mercy, judgment) are favored or emphasized? Does God intervene in our lives? If so, how do we talk about that intervention? How does God relate to evil?

• About humanity. Are human beings essentially good? Essentially sinful? What are our duties to God? To one another? What is the ultimate purpose of our life? What are our responsibilities to one another? To strangers?

• About evil and sin. Why is there evil in the world? How do we account for incursions of evil into our lives? How does the congregation respond to catastrophe or tragedy? What is considered sinful? How do human beings sin? How is sin purged from our lives?

• About the congregation. What is the purpose of the congregation's coming together? What is the most important thing the congregation does? What responsibility, if any, does the congregation have to the community in which it is located? To the larger world?

• About life and its transitions. What attention does the congregation give to birth, coming of age, marriage, old age, and death? What do these practices say about what the congregation believes about life?

You may think of other questions or even sets of questions. Remember that narratives, practices, and texts will all yield answers to these questions. If someone says, "God has blessed our congregation," how has that blessing manifested itself? Or if someone says, "God pulled us through that terrible situation," what does that say about God? Our expectations of fellow human beings—and God's expectations of them—give us a picture of how we perceive humanity theologically.

Important to remember too are the different perspectives that come from the different roles people play in the practical theological process and the different life experiences they bring to it. Positions held in the congregation (both formal and informal), as well as perspectives of gender and generation, education and income, all figure into how people understand the world through God's eyes.

Finding the congregation's implicit theologies helps locate the points of departure for your continuing theological work. You may discover that the theological premise underlying this congregation's life is as simple and relatively uniform as observance of the Golden Rule, or as complex as its practices of the 613 commandments of Orthodox Judaism. Its primary theological assumptions may be captured in the names of the organizations it sponsors (for example, Gideon Ministries). Or they may be scattered and not reconcilable. But bringing them to light is key to the next step in doing theology in the congregation: linking your implicit theologies to the explicit theologies in your congregation, to the wider resources of your faith tradition, and to the actions and strategies you will need for your future.

Theologies at Work in the Congregation

Sometimes congregations try to begin their theological work by collecting and studying the texts that outline what their tradition says a congregation should be and do. Adherents of those communities then try to pattern their lives after those traditions and measure their performance and belief against them. As should now be clear, unless some of the descriptive work laid out in this chapter is done first, the theology that emerges from such a process is likely to be disconnected from the day-to-day experience of members of the congregation.

How, then, do implicit theologies interact with explicit theologies in a congregational study? Recalling our earlier discussion of practical theology, we are now ready for that "dialectical hermeneutic," the conversation between the resources of the faith tradition and the practices of this congregation.

If the purpose of your engaging in a practical theology for your congregation is to clarify identity, you may want to cover the full range of theological questions (God, humanity, evil, the congregation, and so forth, starting with the list above), both as they emerged in implicit theologies and as they emerge in the explicit stories and stated visions of the faith. If, on the other hand, your purpose for engaging in a practical theology is more focused, you may want to examine only certain aspects of your tradition. For example, if you are engaging in theology for the sake of choosing new congregational leaders, you would first surface what seems to shape leadership, authority, and service from the implicit theologies of the congregation. Then you would look at what your tradition says in your sacred texts and books of order or law—or at least select those parts deemed most relevant to your situation.

In either instance, you look for similarities and differences. Do your implicit and explicit theologies more or less match? Are there significant differences? Do your implicit theologies point to things not found in your explicit theological formulations—or point to things your explicit theology finds wrong? Does your implicit theology help you recover lost parts of your tradition that current explicit theologies do not emphasize? Here the theologically trained members can be particularly helpful in understanding the many facets of the explicit theologies of your tradition, some of which may not be known to other members.

Your evaluation of how well your implicit and explicit theologies match is an important part of the practical theology process. You may find that the theology that really shapes the life of your congregation has little to do with the explicit, official theologies of the sponsoring denomination, and that realization may cause genuine concern. Or you may find hidden treasure in your implicit theologies that deserves to be developed and fostered within your congregation. In any case, this conversation between explicit theological traditions and the implicit theological practices of your congregation will lead you toward the "strategic" work of your practical theological process—the actions you take out of your new understanding of your faith. You may decide the divergence between the two theologies calls for a revival or renewal of the spiritual life of the congregation. Or, if you are writing a mission or vision statement, convergence between explicit and implicit theologies may give your congregation a solid sense of its own identity and confidence to express that to others.

Once you have completed the practical theological cycle, you are in a position to make theological reflection an ongoing part of the life of your congregation. You may not need each time to reconstruct the implicit theologies. These will largely stand but will need expansion or correction as things happen to the congregation and as its membership changes. For purposes of discovering and reaffirming a sense of identity, and for purposes of discerning a path toward change, practical theology engages the congregation in discovering its own narratives, matching them with narratives from the sacred texts and heritage, and seeing how this encounter reshapes their identity and strategies for the future. Once having undertaken a major theological review, members and leaders alike can routinely engage in this practical theological conversation. In addition, congregations may occasionally concentrate on specific issues, focusing on one aspect of the congregation's implicit theology and paying special attention to selected portions of the explicit theologies.

what does congregation as community mean when you discover that members participate in several different congregations to meet specific needs? Or in the culture frame, how do artifacts and activities of the congregation support or contradict both your implicit and explicit theologies? Looking through a resources frame at where the money goes in the annual budget or what events consume most of the staff and volunteer time gives an important perspective on the implicit theologies of a congregation. As you study your congregation, remember that all of the work of description and reflection is not a prelude to the theological process, but an integral part of it.

Doing theology in a congregation may seem, at the outset, to be a daunting task. But once a congregation discovers the rhythms of practical theology, it can become an exciting and deeply satisfying undertaking, both to enhance the identity of a community called together in God's name and to create an ever deeper faithfulness to that call.

Your Local Theology and the Frames

In the following chapters, you will encounter various interpretive frames that will help give you a better picture of the situation and circumstances of your congregation. As you use each of them, keep in mind the implicit and explicit theologies of your congregation. Use each frame to ask about what kind of theology the resulting picture expresses and also what kinds of theology it might suggest for the future. For example, as you use an ecological frame,

Resources for Theological Reflection

Whitehead, James, and Evelyn Eaton Whitehead. *Method in Ministry: Theological Reflection and Christian Ministry.* Kansas City, Mo.: Sheed and Ward, 1995.

Killen, Patricia O'Connell, and John De Beer. *The Art of Theological Reflection.* New York: Continuum, 1994.

"The Newsletter." The Center for Theological Reflection, Box 726, Indian Rocks Beach, FL 34365-0726.

NOTES

1. Nancy Tatom Ammerman's *Congregation and Community* (New Brunswick, N.J.: Rutgers University Press, 1997) traces a number of congregations that are facing change in their communities. It is a gold mine of case histories for reflection on issues of change and the theological questions they evoke.

2. See Ammerman, *Congregation and Community*.

3. See Nancy Eiesland, *A Particular Place: Exurbanization and Religious Response* (New Brunswick, N.J.: Rutgers University Press, forthcoming).

4. Thomas H. Groome, *Sharing Faith: A Comprehensive Approach to Religious Education and Pastoral Ministry: The Way of Shared Praxis* (San Francisco: HarperSanFrancisco, 1991).

5. Don S. Browning, *A Fundamental Practical Theology: Descriptive and Strategic Proposals* (Minneapolis: Fortress, 1991).

6. "Praxis" is a word used in two different ways in the literature on practical theology. Ordinarily, it refers to a combination of theory and practice, recognizing that any practice is "theory-laden" in the sense that there is a theoretical position behind every practice. Praxis, then, is practice that is self-aware of the theory that shapes or informs it. Sometimes, however, "praxis" is used as an equivalent for "practice." In this chapter, praxis is used in the first sense.

7. For Groome, reflecting on the implicit theology revealed in a congregation's practices is a distinct step in the process that precedes attention to historical and other sources from the tradition. Hence, his numbering for the subsequent steps is different from Browning's.

8. Browning adds a distinction between "historical" and "systematic" theological work. The first plumbs the resources of the congregation's tradition of faith to find those parallels to its current situation, as well as those instances in that tradition that illumine and challenge the current situation. The second brings the present and past into conversation with one another in order to arrive at a new understanding of the present situation in light of the tradition of faith.

9. Samuel G. Freedman, *Upon This Rock: The Miracles of a Black Church* (San Francisco: HarperCollins, 1993).

10. One should be cautious, however, because every story can be read in a number of ways. The Exodus story is not a story of liberation and freedom for all people: some Native American Christians and Palestinian Christians identify with the Canaanites in the Exodus story, whose land was taken away from them by people who saw themselves as chosen. Similarly, the Exodus story is not read as part of the Easter Vigil in the Coptic Church in Egypt, as it is in other liturgical churches of Christianity.

11. R. Stephen Warner, *New Wine in Old Wineskins: Liberals and Evangelicals in a Small-Town Church* (Berkeley: University of California Press, 1990).

12. See the useful collection by Paul Heelas, Scott Lash, and Paul Morris, eds., *Detraditionalization* (Oxford: Basil Blackwell, 1995). The authors assert at the same time that a retraditionalization is taking place whereby identities are constructed from portions of various traditions.

13. James F. Hopewell, *Congregation: Stories and Structures* (Philadelphia: Fortress, 1987).

14. Gary Dorsey, *Congregation: The Journey Back to Church* (New York: Viking, 1995).

15. These are results of a 1988 Georgetown University study, discussed in Laurence Madden, ed., *The Church Awakening: 25 Years of Liturgical Renewal* (Collegeville, Minn.: Liturgical Press, 1992).

Chapter 2
Ecology: Seeing the Congregation in Context

NANCY L. EIESLAND AND
R. STEPHEN WARNER

Introduction

Each congregation sees itself as a community of God, dedicated to sacred things. Yet congregations are also social institutions. Like schools, factories, police departments, bakeries, and libraries, they are places where people interact, working with one another and serving constituents. This chapter concerns the place of the congregation in society, viewing the congregation through an ecological frame. Later chapters in this book look on the congregation as a culture, as a set of resources, and as an organism with its own internal processes. Here the congregation is analyzed as a unit interacting with other units in society: people, organizations, and cultures. Within this ecological frame, we will ask you to look at the other congregations in your community and try to examine your own congregation from their points of view.

The ecological perspective on religious institutions is a theoretical and practical response to increased religious pluralism and the restructuring of religious life.[1] In other times and places, religious institutions were the overlord, or steward, of society. They played this role, for example, in medieval Europe and Puritan New England, to take two Christian examples, and in precommunist Tibet and postrevolutionary Iran, to use

non-Christian ones. Under such a religious monopoly, it makes sense to ask about the interaction of "the" church with society, focusing on the effect of society on the religious system and the responsibility of the religious system for society. But when religious organizations proliferate and their theologies diverge, as in the United States or India today or the Roman Empire at the time of Jesus, no one of them can claim to be the unique conscience of society. In such times, religious groups have different moralities and missions, and they clamor, collide, compete, and sometimes cooperate with one another to influence their environment. We live in such a time, and therefore the ecological perspective—the recognition that your congregation is one among many congregations and organizations in the community—makes particular sense in our day.

The ecological frame presented here assumes that your congregation is one among many.[2] Other congregations have their place in the community, their own visions, and their particular constituents, and yours and theirs influence each other in many ways, for good and ill. Congregations can consciously cooperate and compete; they can hinder (and help) one another without intending to do so; they affect each other by their very presence as alternative communities of faith.

To recognize the variety of religious voices is not to diminish any one of them but rather to make each more special. The ecological perspective on the natural world has required each one of us to recognize ourselves as one of several billion individuals within a species and our species as one among millions—other mammals, other vertebrates, other animals, other carriers of DNA—in a single web of life. Humans are a unique part of that web, and each of us—vanity claims and faith affirms—is unique among humans. So also with congregations: there are over three hundred thousand of them in the United States, perhaps a hundred or more in your community, and every one is particular.[3]

For our part, we confess our special respect for those congregations which refuse to accept as given the boundaries between themselves and their surroundings, which can see beyond their own problems to the material and spiritual needs of their immediate neighbors and those far away, and which provide space where social distinctions can be transcended. As we shall see, one congregation (Mendocino Presbyterian) expanded its own fellowship in the 1970s to include a greater proportion of the people of its community, some of whom the congregation had previously disdained. The First Congregational Church of Long Beach, California, responded to change by becoming "open and affirming" to the gays and lesbians who represented one of the new constituencies in its community. Another congregation, Hinton Memorial United Methodist Church in Dacula, Georgia, (now known as First United Methodist Church) provides safe and affordable child care for people in the community regardless of their religious affiliation. Congregations that understand their context often make choices to attempt to alter it.

Aspects of Ecological Analysis

We need to be more specific about what it means to say a congregation exists in relation to an environment. We will speak of the environment, or that which is external to the congregation, as wide in *scope*, having several *layers*, and made up of elements that are relatively *invisible* as well as visible. Let us examine each of these aspects to see what is implied for congregational studies.

By wide *scope*, we mean the open-ended character of the congregation's environment—its extension from the local neighborhood to the global community, and from the immediate present to the past and future. A congregation is linked to networks and events across geographic and temporal space. Communities are not only discrete localities with stable boundaries and fixed constituencies, they are also characterized by shared conversations, common practices, and structures that promote cooperation and exchange. These conversations, practices, and structures often connect communities and congregations in what some have called a "global village." Many religious organizations are intimately related to congregations and societies around the world, which may be seen in terms of "foreign" missions or sister communities. Consider, for example, the dense web of social ties and reciprocal relations that characterize Lubavitch synagogues in Crown Heights, New York, and those in Israel; the connections of lay members of one Assembly of God church who travel to Guatemala to construct church facilities; and the ties college students from Korea often form when attending Presbyterian worship services while studying in the United States. This movement back and forth among communities around the world creates transnational circuits of relationship. These relationships, in turn, result in new songs, altered rituals, and new perspectives on global politics, economics, and culture. Whether in exurban Atlanta or rural Nigeria, increasingly congregations recognize their shared conversations, common practices, and structures of cooperation and exchange and find their place within a transnational religious ecology in which their local practices, values, and habits are shaped by far-flung relations.

The religious ecology, however, is not the only context that has become increasingly global in scope. The economic, political, and educational contexts within which congregations exist are intimately related to global circumstances. Whether through international events like the Olympics or media reports of global environmental changes, many communities recognize they are situated within a wider and more complex frame. Crackdowns on dissidents in Cuba result in increased immigration to Miami; economic downturns in Mexico spur increased immigration along the border; and opportunities for American college graduates to teach English as a second language in the Czech Republic create an expatriate glut in Prague. Air travel, Internet connections, and educational exchanges have altered the contexts within which we live. Whether considering our contexts as people of faith, working folk, citizens, or students, we must attend to the global connections that are part of our everyday lives.

To speak of several *layers* refers to the fact that the interaction between a congregation, or any institution, and its environment occurs at different levels. We will use a three-layer conceptualization from the discipline of sociology to speak of the social fabric of any community as a complex web of people, meanings, and relationships, alterations in any one of which can result in social ramifications elsewhere. The first layer is *demography*, or the characteristics of the people in the community, described in terms of numbers, age, and sex distribution; ethnic and racial profile; and changes in these data over time. The second layer is *culture*, or the systems of meaning, values, and practices shared by (and constitutive of) members of the community and groups within the community. The third layer is *organization*, or the systems of roles and relationships that structure the interactions of people in the community. These three levels—demography, culture, and organization—will help us understand the complex dynamics of the community. These concepts will be developed later in this chapter.

The complexity of social ecology is such that many things to which we want or ought to pay attention are relatively *invisible*. Both religious influence and social causation are sometimes open and visible, other times more hidden and subterranean. The pattern of influence is such that changes at one level (for example, demography) can lead to numerous and unexpected consequences at another (for example, organization). When new people move into the community and long-term residents move out or die (these are demographic changes), many congregations' membership rolls (at the organizational level) will show the effects of these shifts. Moreover, new congregations are likely to develop to better meet the needs of the new members of the community (another organizational-level change).

Many processes are less obvious, and we urge you to watch for "invisible" people and intangible forces in your community; these are marginalized people and hidden forces that too easily escape our attention. Depending on your community, poor, homeless, or old people; people with disabilities; people of color; the mentally ill; those who speak other languages; and even people who smoke may be kept out of sight. In some communities, young people are kept off the streets by fearful parents, and girls are seen only in school and church. In some locales, people with disabilities are excluded from much social life because of architectural barriers that prevent their participation. Carl Dudley writes, "Students of the Bible have long recognized the special attention God devotes to 'widows and orphans,' the Biblical symbol of invisible people in every society."[4] Depending on your community and your congregation's values, the "widows and orphans" in need may be pensioners on fixed incomes, latchkey children, victims of domestic violence, racial minorities, or the unborn. Look for them.

"Intangible forces" may be the stuff of legend in your town, "dominating employers, entrenched political figures, dysfunctional educational systems, and the like."[5] But other forces can be quiet and nameless, like the slowly declining real wages that create pressure for both parents of very young children to work outside the home in order to make ends meet, or like the increased cost of real estate in some towns that changes the population mix of the community. (Decreased property values are usually noisier forces!) Other trends that can creep up on us are those that first affect our children, for example, the expectation that everyone in a classroom is computer-literate or the concept that socializing in mixed-sex groups is more "cool" than "dating."

In a complex, interdependent economy, some communities and sectors can do better at exactly the same time as others are doing worse. For example, export-oriented industries may benefit from international trade while older manufacturing towns are seeing massive layoffs. Some congregations may prosper while others wither. At any given time your community may be experiencing social trends that are not the ones talked about on television and in news magazines. The experiences and authority of your own congregation members have a validity that cannot be denied by the "experts." Thus, "a discussion of intangible forces allows members of the congregation to wrestle with the differences between the official information and personal experiences. Sometimes the ripple of a trend is felt first by service institutions like the churches and schools"[6] long before the media notice it. It is important for you to discuss these forces.

In this chapter, we will first discuss three exercises that enlist members of the congregation in the study of the ecological dimension. Then we will consider in turn the demographic, cultural, and organizational aspects of the congregation's context.

Getting in Touch with the Congregation's Context

Even as it is dedicated to God, your congregation is a human institution located in history (the date of its founding to the present), in a specific place in geography (your community), and in the lives of its members (the network "maps" of their lives). We call this time-space-network location the context of the congregation.

We intend to say a lot about context in this book, and your minister and denomination can provide you with other resources to help you analyze and understand your context. Nonetheless, the only final experts on your congregation's context are those who are intimately familiar with your local circumstances—the members of your congregation, your office staff, your clergy, or maybe even a consultant you hire to join you in your self-study. For this reason, we suggest that you begin the study of your context by assembling groups from the congregation to conduct three participatory exercises: one to look at the congregation in time, one to look at it in space, and a third to explore the network maps of members of the congregation.

Construct a Congregational Time Line

One good way to gain a collective understanding of your congregation's place in history is to spend an evening (or a cold winter day) in the social hall making a time line, a structured, collective reflection on the past. It works best to bring together a diverse group from your congregation, youngsters and especially old-timers (who can share their own recollections and serve as a resource for the younger people's questions), women and men, and both those currently serving on committees and those enjoying a well-earned retirement from heavy involvement. Making a time line is fun, and it might be a good idea to begin the session with a simple potluck.

The goal in constructing a time line is to understand how the congregation is situated within an inclusive conception of its history, that is, local, denominational, national, and global history. Also important in this exercise is recognizing that history telling is a collective effort, involving multiple perspectives on those events and processes brought about by demographic, cultural, and organizational change. (For instructions on doing a time line, see pages 209-10 in the methods chapter.)

Figure 2.1 (part I): TIME LINE FOR MENDOCINO PRESBYTERIAN CHURCH, 1957-1968

Location	1957	1958	1959	1960	1961	1962	1963	1964	1965	1966	1967	1968
Church and Congregation	Membership peaks at 160; Rev. Althorpe retires / Preston Hall (classrooms & meeting rooms) opens	Rev. Higginson arrives	Centennial of congregation	Full self-support (first since 1931)	242 Easter attendance is "largest ever recorded"	Rev. Higginson retires / Rev. Hsu arrives	Trustees merged with session / New Preston Hall policy (building open to community)	Youth fellowship folds / Hsu debates Prop. 14	Hsu complains of poor attendance	Rev. Hsu leaves for UPCUSA position	Rev. Kimmerly arrives / Manse refurbished	Sanctuary centennial / Experimental worship
Community			Mendocino Arts Center opens		New highway bridge opens		Wells run dry in regional drought	Larry Redford begins M. H. S. teaching	*Russians Are Coming* filmed in Mendocino			
Region and State		"Pat" Brown elected governor		Sonoma State College opens	Cursillo movement begins in San Francisco	Mumford Fair Housing Law passed		Free Speech Movement at Berkeley	Watts Riot	Ronald Reagan elected governor	S. F. "Summer of Love" / Delano farm strike	Strike at S. F. State
Nation	Interstate Highway Act passed			Freedom rides in South / JFK elected		Cuban missile crisis	"I Have a Dream"—M. L. King in Washington / JFK assassinated	Beatles tour U. S. / Civil Rights Act passed	Voting Rights Act passed / Immigration Law reform passed			M. L. King assassinated / Bobby Kennedy assassinated
World			Cuban revolution		Berlin wall built				Bombing of North Vietnam begins		Israeli-Arab "Six-Day War"	

Figure 2.1 (part II): TIME LINE FOR MENDOCINO PRESBYTERIAN CHURCH, 1969-1981

	1969	1970	1971	1972	1973	1974	1975	1976	1977	1978	1979	1980	1981
Church	Antioch Ranch (Redfords' ministry to ex-hippies) opens; Vietnam moratorium in Mendocino	Membership bottoms out at 124; Kearneys (semi-retired affluent couple) join church	Antioch member David Baker serves on session; Redford resigns high school job	Rev. Kimmerly leaves for new pulpit; Xmas musicale disrupted by interim pastor's anti-war sermon	Rev. Underwood arrives; New organ installed	Attendance soars; New hymnals purchased	Underwoods buy home; manse rented out; Good Shepherd School (Christian academy) opens	Membership exceeds 200; Ben & Carol Weir (UPCUSA workers) visit from Lebanon	Antioch fellowship begins independent Sunday meetings; Many MPC elders make Cursillo	Bruce Douglas begins new youth group; Church resumes occupancy of manse	Bruce Douglas ordained as Assistant Pastor	Membership peaks at 295; Church takes title to "town green"; Rev. Althorpe dies	First membership decline since 1970; Vietnamese refugee family hosted
Local	"Therese's Land" hippie commune opens	Mendocino placed on Nat'l Register of Historic Places	Summer of '42 filming provides temporary jobs in Mendocino	Mass conversions at "The Holy Land"	Mendocino Historical Review Board established		County crackdown on non-standard dwellings	Alternative public high school opens	Local paper (the Beacon) sold to out-of-town publisher	Sinsemilla marijuana cultivation is major business in county	Hill House, large new motel, opens	Fort Bragg lumber mill in steep decline	
California	Delano, Calif., grape boycott	Governor Reagan re-elected				Jerry Brown elected governor		Jim Jones's People's Temple in Ukiah		Cursillo center opens in Santa Rosa			
National	Americans land on the Moon			Nixon goes to China; Nixon re-elected	Roe v. Wade decided by Supreme Court; Watergate hearings	Nixon resigns		Jimmy Carter elected President		Double-digit inflation	Jerry Falwell begins "Moral Majority"	Ronald Reagan elected President	
International		Allende elected in Chile		Xmas bombing of N. Vietnam	Yom Kippur War; oil prices jump		Fall of Saigon	Civil War in Lebanon		People's Temple mass suicides in Guyana		El Salvador Archbishop Romero assassinated	

Figure 2.1 is a time line for the Presbyterian Church of Mendocino, California, as it might have been constructed by members of the congregation in 1982 looking back a quarter century.[7] As they put this graphic story together, the participants could remind each other that their church, the state, and the nation had all experienced radical changes in leadership during that slice of history: pastors Frederick Althorpe, Ward Higginson, Peter Hsu, Mark Kimmerly, and Eric Underwood[8] occupied the Presbyterian manse; governors Pat Brown, Ronald Reagan, and Jerry Brown were in the California statehouse; presidents Dwight D. Eisenhower, John F. Kennedy, Lyndon Johnson, Richard Nixon, Gerald Ford, Jimmy Carter, and Ronald Reagan were in the White House. The time line makes graphically apparent that the twenty-seven-year-old, Chinese American Peter Hsu fit well within the youthful, idealistic, and tragically brief years of the Kennedy presidency and Martin Luther King's 1963 march on Washington. It is not that the national cultural current *caused* a local echo; these correlations are not one-way. Kennedy's election preceded the call to Peter Hsu, whereas the born-again Eric Underwood had been Mendocino's pastor for three years before Jimmy Carter surprised America by declaring himself a born-again candidate for president and six years before Jerry Falwell founded the "Moral Majority."

Similarly, having constructed their time line, the people of the Mendocino congregation could see the import of cultural currents in the connections among the Beatles' tour of the United States in 1964, the coincident demise of the congregation's old-fashioned Westminster Fellowship youth group, San Francisco's hippie "summer of love" in 1967, and the opening of a youth-oriented ministry at Antioch Ranch in 1969. Cultural and organizational alterations in the context also can be seen in the time line: evangelicalism's popularity increased nationwide and local organizations—the Arts Center and the Historical Review Board—were developed both to harness and control the growing tourist trade and to bolster the community's livability.

The mix of memories people bring to a time line exercise is very likely to help participants locate their congregation in world history, and here the histories younger people are learning in school could complement the recollections of long time church members. For example, Mendocino high school students may know that Israel and its Arab neighbors went to war in 1967 and again in 1973, and their parents may recall long lines at the gas station (and a dip in tourist business) in 1973. Some church activists may remember that Presbyterian fraternal workers Ben and Carol Weir, on leave from their duties in Lebanon, spoke at a congregational potluck supper in 1976, two years before Ben Weir was kidnapped in Beirut. Perhaps the young people will be learning in school about the war in Vietnam just when a family from Southeast Asia is being sponsored by the congregation for resettlement in the United States. That will no doubt remind some church veterans of the abortive Christmas Eve musicale in 1972, and they may recall the feelings they had when their interim pastor could not restrain his anger over the bombing of Haiphong Harbor going on at that very hour. In such perhaps small ways, members of the Mendocino congregation become aware of the impact of international currents.

The lesson is not, however, that the congregation is at the mercy of larger political, social, and economic forces, for the time line shows that the congregation's own efforts mattered. For example, the hard work to refurbish the manse was done during the lean year of 1967 in order to accommodate an incoming pastor, and during the next year the sanctuary was restored to celebrate the building's centennial. Another innovation was the opening of the private, outspokenly Christian, Good Shepherd School in 1975. Although the private school was not an organ of the church itself, most of its leaders and many of its students came from families within the congregation who had been caught up in the religious revivals of the time, ranging from the charismatic fellowship at Larry Redford's Antioch Ranch to the Roman Catholic-inspired Cursillo movement.[9] In its own time countercultural, the Good Shepherd School was thus on the leading edge of changes that, for better or worse, have since made their impact on American culture and particularly on education.

These lessons would be better remembered if the completed time line were left up on the wall of the social hall for some months after the time-line potluck. Thus, looking back twenty-five years, the congregation can see that it has been part of history and not merely a bystander.

Conduct a Space Tour

The second aspect of context is your congregation's spatial location in the community. Here, too, members of your congregation can be both enlisted as informants to provide information and encouraged as students to learn more. For these purposes we suggest an exercise best suited for warmer months and daylight hours, a kind of mobile committee meeting. Take a walk, or a ride, around your community. If your congregation is in a new location, you need to look around at this location. If you have been at the same location for a long time, you need to see what and who is new in the neighborhood and to see the familiar with new eyes.

In preparation for this exercise, it is a good idea to map where the congregation's members live. You can have fun doing this in a group meeting, with everyone plotting a page from the congregation's directory. You'll need a large, detailed street map of your area and a bunch of push pins. Post the map on corkboard and place a pin on the map to mark the address of each member household. Use an especially large pin, or a cluster of smaller ones, to indicate the address of the congregation.

You can usefully complicate the exercise and learn something about changing patterns if you use pins of different colors for members who joined at different times (for example, ten-year intervals before the present, or before or after the congregation moved to new quarters, or corresponding to pastorates). If there have been changes in your neighborhood, you may find that newer members come from different areas than do longtime members. If there have been changes in the transportation system (a new highway, for example) newer members may come from longer distances. In some cases, very few members will live nearby the congregation.

The pattern of pins on the map represents the congregation's geographic community, the outlying pins describing the perimeter and the pins around the congregation designating the immediate neighborhood. Depending on the extent of this perimeter, a driving as well as a walking tour, and perhaps more than one of each, may be called for.

Having done the mapping, you are ready to walk (or drive). It does not matter if you cannot get everyone together at the same time: it is a good idea to conduct two or more expeditions at different times of the day and on different days of the week.

Taking a Walk. In many cases, when members live close by or the congregation is located in a built-up area, it will be feasible to survey the community on foot. You should set aside the better part of one or more days to walk through the congregation's neighborhood, absorbing its sights, sounds, and aromas; looking for places people live, work, study, shop, play, and worship; and noticing how people get from place to place.

The purpose of the walk-around exercise is twofold. The first is to discover things in the neighborhood that are new but somewhat hidden, for example, new owners of the pharmacy; new small business establishments, such as beauty parlors and auto repair shops in residential neighborhoods; replacement of local businesses with national chains; new residences; new mailboxes on old houses, evidence that the owners have

Sidebar 2.1
NOTES ON A TUESDAY MORNING
NEIGHBORHOOD WALK-AROUND,
EVANSTON, ILLINOIS

Evanston is an older, medium-sized, midwestern city that is economically, ethnically, and racially diverse; a suburb to a great city; and home to a major university.

There are not many other pedestrians in this period after rush hour and before lunch, but there is plenty of traffic, including sirens, fire engines, ambulances, beat cops on bicycles, commuter trains, and airplanes turning toward O'Hare. An exception to the few-pedestrians rule is the people gathered to smoke outside the two intermediate care facilities for mental patients, which serve five hundred residents. Some of the neighbors are upset with that density, but what do the churches think?

There are some huge mansions in the neighborhood, but it is a mixture of big houses, modest houses, tiny houses, coach houses, two-flats, six-flats, new condo developments, and big old apartment buildings with scores of units. "For Sale" signs, some marked SOLD, and "For Rent" signs, listing apartment sizes from studios to three bedrooms, dot the blocks. What's the asking price? What's the rent? There are many real estate offices, some with black-oriented and some with white-oriented realtors.

Walking down an alley: Are those houses or garages, or is that a workplace—or something else? Hidden people may be people we want to care about, for example, the employees of a sweatshop. But other hidden people such as crack dealers may be seen as a threat to us.

There are lots of cars parked outside a factory next to the tracks. Signs say "Employee Entrance," "No Trespassing," and "Smith Corp." What do they make there? Who works there? Are they good jobs? Where do the employees live?

Who are the new owners of old businesses? Who lives or works upstairs from the storefronts? Are some of these places apartments? Are others professional suites? We don't see many medical or dental offices. Maybe it's the wrong part of town for them, or maybe they're upstairs from the banks.

We don't recognize the names of these banks (Main Street, Grove Street, Chicago Avenue). They're not new, but they've been merged and consolidated. Are the managers the same or new? Would we be able to ask them to help sponsor the neighborhood picnic this summer?

Plenty of eateries, grills, cafes, restaurants, bistros, pubs—plain to fancy, cheap to expensive, fast-food takeouts to sit-down places. What time of day do they open?

---

subdivided apartments or rented rooms; houses with fresh paint and those with peeling paint; places where homeless people try to get shelter; and places the city is spiffing up. Look for evidence of the intangible forces and invisible people mentioned earlier. The second purpose is to recognize things that may have become so familiar that they are not noticed, for example, who else is on the sidewalks at various times of the day and night; who gets on or off the bus at what time; what intersections are particularly busy and at what times; what properties have become such eyesores that they escape attention; and where exactly the firehouse or the police station are located.

Make sure you walk the side streets as well as the main streets and that you survey the alleys, too, in communities that have them. In the course of the walk be alert to your own reactions to what you see and hear, but also try to look at things from the perspective of other people and groups. Put yourself in the role of a newcomer to the community. How apparent are the basic services a person would need to settle into the town? Where does one find a family doctor, an AA meeting, a laundry, a video store, a church, or a pizza parlor? If they are listed in the phone book, can the address be found? What if the newcomer could not read English? How would an older or physically disabled person handle the curbs on the sidewalks or the stairs into buildings? (It may be enlightening to have one member in your group who is a wheelchair user; you may even want to rent or borrow a

Graffiti: Whose is it? What does it say? How long has it been there? Who hasn't yet painted it over? Colorful murals under the railroad tracks—one painted by the girls at the YMCA, another by the kids at the junior high.

What a big junior high school! Kids out at recess make lots of noise. They all seem to be the same height! The clock on the tower still doesn't work! The Youth Drop-In Center across from the school is closed on Monday and Tuesday. The former public school on Main Street (Park School) is now a special school for the disabled. St. Mary's School is now McGaw YMCA Preschool and Day Care Center. It's busy today.

And the churches: There's about one per block. Four in the neighborhood are Methodist. What's the historic relation between the AME Zion church and the African American UMC church in the next block? Four or five are Baptist. There's the Haitian Baptist church and its mother congregation a block away, Calvary Baptist, which now also houses a Korean congregation. According to the yellow pages, Calvary is Baptist General Conference-affiliated, but the Korean congregation, Agape Korean Baptist Church, lists itself as Southern Baptist. Bethany Baptist (an African American church, Progressive National Baptist) is celebrating the sixth anniversary of their dynamic woman pastor this week. They brag about her as "a pastor with a Heavenly Vision with Earthly Focus."

One Catholic church in our neighborhood: St. Mary's; cornerstone says 1891, and the sandstone building looks like it. It occupies a large, well-maintained campus, but St. Mary's School, at the opposite end of the block, is now the YMCA's preschool and day care center.

Two ELCA Lutheran churches: St. Paul's (historically German); cornerstone says 1922. Four blocks away is our church, Immanuel Lutheran (historically Swedish), also ELCA; cornerstone says 1898. But which congregation has been here longer?

Evanston Bible Fellowship meets in a converted office suite down the block from our church. They have "Life Training" at 10:05 on Sunday. The yellow pages lists them as an Evangelical Free Church.

Around the village green are the "Lake Street Church" (which used to be First Baptist, what's the story there?), the First Congregational Church (not UCC but thoroughly New England looking), First Church of Christ, Scientist (a Greek temple, with a reading room open behind the sanctuary this morning), and First Presbyterian, another midwestern sandstone building with a huge plant. Its hundred-plus-space parking lot has forty vehicles on a Tuesday morning.

The Salvation Army is near downtown, a plain office-type building that says 1923 over the door; a regular service schedule is posted. Three Black men are on the front steps looking at letters, referral slips? They are among the few people we see outside any of the churches this Tuesday morning.

The neighborhood's big synagogue, Beth Emet, is six blocks from our church on a busy corner. Does the Meditation Center on Dempster—Zen and Tai Chi—count as a church? Who goes to these churches? Do the people live nearby? Work here? Or just come to church here? What types of programs draw them?

wheelchair if you do not have a volunteer who regularly uses one.) Where would a homeless person spend the night? How does a first-grader get across a busy intersection on the way to school? Where do teens hang out? Are there places and times that feel particularly dangerous? What feels safe? Keep a notebook on what you observe. We will have more suggestions after the next section.

Taking a Drive. The scale of some communities, especially newer ones, may require that you explore by car. The purposes of the drive-around are the same as those of the walk-around—to see for the first time what is unfamiliar and to see anew what is too familiar—but the scale is larger. You may observe more big, new things like shopping malls, industrial parks, and school campuses, or notice changes like the now vacant shops along Main Street. You will also want to ask some different questions. For example, how easy would it be to find your way around if you were a newcomer? Are the roads and streets clearly marked? Are address numbers visible?

Once again, it is important to survey systematically and explore back roads and alleys as well as main thoroughfares. And do not try to go so far that you miss what is close by. Look for mixes of new and old farmhouses amidst strip malls and country churches fronting busy boulevards. Also, get out of your car to explore the malls. Who shops there? What is for sale? Who just hangs around? Does the mall feel dangerous or safe?

In fast-growing communities, there is likely

to be a different mix of people than in more settled towns, and therefore, you have a different mix of perspectives to imagine. For example, put yourself into the role of community old-timers—the people who have been members of that old country congregation for a generation or more—and try to see the changes through their eyes, as well as the eyes of those new to the community. (The figure accompanying the next exercise, "network maps," will prove an aid to your imagination.) Suppose it used to be safe and simple to cross the county road on the way to school or church, but now there are six lanes of traffic in the way.

Talking About Space. Whether you conduct a walk-around or a drive-around, a good exercise for congregations is to set up several teams, each assigned to cover the same geographic area, each with a different perspective in mind: that of a young family newly arrived in the community, a single mother, an immigrant family, a college student, an older couple whose children are gone, or an older single person on a fixed income.

Save time at the end of your excursion for recording your impressions. A simple list with the headings "What I Saw" and "New Questions Raised" will help organize your thoughts. A discussion of what group members observed and experienced is always enlightening.

Observing the Local Religious Ecology. For your congregation, it is particularly important to become aware of the other religious organizations in your community, and this may be done by looking around the community on Friday, Saturday, and Sunday to see what other congregations are doing. Are a lot of people out walking on Sunday morning? Or on Saturday morning? Where is it hard to find parking? How many worship services are advertised on the marquees outside the churches? What languages are represented?

Your committee might notice a lot of activity on Sunday in the parking lot of the high school and find out that a "worship center" or "Vineyard" rents the auditorium to meet

there. One research project first found out about a flourishing Islamic center during a lunch break one Friday by following an unusually heavy stream of traffic down an alleyway between two apartment buildings. What social scientists informally call a "windshield survey"—the signs of activity you can see as you drive systematically along the streets—may provide the first information you have about other religious organizations in town. You may also want to follow up on what you discover by asking members of various committees to visit services or conduct telephone interviews with members or leaders of the congregations in your area. We will talk more about this later in the chapter.

The importance of understanding the local religious ecology has only recently been addressed by scholars like the authors of this book. Indeed, the time line example above (figure 2.1) is flawed by its author's relative neglect of the activities of the other congregations in Mendocino, particularly St. Anthony's Church (Roman Catholic) and the Mendocino Baptist Church (Southern Baptist Convention). But we can no longer ignore the issue. Learning more about your local religious ecology can enable you to think about how congregations within your community may complement one another in meeting needs rather than simply competing for members. It will also help you to understand the increasingly complex religious attachments of congregants.

Explore Members' Network Maps

Though understanding more about the congregation's history and the geographical situation will tell you a great deal, your task of getting in touch with your congregation's context is not yet complete. Not everything that occurs in your congregation's history or within geographical proximity will be equally important. Rather, members have likely transformed these historical events and places into meaningful patterns and networks. They develop "maps" that govern how they move through the community. People organize history and space in different ways. Think, for instance, about how members of your congregation identified different key events in your congregational history. Your congregation's history could be told using a variety of highlights, such as construction projects or pastoral changes. In similar fashion, the geographical context of your congregation can be mapped in multiple ways. To understand your context, you need to know how the congregation fits into the patterns of meaning your members have constructed.

These maps are largely formed by the routines of work, leisure, and consumption. Think of your own weekly routine. If you traced on a map the routes you take, what patterns would be evident at week's end? Likely you would have several dominant routes between home and work, work and day care, day care and grocery store. Other more infrequent routes may also be present, for example, connecting home to place of worship, homes of friends, movie theaters, and gymnasiums.

Each week you and members of your congregation shape your context into distinct patterns that are a result of living in a particular environment and negotiating that environment to meet your needs. These maps not only tell you how congregants get from one place to another, they reveal pictures of community relations and organizational ties. They also may uncover how different constituencies within your congregation—for example, old-timers and newcomers—relate to your geographical context.

For this exercise you will need several detailed maps of your city or locale attached to corkboard, push-pins with colored ends, and yarn. You will also need several large sheets of newsprint or butcher paper and marker pens. Your work may be expedited if you have a copy of your local telephone directory handy as well.

Members can have fun completing this exercise after a Wednesday night supper or as part of various classes or group meetings and then sharing discoveries during an all-congregation gathering. The exercise should take about forty-five minutes to an hour to complete and discuss.

Begin by dividing participants into groups representing what congregants feel are significant constituencies within the congregation. Perhaps your congregation is composed of many long-time residents of the community and numerous newcomers, or perhaps several ethnic groups are prominent. In any case, you will want to ask representatives of each constituency to sit together at a table. Identifying the various constituencies in your congregation will likely be illuminating in itself.

Next you will want to ask for volunteers at each table who are willing to speak about their activities and memberships in the community. You are not trying to find individuals who are strictly representative of everyone around the table. You will have opportunity to talk about the differences later.

When the volunteers have been designated, ask each one to write on the butcher paper answers to the following questions.

- Where do you live?

- Where do you work? Where do the other members of your household work? If you are not currently employed, where do you spend the most time during the day?

- If you have children, where do they attend school?

- If you have pets, where is your veterinarian?

- Where do your parents and siblings live? Or if your parents are deceased, where are they buried?

- Where do your two closest friends reside?

- Where do you do your grocery shopping?

- Where do you purchase your clothing?

- Where are the clubs or voluntary organizations you attend? If you participate in any other groups—for example, Bible studies, yoga groups, or support groups—where do they meet? If you play golf, tennis, or softball; work out at a gym; or attend football, basketball, or baseball games regularly, where do you do that?

When volunteers have written the answers to these questions, you will begin assembling the map for the volunteer at your table. Place a thumbtack on your map at the location of the volunteer's home. Then locate your congregation and place the first pushpin. After that, locate the places the volunteer identified in answer to each of the questions asked above. Insert a pushpin at each location. After each pin has been inserted, group members can cut the yarn to attach to each pin.

After the volunteer's map is finished, encourage those at each table to speak about the patterns revealed. Ask group members how they imagine that their own network maps might differ from or be similar to that of the volunteer. When you reconvene in the larger group, you will want to present each group's findings and discuss the similarities or differences among the maps. What causes these variations? How do these maps help you understand your congregation's context better?

Figures 2.2 and 2.3 are network maps prepared by two families within one congregation in Dacula, Georgia, a community changing from a small town into an exurb of a larger city.[10] Simply comparing the two figures allows one to realize that the context for these two families is quite different. Vernon and Marie England's[11] network map is more concentrated in the changing small town, Dacula, which is the center for their recreation, club meetings, church services, and shopping. Todd and Faith Penner's network map is much more elastic. Leisure activities, meetings, religious participation, and shopping are organized in relation to individual choice—not within a geographic locale.

The network maps of the Englands and Penners illustrate the divergent cultural worlds of old-timers and newcomers. Vernon and Marie England have lived in Dacula since childhood. They are old-timers through and through. Vernon's father was a Baptist preacher in the area, and Marie's father owned an auto repair shop and later a jewelry store in town. The two have known each other all their lives and were married in a simple ceremony in Marie's parents' home when Vernon was nineteen and Marie was eighteen.

Figure 2.2 NETWORK MAP OF VERNON AND MARIE ENGLAND

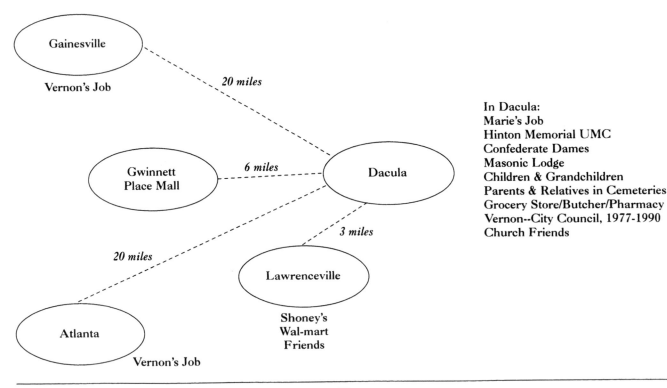

Gainesville

Vernon's Job

20 miles

Gwinnett Place Mall

6 miles

Dacula

In Dacula:
Marie's Job
Hinton Memorial UMC
Confederate Dames
Masonic Lodge
Children & Grandchildren
Parents & Relatives in Cemeteries
Grocery Store/Butcher/Pharmacy
Vernon--City Council, 1977-1990
Church Friends

3 miles

20 miles

Lawrenceville

Shoney's
Wal-mart
Friends

Atlanta

Vernon's Job

Since 1985, when Vernon retired from his job as a machinist, the couple has lived in a subdivision on the right side of the railroad tracks that divide Dacula. Marie and Vernon live only three houses up from their oldest son's family and regularly baby-sit the grandchildren. In 1992, Tom, their youngest son, also moved with his family to another subdivision nearby. With the exception of their daughter, whom Marie and Vernon visit every two or three months at her home in south Georgia, the couple's network of friends and family is tightly bound to Dacula. Most of them are "Saturday night church friends"—a group that for years has been going out for dinner every Saturday and then to church on Sunday.

The Englands have long been active contributors to Dacula's community life. For example, they still attend high school events, such as football games and carnivals. They go to elementary and middle school activities in which their grandchildren are now old enough to participate. Vernon has been active in the local chapter of the VFW and the Masonic Lodge. He also served on the Dacula City Council from 1977 to 1990, during which time he opposed most of the development in the area as well as the installation of county sewer services. Marie has been active in several local clubs as well. Initially after her marriage, she participated in a sewing circle composed of young women who had grown up in the area and whose husbands were in the military. The group, now informally called Ladies' Aid, continues to meet for coffee at least once a month. Then,

in the early 1950s, Marie also helped found the local chapter of the Confederate Dames.

Habit and commitment to local resources shape the Englands' consumption network as well. Vernon shops at a locally owned grocery in Dacula, although he admits that it is does not provide the best selection of produce. Marie and Vernon occasionally dine out close to home at local diners. Marie laments, "Some of these guys aren't going to make it, what with all the newcomers, but it sure seems a shame to see them go after all these years."

Church, too, has been a long-time commitment for the Englands. Vernon's and Marie's active involvement in Hinton Memorial United Methodist Church began in the early 1950s, and, despite their distress about the decline in Hinton's prestige and numbers, the couple has maintained their involvement in and sizable donations to Hinton Memorial. Except for funerals, they do not attend any other religious services in Dacula or the metropolitan region.

As newcomers, Faith and Todd Penner have a different relationship with Hinton Memorial UMC. They joined the congregation in 1993 when Todd and the couple's two children were baptized there. They decided to become members partially in response to their perceived need for assistance in teaching their children about values. The Penners, who are in their midthirties, had lived in the Dacula area for four years when they joined Hinton Memorial and have since moved to Memphis, following a job opportunity for Todd.

Figure 2.3 NETWORK MAP OF TODD AND FAITH PENNER

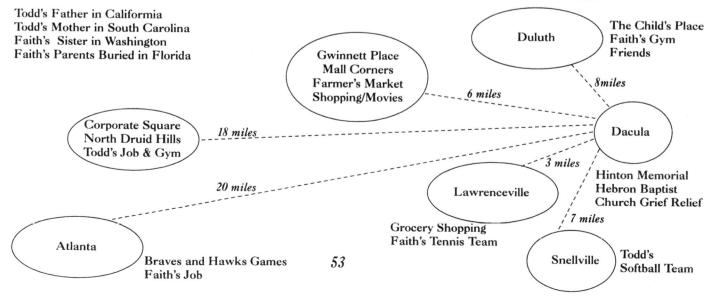

Todd's Father in California
Todd's Mother in South Carolina
Faith's Sister in Washington
Faith's Parents Buried in Florida

Duluth

The Child's Place
Faith's Gym
Friends

Gwinnett Place
Mall Corners
Farmer's Market
Shopping/Movies

6 miles

8 miles

Corporate Square
North Druid Hills
Todd's Job & Gym

18 miles

Dacula

3 miles

Hinton Memorial
Hebron Baptist
Church Grief Relief

20 miles

Lawrenceville

7 miles

Grocery Shopping
Faith's Tennis Team

Atlanta

Braves and Hawks Games
Faith's Job

Snellville

Todd's
Softball Team

Crucial for the Penners in choosing Dacula for their residence was good access to interstate highways. Faith was then working at a downtown Atlanta bank. Todd was working in Lawrenceville and looking for a better job as an engineer, which he eventually landed. Todd was especially keen to find a home on a large lot, yet he wanted to be close enough to the city to make attendance at Hawks and Braves games and other cultural events relatively easy.

The influx of residential development to the area has improved the commercial offerings in Faith's estimate. Todd Penner could think of no business that the family did in Dacula itself. "What's there?" asked Todd rhetorically. On most weekends the couple shopped together for groceries, clothing, and whatever else at or near Gwinnett Place Mall. The Penners were also involved in few voluntary associations—local or otherwise. Faith characterized her husband as "not a joiner." He was, however, an active member of a gym near his work, and he and a colleague from work were on a softball team in another nearby town. Faith, who quit her job in downtown Atlanta when her second child was born, was involved in a women's tennis league. And since late 1992, she had attended weekly Grief Relief support group meetings at Hebron Baptist Church to work through her parents' deaths in an accident years earlier.

For Faith and Todd Penner, the networks that formed their neighborhood spanned the metropolitan region. Though they resided near Dacula, they participated in few local events. Faith, in particular, was very purposive in putting together a network of support, including religious participation, that provided the services she and her family needed. In addition to membership at Hinton Memorial and participation in Hebron's Grief Relief group, she also enrolled their children at The Child's Place, a day care run by a nearby Pentecostal church.

Mapping the activities and involvements of these two families reveals that religion fits into their lives in dissimilar ways. Hinton Memorial United Methodist Church is the only religious organization of which Vernon and Marie Eng-land are members. Their activities and friendships are anchored there. For Todd and Faith, however, Hinton Memorial was one among several religious attachments. Their religious choices were very much shaped by the larger religious ecology. The Methodist church, while a meaningful involvement, was not the only religious gathering of which they were a part.

Examples, such as the Penners', of complex maps of religious participation are becoming more and more common today. Many people are willing to look to more than one religious organization to address their spiritual concerns. Sometimes this willingness stems from a congregation's inability to meet the specialized needs members have. For example, not every congregation can offer numerous support groups, day care, respite assistance, or Bible studies. Thus individuals who seek these specialized services look to other religious groups, joining selectively to meet specific needs.

This trend toward multiple religious associations means that increasingly congregations must think specifically about the local religious ecology. No longer is it possible to think of each congregation as having a constituency that is largely distinct because of either geographical proximity or denominational loyalty. Many individuals are willing to travel some distance to participate in congregations or religious organizations that meet their particular religious or spiritual needs. Furthermore, congregations can no longer count on denominational loyalty to draw congregants to them from their neighborhood or community. The former status and social values of denominations have been disrupted by the proliferation of new religious organizations. Although denominational affiliation is still important to individuals seeking a congregation, prospective members also look for innovative or relevant programs, worship styles, and services, such as Sunday school, day care, and support groups.

What We've Learned

The exercises described in this section are tools that can enable you to better consider your environment. The time line, walk-around/drive-around, and network maps are designed to assist you in doing systematic, careful observation, recollection, and plotting of your context. These exercises are not, however, designed to be contextual calisthenics! Exploring is fun. Your time line may include the laughter and tears of recalling a disastrous Christmas Eve service. A stop for coffee and pie—or the equivalent—is a must during the walk-around/drive-around. And ask network mappers to designate the places that are simply "off their maps," that is, places that they would never think about going, they deliberately avoid, or where they have membership but never darken the door. If the exercises are not at least somewhat enjoyable, your fellow congregants may simply give up the task. As the English poet John Dryden wrote, "For present joys are more to flesh and blood, Than a dull prospect of a distant good." Have fun now.

After you have completed this phase of your research, you should gather committee members to report their initial findings. Do you see patterns in your congregational history? What different *types of individuals* are in your community? What *cultural groups* have you identified? Which *organizations*, including churches, seem particularly influential? You may not have definitive answers, but in the process of brainstorming, your questions may become clearer. You may also recognize the need for further in-depth study of one aspect of your context, such as how political power works locally or the dynamics of the religious ecology. In what follows, we offer additional, more focused resources for sharpening your understanding of the people, cultural meanings, and relations that make up the social fabric in your locale.

Demography

Your congregation is situated in a context of people; who they are matters—and should matter—for you. The exercises in the previous section employed group discussion and visual encounters to sensitize your congregation to the types of people in your community. This section explores this topic in greater depth, using publicly available sources of information, primarily the United States Census. The census is especially valuable for helping us see "invisible" people because of its legally imposed obligation to count *all* people in the United States. True, the extent to which the Census Bureau has fully complied with that obligation has been a matter of dispute for years, particularly as large cities and minority advocate groups have argued that undercounting of homeless people, minority males, and non-English speakers disadvantages both them and the jurisdictions within which they reside. Despite such undercounting, census figures are the best estimates we have for numbers in all population categories, and we will present three illustrations making use of them. (For a detailed discussion of the use of census data, see page 213 in the methods chapter.) Yet, as we shall see, the sheer numbers do not speak for themselves, and they have to be interpreted in light of the sort of site-specific local knowledge that was gained through the preceding exercises.

Population Growth and Decline: The Example of Mendocino, California[12]

Population changes present constraints and opportunities for congregations but do not determine destinies. Although congregations are made up of people, the link between who lives in the community and who attends a congregation is a complex one. When new people arrive, they might be "just the kind of people" for your congregation; alternatively, they may be "not your sort." The people who move out of town are often younger ones. Thus, if your congregation is disproportionately elderly, as many are, it may not feel the effect of negative demographic trends for years. Then, too, a congregation's efforts to reach out to different kinds of people may bring in a higher proportion of a given demographic group; alternatively, the congregation can act in such a way

TABLE 2.1

Population of Mendocino Area and Membership of Mendocino Presbyterian Church, 1900 to 1990

Year	Census Population[1]	Church Membership[2]
1900	4,516	68
1910	5,559	91
1920	5,126	70
1930	3,383	60
1940	3,355	87
1950	4,766	72
1960	5,947	146
1970	5,623	136
1980	8,987	284
1990	9,742	227

1. From decennial United States Censuses. For 1900 to 1950, the unit of enumeration includes the "townships" of Anderson, Big River, and Cuffey's Cove; for 1960 to 1990, the unit is the roughly equivalent Mendocino-Anderson Census County Division.
2. From the Statistical Yearbooks of the Presbyterian Church (USA). Figures shown are averages of end-of-year communicant membership for the three years surrounding the census year.

as to freeze new people out. In the last analysis, a rule that says "no people, no congregation" applies. However, "given people, how much congregation?" remains to be determined.

With this in mind, let us look again at Mendocino Presbyterian. Table 2.1 shows long-term trends for most of the twentieth century for two sets of people, the inhabitants of the surrounding census district and the members of the congregation.

Several things are apparent from these figures. First is that church membership is correlated with community population; they tend to rise and fall in concert. There were especially large increases in both figures during the 1900s, the 1950s, and the 1970s, decades when, respectively, the local lumber mill was busy rebuilding San Francisco after its 1906 earthquake, the entire nation was basking in post-World War II prosperity, and Mendocino was a mecca for back-to-the-land refugees from city life.

Second is that the correlations are imperfect. Church membership declined during the 1940s and 1980s even as population grew, and church growth proportionately outstripped population growth in the 1950s and

1970s. Informants tell of particularly vigorous pastors in these periods of growth and lackluster ones in the periods of decline. Yet the numbers do not answer the question of causality. Did pastoral leadership cause growth, or was it the other way around? It is certainly possible that the enhanced resources provided by favorable demographics made it possible for the congregation to attract and maintain such strong leadership in the years of growth.

The third thing we can see from these figures is that over this century-long stretch of time the church has attracted a higher proportion of the surrounding population to its membership rolls, a proportion varying between 1.5 percent in 1900 and 3.1 percent in 1980. Highways, nonexistent earlier in the century, have been widened and bridges improved, so more people are within a reasonable distance of the church. Cultural changes matter too: as aesthetics have replaced natural resources as a source of property value, Mendocino's historic 1868 sanctuary has greater magnetism for the middle class.

Let us look more closely at the rapid growth of the 1970s, a decade when the parent Presbyterian Church (UPCUSA) was steadily losing members while the Mendocino congregation's evangelism program capitalized on the influx of new residents. Broadly speaking, there were two contingents among the newcomers. First were the semiretired, varying from the quite well-off to those merely making do, all very much middle class, most of them with grown children. These were people middle-aged and older who found in Mendocino a place to enjoy a more leisurely pace of life than they had before. Many of them quite naturally gravitated to the church, some even passing by several other congregations on their five- to fifteen-mile Sunday morning journeys. The other contingent comprised much younger people, some with small children, who came to Mendocino before their careers and fortunes had been established, some in flight from drug cultures and the draft, others drawn away from the alienating structures of universities and cities by the values of rural communes and small town life. Some of them had dropped out of the middle class, others had never arrived.

Two Presbyterian pastors of the 1960s, both liberal, reached out to the newcomers. Early in the decade, Peter Hsu enjoyed the company of unconventional people new to Mendocino (they were called "beatniks" in those days), and he urged a more cosmopolitan attitude on the part of his parishioners. Later in the decade, as things got uglier for young people, Mark Kimmerly was conscience-stricken by the plight of burnt-out hippies, and he tried to find them shelter. However, neither pastor brought the youthful newcomers into the church for more than an occasional visit.

It was the evangelical Eric Underwood who made the church attractive to both the middle-aged middle class and the youthful counterculture. His preaching valorized the humble, small-town ethic both groups sought by moving to Mendocino, and in the middle of the decade, blue-haired ladies and long-haired hippies together filled the church. The mix, however, was difficult to sustain. The economy turned sour in the 1980s, jobs grew scarce, enthusiasm waned, Underwood grew tired, his successor lacked magnetism, and many of the younger, less conventional,

and less settled members of the congregation left Mendocino in search of better opportunities or left the church in search of more spiritual vitality in neighboring congregations. While it lasted, however, the mix of people and their numbers made the church the most vital institution in town.

Changing Population Mixes: The Example of Long Beach, California[13]

The demographic story of Mendocino county in the twentieth century is mostly one of ups and downs correlated with variable economic opportunities, especially opportunities for younger people who are most likely to pull up stakes when things look better elsewhere. The story in Long Beach, five hundred miles to the south, is different, for in that city whole categories of people have come and gone in the past generation. Always a port city, Long Beach used to depend on the United States Navy and a large, aircraft manufacturing company for its economic base. Now it is more oriented to export-import industries, and its people include many more immigrants. Table 2.2, based on the 1970, 1980, and 1990 United States Censuses, reveals the resulting demographic changes for downtown Long Beach and its contiguous residential areas.

In twenty years, the population has increased by about 20 percent, growing only slightly slower than the United States as a whole, but many of the newcomers are minorities, and the previously almost all White population has become highly diverse. Whereas people of color were nearly invisible in this city in 1970—when Long Beach was known as "Iowa-by-the-Sea"—they composed over a third of its people twenty years later. First added to the tiny Black community were large numbers of Hispanics, and in the 1980s other Blacks and thousands of Asian Americans joined the mix. The result is a greater ethnic cross section of the nation's population.

As stick-and-stone units, Long Beach's homes have changed much less than the people who occupy them. Nearly three-quarters of the housing units standing in 1990—single-family houses

TABLE 2.2

Population Changes in Long Beach, California, 1970-1990

	1970	1980	1990
Population	47,432	50,481	57,023
Households	27,547	29,472	29,903
Ethnicity			
White	98.0%	80.2%	62.5%
Black	0.3	2.9	9.4
Asian	——	2.9	5.2
Hispanic	——	12.3	22.0
Other	1.7	1.6	0.9
Percent of current housing units built	73.8	85.9	100.0
Percent of residents living at current address	5.5	15.6	100.0
Age Distribution			
<18	13.3%	15.2%	16.6%
18-64	54.3	60.1	69.4
65+	32.5	25.6	14.0
Types of Households			
Married w/children	33.1%	22.8%	22.9%
Single w/children	8.4	9.2	12.1
Living alone	58.6	57.4	50.9
Unrelated adults	——	10.5	15.3

and apartments—had already been built twenty years earlier. But only one in twenty of 1990's residents still lived where they had in 1970. The story of Long Beach is one of massive population turnover within a physically mature city.

The people of central Long Beach were also younger in 1990 than in 1970, with more children under 18 and many fewer seniors over 65. Many American communities are moving in exactly the opposite direction, finding it worthwhile to remodel unused schools as senior centers. Not Long Beach; it is no longer an enclave of the retired.

The household mix tells more: there has been a decline in people living alone (probably represented largely in the past by the elderly) and a sharp increase in "unrelated adults" living together. Although for census purposes such people may be roommates or cohabiting heterosexual couples, people who live in Long Beach—which has had an annual Gay and Lesbian Pride Day parade since 1985—can infer that many of them are gay and lesbian couples; to judge from the increase in the number of unrelated-adult households between 1970 and 1980, that decade particularly was one of increasing gay and lesbian presence. Thus, although Long Beach's population mix became younger in the 1970s, the proportion of households with children also declined. In the 1980s, as more minorities moved into the city, the proportion of households with children began to grow again.

With greater or lesser intentionality, the congregations of Long Beach have experienced and responded to these changes. Some new congregations have been founded by and for newcomers. Some long-standing groups have made room for newcomers; indeed, some clearly would no longer exist if newcomers had not replaced those who had died or otherwise left the community.

The century-old First Congregational Church felt a particularly sharp drop in attendance in the early 1970s as longtime members moved out or died. In 1974, the church council seriously considered following the people by selling the building downtown and moving to the suburbs. The motion to move was defeated, and church leaders welcomed the legal designation of the sanctuary as a historic landmark, settling in for what they hoped would be a temporary bleak spell before a new upturn. The upturn came a decade later with their call in 1987 of a new pastor, a woman, who spurred the congregation to declare itself "open and affirming" to gays and lesbians. She also welcomed inclusive language and androgynous imagery for God, and she worked closely with the organist and director of music to integrate high quality classical music into the liturgy. These features were particularly attractive to those gay and lesbian Christians who were put off by the theological conservatism of Long Beach's Pentecostal-oriented Metropolitan Community Church.

Since the new pastor's arrival, the church's membership, attendance, and finances have rebounded, and First Congregational witnesses in Long Beach civic life to the values of gender inclusiveness. However, some members are uneasy with the changes, worrying that the congregation might become not just open and affirming but a "gay and lesbian church." Others are concerned that the congregation's middle-class worship style, so attractive to many of its constituents, may be a barrier to greater ethnic and racial inclusiveness. The congregation rents space to a Hispanic Baptist congregation for their Sunday worship and Wednesday Bible classes, but except for the presence of a few interracial families in the congregation, First Congregational's membership is almost entirely white. First Congregational is liberal and anglophone, and as such it is unlikely to reflect the full complexity of the community's population.

St. Matthew's Catholic Church has also felt the impact of Long Beach's demographic changes, but it has responded in a more distinctively Catholic way. Here, too, the early seventies were a watershed when the forty-year pastorate of a beloved Irish American priest ended and the church added a Mass in Spanish to its weekend schedule of six Masses. Twenty years later, three of the six Masses were said in Spanish, with by far the largest attendance being for the Sunday afternoon Spanish service when parishioners overflow the four-hundred-seat sanctuary. The largest turnout for any of the English-speaking Masses is 175.

There is little overlap or interaction between the Spanish and the English speakers, but each group has its own priest, and the Hispanics have their own altar boys. Compared to most Protestant congregations, the so-called Anglo congregation is diverse, with a smattering of Asians and African Americans and a significant contingent of gay men. At the invitation of Cardinal Mahoney in 1986, parishes throughout the archdiocese of Los Angeles, among them St. Matthew's, established formal programs to

Sidebar 2.2
BLACK, BROWN, AND WHITE:
A NOTE ON CENSUS RACIAL AND
ETHNIC CATEGORIES

The United States Census classifies people in terms of both "race" and "Hispanic origin" based on the self-designations they themselves provide in response to census questions. Following the American folk practice that "race" is a biological concept with qualitative categories, respondents are allowed to classify themselves as "White," "Black," "American Indian" (including Eskimo and Aleut), "Asian or Pacific Islander" (including a bewildering array of subclassifications, from Chinese through Asian Indian to Samoan), or "Other." The "Hispanic" question, on the other hand, presupposes a cultural instead of biological basis of distinction, and respondents are asked whether or not they are of "Hispanic origin" and, if so, whether their origins are Mexican, Puerto Rican, Cuban, or other.

Two large groups of Americans have trouble with these choices. First are the increasing numbers of Americans who think of themselves as multiracial. Actually, because adults fill out census forms, we are more likely talking about people having difficulty when asked to classify *their children* into one race or another, which poses a moral and familial dilemma for individuals in interracial marriages. Does a White woman whose husband, the father of her children, is Black classify her children as "White," denying his heritage, or "Black," denying hers, or "other," denying any? If she hyphenates her answer ("White-Black" or "Black-White"), the census department codes only the first term in the pair, reducing the complexity of culture and identity for the sake of unambiguous classification. The same dilemma is posed for the increasing number of Eurasian individuals in the United States, as well as for the large numbers of African Americans who have become aware of almost-forgotten Native American ancestors.

The Census Bureau's either/or thinking is neither arbitrarily bureaucratic nor insensitive to popular concerns. Black/White American racial classification (with no "mixed" option) is a factual legacy of slavery and Jim Crow, and, in the eyes of a racially obsessed society, Americans with as few as one African American great-great-grandparent (those with, as Americans tend to say, "one-sixteenth Black blood") over the years have been classified as "colored," "Negro," "Black," or "African American," all labels carrying the weight of stigma in White society. Given the cultural power of such labels to shape people's lives, many African American leaders argue that they must be recognized by the census and other government bodies. To invite mixed and ambiguous classification would be to conspire in an official understatement of the race problem in America and to dilute the political power of a potentially unified African American constituency.

Notwithstanding this collective imperative, Americans of mixed racial heritage and their advocates have formed a movement to pressure the Census Bureau to allow them to express their identities on the next census in the year 2000. As of this writing, racial classification is a lively issue at the Census Bureau and in the committees of the United States Congress charged with the bureau's legislative oversight.

The other large group for whom the racial and Hispanic items are often problematic are Hispanics. It is not so much that they prefer to call themselves "Latina" or "Latino." Some do; some do not. It is rather that many find no place on the race item to express their distinctive identity. Large numbers of Hispanics think of themselves as White, others identify themselves as Black. But many, particularly those of Mexican origin, think of themselves as of a distinct race, *la raza* in Spanish, whereas the census views race as a biological category and Hispanic as a cultural one. Therefore, a very large percentage of Hispanics in the West and Southwest check "Other" on the race question.

Because "race" and "Hispanic origin" are separate census questions, table 2.2 (Population Changes in Long Beach, California, 1970-1990) could not be read straight off census reports. In order to avoid double counting, those who identified themselves as "Hispanic" were subtracted from those identifying themselves as "White," "Black," "Asian" (a few Filipinos identify as Hispanic), and "Other." The result is a set of numbers that approximates the labels used by people in the society at large to classify themselves and others.

For much of the information above, we are indebted to Jennifer Quick Pool, "Ethnic Identity of Biracial Individuals and the United States Census" (Master's thesis, Department of Sociology, University of Illinois at Chicago, 1996), but Pool bears no responsibility for our use of her findings. For a general discussion, see David A. Hollinger, *Postethnic America* (New York: Basic Books, 1995), chapter 2.

respond to the needs of their gay and lesbian members. At St. Matthew's the eventual result was a group known as *Comunidad*. Despite its Spanish name, the group is English-speaking, and despite its openness to both genders it is overwhelmingly male. Unlike the independent, nationally organized, gay-and-lesbian Catholic group known as "Dignity," *Comunidad* serves more a spiritual than an advocacy function. It provides what some members call a "safe place" where they can congregate without fear of stigmatization for their sexual orientation. *Comunidad* draws many Catholic men who live in neighboring parishes but find a more open welcome at St. Matthew's.

Thus, a self-description one often hears among the English speakers of the congregation is "St. Matthew's is not your traditional family parish." Its incorporation of the diversity of the community has been the occasion for some other Catholics—affluent English speakers formerly registered in the parish—to attend nearby St. Bartholomew's, where they feel more at home.

Neither First Congregational nor St. Matthew's simply "reflects" the increased population diversity of Long Beach. Likewise, neither has neglected that diversity or been untouched by it.

Changing Households: An Example from Gwinnett County, Georgia[14]

The recent change that took place in the area surrounding Dacula, where Faith and Todd Penner and Marie and Vernon England reside, was dramatic. Gwinnett County, one of the two or three fastest growing counties in the nation, was transformed since the late 1970s from a largely rural area consisting of farms and dirt roads to a mecca for exurban families attracted by corporate headquarters, good schools, and proximity both to Atlanta and the north Georgia mountains.

Old-timers, like Elaine Foggs, measure the change in terms of property ownership. While tapping her foot to the music at the Winn House Bluegrass Festival, Elaine, a native of Gwinnett County, spoke of the altered patterns of property ownership in her family. Her grandfather had a big farm in northeast Gwinnett with a cotton gin and sawmill on the premises. Her father had a smaller, fifty-acre farm, also in the county's northeast quadrant. Now Foggs and her husband have only the few acres around their house just off Georgia Highway 316.

Using census data, this transition from rural to exurban status can best be seen in the dramatic decline in the percentage of housing units that are mobile homes at the same time that the total number of housing units increased significantly.

The decline in the number of mobile homes in the area highlights two changes in Dacula's

TABLE 2.3

Population Growth in Northeast Gwinnett County, Georgia, 1980-1990

	1980	1990
Number of persons	7,975	14,458
Number of households	2,507	4,732
Average household size	3.18	3.0
Housing Units[1]	2,603	4,919
Single Family	85.4%	91.4%
Multi-family	1.5	0.3
Mobile Homes	13.1	7.5

1. Housing Unit: A house, apartment, group of rooms, or single room occupied as a separate living quarters or, if vacant, intended for occupancy as a separate living quarters.

context—the decreasing stock of low-income housing and the eclipsing of blue-collar residents. Since World War II, mobile homes have been an important source of low-income housing for rural residents in the United States who may be relatively land-rich but cash-poor. They were also one option for home ownership among blue-collar workers who had worked for local manufacturers in Dacula. As these companies closed or dropped shifts, blue-collar workers were squeezed out of the economy and replaced by white-collar workers of the information age. Although the home values in the Dacula region are still well below those in Gwinnett County as a whole, or in the five-county Atlanta metro area, they increased 133 percent from 1980 to 1990 in the Dacula environs, compared to a 90 percent change in Gwinnett County and a 113 percent increase in the metro area. Today these homes are also much more likely to be frame rather than mobile homes.

Beyond the census data, marketing surveys of the area capture something of its predominant lifestyles. Typical of its blue-collar past, Dacula's residents are also slightly more likely to be members of a fraternal order, to go fresh water fishing, and to buy country music albums than residents of Gwinnett County or the United States.[15] However, these cultural characteristics have changed as more and more newcomers have moved into the area. Dacula resident Lionel Hall predicts that the changing demographics will undermine one of his favorite events in Gwinnett County—the annual county fair. Hall, who moved to the area in 1991, laughingly comments that he is the new representative resident—white, thirty-two years old, married, with a mortgage on a three-bedroom home, and raising 1.3 kids (his wife was beginning the second trimester of her pregnancy). Wandering around the livestock exhibit at the 1993 fair, Hall said that he did not expect to see prize sheep, cows, and hogs in another five years. "Well, look around you. How many of these people do you think are sending their kids to 4-H? Pretty soon this will be just another kinda-country fair for city folk." "Like you?" he was asked. "Like me," Hall

admitted wistfully. As Dacula's population changes, the community's culture is inexorably altered as well.

Although numbers do not speak for themselves, examining census data for your community can help you understand your context in several ways. Comparing the population distributions reported in census tables to those you observe in your congregation, you can see who is especially being served by your congregation and who is missing, and you may discover compelling new opportunities for outreach to groups in your neighborhood who are not members of your congregation. You can use the reports of prior decades to see into the past of your community—the numbers, ages, racial identities, occupations, and living arrangements of the people and the characteristics of the housing they lived in—thus putting the present into perspective. In that way, you may understand better some factors that stand behind your congregation's experience of recent growth or decline. Overall, you will get a better appreciation of the complexity of your community and of the roles of the congregations in it.

As the population characteristics in your community change, so too do the systems of meanings, value, and symbols. Demographic and cultural change seldom comes without some discomfort. Elderly folks may resent the traffic produced by an influx of young families. In other cases, an increasingly aging population may not understand why it should be concerned about the families with children that populate their community, children they are not related to. Whites may feel threatened by African Americans, and African Americans may feel pressured by the arrival of gays and lesbians, Hispanics, and Asian Americans. Yet as the philosopher Heraclitus observed, "You cannot step twice into the same river; for other waters are ever flowing on to you." Viewed from an ecological frame, change, conflict, and discomfort are the natural and expected consequence of continued existence and, indeed, vitality. Acknowledging that change (even inevitable change) is difficult can alleviate resentment between old-timers and

---

Sidebar 2.3
INTERSECTING CULTURAL WORLDS IN 1970s NORTHERN CALIFORNIA

The fog had lifted early in the morning of July 4, 1976, so the town was visible as I crested the hill on the highway coming in from the south. The view struck me as spectacular but incongruous. The town—false storefronts, high-pitched roofs, rickety water towers, and especially the tall church steeple—was a transplant from New England. But the setting—the crisp air, the browned hillsides, the blooming wildflowers, the brilliant light, and the deep blue of the ocean—was Mediterranean. It was, in fact, California....

There were many temporary residents. Along Main Street were parked the cars of weekenders and summer vacationers. There were station wagons from Washington and Arizona, sporty cars from Nevada, a smattering of sedans from points east, and California Winnebagos, Peugeots, and BMWs. Bumper stickers on some cars announced that the occupants were for Ford or Carter or would rather be skiing. These tourist vehicles competed for streetside space with beat-up vans, buses, pickups, and VW bugs that bore the dust of country roads and bumper stickers that implored onlookers to save the whales or honk if they loved Jesus. In the driveways of the white-painted houses, or under the flowered trellises of their carports, were the Chevrolets and Toyotas of those who lived in town.

People were out walking and wandering into galleries and boutiques. Some stopped by the displays of the jewelry and pottery vendors who set up their tables on the wooden sidewalk. A dark-haired woman in a richly colored poncho presided over a mobile burrito stand. Garlicky smells came out of a store that called itself The Deli, and people paused to read announcements on the bulletin board outside. The World's Largest Salmon Barbecue had been held on July 3 in Fort Bragg. The Mendocino Bicentennial Parade and Birthday Celebration, featuring floats, a marching band, songs, and a recitation of the Declaration of Independence, was to begin at noon. Someone had puppies to give away, and a Tai-Chi class was forming. Next to The Deli, other strollers stopped to look down on the ducks swimming in the remnant of a drought-stricken pond.

The busiest place that morning, though, was not the street, the galleries, the shops, or the brushy path above the ocean cliffs. It was the parking lot beneath that tall steeple, the parking lot of Mendocino Presbyterian Church.

R. Stephen Warner, *New Wine in Old Wineskins* (Berkeley: University of California Press, 1988), pp. 1-2.

---

newcomers, easing the transition as newcomers themselves become old-timers.

Cultural Worlds

The kind of demographic information we can get from the census—numbers of people by age, race, Hispanic origin, income bracket—is very valuable. Yet we need much more than demographic data in order to understand the cultures of the community, that is to say, how people recognize themselves and others as divided into meaningful groups, subcultures, classes, and communities—some of which they belong to, some of which are the proper place of the "other person," and some of which are shared.

For example, in the case of Long Beach, the census data about a large number of unrelated adults sharing households could not alone tell us that these include many gay and lesbian couples. If Long Beach were still a military town, those households could be enlisted men sharing cheap apartments, or in a college town, they could be conventional roommates. Because we have site-specific knowledge of the social worlds of Long Beach and know that gays and lesbians have come out in the last generation, we can be confident that those numbers include substantial proportions of same-sex couples living together.

The grounds on which people form subcultures include race, language, national origin, religion, occupation, organizational memberships, political conviction, age, gender, sexual orientation, and that catch-all called "lifestyle." Various social theories expect one or another of these statuses to predominate in people's lives. Thus, Karl Marx expected (and hoped) that the way people made a living ("social class," in his terms) would be the basis of identity and community. ("Work-

Sidebar 2.4
SEEING THE WORD IN A CHURCH FOR THE DEAF

Since 1977, the pastor of Chicago Catholic Ephpheta, the archdiocesan Deaf Center, has been Father Joe Mulcrone, a hearing person who grew up with deaf grandparents, and for most of that time the Deaf Center masses have been held at the chapel of St. Francis Borgia parish. For the benefit of hearing relatives and visitors, Father Joe provides a simultaneous oral/aural interpretation of the proceedings.

Though a boxy, plain, small room seating only three hundred, the space works. The language of the mass, American Sign (ASL), requires visual access to the face, hands, and torso of the speaker, so the long nave and cruciform plan of Chicago's grand nineteenth-century parish churches and in-the-round seating of some contemporary ones would leave many deaf parishioners out of communication. Yet as small as the room is, people do not pack in, for their speaking requires rapid gestures with the arms and hands, even when they are only responding "and also with you" to the priest or conversing with a neighbor. What the mouth and ears are to the hearing, the hands and eyes are to the deaf.

Standing and kneeling are minimized to maintain visual access, and people do not bow their heads for prayer. Nor do they look at the ceiling: Father Joe likes to say that the deaf congregation is the most attentive he's ever served.... The Lord's Prayer requires an astonishing amount of communal motion, and the passing of the peace, the sign for which is made by crossing the palms twice—right over left and left over right—connects people visually and tactually. (If you are facing in the wrong direction, you may be tapped on the shoulder from behind to gain your attention for the rite. Sound is broadcast, but signing and touching connect sender and receiver.)

The mass is by no means silent. Plenty of sound, much of it liturgically random, comes from restless preteens, the hearing children of deaf parents, crying babies, deaf people educated under oralist regimes, the clap of hands signing "amen," and the voices of hearing guests. At one point Father Joe jokes bilingually that "sometimes you're lucky to be deaf" not to have to hear the "singing babies."

Father Joe pronounces the Communion rite simultaneously in two languages, ASL and oral English, holding the wafer with one hand while signing with the other. His signing is smooth and crisp and the routine of the liturgy allows him to accentuate meaning in three dimensions and extend the Words of the Institution to add greater depth to the Eucharist. There is usually a time for announcements after Communion, and at one September mass, Father Joe alerted parishioners to the imminent voter registration deadline and told them where deaf people could get help to register.

The congregation does not disperse as soon as they are told "the mass is ended" but stays, especially for the extended coffee hour that follows, where the air is full of the hands of hundreds of deaf people catching up with each others' week. Father Joe understands the importance of after-church socializing from the experience of an uncle who was pastor to a rural parish in the days before widespread telephones. His uncle's congregation and his own are made up of people whose life conditions isolate them, and seeing one another is special to these people. The leaders of the parish also make sure that a literature table carries publications, religious and otherwise, directed to the public concerns of the deaf.

As we looked over the congregational conversation—people White and Black, Latino and Asian, young and old, well-dressed and casual, raised in English-speaking and non-English-speaking families, physically able and disabled, people gathered from homes all over the metropolitan area—it occurred to us that deafness, like mortality and sexuality, and unlike race and class, is a sociological wild card, confounding rather than reproducing social divisions. Thus, although in one sense the congregation is homogeneous, in another it draws people from every background and station in the city. The Christian celebration of ecclesia, union-out-of-difference, took on a new meaning for us in this congregation.

ingmen of all countries, unite.") Max Weber and Emile Durkheim also expected occupation to be salient grounds of group identification. Many theorists who focus on the United States have thought that ethnicity and race compete with social class as meaningful, and especially political, identifiers. Recently, feminist theorists have stressed the salience of gender and sexual orientation as providing basic grounds of meaning in people's lives. It is not just that we need more detailed objective information, that is, data on the national oriigin of individuals' parents and grandparents, in order to know how individuals classify themselves ethnically. Because of intermarriage, high rates of mobility, multiplicity of associations, the persuasiveness of mass media, and the activities of social movements—among other factors—American identities are increasingly protean or lacking clear boundaries. Thus, not all of the gays and lesbians whose presence is hinted at by the Long Beach census think of themselves as members of "the gay and lesbian community," and, among those who do, that may be one identity among many others they embrace (for example, Catholic, Irish American, musician, student, and so forth). In truth, many different and particular subcultures may coexist in each local community. "The gay and lesbian community" is itself a social construct, and the willingness to identify with it is an option for gay and lesbian (and other, including straight and bisexual) individuals.

In the case of Mendocino, California, the excerpt in sidebar 2.3 from *New Wine in Old Wineskins* uses clues about people's automobiles to determine the presence of the three major subcultures—longtime townspeople, hippies, and affluent newcomers—that formed recognizable constituencies of the local Presbyterian congregation in the mid-1970s.

In her book *Cities on a Hill*,[16] Frances FitzGerald samples four different American subcultures and suggests a theory to explain the shifting processes of group identification that are increasingly characteristic of American society. The four subcultures FitzGerald describes are the senior citizens of a retirement community in Florida, the sanyassins of Rajneeshpuram in Oregon, the fundamentalist Christians of Liberty Baptist Church in Lynchburg, Virginia, and the gays of San Francisco's Castro district, the first gay-dominated neighborhood in the world. FitzGerald sees in these communities not evidence of social disorganization but of a new organizational principle in our society, a social "centrifuge," which she imagined as she stood on a hill high above San Francisco Bay in the late 1970s and looked out on the streams of movement below.

A centrifuge spins so rapidly that the elements within it are hurled about and first separated from their matrices but then deposited alongside elements of similar density. A centrifuge is a way of purifying different essences out of haphazard

mixtures. FitzGerald's social centrifuge is a metaphor for the process by which people leave their older identities and sort themselves into new ones. While the identities of the past were based around occupation and ethnicity, FitzGerald argues that those of the future will be based around lifestyle and ideals. To return to the example of Mendocino, it was the small town ideal itself that drew people from very different backgrounds—young hippies and affluent retirees—to rural California, and it was the genius of the Presbyterian pastor Eric Underwood to work with what they had in common in that ideal, their "elective parochialism."[17]

Whatever we may think of FitzGerald's examples, she helps us understand two features of contemporary American identities and subcultures: that they are more diverse than ever, based on whole new categories of association, and that they are organized, not random. Age, disability, environmentalism, and, of course, gender and sexual orientation, have joined social class, race, and ethnicity as grounds of meaning and social identity. Not all but some of those identities bring people together in subcultures that give texture to the particular local context. In sidebar 2.4, we look at some of the particular ways that members of one subculture—the deaf—share their religious lives.

Despite all the expansion of subcultures and the ambiguities among multiple identities, class, race, and ethnicity do continue to be potent factors in shaping individual identity and group identification. Furthermore, we recognize that all identities and groups formed around class, race, and ethnicity are not equally valued in society. Marx and Weber were at least partially right when they argued that class standing and occupation are important because they help determine the possible opportunities for, or constraints inhibiting, future achievement by any individual or group. We are most inclined to agree with Weber, in particular, who noted that the economic factors of class status, such as the type of occupation or monetary resources an individual or group possesses, are not the only determining factors in overall social status. Standing in society's hierarchy also depends on particular cultural characteristics related to nonquantifiable but nonetheless very real qualities of prestige or respectability. Finally, access to political power is another important factor in considering social status. This combination of wealth, occupation, education, gender, race, ethnicity, prestige, and power—among other factors—is often called socioeconomic status (SES). Some shorthand designations for groups of individuals who fall into various SES categories have become commonplace, such as yuppies (young urban professionals), or buppies (black urban professionals), and DINKS (dual income, no kids). Although these designations easily become stereotypes, their utility is in their ability to communicate information about lifestyles. Rightly or wrongly, we are apt to believe that yuppies are likely to eat at restaurants, belong to a health club, vacation abroad, and employ a housecleaner.

The socioeconomic standing of groups in relation to one another forms the basis of the stratification system of any society. This ordering of groups based on SES is often pictured as a pyramid. Those groups at the very top of the pyramid control most of the society's resources, have the most access to opportunities and symbolic prestige, and possess the greatest entree to political power. For example, in the United States the top 1 percent of the population controls over 70 percent of the wealth—capital and investment—and the top 5 percent controls over 90 percent. Likewise, cultural practices like driving an expensive car, living in a large home, taking fabulous vacations, and wearing expensive clothing— all derived from media images of affluence and what life is supposed to be like at the top of the stratification pyramid—become prestigious, and doing these things increases social status. Finally, one need only read the newspapers to realize that having money to contribute to political candidates increases access to political influence. Power, prestige, and wealth accrue to those at the top of the stratification pyramid, and those lower in the pyramid, such as female heads of households, immigrants, and the poor, have a much more difficult time gaining access to these social goods.

It may be easier to see stratification when considering the national or global context, but it is also at work in your local context. SES differences are often visible in a specific environment: a ghetto, a shopping mall, a gated community, or golf course. During your walk-around and drive-around, you noted the ways in which people are dispersed around your community. Now think about the possible reasons for this dispersal. What are the social factors—for example, income, age, race, ethnicity—that are behind the housing, commercial, and recreational spaces you saw? Most of us can point to places on a map of our community to identify lower income neighborhoods, racially segregated blocks, and high status addresses. Which social groups live in the prestigious parts of town? Who resides in low status areas? The answers to these questions provide the basis for grasping your local system of social stratification. Clearly in the complex world of shifting economic and cultural categories, the status value of places changes over time. For example, a slum may become an attractive place for gays and lesbians who begin the process of gentrification. Nonetheless, it is important to remember that stratification takes place as the meanings we give to places, people, and groups shape their access to opportunities, power, and prestige. To understand your environment, you will want to be attentive to the status values of the places near and distant from your congregation, the lifestyles that predominate in those places, and the ability of residents in various locales and from different groups to get done those things that will benefit them.

Organizational Ecology

This last matter of "getting things done" raises questions about what type of and how much political power various groups have. It also raises the larger question of how groups fit within a local organizational ecology. Understanding how decisions are made, consensus built, or problems addressed within your community requires that you carefully examine the various organizations that meet to shape civic life and consider how these associations relate to one another. These various groups are stakeholders in your community, that is, they have interest—whether financial, moral, or social—in community life. Thus the local organizational ecology consists of the various groups that organize people's connections with the life of their communities and actively promote their vision of community life.

Often organizations that have a stake in the community differ in their views about what is good for the community. When such differences occur, organizations and individuals use what power they can muster to sway decisions.

Power is a slippery concept and merits careful consideration as you take measure of your context. Sidebar 2.5 tells the story of a grassroots protest to the expansion of an airport near Dacula and illustrates the varieties of power deployed by various citizens and groups.

Obviously the story does not end here, but let us stop to consider the place of religious groups, in particular, in community power relations. Many congregations and their members want to use their resources and moral suasion for the betterment of their community. Thus it is vital that they consider how political power works locally. Sociologists N. J. Demerath III and Rhys Williams studied the relationship between religious groups and political power in Springfield, Massachusetts, and their research offers much that can enable any congregation to think systematically about the politics in their context.[18]

Power in the political arena can be described in several ways. It can be either primary—getting specific things done directly through political processes—or secondary—altering and adjusting general policies. Power can also be positive or negative. The former entails creating change, while the latter is, to quote a Dacula old-timer, "putting on the brakes." Demerath and Williams also identify a few factors to bear in mind when considering how political power works in your context, for example, community size, differentiation of the major institutional sectors in the community such as political, economic, educational, and religious and the nature of the political issues under consideration. Using the airport controversy, let us explore each of these factors.

First, religion is likely to exert more political power in towns than in cities, argue Demerath and Williams. In towns, citizens and worshipers are likely to interact within a number of settings. A resident can buttonhole a local official on a first-name basis over coffee, rather than calling a secretary for a place on the politician's calendar. In Dacula, Hinton Memorial UMC could have a political impact, in part, because of the relatively small size of the town. Locals knew the home phone numbers of their representatives on the city and county councils. Concerned citizens and worshipers worried, however, that they would not be able to get the attention of politicians within the Atlanta metropolitan region, of which Dacula was becoming a part. Political power was no longer primarily in the hands of local governments, such as the Dacula City Council. The things that really mattered to local folks were increasingly being decided in metropolitan-wide discussions to which newcomers often had greater access because of their network ties and professional resources. Congregants at Hinton and other concerned citizens could not rely primarily on their intimate ties with local politicos, rather they had to rely on new strategies that garnered the attention of remote, unknown officials. Dacula's political context was changing in ways that could decrease the influence of religiou groups, like Hinton Memorial. In this instance, however, the congregation's mix of old-timers and newcomers enabled it to take multiple tacks and thus to maximize political influence.

Second, religion is likely to have greater power in contexts in which there is significant overlap of people and activities from one institution to another, that is, among familial, economic, political, educational, and religious sectors of the community. When relatively close connections exist among the voting booth, the pew, the classroom, and the living room, what happens in the pew is more likely to affect what occurs in the classroom, living room, and voting booth. In other

---

Sidebar 2.5
AIRPORT FLY AWAY

"The people in the general area of Lawrenceville, including those in the Dacula area, raised their voices against enlarging Briscoe Field to handle passenger service. The whole area had sort of a town meeting atmosphere. This was a fine hour of democratic action.

"The representatives of our republic-style government got the loud and clear message. Our people can be proud of their response to this issue. The response also serves notice on elected officials that the electorate ain't dead yet."

That announcement, printed in the Hinton Memorial United Methodist Church "All Around Town" community newsletter in March 1994, signaled the end of a controversy in the congregation and the community. The proposed expansion of Gwinnett County-Briscoe Field to create a new regional airport was met by members of Hinton Memorial UMC with immediate grassroots action. As one longtime resident said, "There was a rumble you could hear all the way to the statehouse. This was one place that was not going to be railroaded." The issue united newcomers and old-timers in a common effort to redefine their relationship with the metropolitan region and to protect what they perceived as their superior quality of life. At the center of the conflict was Hinton Memorial UMC.

The airport controversy began in 1991 when the Gwinnett County Airport Authority began studying the feasibility of commuter air service at Briscoe Field. Response to the report fell along lines of economic interest: about 250 local homeowners, mostly old-timers, were opposed. Local boosters and large landholders saw the potential advantage of offering commercial service to accommodate local corporations whose employees wished to avoid traveling across Atlanta to Hartsfield International. Before the panel made much headway, however, an economic recession set in and the issue was dropped. In 1993 and 1994, when the proposal to expand the airport was revived, the grassroots opposition was different. In addition to local homeowners, opposition came from local civic organizations, including congregations, which reframed the proposal as an assault on the community's quality of life.

At Hinton Memorial UMC, the airport controversy again placed the congregation at the center of the community. Congregational old-timers involved in this most recent battle recalled a time prior to the 1970s when the Hinton Memorial UMC was the most prestigious church in the community with a say in almost everything that occurred in the area. In recent years, however, Hebron Baptist Church—the local megachurch—had usurped Hinton's position as the high status congregation, according to most local observers. Hinton congregants had developed a niche identity as the area's historic church.

The organizing efforts at Hinton Memorial were extensive. They first came to my attention when I received a call from a Hinton newcomer. She asked, "Do you know any state representatives or appointed officials you can call?" No, I had to admit, I did not. "What's going on?" I asked. Carol went on to tell me the news of the proposed airport. "We have to stop it or we'll be just like Union City," she said, referring to a town south of Atlanta in the Hartsfield flight path where an exodus of middle-class families had depressed the town's economy and hastened White flight. Carol made it clear to me that the congregation's survival and Dacula's quality of life was at stake in this issue. "Call anybody you know and tell them to stop the airport expansion," she pleaded. Carol had organized a petition drive, called all the members in the church directory, and was now working her way through the congregation's visitors cards.

---

words, religion will have more power because it will be linked to other important institutions. When little overlap exists, however, each institution may function without regard for the values, practices, and needs of the other institutions.

During the airport controversy, activists sought to identify how government, education, and religion were intimately related. In truth, Dacula's institutions were becoming increasingly separate and specialized. Residents had complained that the school system no longer respected "church night" on Wednesday evening by refraining from scheduling activities. Hinton members complained about the

Reverend Luther Dawson's sermons opposing the state lottery. Nonetheless, the looming threat to their community brought people and institutions—with the exception of business interests, such as those represented by Todd Penner—together across their developing boundaries into a common cause. For this reason, people of faith did have greater influence than might have been expected.

In considering the role of religion in the organizational ecology, attention must also be given to the symbolic power that religious professionals may have. In sidebar 2.6, Demerath and Williams relate an incident in Springfield

The Sunday after the airport proposal was announced publicly, the announcement time during the Hinton Memorial UMC worship service was filled with discussion of the organizing efforts to stop the airport expansion. Celia Dent, a congregational newcomer who worked as a public relations officer for a state environmental agency, had designed posters announcing a public forum to be held at the church. Some Hinton Memorial old-timers, who had previously opposed the Reverend Luther Dawson's mixing of religion and politics when he spoke out against the state lottery, now joined efforts with newcomers to distribute posters and invite local residents to the forum. "This is different," argued one vocal old-timer. "This isn't about opinions; it's about our homes."

A forum opposing the airport expansion was attended by a near capacity crowd at Hinton Memorial. As the meeting got underway, Reverend Dawson opened with a prayer for mutual understanding and peaceableness. Celia Dent began the forum by asking those in attendance about what they thought this battle was about. Several opponents to the proposal argued that this was not simply a NIMBY (Not In My Back Yard) opposition. Rather, local residents were organizing because they were tired of having changes "shoved down our throats by Atlanta officials," as one individual shouted. "It's time we take control of the growth," said someone in the audience. "Our way or no way!"

Only one Hinton congregant stood during the meeting to support the airport expansion. Todd Penner, whose job required extensive travel, spoke in favor of the airport expansion. "I know that it's not popular, but I think there are a lot of people like me around here who could use some relief from that hour drive to the airport and another half-hour finding a parking place," stated Penner. "There's no denying it now. Dacula's a part of metro Atlanta, and we've got to take the bad with the good." "But what's the good?" a middle-aged man in a sweat suit asked. "We get more traffic, more crime, more taxes. When are we going to start getting to the good stuff?"

Based on research for Nancy L. Eiesland, *A Particular Place: Exurbanization and Religious Response* (New Brunswick, N.J.: Rutgers University Press, forthcoming).

during which an imperious Roman Catholic sister was able to intimidate publicly the city's mayor and in the process to achieve her desired end—the opening of a homeless shelter. In orchestrating a public confrontation with the mayor, this sister also employed a bit of "theater" in order to define the situation and to force action. It was a theater in which her symbolic role as a nun was highly effective.

Symbolic power and the ability to use that power to create attention can be important sources of community influence for religious professionals. Recall images from the civil rights marches with priests, rabbis, and ministers in their religious garb facing angry mobs. Though these religious leaders may not have represented large constituencies who supported their actions, nonetheless they invoked a moral authority that increased their power to create change locally and nationally.

Another factor that Demerath and Williams point to in considering religion and political power is the nature of the issues under consideration. They contend that religion has more influence when the issues being addressed are dominant rather than minority issues and when they are about cultural rather than structural concerns. Dominant issues are those that are perceived to be in nearly everyone's interests. When religion backs dominant issues, it is likely to be more successful than when it backs minority issues—those that benefit only a small group or are perceived to be divisive in the community. Cultural issues are about beliefs, values, and meaning, whereas structural issues involve votes, budgets, personnel decisions, and coalitions. Religious groups are often most successful in influencing politics when the issues are framed in cultural terms, rather than in structural terms. During the airport controversy, having organizational meetings in the community's self-proclaimed historic congregation was symbolically important in reframing the issue as not being about personal interests ("Not In My Backyard") but about the community's quality of life, especially the values of small-town life that united newcomers and old-timers.

Sidebar 2.6
THE MAYOR AND THE SISTER

In December 1983, Service Providers, Inc., opened a shelter on Prospect Street for homeless families. That brought the total number of beds available for [Springfield's] homeless to some one hundred and fifty. This still fell short of caring for all the city's estimated homeless population at the time, and because it included beds committed to families for up to three weeks or so, there remained an acute shortage of overnight facilities available on an emergency basis. Thus began a protracted political struggle during which religious groups and social service agencies alike pressured the city to acknowledge the problem and provide an overflow shelter in response.

The crisis was first catalyzed by a religious reaction. In February 1984, the dean of the Episcopal cathedral announced a plan to open an emergency shelter in the basement of Christ Church Cathedral. The Council of Churches' Downtown Ministry agreed to help by donating the $10,000 it had received from the state Department of Public Welfare. But the Episcopal shelter did not sit well with city hall, presumably because it would attract the homeless to the "quadrangle"—one of the downtown's most prestigious areas that the cathedral shared with the municipal library and museum complex—and perhaps more important, because it threatened to lift control of services for the homeless out of the hands of city political officials.

The city administration reacted in two ways. Health department officials responded to the church's application for a "lodging house special permit" by inspecting the basement of the cathedral, finding it unsuitable for such a shelter, and threatening to padlock the church if a shelter were opened. But in addition to a stick, there was a carrot. The mayor asked the Episcopal rector to co-chair a newly created "Mayor's Task Force on Homelessness." As an intimate of the rector put it: "He knew he was being co-opted—those were the rules going in—but he wanted to get something done." His co-chair was the city councillor and United Way employee who considered homelessness "his" issue. The task force was charged with studying the problem and presenting recommendations for city action.

By October 1984, the task force had made some progress. It applied for and received a multipart $100,000 grant from the state. The grant included money to expand the Open Pantry's Loaves and Fishes soup kitchen and move it out of the immediate downtown business area. It also funded the opening of a day program for the homeless, to be staffed by volunteers from a United Methodist church. Finally, $31,000 of the grant was allocated to begin an emergency overflow shelter, as soon as the task force could locate an appropriate site and administering agency.

The symbolic overtones of the site the task force selected were readily apparent; it was the old isolation ward of the city's municipal hospital. However, the city spent a reported $28,000 renovating it for the task. Meanwhile, the Salvation Army and Service Providers, Inc., contracted jointly to operate the facility, and SPI agreed to apply to the state Department of Public Welfare for an additional $30,000 to keep the shelter open throughout the winter. To many, it seemed the problem of the homeless had been more or less "handled."

On November 27, 1984, the mayor called a press conference to announce the shelter's opening, even though the actual opening was to be delayed. The announced problem involved difficulties in obtaining necessary insurance for the staffing agency, though there were suspicions city officials were "dragging their heels." These suspicions erupted at the press conference itself when the sister-director of Open Pantry interrupted the proceedings to press the mayor repeatedly for a specific date when the shelter would open. For every reason he offered for the delay, she and her colleagues provided rapid rebuttal. Thus, when the insurance issue came up, the sister-director offered to staff it at once with the Sisters of Providence, one of whom testified that she had checked with their own insurance company and learned that it would provide an immediate rider until SPI was ready. Moreover, the sister-director had brought along ten homeless people to dramatize the problem. Word of the shelter's opening had reached the streets, and homeless people were swamping the Loaves and Fishes soup kitchen in search of assistance. Ten people even paid an unannounced visit to the mayor's office, a move that some city hall insiders thought was choreographed by the sister. One of the homeless people remarked later, "Maybe now they [city officials] know there is a need."

From N. J. Demerath III and Rhys H. Williams, *A Bridging of Faiths: Religion and Politics in a New England City* (Princeton, N.J.: Princeton University Press, 1992).

Opponents to the planned expansion of the Gwinnett County-Briscoe Field airport were able to stop the development. The involvement of Hinton Memorial UMC in this controversy highlights the role of local religious institutions in shaping debates about quality of life locally. It also underscores the challenges faced by religious groups trying to use their political clout within their context. Todd Penner's support of the airport expansion highlights the dilemma congregations face when they support one side within a political debate. Congregations are internally diverse, and often members disagree on political issues. Even when that is less true, many members are unwilling to have their religious leader act on their behalf in matters of politics. Knowing about the various groups present in your community and congregation is vital to getting things done in your community.

In every community there are more things to be done to promote justice, equality, and mutual understanding than can be done by any one congregation. Thus, understanding the diverse callings and gifts of the congregations and groups within your religious and social ecology can enable your congregation to concentrate its efforts and resources on those issues for which members have passion, whether providing a homeless shelter, respite services, or day care; advocating pro-life causes, ordination of gays and lesbians, or access for people with disabilities; or sponsoring Scouts, softball leagues, or AA. By discovering the mission, culture, and program of religious organizations in your area, your congregation may not only concentrate its efforts on what you can do best, but you may also establish networks for future collaboration.

Having done the windshield survey of religious organizations discussed earlier, you will now want to be more systematic in exploring your religious ecology. A good place to start is the local ecumenical ministerial association. Your minister, and perhaps some of your most active members, may be participants. If you are Protestant, through these contacts you may have a good idea what Baptist, Methodist, Lutheran, Presbyterian, and Episcopalian churches—and maybe also the Catholic parishes and Jewish synagogues—in town are doing. There may even be a ministerial association that includes local Muslims. In recognition of America's increasing religious diversity, the venerable National Conference of Christians and Jews has shortened its name to The National Conference. And in some cities, the organization sponsors interfaith Thanksgiving services bringing together Christians, Jews, Muslims, Buddhists, Hindus, and others. If your congregation represents a religious minority group, you probably do not need to be reminded that it is important to pay attention to the larger groups around you.

Ecumenical ministerial associations usually publish an address list of local religious groups. A simple exercise is to distribute this list to a select number of congregants. Ask each person to write several sentences about the mission, culture, and programs of any of the congregations with which they are familiar. Later, when you gather to discuss your impressions as a group, list which congregations individuals have visited for worship services, revivals, baptisms, bar mitzvahs, or funerals. Those congregations that are relatively unknown to your congregation—maybe because they are new or outside your denominational or religious tradition—are good candidates for a get-acquainted visit or—as a poor substitute—a telephone interview with members or leaders of the congregation. (The observational protocol in the methods chapter [pages 200-201] can orient you as you visit these congregations.) If you are unfamiliar with the history, customs, and practices of the group you will visit, you may also wish to consult *How to Be a Perfect Stranger: A Guide to Etiquette in Other People's Religious Ceremonies*, volumes 1 & 2.[19] These helpful texts provide a brief history of a variety of religious groups (from Assemblies of God to Hindu); an overview of a typical service for each religious group; and descriptions of holy days, festivals, and life-course ceremonies. While this resource offers broad sketches of religious groups, remember that the congregations you visit will have their own local and distinctive customs.

Also remember that congregations are not the only religious groups within your ecology. Religious special purpose groups—such as Christian Coalition or Catholics for a Free Choice, support groups, and evangelistic organizations—are likely represented in your community. Look in the yellow pages, the activities listings of the local paper, and the bulletin board at the supermarket.

Learning more about your religious ecology will help you to understand the indirect and unintentional influences the religious ecology has on your congregation. Think about, for instance,

Sidebar 2.7
MENDOCINO PRESBYTERIAN
AND THE LAND SWAP[1]

In the 1970s, the outstanding public issue in Mendocino was "growth." Not only church membership was skyrocketing, so also was the town's population, with the area's population growing by over 60 percent in that decade. The chance to partake of rural, small-town America, to recapture a past many had never known, lured newcomers in such numbers as to threaten the very values they came in search of.

One of the newcomers was John Heider, a clinical psychologist by trade but better described as a leader of leaders in the human potential movement.[2] With the backing of philanthropic friends, he founded the Human Potential School of Mendocino in 1974, buying several properties for the new venture—houses, barns, a garage, and a two-acre vacant field in the heart of town.

For four years, what he and his friends called HumPot U brought clients to Mendocino for three-month workshops in Gestalt therapy, group process, meditation, and Tai Chi. Some of the participants worked off their tuition by helping to fix up the properties. But the vacant lot was a white elephant. Although zoning regulations would have allowed Heider to build on the property, Mendocino's no-growth partisans would have thrown one roadblock after another in the path of any building and made the owner's life miserable in the process.

Although Heider deplored confrontational tactics and personally disliked some of the no-growth activists, he could not ignore them. He eventually came to think that "the highest and best use" for the field was to remain open space. But when his own plans had changed and he wanted to move his base of operations out of California, he could not be the steward of what had come to be called "the town green." Nor was there a municipal government to assume such a responsibility, because voters of Mendocino had defeated the latest proposal to incorporate.

Of all the institutions in town, such as the Presbyterian, Catholic, and Baptist churches, the Masonic lodges, the Historical Review Board, even the Mendocino Land Trust (newly established as a fiduciary for publicly accessible properties willed in bequests), Heider trusted the Presbyterian church as "the most unbiased of all the parties in town." Although he was not a member of the congregation, he sensed that Pastor Eric Underwood "most nearly stood at the center of the town's various factions." Heider and his board offered to turn the gift over and deed the field to the church for use as a public park.

The congregation had its own obligations and needs. Trustees worried about their liability for injuries in the field, which sat four blocks from the church itself. They knew they could not claim the park as integral to the church's religious function; it was therefore subject to taxation on its market value. They were also less convinced than Heider that the land ought to be kept open in perpetuity. Who knew what needs might arise? Many people were worried that town youth had no wholesome, supervised center where they could gather after school. Nonetheless, after prolonged negotiations, the trustees accepted the gift, agreeing to hold the land undeveloped for at least five years. Heider signed it over in 1980.

For several years, the church-owned field sat vacant. Meanwhile, the congregation's most pressing need for space was parking, because the membership had grown from 124 to 295 between 1970 and 1980. Yet the church was hemmed in. The most obvious direction to expand the campus was toward Mendocino Headlands State Park. That land, however, was legally dedicated, in perpetuity, to the people of California.

Then Underwood proposed that the church could swap Heider's field for a piece of state park: the state park system could assume responsibility for the open field at the center of town and the congregation could get an acre of open land adjoining its property. State park officials would have to be persuaded, however, and the state legislature would have to pass enabling legislation.

what might happen when the congregation down the block begins a men's Bible study over breakfast on Sunday. It may not be long before someone in your congregation suggests that you do the same. A more dramatic but increasingly common example may be the emergence of a megachurch—a congregation with two thousand or more members—in your locality.[20] While your congregation may not want to copy practices and programs of the megachurch, members will surely not be able to ignore its presence.[21] Developing information about and insight into the religious ecology enables your congregation to make better decisions about which programs and practices to develop—perhaps according to a congregational mission statement—rather than being swayed by

The state park district superintendent set his conditions. Any building the congregation might erect on the property must not obstruct the famous view of the church from the highway exit. If used for parking, the lot deeded to the church must be open to the public, except on Sunday morning. Additionally the church must allow pedestrian access through it to the headlands and the beach.

The local state assemblyman managed a bill through both houses of the legislature, but it was vetoed by the governor on a technicality. Bob Raymond, past ruling elder and prominent Mendocino attorney, carefully drafted a revision, and it was signed into law by Governor Deukmejian.

On December 30, 1988, John Heider returned to Mendocino for the dedication of the new park. Concluding his brief remarks, he said, "May I ask you to join with me in a minute of silent meditation, sensing this time, this place, the people gathered here today as well as those who will pass through this field in years to come, blessed by what you have done." Heider Field, identified by a rustic wooden sign, lies in the center of Mendocino today, unfenced, uncultivated, open to all and a reproach to commercialism.

1. Based on research conducted for this chapter. The authors are indebted to William Mangrum and Annelle Karlstadt for research assistance and to Ronn Garton, John Heider, and Robert Raymond for their frank recollections of long-ago events.
2. See John Heider, *The Tao of Leadership* (Atlanta: Humanics Ltd., 1985).

outside pressures to follow the leader. Your congregation may even decide that another congregation is meeting a particular need, whether it be outreach to pregnant teens, Spanish services, or jazz vespers, and your congregation can best assist by lending support to their efforts (and by staying out of their way).

In addition to its relations with other congregations, your congregation is also linked to other cultural organizations. Think for a minute about all the organizations in your community that shape local webs of involvement. Are bowling, softball, soccer, or tennis leagues active? Which support groups are advertised in the local paper? Does the PTA have a strong presence? Do the Hibernians sponsor the annual parade? What country clubs, symphony guilds, fraternal or veterans groups, or labor unions are in the area? By answering these questions you will begin to identify the various organizations that promote civic involvement and social connectedness. Considered together with congregations, reading groups, choirs, and Scout troops—to name only a few of these groups—form a local social ecology, that is, the systems of roles and relationships that structure the interactions of people in the community. Your congregation is one among many organizations that shape the culture of your locale.

As an environment changes, the mix of cultural organizations is also altered. For example, when Long Beach experienced an inflow of large numbers of Hispanics, Asian Americans, African Americans, and gays and lesbians, the organizational milieu of "Iowa-by-the-Sea" became more culturally diverse, including a local chapter of the NAACP, a Spanish language newspaper, and gay men's choruses. The Mendocino example in sidebar 2.7 highlights the community's dense and changing social ecology, which includes the Presbyterian, Catholic, and Baptist churches; the Masonic lodges; the volunteer fire department; the cemetery society; the Arts Center; the Historical Review Board; the sewer board; and even the Mendocino Land Trust.

A community's social ecology provides the basis for its social capital—those features of organization, like network, norms, and social trust, that make civic life possible.[22] Nancy Ammerman notes that social capital "consists, in part, of trust and mutual obligation, in part of information gathered and available, and in part of norms that encourage prosocial and discourage antisocial behaviors."[23] The people, meanings, and relations within your community combine to create social capital. This social creation, in turn, makes for a stronger community, which enables basic human survival as well as provides opportunities for meaning making, aesthetic pleasures, and social interaction.

We recognize that social capital sometimes is not as abundant as would be optimal. Too often neighbors are suspicious of one another, churches fleece the fold, and politicians are caught with their hands in the public till. Yet our research confirms and our theological interpretation affirms our strong belief that considerable social capital exists within many contexts. Many communities are ecologically healthy, adapting and thriving as changes in their environments necessitate. Even when some organizations—including congregations—cease to be, others emerge in their place, serving other needs and people. These social ecologies provide the context within which people develop trust, hope, and faith. And in communities so beset by disadvantages and disintegration that the habits of social cooperation have atrophied and signs of hope are few, faith communities can bolster hope with religious vision, hard work, and collaboration. But strategic action and prayer are best accompanied by a careful assessment of the social ecology and the social capital within that context.

Conclusion: Congregations and Their Communities

Using an ecological frame enables us to step back to see the rich and complex environment within which each particular congregation is embedded. A broad range of individuals, cultures, and organizations makes up each context. By carefully studying this context and discovering a place within it, congregations can work together for good. The exercises, theories, and examples offered here are intended to equip you for further exploration.

We will conclude with some recommendations for further reading, for the relationship between congregations and communities has received increasing attention in the past decade. In this chapter, directed to members and leaders of particular congregations, we have focused on case studies, particularly the congregations of Dacula, Georgia, and Mendocino, California. We, the authors, are intimately familiar with these communities, just as we expect you, our readers, to be familiar with your congregations, which it is our purpose to invite you to study. Nonetheless, as we conclude, we will offer some observations based on a growing literature that compares congregations in their relationships with their communities.

The earliest study is *Varieties of Religious Presence*[24] whose authors, David Roozen, William McKinney, and Jackson Carroll, have long involvement in congregational studies. Based on 1981 quantitative survey data from 177 congregations in the greater Hartford, Connecticut, area and a closer look at ten representative congregations (Protestant, Catholic, and Jewish), *Varieties* stated an influential fourfold typology of mission orientations. A few years later, Carl Dudley and his associates in the Church and Community Project, building partly on the work of Roozen and his colleagues, worked with more than one hundred congregations in Illinois and Indiana. It was their goal not only to study these congregations' involvement with their communities but also to empower them to be more effective, and their book, *Energizing the Congregation*,[25] focuses closely on six Protestant congregations that represent five types of orientation to community ministry. (See sidebar 3.5.)

In the early 1990s, Penny Becker studied twenty-three Protestant, Catholic, and Jewish congregations in a large, midwestern suburb. Her focus was on determinants of conflict within congregations, and she discovered four types of congregations according to what they claimed was *The Way We Do Things Here*.[26] (Chapter 4 draws on Becker's work.) Finally, in the broadest scale study to date, *Congregation and Community*,[27] Nancy Ammerman and her associates studied twenty-three Christian congregations in five metropolitan areas nationwide to determine their response to dramatic changes in their communities.

Roozen, McKinney, and Carroll's typology crosscuts two dimensions—whether the congregation's approach to mission is "this worldly" or "otherworldly" and whether it is "member-centered" or "publicly proactive"—to derive four types: the "activist" orientation this-worldly and proactive); its polar opposite, "sanctuary" orientation ("otherworldly" and membership-centered); and two intervening types, the "evangelistic" orientation and the "civic" orientation. A major claim of the study is that the four orientations, representing congregational self-understandings, are fundamentally theological orientations that matter for the way the congregation interacts with the community. In this sense, congregations are not at the mercy of their environment but can affect it.

Dudley and Johnson's methods were less structured than those of Roozen and his colleagues and their resulting types are not as neat, but they also claim to have inductively discovered a limited number (five) of self-images congregations have about their place in the community. They are the "prophet" self-image (similar to the "activist" orientation) and the "pillar" (likened to the "civic" orientation) and three other congregational self-images—the "servant," the "survivor," and the "pilgrim"—which represent variations not identified by Roozen and his colleagues. The servant cares for the needs of others in a charitable, nonpolitical way. The survivor hangs on to life in a situation of constant crisis. The pilgrim looks after its own people wherever they may move. One special feature of Dudley and Johnson's work is that for each self-image they highlight a positive, forward-looking aspect, and a negative, defensive one.

Becker, like Roozen and his colleagues, discovered four types, and like Dudley's and Johnson's, her discovery process was inductive. Looking for determinants of congregational conflict, she found that the most intractable conflicts occur when members of the congregation have no consensus on their fundamental identity. There were four such identities, depending on answers to two questions—whether the congregation fosters debate about issues and whether they expect their internal relationships to be close or remote. The "leader" congregation, like Roozen's "activist" and Dudley's "prophet," is devoted to public issues but does not expect intimacy in its internal life. Its polar opposite,

the "family" congregation, expects intimacy even at the cost of issue-centered engagement. The "community" congregation is issue-centered and close-knit and is therefore prone to conflict, whereas the "house of worship" is interested neither in debating issues nor in group intimacy. A special feature of Becker's work is that the congregations she studied cluster in a built-up, stably integrated, middle-class community, most of whose residents could choose any one of them as their congregation. These twenty-three congregations are not only different, they can be thought of as feasible alternatives to each other.

Any one of these books, the cases they are based on, and the typologies they offer, may help members, or a study group, of your congregation understand your place in the community and learn ways to be more faithful in what you do. Perhaps, like the Presbyterian church of Mendocino, your congregation has changed its "type" over time.[28] Perhaps you would find that your congregation combined two or more of the types in its various programs or subgroups. More likely, you would recognize some ways that your congregation shares God's work in your community. That work may well call for an "activist" approach to change unjust structures, an "evangelist" effort to change individual lives, a "sanctuary" that provides safe spaces in the midst of dangers, as well as a "civic" encouragement to good citizenship.

Ammerman's findings are especially pertinent here. She broke down her twenty-three congregations not according to their type but according to the kinds of response they made to dramatic changes in their communities, changes ranging from downsizing in the town's biggest factory (as in Anderson, Indiana) through rapid suburbanization (as in Dacula, Georgia) to the influx of whole new categories of people (as with the gay and lesbian presence in Long Beach, California). The congregations' different responses were: to ignore the changes or resist addressing them (which usually spelled decline for the congregation), relocate the congregation, sharpen the identification of the congregation's constituent population (becoming a "niche" congregation), innovate by welcoming newcomer populations, or adopt a wholly new identity. Ammerman and her team did gather survey data on theological orientations so that she could categorize the congregations according to Roozen's mission orientations, but she found that the congregation's responses to change were not determined by what type they fell under. "Civically" minded congregations could only adapt effectively if they understood the complexity of the community they sought to represent and benefit. Similarly, "evangelist" congregations could effectively reach out to save souls only if they were willing "to deal with the diversity of cultural and physical packages those souls come in."[29] Helping your own congregation to understand community complexity and population diversity may well occasion conflict, and here Ammerman's most general finding stands out: the only congregations that avoided conflict were those that refused to change, a refusal that would ultimately mean their demise. The only sure way for a congregation to die is for it to close itself off from its context.

NOTES

1. Robert Wuthnow, *The Restructuring of American Religion* (Princeton: Princeton University Press, 1988).

2. The present chapter is diffusely indebted to the chapter on context, attributed by the editors (p. 3) to William McKinney and Wade Clark Roof, in the *Handbook for Congregational Studies*, ed. Jackson W. Carroll, Carl S. Dudley, and William McKinney (Nashville: Abingdon, 1986). This chapter, however, represents a new point of view, highlighting the congregation in relation to religious and other organizations in the community.

3. R. Stephen Warner, "The Place of the Congregation in the American Religious Configuration," in *New Perspectives in the Study of Congregations*, ed. James P. Wind and James W. Lewis (Chicago: University of Chicago Press, 1994), 54-99.

4. Carl Dudley, *Basic Steps Toward Community Ministry* (New York: The Alban Institute, 1991), 25.

5. Ibid., 28.

6. Ibid., 29.

7. Based on R. Stephen Warner, *New Wine in Old Wineskins: Evangelicals and Liberals in a Small-Town Church* (Berkeley: University of California Press, 1988); idem, "Mirror for American Protestantism: Mendocino Presbyterian Church in the Sixties and Seventies," in *The Mainstream Protestant "Decline": The Presbyterian Pattern*, ed. Milton J. Coalter, John M. Mulder, and Louis B. Weeks (Louisville: Westminister/John Knox, 1990), 198-223, 250-53; and idem, "Oenology: The Making of *New Wine*," in *A Case for the Case Study*, ed. Joe Feagin, Anthony Orum, and Gideon Sjoberg (Chapel Hill: University of North Carolina Press, 1991), 174-99.

8. These are pseudonyms.

9. Some church members in the 1970s saw how religious enthusiasm could go too far in the example of Jim Jones, whose United States base of operations was on the county road several miles east of Mendocino. See Warner, *New Wine in Old Wineskins*, 228.

10. The following section and figures 2.2 and 2.3 are based on Eiesland, *A Particular Place: Exurbanization and Religious Response* (New Brunswick, N.J.: Rutgers University Press, forthcoming).

11. All names in this account are pseudonyms; some distinguishing characteristics of individuals and events have also been altered to protect anonymity.

12. Based on Warner, *New Wine in Old Wineskins* "Mirror for American Protestantism"; and "Oenology: The Making of *New Wine*."

13. The following section is based on research conducted by Nancy Ammerman and her associates and reported, with different emphases, in her *Congregation and Community* (New Brunswick, N.J.: Rutgers University Press, 1997). We are grateful to Ammerman for sharing her notebooks with us, but we alone claim responsibility for the interpretations offered here.

14. See Eiesland, *A Particular Place*.

15. These data come from a nationwide survey conducted by Mediamark Research Inc. (1991-1992).

16. Frances FitzGerald, *Cities on a Hill: A Journey through Contemporary American Subcultures* (New York: Simon and Schuster, 1986).

17. See Warner, *New Wine in Old Wineskins*, 86-87, 201-8, 292-93.

18. N. J. Demerath III and Rhys H. Williams, *A Bridging of Faiths: Religion and Politics in a New England City* (Princeton, N.J.: Princeton University Press, 1992).

19. Volumes one and two contain information on different religious groups. Arthur J. Magida, ed., *How to Be a Perfect Stranger, Volume 1: A Guide to Etiquette in Other People's Religious Ceremonies* (Woodstock, Vt.: Jewish Lights Publishing, 1996); Stuart A. Matlins and Arthur J. Magida, eds., *How to Be a Perfect Stranger, Volume 2: A Guide to Etiquette in Other People's Religious Ceremonies* (Woodstock, Vt.: Jewish Lights, 1997).

20. Much of what the authors know about megachurches is indebted to the work of Scott Lee Thumma; see his chapter, "Megachurches of Atlanta," in *Religions of Atlanta: Religious Diversity in the Centennial Olympic City*, ed. Gary Laderman (Atlanta: Scholars Press, 1996).

21. For discussion of the effects of a megachurch on one community's religious ecology, see Nancy L. Eiesland, "Contending with a Giant: The Impact of a Megachurch on Exurban Religious Institutions," in *Contemporary American Religion: An Ethnographic Reader*, ed. Penny E. Becker and Nancy L. Eiesland (Walnut Creek, Calif.: Alta Mira, 1997).

22. For a recent discussion of social capital, see Robert D. Putnam, "Bowling Alone: America's Declining Social Capital," *Journal of Democracy* 6 (January 1995): 65-78. Compare with Nicholas Lemann, "Kicking in Groups," *The Atlantic Monthly* 277 (April 1996): 22-26.

23. Ammerman, *Congregation and Community*, 347.

24. David Roozen, William McKinney, and Jackson Carroll, *Varieties of Religious Presence: Mission in Public Life* (New York: Pilgrim, 1984).

25. Carl S. Dudley and Sally A. Johnson, *Energizing the Congregation: Images That Shape Your Church's Ministry* (Louisville: Westminster/John Knox, 1993).

26. Penny Edgell Becker, *The Way We Do Things Here: Cultures and Conflict in Local Congregations* (Cambridge: Cambridge University Press, 1998).

27. Nancy Tatom Ammerman, *Congregation and Community*.

28. See Warner, *New Wine in Old Wineskins*, 283-89.

29. Ammerman, *Congregation and Community*, 342.

Chapter 3

Culture and Identity in the Congregation

NANCY T. AMMERMAN

No two congregations are alike. Each gathering of people creates its own ways of doing things, its own ways of describing the world, its own tools and artifacts that produce its distinctive appearance. Congregations, in other words, are subcultures within a larger culture. They have distinct identities that can be seen in what they make and do together. One of the perspectives one can bring to the study of a congregation, then, is that of the student of culture who looks for the everyday patterns of life that make each congregation itself, that give it its identity. James Hopewell begins his book *Congregation* with the observation that "a group of people cannot regularly gather for what they feel to be religious purposes without developing a complex network of signals and symbols and conventions—in short, a subculture—that gains its own logic and then functions in a way peculiar to that group."[1]

Defining Culture

Culture is who we are and the world we have created to live in. It is the predictable patterns of who does what and habitual strategies for telling the world about the things held most dear. The *Handbook for Congregational Studies* talked about a congregation's identity, and culture is not unlike what the *Handbook* meant by that concept. But thinking about a congregation's culture reminds us that it is something this group of people has created, not a fixed or normative category. Unlike our usual notions about identity, a culture is neither who we always will be nor who we ought to be. It is who we are and all the ways in which we reinforce and recreate who we are. A culture includes the congregation's history and stories of its heroes. It includes its symbols, rituals, and worldview. It is shaped by the cultures in which its members live (represented by their demographic characteristics), but it takes on its own unique identity and character when those members come together.[2] Just as our larger culture tells us how to greet people and how to eat properly and what sorts of clothes to wear, so a congregational culture gives those rules its own special twist. Understanding a congregation requires understanding that it is a unique gathering of people with a cultural identity all its own.

Congregations, of course, do not create their cultures from scratch. They have a rather large store of ingredients from which to borrow. In some cases, they may get both the ingredients and an elaborate recipe from their specific religious tradition. When one walks into a Catholic or Presbyterian or Lutheran place of worship, or enters a Jewish or Muslim or Hindu sacred space, it is clear that the place or space belongs to a tradition, that it is identified with the ideas and practices and symbols of that larger religious whole. It may seem, in fact, that congregations have little room for creating anything on their own, given some traditions' prescriptions for how rituals are done, what sort of governance structure is allowed, what lessons are studied by the children, and even what the building looks like. Congregations, after all, act as carriers of some larger tradition. Even the most independent church, which claims to be free of denominational interference, nevertheless sees itself as a carrier of the Christian message and participates in networks of affiliation that shape its life. What each congregation cooks up, then, is always a mix of local creativity and larger tradition. What we see in a given locale is that group's selective retrieval of their own theological heritage, along with the local inventions that have been necessary to make sense of life in that place.

In addition to being shaped by a theological tradition, congregations are also, of course, shaped by the larger secular culture in which they are located. Most obviously, they usually borrow the larger culture's language. Anyone who has visited congregations at a distance from his or her home immediately recognizes that congregations borrow more than language. The rhythm of the music may be different, even if the hymns are the same. The order and timing of the service may vary, even if all the usual elements are there. The arrangement of the space, the dress of the worshipers, and who is honored and how—all signal the distinctiveness that comes from a particular local culture. What we see in those distant locations is both the particular inventions of those local worshipers and the ways they borrow from the habits and tools of their larger culture.

In the United States, congregations build their culture out of well-defined expectations for what local religious bodies are supposed to be like. We expect, for instance, that congregations are voluntary gatherings, that people can choose where they belong. Religious groups that attempt to assign people to a given parish must contend with this larger cultural norm.

We also expect religious buildings to be distinctive and worship services to be at a predictable time. We expect that there will be a "pastor" of some sort and a certain predictable range of activities—worship chief among them, but educational, fellowship, and service activities, as well. When a congregation engages in activities outside the expected range—political activities or economic enterprises, for instance—it has to explain itself. Likewise, when a congregation fails to engage in the expected activities, it is suspect. Certainly lots of groups manage to be different, but the point is that they (and we) recognize that they are *different*.

We can remind ourselves that how we do things is shaped by our culture by noting that "it has not always been so." Sunday school is a relatively recent invention, for instance, and only in the last century or so have churches had picnics and outings, not to mention gyms and bowling alleys.[3] We can also remind ourselves of the strength of these cultural patterns by looking at the non-Christian immigrant groups who are increasingly present in the United States. Despite the traditions for gathering (or not gathering) that may have been present for Muslims or Buddhists in their home countries, in the American situation these groups are organizing congregations that look very much like the voluntary gatherings that are characteristic of American religious groups.[4] They, like everyone else, construct their congregational culture out of the materials available, and those materials come from the particular cultural stockpile where they are located.

Not only are congregations in the United States shaped by this institutional blueprint, they also borrow from their own social and cultural locations. Folks in rural areas may arrive in overalls that would be shocking in a suburban congregation. The pastor of a university church may include contemporary poetry in her sermon that would be bewildering to another congregation. The participants in a Hindu temple will bring food for a temple gathering that would taste odd to members elsewhere. And when all the members of the committee pull out their computerized pocket calendars or exchange E-mail addresses, they are bringing the habits of their particular social worlds into the mix of the congregation's activities.

Sometimes the outside culture people bring to the congregation is based on region, ethnicity, and social class. Congregations in the South are different from those in the West, while gatherings of *Latinos y Latinas* are distinct from those of African Americans or those of European heritage. But even within, say, an African American and southern subculture, there are also divisions based on education and occupation and social class and generation. Having been to college gives a person different experiences from those who have not been. People who do similar types of work may discover that they have much in common. Similarly, people who have been brought up in a particular time (such as the Great Depression or the period following World War II) share some common experiences. From all the different social settings in which we have learned to be who we are, we bring skills and assumptions into the culture of the congregation.

It is not unusual, in fact, for the people who gather into a congregation to share a common social and cultural heritage. They are likely to speak the same language, probably with the same accent. They are likely to be quite similar in educational, occupational, and status backgrounds. And they are quite likely to share a common ethnicity. Because the United States allows for the voluntary gathering of religious communities (rather than having an official state church with prescribed parish boundaries), members sort themselves into groupings in which they feel at home, where the people in the pews are like themselves. As a result, all the cultural elements that create that feeling of at-homeness also shape the congregation's particular ways of doing things. Their ethnic and status culture will affect the kinds of music they like, the kinds of literature the pastor can cite in a sermon, the way they expect to be involved in decision making, and the sort of decor they see as appropriate—among other things.

One of the most basic cultural differences that finds its way into congregational life is the difference between traditional rural ways of life and the fast-paced life of the modern city.

Rural communities expect everyone to know everyone else and are not surprised when family, politics, and business spill over into each other. They expect to get things done informally and in their own good time. Urban communities, by contrast, are places where people tend to live by the clock and by the book. People do not expect others to know their business, but they do expect to have clear job descriptions and definite lines of authority. These expectations naturally find their way into congregational life.[5]

One of your first tasks in understanding the culture of your congregation is to take an inventory of the important pieces of the outside culture your members share. You may get some of this information from a parish survey that includes questions about education, occupation, ethnicity, and residence, for instance. What social and cultural characteristics do they share? In what ways is it easy for people to talk to each other because they already have so much in common? Understanding the culture in which they live most of their lives, in neighborhood and family and workplace, will help you to understand the cultural expectations and patterns they bring into the congregation. A survey will give you important outlines of the differences, but a closer understanding of different cultural ways of life will probably require more in-depth interviews and observation.

One of the things you may discover rather quickly, both from surveys and from interviews, is that no congregation is ever really just one unified culture. There are subcultures within that may be more or less distinct, groups that spend a good deal of time with each other and perhaps relatively little with others in the congregation. A subculture may be organized around commonalities of age or longevity, with older widowed women participating in a world of congregational activities that is quite different, for instance, from the world inhabited by a young adult, activist group of professionals. Subcultures in the congregation may also be defined by where people live or what they do for a living. You will need to discover the lines along which such subcultural differences are drawn. Is there one small minority or several?

Are there two or three large blocks of people with some significant differences: Italians and Irish, managers and line workers, new residents of subdivisions and older town residents, and so forth? Each subculture may see different parts of the building as sacred, may enjoy different parts of the worship service, and may engage in very different mission activities. As you try to understand the culture of a congregation, remember that there are probably significant variations on the themes you discover.

As you are looking for the ways in which outside statuses define lines of difference inside the congregation, it is important to keep in mind that congregations vary enormously in how they relate to the world outside their doors. Some congregations pride themselves on being set apart from the world.[6] They are very aware of their boundaries and talk often of what makes them different from other groups of believers and from the outside world. They offer their members as many alternatives to the outside culture as possible, and they absorb large amounts of their members' available time, often minimizing differences in the backgrounds people bring into the congregation. Most of their members' significant relationships are likely to be congregation-related as well. Whether set apart by distinctive food and dress or by distinctive morals and language, these congregations have cultures that are sustained by the high investment of their members in the congregation's common life.[7] Their stories, views of the world, habits, and rituals are likely to be relatively unusual, in contrast to congregations that have more permeable boundaries with the larger culture.

In contrast, where the congregation emphasizes being part of the culture rather than set apart, movement in and out of the congregation is relatively easy, and the congregation can speak to and with the community in terms seemingly understood by everyone. What people do because they are members and what they do just because they are good citizens are hard to distinguish. These congregations have little apparent sense of boundary, of what sets them apart—except perhaps their shunning of the strictness and intolerance they see in other

groups. These congregations have fewer requirements for membership and absorb less of their members' time and energy. As a result, their cultures may seem less distinctive, more ordinary. When we observe such a congregation, it is important to remember that even what seems unremarkable is still a distinctive culture. There are still boundaries that define who is an acceptable member and who is not. Even the most apparently boundaryless congregation probably has a well-tuned but unspoken sense of what belief and behavior would be out of place among them.

The shape of a congregational culture is also affected by its size. The larger the congregation, the more diverse the cultures within it and the more subcultures there are likely to be. While there may be many elements everyone shares, large congregations are likely to have subgroups that are defined by the unique activities that they do not share with other groups in the congregation. For instance, an older adult Sunday school class may carry on a way of being church that was pervasive fifty years ago, but not (in the rest of the congregation) today. In other congregations, a singles group may have a life of its own, or the people who attend the 11:00 service may barely know those who attend at 8:30. In small congregations, there is little opportunity for such special interest groups to become isolated, but in large congregations, there are often many subcultures relatively independent of one another.

Finally, a congregation's culture is shaped by its own history. We will return to this in more detail below, but it is important to remember that the culture we see today is but a chapter in a much longer story that has both a past and a future dimension.

Each congregation is, then, a unique culture, but it is a culture constructed out of many different kinds of materials. And it is never static. Each time a new person joins, each time a new pastor or priest or rabbi arrives, each time something changes in the neighborhood, and each time the members themselves change (have children, grow older, lose their jobs, and the like), the life experiences out of which the congregation's culture is made have been altered. A congregation exists in the tension between long entrenched patterns and new contingencies. In fact, there is often active negotiation going on over what sort of place a congregation will be. In some places the weight of history and continuity is much stronger than in others. Where people's lives seemingly change less and there is little movement in and out of the congregation, the culture seems to remain unchanged. But in no place does the existing culture survive unchanged forever (we promise!). A congregational culture is constructed out of all the materials we have been discussing—theological and denominational traditions, expectations from the larger culture, patterns of social class and ethnicity, and the like. All those things are carried into the congregation by its members and leaders. Whenever any of those elements changes, the congregation will inevitably change as well.

As we suggested in the beginning, however, congregational culture is more than the sum of what people bring with them and more than a mirror image of the theological tradition they represent. It is a unique creation, constructed out of their interaction together over time. Your job in understanding this culture, then, is to observe that interaction and talk with people who can explain to you "how we do things here."

Reasons for Studying Culture

Some people may want to study a congregation's culture just because they are fascinated and want to understand these unique human institutions. But others may have much more specific and practical goals in mind. One of the most common times when a congregation's culture needs to be understood is when any new person arrives. Especially when clergy begin their work in a new place, they need to know much more than mere annual reports and orders of worship can tell them. They need to know the congregation's stories and its idiom, its ways of feasting and its ways of bestowing honor. The new pastor needs to learn the often unspoken expectations of the insiders and elites, as well as the expectations of those who attend more sporadi-

cally. Immediately after a pastor or priest or rabbi comes to a congregation, a careful study of its culture can be invaluable.

Similarly, any new person who joins the congregation will have to learn his or her place in it. A careful study of the congregation's culture can help those who work with new members to know how to help them through the process.

Understanding culture is also critical to making any sort of change. Before new programs can be implemented or administrations reorganized or new ministries begun, clergy and other leaders need to understand the well-established ways of life that will be disrupted by these changes. Understanding what will be lost can often help leaders find rewarding substitutes in the new system. Seeing clearly how people's lives will be changed can help leaders know how to communicate about what will happen and avoid unpleasant surprises for everyone involved. Studying the culture may also uncover stories and symbols from the congregation's past that may help to bridge the way into the future. There are both hidden riches and lurking land mines in any culture, and it pays to know where they are.

Methods for Studying Culture

When an anthropologist enters a new culture, the most important thing he or she does is to observe—to watch and listen long enough to know something of what people intend by their actions and what they mean by their words. You, unlike some anthropologists, are not going off to a tropical isle, however, and that is both an advantage and a disadvantage. The advantage in time and energy is obvious. The disadvantage is that congregations seem so familiar to most of us that it is hard to have the patience and discipline to get past our assumptions. We are the proverbial fish that does not notice the water. For that reason, a visit to another congregation may be a helpful exercise at the beginning of your study process. Refer to the section on observing worship in chapter 7 of this book for guidelines for this task. By watching how a group quite different from your own gathers for worship, for instance, you may begin to see some of the distinctiveness of the congregation to which you are giving your primary attention.

Many times those who study a congregation's culture and identity will be members and leaders of that congregation. If that is the case, you should pay special attention to the advice for insiders given in the chapter on methods. You will be uncovering and giving voice to many of the unwritten assumptions of your congregation's life. You will want to proceed with great care and respect while also working hard to see the things you need to see.

Other times, a congregation calls on an outside consultant for advice on seeing themselves more clearly. Just as it may help members to visit another congregation as a way of gaining perspective, so an outsider can often see and say things an insider cannot. A consultant will need to know, however, that the congregation itself is fully involved in setting the agenda and helping to provide the information necessary to understand something an outsider can only begin to comprehend in the short time usually available for such studies.

If you are studying your own congregation, your first task as an observer of culture will be to identify the focus of your activity and to organize your work. It is easy to get overwhelmed by the complexity of a culture, and your task will be made easier *if you develop a focus* that will help you narrow your work. You did not start out to learn about this congregation so that you could write a book! You started out with a specific concern, a puzzle you wanted to solve. You might be interested in understanding what the congregation is passing along to its children or what newcomers are perceiving when they arrive or why the youth group is thriving or why money is a taboo topic or why certain community service projects generate no enthusiasm. Depending on your focus, you can be selective about the events you observe, the people you interview, and the artifacts you collect. You can also be selective in the themes you choose to highlight in the material you have gathered.

As you decide on what you want to know, you will also need to think about how you will find out. You will almost surely want to do some *systematic observation* of events in the congregation. You want to know what people are actually doing when they gather in this place. Likewise, you will discover that the events do not always explain themselves. *Interviews* will be important aids to filling in the cultural picture. Some of those may be in the form of *focus groups,* or you may choose to focus on the congregation's history through the use of a *time-line exercise.* You may even decide that some of what you need to know can be gathered through the use of a paper-and-pencil *questionnaire.* Alongside your observations and conversations, do not forget to gather the *artifacts*—from old pictures to worship books—that may give you an additional window on this congregation's identity. For specific guidelines on each of these ways of gathering data, refer to chapter 7 on methods. But before you undertake any specific method of gathering information, make sure you know what you want to know and how a given activity will help you find it out.

Also, this should not be a solo operation. At the very least, a group of advisers from the congregation should help to develop the focus, design the methods to be used, and serve as interpreters along the way. Indeed, a team of people from the congregation can divide up the tasks of data gathering as well. Some can observe one event while others concentrate on other events. Each person might conduct only three or four interviews. And everyone can be on the lookout for important documents and other materials. If you do proceed as a team, it is important to meet regularly together so that you are clear about your assignments and your focus. It is also important that everyone agree to keep good notes. Although several people can gather data, it is still essential that one person be responsible for compiling it. As that person reads notes and interview transcripts, however, the team of other information gatherers can be valuable consultants in understanding the themes and patterns that emerge.

Before you design your study, you will need

to take into account all the various dimensions of the congregation's culture and identity. One way of thinking about those dimensions is to look at *activities, artifacts,* and *accounts.* Our sense of who we are is shaped by what we do, what we make, and how we talk about ourselves. Let us look more closely at each of those aspects of congregational culture.[8]

Activities: What the Congregation Does Together

Congregations create their culture, in large part, through the things they do together. Whenever they gather, inside the congregation's building or scattered throughout the community, they act within (and sometimes stretch) the boundaries of what their culture has established as normal. It even happens when just one person is representing the congregation. Sometimes, in fact, the congregation acts even when no one is present, for example, through its gifts and other forms of presence in the community. The most visible—and the most invisible—of those activities are the congregation's rituals.

Rituals

All cultures have rituals that give shape to people's common life together, and congregations are certainly no exception. The single most common congregational activity is, in fact, the ritual of a weekly worship event. It is in this event that congregations engage in their most dramatic rituals, their most intentional presentation of who they are. In a powerful sense, worship is an event that is meant to express the unifying vision of the congregation. It is this expressive character that makes something a ritual. It is predictable activity that is intended to express something beyond itself. Ordinary activities like turning on the lights or taking out the garbage may take on some special meaning, but they usually remain relatively meaningless, mundane tasks. But other ordinary activities can take on special meaning by being enacted in the context of a congregation's life together. Note what Dodson and Gilkes have to

say about the routine act of eating (see sidebar 3.1). Rituals are more than utilitarian, then; they communicate meanings and relationships that are central to the very identity of the congregation. Rituals point beyond themselves. All rituals, in fact, help to create the community that enacts them. They both *express* who we are and *make* us who we are.[9] From how someone is greeted at the door, to the congregation's most holy events, rituals say more than what can be communicated in words.

Sidebar 3.1
RITUALS OF FOOD IN AFRICAN AMERICAN CHURCHES

Since the meat most often served in United States African American churches is chicken, it is referred to by many as "gospel bird." The sale of chicken dinners was a principal means whereby churches raised money to build their sanctuaries and schools and generated income for a variety of activities. The image of chicken dinners, dinners featuring "gospel bird," is so fixed in the United States African American imagination that some see it only as a negative stereotype. Many people will not eat chicken precisely because of the negative dimensions. Yet, the popularity of church dinners featuring chicken as a source of fund-raising and sociability remains strong. Regardless of attempts to diversify the fare, chicken dinners are most in demand, and the chicken usually runs out first. The preference is still for gospel bird. (p. 523)

The importance of feeding the preacher is expressed in a variety of ways. In one congregation we observed that a special potluck was being organized to celebrate the installation of an assistant pastor. Every member was asked to bring a dish. The kitchen team was voted in at a special church meeting. A deaconess of the church, who was also a member of the kitchen team for that dinner, announced for several Sundays during the worship service that all contributed food was to be brought to the kitchen and there would be no acceptance of special dishes designated "only for the pastor's table." On the Sunday of the dinner, members complied with the kitchen team's request and did not attempt to designate their dishes for the pastor's table. However, many brought dishes separately prepared for the assistant pastor, each wrapped for carry out and in shopping bags. (p. 531)

From Jualynne E. Dodson and Cheryl Townsend Gilkes, "There's Nothing Like Church Food," *Journal of the American Academy of Religion* 63 (Fall 1995): 519-38.

Even "low church" congregations, who pride themselves on less formal rituals, nevertheless have their own version of the worship drama. Whether a congregation is "high" or "low," there is a routine order of songs and prayers and sermons. People wear special costumes (even if it is only their best Sunday suit), they know their places (fourth pew on the right), and they know what props are needed (Bibles, hymnals, prayer books, head coverings, and the like). In fact, one way to observe a worship service is to imagine it as a theatrical event, looking for the settings, props, costumes, actors, and scripts.

One of the most important things to notice about any ritual is that it involves all the senses. It involves things we see, touch, smell, and taste, as well as what we hear.[10] Look for the banners and flags, furniture, linens, clothing, and other implements that draw your attention to the specialness of the ritual. Open your ears to the array of sounds that accompany worship—the sounds of children wiggling in their seats, of a mass of bodies bowing to the floor, of bells and calls to prayer. Then close your eyes and note the smells that surround you. You do not need incense to have special smells that remind you of where you are and what you are doing. It may just be someone's characteristic perfume or the mustiness of old hymnals. The things you smell and touch, along with the bodily movements that are required of worshipers, are often part of a deeply held memory. Kneeling, washing one's hands, walking forward to receive Communion or give one's offering, the touch of the *tallit* on the edge of the Torah, being immersed in a baptismal pool, even the rhythm of standing and sitting—all form part of the texture of a congregation's cultural memory.

Likewise, ritual music is a deeply sensual experience that often touches people in ways words cannot.[11] In his book on current Catholic musical practices, Thomas Day notes that "congregational singing always begins as a sensuous experience, not an intellectual one; it flourishes wherever the congregation can feel the sensuous pleasure of musical vibrations."[12] Singing and chanting call worshipers to enact and relive—together—the faith they are recounting in song.[13]

In addition to paying attention to the sights and sounds of the congregation's rituals, the observer should also pay attention to the actors. Not everyone is an equal participant in all the ritual events of the congregation. Within every group there are differences in status and in levels of participation. Some differences in status are marked by ordination or some other setting apart, and they give some members specialized worship roles. These leaders may be permitted access to sacred spaces and expected to utter sacred words or read sacred texts that are forbidden to ordinary members.[14] In addition, there are more ordinary roles and positions of honor that reflect the congregation's identity and culture.[15] Singers, readers, ushers, offering takers, and announcement makers are likely to be otherwise influential members of the congregation, for instance. The presence or absence of certain members or guests may be especially marked, acknowledging their importance and honor in the community. Even the way people greet one another reveals much about who defers to whom—whether by gender, social class, seniority, or spiritual categories defined by the congregation itself. Both in these routine activities and on special occasions, some people are singled out for special recognition. That recognition, in turn, says a lot about the sorts of behavior the congregation values and wishes to encourage. All the things people do as they gather for worship signal both the ways they are bound together into one community and the ways that community itself is divided.

Of particular note are the ways worship and other rituals are likely to reveal the differing roles of men and women, gendered differences developed by either habit or fiat. There may be spaces inhabited by one gender and not the other—separate seating or places off limits to women (or men). Women and men may have distinct roles, some things permitted to one and not the other. Just as people bring their outside status and cultural identities into the congregation, they also bring with them all the experiences and expectations that go with being male and female. Even congregations that pride themselves on equality may be experienced differently by women than by men. A careful observer will both watch for what men and women do and listen for how they describe their experiences.

The scheduling of worship can also tell you about the congregation's culture. Even if the service is at a rather predictable time, you should notice, for instance, whether there are early services, what the rhythm of children's and adult activities is, and what people seem to expect to do with the rest of their day. A congregation sends (usually unconscious) signals about itself in the very schedule of services it posts (if it does) on its outdoor bulletin board.

Beyond the mere worship schedule, worship is important because it is a ritual, and rituals say something about who we are. They point beyond themselves to deeper meanings. In the case of religious gatherings, those meanings are, at heart, about the deity being worshiped and proclaimed. The congregation's rituals are one way that it tells the story of God's activity. What and how members pray says a good deal about their understanding of their god. Listen for how God is addressed, what God is asked to do, what God is thanked for, and what is simply assumed about God's nature. Beyond these direct verbal cues, allow yourself to experience the sensual and emotional weight of the gathering you are observing. Does it feel joyful or solemn, awe-inspiring or comforting, or some combination thereof? In addition, talk to your informants about what they experience and how they understand what they do when they worship.

The experience of worship is also sometimes expected to change things; but the degree to which that is the case varies enormously—from person to person, event to event, and congregation to congregation. At the least, times of worship offer moments of quiet reflection about life. But they may also offer extended periods of ecstatic religious experience, deep insight into one's own soul, or renewed passion for trying to change the world. Not every person who attends expects to have a mystical or ecstatic experience at every service, but most people who choose to attend religious services expect that at least occasionally they will feel close to God. At the very least, they expect congregations to invoke

God's presence, and part of a congregation's culture is its mode of doing so. Does God's presence depend on the individual worshiper or on the leader? Is it simply there in the building and the ritual, or must it be experienced by each person? Does it require special actions or objects, or it is readily available in ordinary time and space?[16] Is it something that happens constantly, or something that is a surprising rarity? A congregation's sense of transcendence is an important aspect of its culture and something often observable in its rituals.

Rituals define the congregation and the people who participate in them. Some rituals focus on the group. They have been called *rites of intensification*. They intensify the group's commitment to its shared beliefs and meanings. They include a variety of occasions in which core values of the group are celebrated. For the nation, those might include the Fourth of July, Thanksgiving, or Mother's Day; for Christian churches, the celebrations of Christmas and Easter; and for Muslims, the fasting of Ramadan. In addition, local congregations may have their own special days—homecomings and anniversaries and fairs and barbecues and other local rituals. At an annual meeting, the events of the year may be recounted. At an anniversary, the congregation's history may be told. At the Jewish Passover, the history of Israel's most formative events are enacted. Such events provide opportunities for members to learn about the group they belong to, for children to be brought into the faith, and for everyone to experience a sense of unity and accomplishment.

Other rituals focus on the individual's life, especially as defined by her or his participation in the group. These have been called *rites of passage*. They are transition events that mark changes in the individual's life or changes in the life of the congregation. They are moments that mark our passage from one status to another. The child passes into adulthood, the congregation passes from one pastor or rabbi to another, the member passes from this life to the next, the person being ordained passes from laity to clergy, and the visitor passes into full membership. Confirmations, bat and bar mitzvahs, installations and ordinations, funerals, and many other rituals define the contours of our individual lives in ways that also define us as members of a congregation. A funeral not only marks the death of an individual but also signals the continuing life of the group gathered to mourn. How families are comforted and cared for and what is extolled in the eulogy, even how the body is treated, communicate volumes about those left behind.[17] Such times let us ask ourselves all over again who we are and who we want to become.

Anthropologist Victor Turner noted that rites of passage often include a time "between" (called *liminal,* meaning "on the threshold"), when we are no longer who we were but not yet who we will become. These times often allow for experimentation and breaking the rules.[18] Newness can break into the congregation's routine, requiring people to be more intentional than usual about what they do and why. The congregation itself may take the transitional time between pastors as a liminal time, for instance. It can be a time of self-study and reflection, not just on what pastoral skills are needed, but on what sort of congregation this is. In observing important rites of passage, then, we should pay attention to the time leading up to the big event, as well as the event itself. We can learn a good deal about how the congregation defines a virtuous life, as well as about its own sense of identity and purpose.

Other Activities

Worship, while the most central event for most congregations, is certainly not the only important activity to observe. In most congregations, there are at least some additional activities that bring together all or part of the group. Most congregations have some sort of *religious education activities.* For most Christian and many Jewish groups it is a Sunday school (Sabbath school for Seventh-Day groups). There children learn basic scriptural knowledge and are taught the principles of their faith. In congregations that also have adult classes, those groups often function as support groups, as well as forums for study and discussion. Indeed, Robert Wuthnow reports that adult Sunday school classes are the single most common form of small group in American society, with perhaps 25 million adults participating.[19]

In some churches the educational opportunities are much more extensive—lecture series; missions education groups; special men's, women's, and children's groups; and weeknight Bible study groups. For Jewish children, education includes learning Hebrew and preparing for a bar or bat mitzvah. For Muslims, it includes Arabic and study of the Qu'ran. Observing educational activities reveals both *what* is being taught about living a virtuous life and about the history of the faith, but also *how* members expect to participate—whether they expect to learn by memorization or interaction, or whether the emphasis is on personal experience or learning the facts, for instance.

Many congregations also engage in *fellowship* activities. They want their members to know each other and care for each other, so they plan church suppers and holiday parties, lunch after sabbath services or grand feasts for the end of Ramadan, outings, sports events, bingo nights, and coffee hours. Just which holidays are celebrated, which sports organized, and what foods brought to potluck dinners are—no less than worship rituals—elements in the congregation's culture. Whether the coffee is instant or brewed, served in china or foam or paper cups, and paid for by the congregation's budget or by individual contributions may say a good deal about the resources and political sentiments of the members.

While some of what a congregation does is explicitly planned with fellowship in mind, a great deal of what it does has fellowship as a byproduct. Whether participating in a weekly Bible study or serving together on a soup line, representing the group's interests before a town board or painting the nursery, when members gather, they inevitably share bits and pieces of their lives with each other. That shared activity, in turn, creates an additional base on which the culture of the congregation can be built.

What and how much is shared, however, will vary with the culture of the congregation. In some places members are accustomed to a great deal of privacy. In others, members expect to talk extensively about their work and family life. When a member is in need, others are likely to respond with tangible forms of assistance, as well as with emotional support—with casseroles and hugs.[20] They share face-to-face discussions of life's issues and become intimate companions, forming a familylike bond of obligation. Other congregations, however, simply do not expect such social bonds to be important. They see themselves primarily as worship centers, and they do not seek to foster ongoing relationships among those who participate.

Beyond the intimacy, fun, and sharing of fellowship times are the day-to-day *task-oriented activities* that keep the congregation going. Committees and task forces meet to plan the congregation's programs. Deacons or elders or a council are charged with overseeing the spiritual and programmatic affairs of the congregation. Each working group has its own culture, its own habits and routines—when they meet, who takes minutes, whether there is coffee or tea, who talks the most, how they report to the rest of the congregation. These routines for *how* work is done are intimately related to assumptions about who can make decisions and why (all subjects taken up in much more detail in chapter 4 on process). These small cultural elements are as much a part of the congregation's authority structure as are the official patterns contained in the group's bylaws.

In addition to decision-making bodies, there are also often *ministry activities* aimed at serving people outside the congregation. Members come together to staff food pantries, organize support for the nation of Israel, visit people they want to recruit, build a Habitat for Humanity house, or go on an overseas mission trip. The shape of these ministries is also a reflection of the congregation's sense of identity and its sense of its place in the world. What problems are noticed reflects the particular cultural blinders (and telescopes) of the congregation. What members choose to do in response reflects the congregation's sense of mission along with its perceived cultural resources.

Finally, there is what we might call the *kitchen work* of the congregation. Often it is literally in the kitchen, but it might also be in the office or in the yard. It is the behind-the-scenes support work that makes congregational life possible. It is the dish washing and envelope stuffing and hedge trimming that are no less a part of the congregational culture than the highest holy moment. It is the work of the altar guild and the usher board, for instance, in setting the stage for worship and making sure the service goes smoothly. How all this is done and by whom will be shaped by often unwritten expectations in each congregational culture. Often these tasks are done by women, women who may have few public roles in the congregation but expend themselves for the good of the community in these seemingly small tasks. Joanna Gillespie's interview with such a woman (see sidebar 3.2) gives us a glimpse of how mundane work is given meaning by its place in the very special culture that is the congregation.

Sidebar 3.2
THE EVERYDAY WORK OF THE CONGREGATION

One older woman, farm-born and -raised, spoke fervently about the rewards of her thirty years "on the altar." She had always found great satisfaction in making things "pretty" and "shiny." "Sometimes, when I'm alone in the church, and just polishing the brass till it glows, and I'm praying . . ." Her voice broke and her eyes filled with tears. She added, almost in surprise, "That's when I know He's there." After a silence, I said, "It's lovely to hear you say that." She spoke thoughtfully, "Never said it before. No one ever asked me before." When asked what it is about "altar work" that transforms it into a kind of worship for her, she responded, with deep emotion: "I was doing it for Him, and for our priest, and for our people . . . I just always felt that it was *one* thing I could do for my religion, that I loved."

From Joanna Gillespie, "Gender and Generation," in *Episcopal Women* (New York: Oxford University Press, 1992), 202-3.

When observing all of these routine activities of the congregation, you can use the same sorts of questions you used when watching more formal rituals. You can look for who is participating and how they use their space, what props they need, how they are dressed, and the like. You can note the congregation's use of time—when things are scheduled and what the rhythm of events is. And you can note the way tasks are divided and the way different types of people (by gender or age or longevity, for instance) participate. After observing for a while, you may also be able to discern the unspoken assumptions and see the activity that goes on behind the scenes to make any given event possible.

It is through all these patterns of activity that the congregation communicates to itself and others what it is about. Symbols of identity and transcendence are most visible in a congregation's most ritualized events, but all sorts of things can be rituals, and all sorts of objects and gestures can carry meaning beyond themselves.[21] Every time members greet each other or call a meeting to order, they signal their participation in the culture that makes those words and deeds sensible. Whenever they arrive with Bible in hand or sneak out for a cigarette between Sunday school and worship, they signal that they know and accept the norms that govern this community's life together. And whenever they genuflect and cross themselves, join hands in a prayer circle, or bow to the ground in prayer, they indicate that they are connected both to this particular group and its traditions and to a sacred reality beyond them all. Observing what people do together is also a way of understanding who they are and what they think is important.

Introducing Newcomers to the Culture

The culture of a congregation emerges in what it does together, but the people who constitute any congregation are constantly changing. Congregational cultures are constantly being remade and passed along to newcomers, whether intentionally or unintentionally. No congregation can count on its current members to last forever, nor can it count on a guaranteed pool of potential members from its community or even from its own progeny. Congregational membership in the voluntary system of the United States is neither prescribed by law nor inherited in unbroken line from ancestors. The last several decades have, in fact, seen a vast increase in the degree to which religious affiliation (including the decision not to affiliate) has become a matter of individual choice, a matter indeed of several choices across a lifetime, as people move about and switch from one religious group to another.[22] All congregations, then, are faced with the ongoing task of integrating newcomers into the existing culture of the place.

Sometimes those newcomers are newborns, and the congregation's efforts at teaching their young are good indicators of how they think about themselves. Children's Sunday school classes often help us see what members are willing to say about the nature of God, about what is expected of members, and about what constitutes a virtuous life. Even more explicitly, confirmation and bat and bar mitzvah classes teach the essential practices and doctrines of the congregation and of the faith. Beyond these obvious opportunities for observing explicit cultural transmissions, you can watch for where children are included and excluded, when they are reprimanded or rewarded. What adults tell their children is often a reminder to themselves about what is supposed to be important.

Given current levels of geographical and religious mobility, few children born into a congregation today can be expected to grow up, marry, and raise their own children there in the years ahead. But raising children is still a key ingredient in the culture of most congregations. Many people join a church or synagogue "for the children." Congregations that orient themselves to this impulse are often identified by their emphasis on children's activities and on their description of themselves as "family" places. The degree to which this is the case (and the degree to which that fits the demographic realities of the community) will be an important piece of understanding a congregation's culture.

Not all newcomers are newborns, of course. But recruiting members from beyond the households of existing members is not something many congregations do with any real intentionality. Observing this aspect of a congregation's culture may require looking for assumptions, rather than for established programs. Most congregations rely on their recognized position in the community to bring them a steady supply of new members. Understanding the culture of a congregation will require assessing the way people beyond its membership routinely come in contact with it. That is, do people in the community have a clear perception of what sort of congregation this is and who is most likely to belong here? Where is the congregation located—both physically and socially—in the community? Who routinely encounters the congregation and its members in their usual round of activities and relationships? It is those relationships, activities, networks, and presence that create the social pool out of which the congregation will naturally draw its new members.

More than most other religious groups, evangelical Christians are likely to make recruitment of new members and converts central to the congregation's culture. Members talk to their neighbors, coworkers, and friends about making a religious commitment and joining the church. The degree to which such explicit recruitment activities are encouraged is another important aspect of the congregation's culture. A more reserved congregation might find any sort of advertisement offensive, while still others might encourage door-to-door witnessing. It is important to pay attention both to what people say about proper methods and targets of recruitment and to *what they do* to bring people in.

In addition to both passive and personal contacts, congregations can also engage in various media efforts at communicating with the community. Many congregations put advertisements on a local newspaper's church page or in the telephone yellow pages. They may try to convey in a few words or images the theological and programmatic emphases that make them distinctive. They explicitly try to describe themselves in ways that can provide clues to their culture. These are among the artifacts you should collect.

Congregations also communicate with the community through their various efforts at ministry or service. Some congregations may offer food and shelter, while others offer space for public recitals. Some may be the place the town or neighborhood comes together in times of crisis, while others offer individualized psychological counseling or family crisis assistance. Understanding the congregation's culture involves looking at who is served, by whom, and with what intended effect.

Whenever and wherever a congregation communicates about itself with those beyond its domain, the congregational culture is being heralded—and remade. When those outsiders choose to become insiders, they have to be turned into practicing members of the culture, and observing the socialization process is another excellent window on a congregation's life. Congregations with especially distinctive cultures may have to work hard at training their new recruits, while more ordinary congregations may absorb members with ease. Catholic parishes routinely require an extended period of study and reflection in "Rite of Christian Initiation for Adults" (RCIA) classes. Evangelical churches may require a period of new member classes but also expect that new converts will be shepherded by experienced members in their first months and years of participation. Orthodox Jewish congregations have to teach their recruits Hebrew, in addition to the intricacies of dietary and other distinctive practices.[23] Along the way, congregations also pass along their subtle expectations about decorum, how much enthusiasm is permitted, what the most important obligations of membership are, and the like.[24]

Not to be missed, finally, are the ways new members change the culture of the congregation. They bring in new expectations, new experiences, and new connections to other parts of the community. A picture of recent recruits and their connections in the congrega-

Sidebar 3.3
SPACE, PROPS, AND IDENTITY

Spring Hill Church rapidly developed a reputation in its early years as the performing arts center of its growing suburban community. They hosted concerts and recitals and the annual community arts festival. As they planned for new buildings, they decided to build a performing arts center first, followed by a sanctuary. Once it was built, the old sanctuary was torn down, and worship services moved into the new center. To accommodate the multiple uses of the building, the pulpit, lectern, and altar table were constructed on rollers, and they moved about very easily (sometimes too easily!).

In the years that followed, however, the community continued to grow, and the musical groups found other spaces for rehearsal and performance. At the same time, the church suffered a financial scandal over money missing from the organ fund. And finally, a succession of sexual scandals destroyed the last shreds of trust members had in their leaders. In a few short years they had lost their sense of identity. They were no longer the respected center of the community's arts activities, and they did not have leaders they and others could trust.

Unsure of what story to tell about themselves, their worship also took on a flat, detached quality. Interviewed about worship at Spring Hill, members seemed uninvolved, almost unable to remember what had happened last Sunday. They did not notice changes and could not think of what they especially liked or disliked. The seminarian who interviewed them wondered what this apparent lack of passion could mean. She finally concluded, "They are no longer sure how they fit in the world as a congregation, therefore they are detached from their ritual. All the meanings previously attached to their ritual have been called into question by the loss of their civic identity, the problems that undercut or destroyed trust in their leaders, and the discontinuity of four pastors in five years."

Like the pulpit and altar table that are dislodged at the slightest sudden gesture, worship at Spring Hill seems transient and untrustworthy. Things will not be nailed down again until the painful stories are told, the old identity mourned, and a new one consciously constructed. Only then will new stories *and* new rituals be possible. At that point, the rollers may finally come off the furniture.

This case is drawn from the work of a student at Candler School of Theology who asked to remain anonymous. The name of the church has been changed, as well.

tion is often a very good indicator of the future direction of the congregation's culture.

Artifacts: The Things Congregations Make

Congregations are both producers and consumers of vast arrays of material objects. The congregation's culture is not just the activities in which it engages, but also the props for and residues of those activities. Just as rituals and activities structure the congregation's time together, so its buildings and furnishings, altars and holy books, even cribs and dishes, structure its space. Archaeologists can often reconstruct amazing details of everyday life from the shards of pottery and bone they dig up. When we look at a living congregation, we do not have to use our imaginations quite so much, but the physical environment can still tell us a great deal about those who created it.

The building itself is perhaps the most obvious of the congregation's artifacts, speaking silently about the congregation's patterns of activity and its values. Its surrounding landscaping and parking, along with the visible religious symbols it displays, establish the place of the congregation in the community and reflect its assumptions about God, nature, humanity, itself, and others. Buildings, furniture, and grounds are the visible, sensual reminders that offer clues to observers about the group that uses them.[25] Is there a high fence or a wide driveway around this property? Is the children's wing deserted and musty, or is there a high-tech nursery? Taking a walk around the neighborhood, perhaps with someone who lives or works there but is not a member, can often help you to see the congregation's property with new eyes.

The layout and furnishings of the building help to shape the patterns of interaction contained in it. The size and condition of gathering spaces and their accessibility to people with various handicapping conditions determine what sorts of social interaction is possible, among what sorts of people. A trip through the building in a wheelchair can be a very revealing experience. You might also want to do an inventory of gathering spaces, including their size, location, condition, and use. A look at the worship space is also helpful. A visually rich environment may encourage silent individual meditation, while a visually neutral one may encourage human interaction. Thinking about how the space encourages different sorts of interactions with God and others will be a step toward understanding the culture that occupies that space.

Buildings convey meanings, but like all meanings, these are dependent on the audience receiving them. For that reason, a walking tour with a small group of informants can be a very useful activity. Ask them to tell you stories about events they associate with various areas of the group's building and grounds. Ask them to stop occasionally to talk about what makes a given spot special, even how it feels to be in that place and who it reminds them of. Going to the places they find most holy or the places associated with their fondest memories can be extremely revealing. The members of Spring Hill Church (see sidebar 3.3) might have had interesting stories to tell about why their building was built as it was and why the altar table is on wheels. Their situation reminds us that buildings are sometimes more appropriate to a congregation that once occupied them than to the needs of the current group that gathers there. As you tour buildings, watch for the spaces that are unused, as well as those that are busy.

Some of the congregation's space, of course, is marked off as sacred.[26] There are the obvious symbols contained in altars and banners, prayer rugs and ark, crosses and stained-glass windows, pulpits and organs. Those items tell stories about the faith tradition of the congregation. They honor the heroes and saints, and they mark off the spaces that are especially holy. The symbols that highlight these spaces usually have official theological meanings, but they also have meanings embellished by the given local congregation that has constructed them. We already noted that worship services are especially good times for observing the congregation's use of its space and its deployment of sacred artifacts. But the congregation's culture usually involves more than what is brought out on such special occasions. All the congregation's activities require physical space and props, all of which tell a story. Try taking one room in your congregation's building—the nursery or kitchen, for example—and do an "excavation." See what the objects in that room can tell you.

You also may want to draw a map of important spaces, especially after you have a good sense of how they are used and by whom. When Melvin Williams was studying the culture of the church he calls Zion, he discovered that space and status were very closely related to each other. The map he drew of the sanctuary (see figure 3.1) was also a map of the relationships of the members to the congregation and to each other. One way you might find out about the congregation's space and important objects is to ask one of your informants or a focus group to take you on a walking tour of the property, pointing out the important memorials, the sacred spaces and decorations, the significance of the arrangement of the pews or the placement of the lectern, and the like.

Like all cultures, congregations invent material objects that aid them in performing their routine tasks and express the values they hold dearest. Whether it is the set of accounting books and office equipment, the dozens of baby cribs in the nursery, or the extensive athletic equipment in the gym, physical objects tell us a good deal about the culture that uses them. The arrangement of buildings, furniture, landscaping, and ritual objects is critical to understanding the group's identity and its relationship to its community.

Accounts: The Stories Congregations Tell

Cultures are patterns of both activity and objects, but they are also patterns of language

Figure 3.1 SEATING CHART OF ZION'S AUDITORIUM

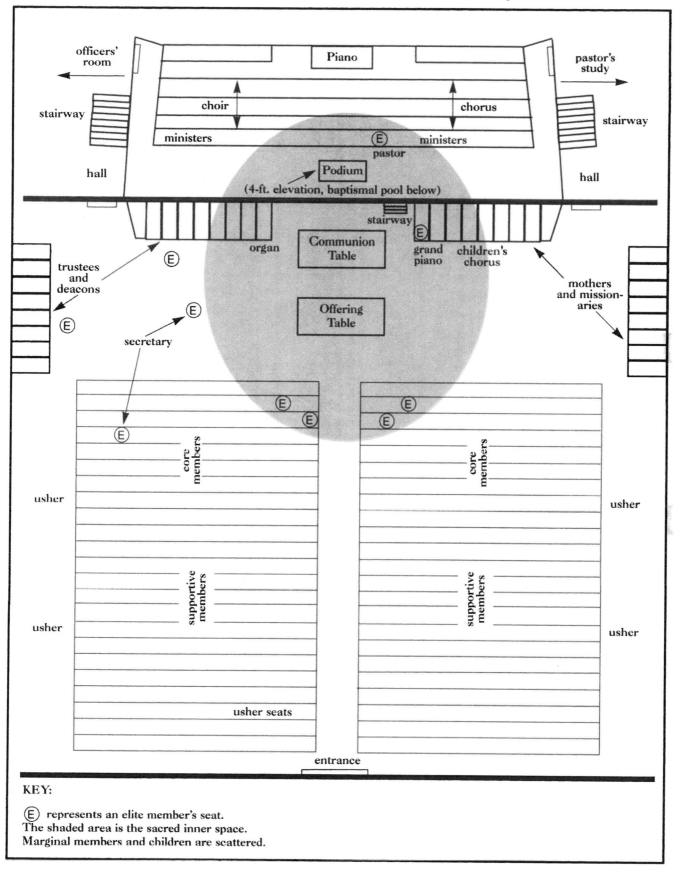

and story. Language is a basic social process, a way we relate to each other and a way to agree on what our world is and means. Whenever we share experiences, we talk about them, and in the talking we come to understand more about what the experience meant in the first place. Congregations, too, are full of talk—sometimes mundane and sometimes holy. Listening for how people talk to each other is critical to understanding their culture.[27]

Language

Congregations develop distinctive words and phrases for their surroundings and their activities. They naturally develop shorthand ways of alluding to the ideas, people, and events they care about. One learns that it is the "narthex" and not the "vestibule"; a "carry-in," not a "potluck." A new member may even learn to speak (and think) of himself or herself differently—as a communicant, a *ba'alat teshuvah*, or a believer, for instance.

When learning about your congregation's culture, you might start by creating a lexicon of the names for their sacred objects, actions, times, and spaces. Are there words for different parts of the building and words for various aspects of the worship service? Are there names for the officials of the congregation, both clergy and lay? And are there designations for the seasons of the year, the clothing worship leaders wear, the people who assist in worship, and the ceremonies used when people are inducted into full membership? Some churches, for instance, have Communion, while others celebrate the Eucharist, and still others commemorate the Lord's Supper. Some have homilies, and others have sermons. Some know exactly what a lectionary is, and others would be bewildered. Each religious tradition's language gives voice to the particular ways that tradition seeks to connect people with God. Once you have constructed your lexicon, note the degree to which this lexicon sets the congregation apart from the larger culture in which it is situated and the degree to which everyone in the congregation shares in its use. Do only the specialists know the correct terms to use, or does everyone share a common jargon?

History

In addition to the words that name and order the congregation's time and space, there are also stories that transmit the lore of the group.[28] These tales may be about their founding, but they are also likely to be about times of great success or of crises that have been overcome. They are stories passed on from old members to new as a way of telling what this congregation is all about. Denham Grierson has written, "The act of remembering is essential for the creation of identity and corporate integrity in any community. A community is by definition a sharing together of significant happenings."[29]

Not everything, of course, is of equal significance. Thousands of events happen to us each week; relatively few are worth remembering for their capacity to disclose who we are. A congregation's history is actually quite pliable. There are always stories to be told. Which stories get told at which time depends in large part on both the needs of the hour and the memories of those present. Knowing those stories can often be helpful when planning for the future. When people can make connections between proposed changes and some episode in their past, the new activities are often more comprehensible. Similarly, telling the congregation's stories may allow themes, images, and symbols to emerge that can be energizing for the future.[30]

Many attempts to articulate a congregation's history, unfortunately, get trapped in the details and miss the grand stories of its heroes, heroines, turning points, and significant symbols. Annual reports may contain the nuts and bolts of a congregation's life but little of what makes it distinct from any other group with 343 members and $600,000 worth of property. Parish profiles prepared to guide the selection of a new pastor may not get past the congregation's average income and predominant view of the Bible to tell how this group came to think that way. Locally written histories often contain valuable information about leadership, property, and program but little about the stories that give those objects their meaning.[31]

One way to discover those stories is to do *oral history interviews.* Long-term members of the congregation can be given an opportunity to reminisce about the history of the group. The person who conducts the interview may begin with some general orienting questions and then focus on specific themes or tales. The general questions may be quite simple.

- *Tell me what this congregation was like back when you first started to attend here.*

- *How have things changed around here since then?*

- *What do you think a new member ought to know about the history of this congregation?*

The specific themes you explore might include descriptions of worship services or what the religious education program was like or what sorts of buildings they had and how money was raised. In addition to listening for the general contours of the congregation's history, keep the interview focused in ways that serve your attempts to understand this particular culture. Along the way, keep the people oriented by asking them to relate their stories to other events you know about.

- *Was that before or after the big fire?*

- *Was that while Father Kowalski was here?*

Encourage them to tell stories, not just to relate facts. You are interested in the facts, but it is the stories that will tell you about this congregation's sense of identity.

Another useful exercise when uncovering a congregation's history is to *construct a time line.* Here the story telling is collective, rather than individual. The specifics of this exercise are described in more detail in the chapter on methods, but recall that you will be visually marking off significant events in the congregation's history and in the surrounding community and world. While a time line used to understand a changing context might focus especially on events outside the congregation, a time line exploring history

will understandably focus inward. You might start by placing key information about clergy and buildings along the top. Then prompt the participants with questions about the people who were part of the congregation, the activities and programs that they remember and the crises that affected them. As events are recalled, encourage the participants to elaborate, tell stories, and make connections. The visual image you construct, as well as the stories told along the way, may help the congregation see its history in a new way. Leave the paper up as long as feasible, and encourage further additions, even after the initial session. Make your own notes, transcribing the time line and recording the stories. At some point, you may want to distribute a version of the time line to the whole congregation.

Myths

In the telling of congregational stories, certain tales rise above the others to take on the special quality of myths. Myths are stories that ground our history in something bigger. They speak of divine actions in ways that define who we are. When members tell about the congregation's founding or its survival of a crisis in terms of God's unfolding will, they are giving the story mythic quality. It is not less true for being a myth, but more so.

The stories told as myths may come from a denomination, from the larger faith tradition, or from the Scriptures. Rabbis are never without a story to illustrate one of life's truths. Methodists hear stories about the Wesleys, Baptists about Luther Rice and Lottie Moon, and members of AME churches about Richard Allen and Jarena Lee. Christians in all sorts of traditions share stories about the saints and mystics and teachers of the early church, as well as the foundational stories of Jesus' life. And Jews, Christians, and Muslims alike hear the great sagas of kings and prophets from ancient times. Pay special attention to which stories from sacred texts are particular favorites, retold in sermons or children's plays or sung in hymns. Those stories are likely to tell you something about whom people identify with and how they understand their own lives. Each group is likely to find in the stories elements that make sense of their own situation, and as situations change, new meanings are likely to arise. As congregations change, there will be new stories to tell and new people who need to hear old tales. But people are also likely to find themselves listening to old stories with new ears.[32] Stories have a great deal to do with who we think we are and who we can imagine becoming. Stories often have multiple plots, with multiple trajectories, and they can either constrain or enliven a group's future. Watch for how new people suggest different ways of hearing old stories.

Worldviews

The mythic story line adopted by a congregation has within it a basic view of the world that may be—according to James Hopewell's appropriation of Northrop Frye's literary theory—comic, romantic, tragic, or ironic (see sidebar 3.4). Individuals and congregations have characteristic ways of looking at the world and characteristic explanations for why things happen as they do. Hopewell's idea was that all of us have in our minds ways of answering some of life's most important questions. While not everyone will be easily categorized, there are often dominant worldviews in a congregation that follow one of these themes more than another.

These worldviews may be discovered in interviews by asking people how they make sense of a death or illness, what they think God is up to in the world, or how they see their own faith changing over the years. Looking for themes in the interviews may give the observer clues about the typical ways people in this congregation understand the grand unfolding of life's story. One might also use a survey that includes the questions designed by Hopewell.[33] In either case, a visual accounting of your findings (see figure 3.2) may help you to see how the people in this congregational culture shape their view of the world. By literally mapping where a representative selection of members falls on these worldview dimensions, you may learn a great deal

about the assumptions and storylines that shape your congregation's culture.

Figure 3.2 DISTRIBUTION OF A CONGREGATION'S WORLDVIEWS

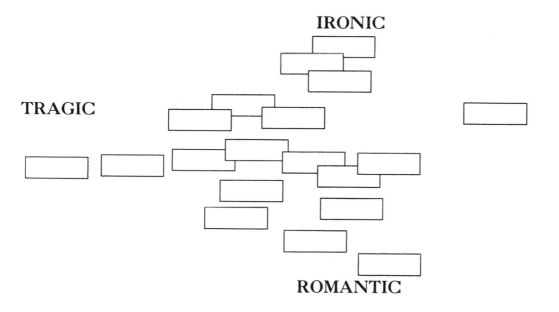

Symbols, Images, and Metaphors

Sometimes the congregation's identity is captured not so much in a story as in an image or metaphor. When members say, "We are an ark," they may be signaling the degree to which they feel isolated in a hostile environment, and that image will affect their planning and behavior. If they say, "We are the center of this community," it may signal something very different, as will an image of rescuing people with a life raft. Those images can be multivalent, interpreted differently by different people at different times in a congregation's history. But images and metaphors are to be taken seriously as shapers of a congregation's culture. Note the recurrent images Dudley and Johnson discerned in their study of congregations seeking to minister to their communities (see sidebar 3.5). Do any of these sound familiar?

While images and metaphors are often implicit, other gestures and objects are more explicitly used by the congregation to signal something beyond themselves, something that the congregation considers important. Anything carrying that sort of meaning is a significant symbol. Every word or gesture, of course, represents something more than mere sounds and movements and is therefore a symbol

defined by the culture in which it is located. Everything from the words we use to the building directory to gestures of greeting are signs that stand for social realities beyond themselves. We are interested here, however, in more than the everyday symbols of the culture. Most helpful to the interpreter of a congregational culture are the more potent reminders of the values this group holds dearest, the symbols that evoke a more visceral response which is less easily pinned down. The symbols we are looking for are the ones with high levels of emotion and low levels of specificity about their explicit meaning. Symbols, in Victor Turner's terms, are multivocal: they evoke a mysterious complexity of meaning and do so in such a way that one's identity is itself caught up in them.[34]

Often these symbols are directly related to the congregation's theological tradition: the cross, the open Bible, a baptismal font, the Torah scroll, the menorah, and the like. Asking people to draw a mental (or actual) sketch of the congregation's worship space may elicit mention of items they see as significant. Talking to various members about what key symbolic items mean to them can help to outline the contours of the operative theological traditions in the congregation. What does the Communion table remind them of? What do they feel and think when they

---

Sidebar 3.5
CONGREGATIONAL
SELF-IMAGES

The *Pillar church* is anchored in its geographic community, for which it feels uniquely responsible. The architecture often reflects this self-image: the strong pillars that lift the roof physically reflect a membership that lifts the community spiritually. Like the building, the members are pillars of the community, good citizens individually and corporately.

The *Pilgrim church* dwells with its own people wherever they are, sustaining them as a community in their pilgrimage. Their culture and their Christian faith are woven into a single fabric of church life. Some Pilgrim congregations have moved with their people from one dwelling place to another. With a strong pilgrim theology some churches embrace waves of immigration or racial change.

The *Survivor church* loves to tell stories of the storms it has weathered. Often the congregation attracts and sustains people who take pride in their survival time and again. Survivor churches live on the edge, always on the verge of being overwhelmed by emergencies. They do not expect to conquer their problems, but they will not give in.

The *Prophet church* attracts members who feel called to challenge the evils of the world from communities to corporations, from individuals to national governments. Independent, often entrepreneurial in style, Prophet churches or prophetic segments in a larger church draw strong support from members who share their commitments. Prophet churches share with Survivors a sense of crisis that demands high levels of commitment.

The *Servant Church* attracts people who like to help others in modest ways of quiet faithfulness. They visit the sick, take meals to the bereaved, and send cards to the shut-ins. Beginning with their own members, they naturally extend their service to provide food, clothing, and other basic needs to their neighbors.

In summary, then, the images reflect the ways congregations respond to human need: The *Pillar* church has a sense of civic responsibility that embraces the community. The *Pilgrim* church cares for the cultural group as extended family. The *Survivor* church reacts to crises in an overwhelming world. The *Prophet* church is proactive to translate crises into causes. The *Servant* church reaches out to support individuals who need help.

From Carl S. Dudley and Sally A. Johnson, *Energizing the Congregation: Images that Shape Your Church's Ministry* (Louisville: Westminster/John Knox, 1993), 4-7.

---

see the opening of the Torah scroll? How do they feel when someone is baptized?

Other symbols may have no explicit *theological* connections. Yet a particular arrangement of furniture, the way the annual report is printed and bound, projecting the words of praise choruses with an overhead projector, who moves through a reception line first, or even what color the restrooms are painted—all may have meanings that tell us a great deal about the culture we are observing. The importance of these more mundane symbols is often discovered when inadvertent changes are made. A new printer is selected, new paint is applied, or furniture rearranged. Suddenly people realize something is awry. The old arrangements were not just functional but symbolic of the congregation's sense of identity. Observing such disjunctures and asking people to reflect on them can often be a helpful window on the congregation's culture.

Theologies

As we already noted in the chapter on theology, congregations have both official and unofficial ideas about what God is like, how human beings are related to God, what constitutes sin and salvation, and other questions about the nature of the world and where it is headed. Understanding the congregation's culture requires attention to this dimension, as well. The official ideas are usually fairly easy to find. A congregation may recite a creed or a set of prayers. Preachers may expound on proper doctrine. Teachers may explain the ways of the faith to children, especially in confirmation or bar and bat mitzvah classes. There may be pamphlets or banners with key covenants on them, and new members may be given guidebooks to the faith. Books of procedure may also take their place alongside sacred scripture as guides for congregational life. In all sorts of ways, congregations spend

Sidebar 3.6
MISSION ORIENTATION
QUESTIONS

For each of the following statements, indicate whether it is Basic, Quite Important, Somewhat Important, Not Really Important, or Contrary to your congregation's sense of mission.

1. Providing adult education that brings laity face to face with urban problems, racial discrimination, world poverty and hunger, and other social issues.

2. Providing for members an earthly refuge from the trials and tribulations of daily life.

3. Cooperating with other denominations and faith groups to achieve community improvements.

4. Helping people accept that their condition and status in life is determined and controlled by God, and that therefore one has only to accept it and live the best life possible.

5. Promoting social change through *the use of organized, collective* influence or force.

6. Helping people resist the temptation to experiment with the new "pleasures" and "life-styles" so prominent in our secular society and media.

7. Providing aid and services to those in need within the local community.

8. Maintaining an active, organized evangelism program; inviting the unchurched to participate in the life of the congregation.

9. Actively reaching out to members of other religious groups with an invitation to participate in the life of the congregation.

10. Encouraging the pastor to speak out in public and from the pulpit on controversial social, political, and economic matters.

11. Preparing church members for a world to come in which the cares of this world are absent.

12. Encouraging members to make specific declarations of their personal faith to friends, neighbors, and strangers.

13. Providing financial support to political or social action groups and organizations.

14. Maintaining a proper distance between the congregation and governmental affairs.

15. Helping people to understand that they are "agents" of God's hope, responsible for actualizing the good and humane as they share in the development of history and society.

16. Fostering a sense of patriotism among the congregation's members.

17. Encouraging members to reach their own decisions on issues of faith and morals.

18. Involving the congregation corporately in social and political activities.

19. Organizing social action groups within the congregation to directly accomplish some social or political end.

20. Protecting members from the false teachings of other churches and religious groups.

21. Listening to what the "world" is saying in order to understand what the congregation's ministry should be about.

22. Encouraging and inspiring members, as individuals, to become involved in social and political issues.

23. Encouraging members to adhere faithfully to civil laws as they are mandated by governmental authorities.

From David A. Roozen, William McKinney, and Jackson W. Carroll, *Varieties of Religious Presence* (New York: Pilgrim Press, 1984), 84-86.

time highlighting their ideas about God. The observer interested in the explicit theological teachings of a congregation will likely have little trouble finding occasions for study. If you do, that may tell you a great deal about the culture of the congregation. The degree to which theology is an explicit topic of conversation does vary, and that is part of how a group identifies itself.

Theology is not only contained in creed and scripture, however. It is also heard, as we have already noted, in stories. Both the stories of the individual congregation and the stories members tell and retell from their larger tradition say a great deal about which aspects of God's character they find most compelling, how they think humanity should be related to God, and what they care most deeply about. Are they fond of the stories of conquest or the stories of sin and forgiveness? Do they focus on the martyrs or on the wisdom characters? Do they tell the miracle stories over and over? Listening for favorite characters and stories can help the observer discover what people really believe.

In addition, concentrate your observation on looking for the ways people's routine actions reveal what they believe about the nature of human life, who God is, and what God expects of them. How do they treat each other? How do they treat outsiders? What objects and events get special care? When do they punish their children, and when do they reward them?

Closely related to its theology is the congregation's "mission orientation," its sense of how God works in the world and what God wants people to do. When Roozen, McKinney, and Carroll studied congregations in Hartford, Connecticut, they discovered there were four typical ways of relating the congregation to its context, ways in which the congregation was present in the community.[35] Some congregations see their presence largely in terms of providing sacred space that is a safe haven from this world (the *sanctuary* orientation). Others see themselves as actively involved in seeking individuals who need salvation and thereby changing the world one person at a time (the *evangelistic* orientation). Still others see themselves as the promoters and preservers of what is good in this world (the *civic* orientation), while the last group seeks to change the structures of the world that cause suffering and injustice (the *activist* orientation). These orientations flow from a congregation's understanding of God's actions and their own, of where that action is located (in this world or another), and of whether or not congregations are primary actors in the drama. Sidebar 3.6 contains a set of survey questions that can be used in identifying a congregation's dominant understanding of its mission.

It is important to remember that theological exposition does not happen only in the official venues and is not done only by official clergy. When teachers explain the ways of God to four-year-olds and when adults reprimand teens for their lack of seriousness, theological exposition is taking place. Similarly, when one member attempts to comfort another or explain a ritual to a newcomer, or when an adult discussion group tackles a difficult scripture, more theological work is being done.

In addition, much of the congregation's theology is implicit in what it values and how it does its work. Who is welcome and what behavior is condemned says much about how God's family is defined and what constitutes a virtuous life. The stories and metaphors you have been gathering also contain themes of God's presence and action in the world. Even the minutes of a board meeting may contain hints of this congregation's ideas about what a church or synagogue is really supposed to be about. Most assuredly, their budget fights reflect underlying theological assumptions. Listening for the theological dimension of the congregation's culture means listening for what is valued most highly, what people really care about. The chapter on theology offers additional guidelines for how observers can discern the operative theologies in a congregation.

Finally, a word about surveys. *Many* questionnaire items have been developed for discovering various aspects of people's beliefs about God. Some representative questions are contained in the chapter on methods and in appendix A. Seeing how your congregation responds to such a set of questions can often be very revealing. One should always, however, take actual observations more seriously than, or at least alongside, responses to a survey. How people actually use and talk about the Bible is far more important than which preset response they choose on a questionnaire. In addition, the questions asked on the survey may not really reflect either the particular questions most pertinent to this congregation's operative theology or the way they would put things. The range of responses may not be their range at all. Finding out that 60 percent of respondents chose a given answer to a question about faith may only tell you that that answer was the least unpalatable of the alternatives. If you use a survey to find out about your congregation's theologies, choose the questions with care. Avoid items that contain language or presuppositions that seem foreign to you. Keep the language as close to what is familiar as possible. And then use the results more as a conversation starter than as a final verdict on what the congregation believes.

Understanding the culture of a congregation means taking seriously the language it uses, the history it has available, the myths and stories and worldviews that ground it, and the theologies that occupy both center and backstage. All the things they say about themselves stand alongside what they do and what they make as clues to the patterns of relationship and meaning that characterize this particular people in this particular place.

Interpreting the Congregational Culture

Having observed and interviewed the congregation to gather information about what the congregation does, what it makes, and how it speaks of itself, the time will eventually come when interpretation is in order, when you will want to be able to say something about what it all means. If you have been taking good notes and reviewing those notes along the way, you probably have a good idea already about what the dominant themes are. If you have been working with a group of advisers and cogatherers of data, the process of interpretation should include them, as well.

One way to begin the task of summarizing the information you have gathered is to make a list of statements for yourselves that begins with, "People in this congregation tend to" You might organize those statements around the various types of things you have observed: "Worship services tend to ..." "The building tends to ..." "Newcomers tend to ..." "Beliefs about God tend to ..."

Another way to approach this task is to think about what one might write in a handbook for newcomers to a congregation. What cultural knowledge does one need to survive here, assuming the newcomer knows *nothing* before coming here? These statements are not where you want to end your interpretation, but they can be a good beginning place, a way to begin to summarize the mounds of information you have collected.

As you begin this process, remember your focus. Using that focus, you might organize the information you have gathered around the various elements of culture we have identified.

- Which rituals are most predictable and central to the congregation's culture?

- Which other activities are most instrumental in shaping the people who participate and in influencing what this group thinks of itself?

- What symbols best describe who they are? What objects, people, and events carry meanings linking them to the ideals of this group?

- Which routine practices and styles of relationship best capture what this congregation values most?

- What stories are the essential myths of this people?

- What beliefs and ideas best describe what they think a practicing member ought to be like?

How you ask these questions will be shaped by the curiosity or dilemma that sent you on this search in the first place. What does the ritual life of this congregation tell us about that issue? What do its key symbols say? And so forth. But be open to surprises. With all the information you have gathered, you may learn valuable things about this congregation that are quite peripheral to the actual focus of your study!

As you try to make sense of what you know, be aware that studying a congregation's culture nearly always generates more information than you really need. While some of that information may turn out to yield surprising insights, you need to remind yourself again of the questions with which you began, reformulating those questions in light of what you now know. Having gathered fascinating vignettes of congregational life, it is often hard to set them aside, but for the sake of coherence (and time) some triage is always necessary. Do not throw extraneous material away! Simply file it for later review and move on with the task at hand.

In addition, you will have learned along the way that not every activity or every behavior you observed is meaningful. Sometimes what you saw was a meaningful wink, but sometimes it was just an idiosyncratic twitch. While you may have uncovered many interesting details about the congregation's story and its patterns of life, not all of them tell you about the particular patterns of culture that stand at the center of the congregation's life or that bear on the issue in which you are interested. An important interpretive task is that of winnowing down all the things you now know to the key information that needs to be communicated to others.

Go back through all the information you have collected, then, looking for what is most significant, which ideas and activities and artifacts seem to be essential to this congregation's identity and to answering your specific questions. One way important discoveries are often made is by asking yourself about the surprises and unexpected happenings you have encountered. Where did you find things that were not as you thought they would be? What has happened that surprised everyone and made the whole congregation see itself more clearly?

You will also have discovered that there are many stories and many meanings within any given group of people. You may despair of ever finding the threads that weave through the tapestry of the whole. Those threads, in fact, may be very thin. A description of any congregation's culture will include the ways in which that culture is subdivided, the ways varying groups within the congregation tell different stories and practice the ways of the faith differently.

But in the midst of all the detail and diversity, you should have found some recurring patterns and themes. Perhaps it is an insistence on decorum and proper observance of the commands of the faith. Perhaps it is support for families. Per-

haps it is the presence of the Spirit. Perhaps it is a sense of survival in an alien land. Perhaps it is a story of congregational rebirth. Or perhaps it is an ever-present struggle to be inclusive of diversity. You may also discover that the patterns in your congregation, its typical ways of doing things, are similar to the patterns described by Hopewell's worldview types, the "mission orientation" types, Dudley's and Johnson's "congregational self-images," or some other set of congregational descriptions you have discovered. Although each congregation is certainly unique, discernible similarities across congregations often help observers make sense of their own situation. A careful look at what others have written about congregations can often help you see your own congregation's culture more clearly.

Once you have decided what the key lines of your findings will be, you will need to communicate what you know back to the congregation. A report from observers to congregations can take a number of forms. If it is written, it may take the form of a story (or collection of stories). It might also be an outline of answers to questions or simply a descriptive essay. Or it might take oral, visual, or even dramatic form, depending on the talents of those doing the reporting. But it is important to bring the congregation itself into this process. As you offer back what you have observed about what the congregation most values and how it identifies itself, the members need opportunities to respond. Your systematic observation of the congregation's culture should exist in dialogue with the ongoing life of this particular gathering of people. They can offer further nuances and corrections, but they can also receive a new understanding of their own assumptions and uniqueness, having seen themselves through the eyes of a cultural observer.

NOTES

1. James F. Hopewell, *Congregation: Stories and Structures* (Philadelphia: Fortress Press, 1987), 5. Another helpful treatment of the congregation as a culture is Denham Grierson's *Transforming a People of God* (Melbourne: The Joint Board of Christian Education of Australia and New Zealand, 1984). He suggests that pastors pay attention to, among other things, the congregation's remembered history, hero stories, artifacts of significance, symbols, rituals and gestures, myths of destiny, and images of hope.

2. The *Handbook for Congregational Studies* spoke of history, heritage, worldview, symbols, ritual, demography, and character as the elements of a congregation's identity (p. 23).

3. E. Brooks Holifield, "Toward a History of American Congregations," in *American Congregations: New Perspectives in the Study of Congregations*, ed. James P. Wind and James W. Lewis (Chicago: University of Chicago Press, 1994), 23-53.

4. R. Stephen Warner, "The Place of the Congregation in the Contemporary American Religious Configuration," *American Congregations*, 54-99.

5. A vivid example of the way images from rural life can pervade even an urban congregation is found in Melvin Williams *Community in a Black Pentecostal Church* (Prospect Heights, Ill.: Waveland Press, 1984).

6. This is the distinction sociologists of religion label "sectarian." See Rodney Stark and William Sims Bainbridge, *The Future of Religion* (Berkeley: University of California Press, 1985), chapter 2, for a summary of the social characteristics that define "sects."

7. Daniel V. A. Olsen, "Fellowship Ties and the Transmission of Religious Identity," in *Beyond Establishment: Protestant Identity in a Post-Protestant Age*, ed. Jackson W. Carroll and Wade Clark Roof (Louisville: Westminster/John Knox, 1993), 32-53.

8. This framework for analyzing congregational culture was developed for the study of the congregations described in Nancy Tatom Ammerman, *Congregation and Community* (New Brunswick, N.J.: Rutgers University Press, 1997). The section below draws heavily on ideas elaborated in chapter 1 of that book.

9. Clifford Geertz, *The Interpretation of Cultures* (New York: Basic Books, 1973).

10. Keith Roberts has written about the different ways in which congregations acknowledge and highlight the sensual aspects of their rituals in "Ritual and the Transmission of a Cultural Tradition: An Ethnographic Perspective," in *Beyond Establishment*, 74-98.

11. The importance of bodily ritual and singing in creating communities across cultural boundaries is discussed in R. Stephen Warner, "Religion, Boundaries, and Bridges," *Sociology of Religion* 58, no. 3 (Fall, 1997): 217-238.

12. Thomas Day, *Why Catholics Can't Sing: The Culture of Catholicism and the Triumph of Bad Taste* (New York: Crossroad, 1991), 163.

13. Linda J. Clark, "Hymn-Singing: The Congregation Making Faith," in *Carriers of Faith*, ed. Carl S. Dudley, Jackson W. Carroll, and James P. Wind (Louisville: Westminster/John Knox, 1991).

14. Pierre Bourdieu notes the way in which legitimate religious authority is constituted in the ability to say the right words, use the right gestures, occupy the right space, and in so doing represent the whole institution, rather than merely oneself. See *Language and Symbolic Power*, trans. John B. Thompson (Cambridge, Mass.: Harvard University Press, 1982), chapters 3-4.

15. Samuel Heilman describes in vivid detail the "cast of characters" and their predictable roles in the synagogue he studied. See *Synagogue Life* (Chicago: University of Chicago Press, 1973).

16. R. Stephen Warner has made the distinction between what he calls "monistic" and "dualistic" modes of religious experience. The latter has highly formalized routines at times set aside for invoking God's presence. The former sees divine presence permeating everyday time and ordinary objects. No special ritual formulae are necessary; ordinary speech and everyday dress will do. See "Dualistic and Monistic Religiosity," in *Religious Movements: Genesis, Exodus, and Numbers*, ed. Rodney Stark (New York: Paragon, 1985), 199-220.

17. Clifford Geertz recounts the story of a death and funeral in Java as a way of illustrating the intricate ways in which ritual, death, and social life are intertwined. See "Ritual and Social Change: A Javanese Example," in *The Interpretation of Cultures* (New York: Basic Books, 1973).

18. Victor Turner, *The Ritual Process* (Ithaca, N.Y.: Cornell University Press, 1977).

19. See Robert Wuthnow, *Sharing the Journey* (New York: Free Press, 1994), 66-68.

20. Wuthnow's *Sharing the Journey* examines both the emotional support and the spiritual formation that happens in small groups. For a discussion of the ways in which these bonds of mutual aid constitute a system of "pastoral care" in the congregation, see Don S. Browning, "Pastoral Care and the Study of the Congregation," in *Beyond Clericalism: The Congregation as a Focus for Theological Education*, ed. Joseph C. Hough, Jr., and Barbara G. Wheeler (Atlanta: Scholars Press, 1988), 103-18.

21. In *Meaning and Moral Order* (Berkeley: University of California Press, 1987), Robert Wuthnow argues that there need be neither gathering of people nor setting off of special objects to have a ritual. Wherever people engage in behavior that communicates (often dramatically) about their social relations, ritual has occurred (pp. 98-109).

22. For a recent report on patterns of denominational switching, see C. Kirk Hadaway and Penny Long Marler, "All in the Family: Religious Mobility in America," *Review of Religious Research* 35, no. 2 (December 1993): 97-116.

23. Lynn Davidman, *Tradition in a Rootless World* (Berkeley: University of California Press, 1991), describes the process of becoming Orthodox as it was experienced by two groups of young Jewish women.

24. Some religious educators recognize the power of congregational and familial cultures in forming religious people in unintentional, as well as intentional, ways. Children learn by participating in events and activities—official and unofficial—that give the tradition its identity and substance. See, for example, John H. Westerhoff and Gwen Kennedy Neville, *Generation to Generation: Conversations in Religious Education and Culture* (Philadelphia: Pilgrim Press, 1974).

25. For a discussion of the importance of artifacts in understanding organizational cultures, see Pasquale Gagliardi, "Artifacts as Pathways and Remains of Organizational Life," in *Symbols and Artifacts* (New York: Aldine de Gruyter, 1990), 3-38.

26. See Michael Ducey, *Sunday Morning: Aspects of Urban Ritual* (New York: Free Press, 1977), 94-97, for a discussion of the uses of sacred space in the churches he studied. Heilman also offers a very instructive look at the physical setting of the synagogue in *Synagogue Life* (Chicago: University of Chicago Press, 1973).

27. See Peter L. Berger, *The Sacred Canopy* (Garden City, N.Y.: Anchor Doubleday, 1969), chapter 1, and Peter L. Berger and Thomas Luckmann, *The Social Construction of Reality* (Garden City, N.Y.: Anchor Doubleday, 1967). Hopewell (*Congregation*) discusses the importance of the congregation's "idiom" (pp. 5-9). See also Ducey's description of the use of language, music, and styles of speaking in *Sunday Morning*, 116-22. In *Bible Believers: Fundamentalists in the Modern World* (New Brunswick, N.J.: Rutgers University Press, 1987), 86-88, I note the way language helps to maintain the boundaries of a conservative congregation.

28. Heilman (*Synagogue Life*) notes that the story of Kehillat Kodesh's beginnings is known by every member, and "the very knowledge of these facts seems often to be the best evidence of one's membership in the group" (p. 9). He goes on to include gossip and joking as modes of storytelling that shape that community's life, alongside the prayer and study that are at the heart of a synagogue's identity.

29. Denham Grierson, *Transforming a People of God*, 55.

30. The uses of story and image in moving a congregation toward change are noted in Carl S. Dudley and Sally A. Johnson, *Energizing the Congregation: Images that Shape Your Church's Ministry* (Louisville: Westminster/John Knox, 1993), especially chapter 7.

31. James P. Wind, *Places of Worship* (Nashville: American Association for State and Local History, 1990) is a useful guide to writing congregational histories.

32. Carl Dudley tells a story about a Norwegian church that sold its building to a Black congregation. The Norwegian congregation, as was traditional, had a boat over the altar, and planned to take the boat with them to their new building. The Black church, however, had immediately adopted the boat as part of *their* heritage and refused to let it go. The boat was the same boat, but meant something very different and no less important to this new constituency.

33. See Hopewell, *Congregation*, pp. 203-11.

34. Victor Turner, *Drama, Fields and Metaphors* (Ithaca, N.Y.: Cornell University Press, 1974), 29. For a more extended discussion, see Victor Turner, *The Forest of Symbols* (Ithaca, N.Y.: Cornell University Press, 1967), 19-41.

35. David A. Roozen, William McKinney, and Jackson W. Carroll, *Varieties of Religious Presence* (New York: Pilgrim Press, 1984).

Chapter 4

Process: Dynamics of Congregational Life

CARL S. DUDLEY [1]

Strong feelings and sustaining forms of congregational life come into focus through the lens of process. Whether you are examining the formal structures of the organization or the expectations of those who belong to it, the analytical tools of process thinking expose the lively interaction that links behavior with beliefs, and values with actions. By using a process frame, you can see the ways in which a congregation plans and makes decisions, rewards and punishes its members, and fights and solves its problems. You can see how a congregation translates faith into its common life and how the process of its common life in turn shapes its faith.

Through the process frame you look at social dynamics, from the subtle norms of community assumptions to the legal structures that encourage order and challenge injustice. A process frame offers tools to manage interpersonal divisions, heal fractured relations after a fight, or aid individuals in better understanding one another. Because processes often operate at a taken-for-granted level, the tools in this chapter are designed to help you name and examine some specifics of your congregation's processes. With this knowledge you can intervene to strengthen or change congregational dynamics. Because here we can but

sketch the contours of its possibilities, we encourage you to take the initiative to follow leads and expand resources in those areas that speak to your conditions.

This chapter begins with a basic discussion of the distinction—and constant interaction—between formal and informal processes. Because process is best understood in the real situations of congregational life, we then introduce three common congregational activities in which processes can be seen at work: program planning, group building, and conflict management. These activities provide windows to some ways process permeates every dimension of congregational life, from explicit and formal public worship to simple and often unconscious norms for authority and participation.

When Understanding Process Makes a Difference

Of all the elements of congregational study, process appears to be at the same time the most available and the most elusive. It seems accessible because everyone who is present participates in it. From the worship leader to the hymn singer, from the energetic organizer to the marginal participant, everyone is an actor in the flow of social process. Because process is embedded in the exchange, however, the elusive moment is gone as quickly as it appears. Through the frame of process thinking, you see patterns in the passing moment, the shape of ministry, the drama of human interaction. Whether you are dealing with selecting new carpet or starting a new ministry, you will need to understand the "hows" of action—how resources get mobilized and how new ideas get interpreted. By naming "how we do it," you have tools to critique and then support or modify a wide variety of activities.

At times congregations feel the need to change but are not sure how to do it. In the every day decisions of congregational life, process dynamics may look like this: After the council meeting when a few members gather at a favorite restaurant, they may talk about their troubled feelings about tension they are experiencing. The tone of the conversation is complaining, with a focus on bad feelings. Sides are formed and members try to influence others to join their side long before there is any action to call the congregation or its leaders to make a clear decision. Even clergy may be caught up in the situation and seek advice from individual members and professional colleagues. At some meetings there will be the appearance of progress, but no one is exactly sure what progress means—unless it is the absence of acrimony.

When these symptoms appear, how can you as congregational leaders get the information you need to move into and through this frustration? How can you make it a learning experience, an opportunity for insight into yourselves, and a chance to develop skills and resources for facing similar situations when they occur in the future? Taking a look at the congregation through the lens of process thinking may reveal the roadblocks that stand in the way of change and the sources of the congregation's discomfort.

Sidebar 4.1
SIGNALS INVITING PROCESS REVIEW

Among the signals that a better understanding of process is needed:

- The effectiveness of committees is decreasing.

- The number of programs is declining.

- Participation at social functions is decreasing.

- Members seem sour, withdrawn, or simply exhausted.

- There is frequent minor conflict, the cause of which is difficult to determine or understand.

A process audit might also be appropriate for single committees or groups, especially when particular symptoms persist:

- It is very difficult to find a chairperson.

- Attendance at meetings is spotty.

- When assigned tasks, members forget to do them.

- Meetings are boring or definitely unpleasant.

- The committee does not meet.

- The work of the committee does not get done.

- Members complain not only about the groups but about many issues not related to the work of the group.

Process study is more apparently important in troubled times, from mild discomfort to major crises (as suggested in sidebar 4.1). Process analysis can be essential in times of conflict, but you do not need to wait for crises. Congregations can initiate periodic reviews, committee by committee, group by group, to assess the strengths and weakness of routine patterns of work and to examine the extent that members are included and satisfied. Such a regular process audit not only forestalls many problems but removes the stigma of "crisis evaluation" when problems arise.

The process frame can help you to better understand any congregational activity, such as worship and prayer, difficult decisions and controversial elections, and harmony or hostility in public events and personal behavior.

Whether you use the process frame in good times or bad, you need to develop enough information to suggest both strengths and weaknesses, to affirm what is right as well as to reveal what is wrong. Armed with this wide variety of process perspectives, you should be able to understand the activity more fully and act accordingly.

Formal and Informal Dimensions of Process

Using the process lens allows you to see many dimensions of social dynamics in congregational life that occur simultaneously. One distinction that permeates almost all of process thinking is the difference between formal and informal processes. *Formal process* includes practices, procedures, and policies that have been openly considered and officially accepted by the congregation either by its own action or through membership in a larger denominational body. These are the legitimate, written rules that organizations adopt to define their leaders and prescribe essential procedures such as delegating authority, holding property, and allocating resources. Such formal policies become especially important when congregations are faced with controversial decisions, disagreements, or open conflict.

Most congregational process, however, remains unwritten. *Informal process* refers to the social interaction that occurs without guidelines or instruction—it just happens. You can see these dynamics throughout the congregation. They are open to inspection, yet a pattern persists: the chair begins the meeting with prayer (there is no agenda) and asks that the minutes be read. Once that is done, the leader asks what the group wants to talk about, and the conversation wanders wherever the members of that group lead it. When the minutes are read at the next meeting, they may bear little resemblance to the dialogue that actually occurred, but old-timers also take that for granted.

Such patterns of social continuity, although unrecorded, are convenient, functional, sometimes ingenious, and often revealing. Powerful and pervasive, these informal elements often fit comfortably within more formal congregational procedures. Unfortunately such processes can become dysfunctional and sometimes destructive. They may change naturally in response to new conditions. Often by benign neglect, they are conveniently forgotten. But sometimes the entrenched and unproductive process needs to be challenged and intentionally altered. Worn out habits can be reassessed and intentionally renewed.

Strain between formal authorities and informal dynamics often reveals the assumptions about process that members and clergy hold. This may be more evident in times of transition when the presence of someone new makes obvious the fault lines of tension. New leaders can feel this strain at the level of informal process, where assumptions about goals, authority relationships, and the proper distribution of resources are first revealed in the course of making a decision. New pastors also face the challenge of "reading" these informal dynamics of interaction in order to exercise effectively both pastoral care and congregational leadership.

Authority, for example, has both formal and informal dimensions. Imagine a pastor who has decided it is time to set new goals for the congregation but does not bother to review the informal process by which decisions are made. At the annual retreat with members of the governing board, through an opening meditation (which reminds them of their historic commitments and his formal position of leadership), the pastor challenges the board, asking, What new programs should we initiate? He leads them in studying Scripture, reviewing church purpose statements, and writing several new goals for the coming year. The pastor has used the formal structures and appealed to recognized sources of authority. After the retreat the pastor takes pride in their accomplishments. Yet, alas, the newly minted goals are comfortably ignored by the groups within the congregation throughout the following year, and a dusty copy of the unused goals may be rediscovered by the new committee formed to plan the next annual retreat.

Formal process was insufficient to penetrate the informal dynamics of the several groups that compose the congregation.

Informal process can be entrenched in the congregation. New goals, although officially approved, will not be actualized until the informal practices have been exposed and intentionally amended to provide space for something new to be incorporated. To alter present conditions, then, you must begin by looking closely at existing patterns.

When you study process, you expose the dual guidance system of the congregation. Sometimes it appears to be as formal as the sharp phrases of a ship captain's commands, but more often it is as unseen as a gyroscope that keeps the ship on course or the automatic pilot of an airplane. Although formal rules must be articulated and often need to be reinforced, informal processes keep the congregation moving with minimum effort. These practices have been in place so long that they retain their stability even (or especially) under pressure.

Informal process needs to be experienced and absorbed by living in the community. It is easier to discover than explain, more a spirit to be caught than a lesson to be taught. It is woven into the habits and routine living of the congregation. To study process, you need several perspectives and different analytical tools to better understand the continuing, complex interaction through which a congregation does its work. Bringing these patterns to consciousness is an essential initial task in the study of congregational process.[2]

The fleeting moments of informal process can never be repeated, and every recounting by leaders, participants, or observers is an interpretation. Like the videographer looking through the lens of a video camera or the editors of a documentary piecing together the final film, you study process by filtering many impressions in order to focus on a few. As suggested by sidebar 4.2, although you are using common analytical tools, you will see different things through the process lens. Naming the dynamics of process carries ethical implications. Gathering

---

Sidebar 4.2
SENSING CONGREGATIONAL PROCESS

Flow: What are the patterns of social interaction in the organization? How is information shared, and with whom? Through whom must decisions pass to be accepted?

Style: How careful are the members about sticking to formal, agreed upon means of deciding? Are the patterns stiff and formal, easy and quick? When do you see formal procedures in action, and when do informal patterns take over?

Incidents: What sorts of events cause people to react, and in what way? For example, do apparently minor incidents create substantial response, or do major occurrences generate little reaction?

Consensus: Do members agree on basic goals, policies, and the direction the congregation should take in the future? Are disagreements based in subgroups or friendship circles?

Success and Failure: The ways members discuss success and failure gives clues about how things get done. Can you list the differences between a meeting described as "a great success" and another called "a waste of time"?

Hunches: Hunches are intuitions from experience. When you undertake long-term observation of a congregation, your hunches are important data about what is happening and why.

Surprises: The gap between expectation and occurrence is usually significant. You can explore who is surprised (leaders? members? outsiders?) and why.

---

information is itself an intervention, since you are inextricably involved as part of your own study. Such personal intervention may increase the accuracy of your information, but at a price. You may become less sensitive to alternative views, for example, or biased in the eyes of members. As you study your congregation, especially through the lens of process, you should make every effort to demonstrate your respect for existing situations and differing views. Unless members believe that you appreciate their views, you reduce your credibility and capacity to suggest new ways of thinking and working.

Three Congregational Activities

Three familiar congregational activities can serve as windows to understanding process: congregational planning, group building, and conflict management. In Samuel Freedman's dramatic description, we see the intersection of these as a new pastor enters an established congregation:

One morning in June 1974, on his third Sunday as pastor of Saint Paul, Reverend Youngblood was standing in the lobby after service, shaking hands with his departing congregants. As the sanctuary emptied and the receiving line thinned, he noticed a white man lurking near the radiator in the corner, dressed on this formal occasion in a windbreaker and khaki slacks.

"Who is that?" the young minister asked a deacon.

"Mr. Poulos, the contractor. He came to collect the check."

"A check for what?"

"He says we owe him a thousand dollars."

Without knowing more, Reverend Youngblood knew Saint Paul could not pay. Already this morning he had learned that two other checks had bounced, each for only seventy dollars and one to the church's own musician. The chairman of the board of trustees, leading a rebellion against the new pastor, refused to even show him the books. Those records remained with the chairman, a man named Josh Sanford, into whose shoe store, it was rumored, a share of the weekly offering found its way. And now, when Reverend Youngblood asked the contractor why he had come dunning on a Sunday, the man replied, "Josh Sanford told me to."

... Reverend Youngblood now had to act. He persuaded the contractor to wait until the end of the month to be paid, giving him two Sundays to appeal to the congregation. Then he summoned Josh Sanford to a meeting of the board of trustees two evenings hence. After songs and prayers, they faced each other across the table, the preacher with the muttonchops and billowing Afro that advertised his youth, the trustee old enough to be his grandfather, all gray hair and tanned leather skin. Reverend Youngblood had already decided on confrontation; if he was going to get fired, it might as well be now.

"How could something like this happen?" he began.

"I didn't know—"

"You didn't know?" Reverend Youngblood said, cutting off the older man.

"I thought—"

"You thought? You thought? How can you tell me you thought and made a mistake like that?" He was shouting and hammering the table, his fury displacing his fright. "If I'd done that, y'all would tar and feather me and ride me outta town on a rail!"

"Then I quit!" Sanford shouted back, tossing his ring of church keys across the table. The jangling ceased and the keys lay on the varnished wood, as tangible a challenge as any knightly gauntlet. Reverend Youngblood snatched and pocketed the ring before Sanford could change his mind. "Next item of business," he announced, and two more trustees resigned.

After they stalked home and the three bewildered holdovers voted to adjourn, the pastor remained in his office, free now to tremble with terror. What if this victory was only temporary? He was still a stranger to his own congregation, while Sanford was a veteran of countless coups and palace revolts. He prayed for a sign that he had acted wisely, and as he looked up from his desk he saw a deacon, Thad Johnson, passing in the hall. At Reverend Youngblood's invitation, Johnson stepped into the office, lifted his arms and started to speak, then fell mute. He tiptoed back to the door, closed it on the prying world, and said, "Pastor, we been tryin' to do that for twelve years."[3]

All process is not so precipitous, but this story combines essential elements of entry and community building, of leadership styles and necessary conflict, and of oppressive silence and expressed affirmation.

We begin, however, with the dynamics of planning because it allows a view of process in slow motion. By then moving through the more complex dimensions of community building to the emotionally charged elements of conflict, we will witness the shift that becomes evident in "unsettled times."[4] Although these three situations are only a few of many ways to examine process, they demonstrate a variety of places to look and tools for examining the social dynamics embodied in congregational life.

Congregational Planning

Each lens of this handbook yields different information about planning. For example, a planning committee may look at the human needs evident in its social context and develop a plan to respond in ways that are consistent with congregational culture, shaped by normative theology, and supported by available resources. In process dynamics we examine the social interactions that facilitate or frustrate participation in the planning exercise.

Sometimes planning is not a formal activity but appears as a spontaneous necessity. Planning may be called for when the congregation feels stuck yet insists on defending its routines, using such phrases as:

"We've always done it this way."

"The pastor knows best and explains what to do."

"It just seemed like a good idea at the time."

"You old-timers know your way around."

"Who did that last year?"

"Sandy just wanted to do it."

"We never argue, we just keep quiet."

Although planning is a relatively simple process, when you seek to make changes you may threaten the unexamined habits of thought and action embedded in many congregations. Ethically, the planning process takes sides by placing priorities on analysis over assumption, on intent over habit, on change over status quo. Planning asks the congregation to look at itself. By naming process dynamics, a congregation can examine *the ways* it looks at itself.

Planning requires that leaders become self-conscious about their roles and responsibilities, examine alternatives, and act on their conclusions. Although planning may appear to be a simple and natural activity to some members, it may be difficult for other members to visualize, disruptive when put into practice, and simply not worth the effort.

Observing the planning process can reveal situations when the formal and informal processes are "out of sync." Sometimes participants feel frustration at the gap, often for opposite reasons: Some had expected the formal procedure to work, and others had assumed that the informal would naturally prevail. In the experience described above, the pastor experienced significant frustration because he expected that formal process would prevail. In other situations, congregations conspire to separate the formal from the informal, such as when congregations formally adopt evangelism goals but informally resist any organized effort to implement an evangelism program.

Power issues often emerge in the planning process. You might be able to distinguish the formal and informal power in a congregation when an elected board decides to use democratic planning procedures involving the participation of many members in systematic planning. Although this may satisfy those who want an open process, the procedure may be sabotaged by certain entrenched people or groups who have always been influential in congregational decisions. The saboteur can be an entrenched trustee (as in St. Paul Church, above), large donors, choir members, volunteers, or even the clergy. The saboteur's authority is often well-known to old members but hidden from new leaders.

Power is not the only reason planning produces tension. The structural, democratic procedure may seem rational enough for those who are goal oriented, but members who participate on the basis of personal relationships may find that voting creates divisions among friends. Until they are convinced that personal conflict can be avoided, members may derail the planning process. They may say in effect, "Let change come in God's good time—when we all agree that it's right."

Church leaders need to be prepared for the fact that some people love planning and others find it difficult or irrelevant. If you concentrate on process, however, planning will give you an opportunity to appreciate the widely different

Sidebar 4.3
CONGREGATIONAL CORE TASKS
AND PROCESS

Type	Core Tasks	Process Style
Family	Care and nurture of members	Closed, informal decisions
Community	Engage public issues and nurture members	Extended democratic debate
House of Worship	Public worship	Formal debate with heavy reliance on staff
Leader	Speaking out and seeking change	Democratic but invest more and expect more from pastoral leaders and are willing to act while strong disagreement remains

See Penny Edgell Becker, *"The Way We Do Things Here": Culture and Conflict in Local Congregations* (Cambridge: Cambridge University Press, 1998).

ways people participate in the life of your congregation. You can begin with two beguilingly simple questions: What is the task? and Who will do it?[5] Each question in turn introduces a variety of analytical tools.

Deciding Task Priorities. How a congregation makes decisions about spending its time and energy is an important window on the inner dynamics of its life together. You will find great differences between one congregation and another—and within a congregation—in the priorities members assign to various tasks. Is worship most important? Or making an impact in the community? Or the congregation's social life? Or study of the Scripture? The way these priorities are established strongly affects the congregational climate—its general feeling of warmth and support, its overall morale, its general openness to change, its usual levels of conflict, and its habits for including people in decisions.

Penny Edgell Becker[6] shows how analyzing the congregation's core tasks, or its definition of its mission, provides a useful shorthand for capturing important elements of process (see sidebar 4.3). Congregations that think of themselves as a *family* see the care and nurture of members as their core task, and they do things differently from other congregations. For example, they are more likely to favor relatively closed and informal decision-making processes and to rely on personal authority and experience.

Community congregations also put an emphasis on the relationships of the members to each other, but they combine that emphasis with concern for all the various issues of the day. The result is a process like a continuous democratic forum. People talk and debate until they find a strategy that will address the issue without alienating anyone.

Although all congregations see worship as a core task, some define themselves primarily as a *house of worship.* They are less interested in issues, and even their own relationships to each other are subordinated to their primary goal of worshiping God. As a result, they do not spend great energy on making decisions. Their process is shorter and more formal, and they rely more heavily on the staff and a few core members for leadership.

Still other congregations *(leaders)* are activists who take it as their task to speak to the world, seeking to change it according to their understanding of their religious tradition. They are just as interested in current issues as community congregations, but they are more willing to shorten the debate process, rely on their pastor for religious direction, and move ahead even if real differences remain.

Identifying these core tasks, then, lends a particular advantage to studying process. Mission and goals are sometimes easier to identify than process itself. They can provide a useful place to start, a window into more elusive aspects of process.

If your congregation has committed significant energy to planning, you may wish to provide a survey to the widest possible number of your members and invite them to express their views and become involved in the planning. By assessing the strength of support for various kinds of program activities and how people feel about the way decisions are made, these instruments can be helpful in understanding your congregation's ways of working. Numerous questionnaires to assist congregations are available through bookstores and denominational offices. As models for your use, we have included survey questions from Hartford Seminary (see appendix A). More than a vote for or against possible tasks, these instruments allow you to measure members' feelings about procedures and commitments to congregational program priorities.

This information can often open the door for change. Defining the primary tasks can release congregational energy—when the congregation, using its own decision-making style, agrees to the tasks themselves. As the work of Kennon L. Callahan[7] has demonstrated, simply naming central tasks has energized many congregations with

renewed hope in their future. In one church, a member survey showed that they had substantial agreement about priority tasks and warm support for one another. Yet they also found that many members felt neglected and ignored when congregational decisions were being made. In other words, the goals were supported, but the process was weak. With this information, congregational leaders were able to build unity around their goals while they worked to find ways members could participate more fully in making decisions.

Sharing the results of such studies is both an ethical and practical decision. Because process issues reflect attitudes and perceptions, you will need to share them in a pastoral way, giving members ample opportunity to explore and digest the material. Retreat settings offer ideal arenas for such discussion because they allow time for intense presentations, reflection, informal discussion, and continuous participation by members.

Leadership Roles. All organizations divide tasks among various leadership roles, allocating responsibilities to specific people or groups. Edgar Schein notes that people fill roles in their own unique style, which is essential to healthy process:

The network of positions and roles which define the formal organizational structure is occupied by people, and those people in varying degrees put their own personalities into

---

Sidebar 4.4
ROLE EXPECTATIONS

- *Denominational* role expectations are defined by the official polity and practice of the larger body.

- *Contractual* roles are defined by local congregations through explicit written agreements.

- *Traditional* role expectations have been expressed in congregational practice but remain unwritten.

- *Tacit* role expectations reflect the procedures that participants assume without discussion or agreement.

getting their job done. The effect of this is not only that each role occupant has a certain style of doing his work, but that he has certain patterns of relating to other people in the organization.... It is important to have the right structure of roles for effective organizational performance, but at the same time, people's personalities, perceptions, and experiences also determine how they will behave in their roles and how they will relate to others.[8]

Understanding how your congregation plans its work requires looking at who occupies what roles and how the people who occupy the roles relate to others. In congregations, special attention must be given to the roles and styles of clergy and other very visible leaders. Often member expectations become most obvious when they are violated. When congregations want to rationalize the roles of leadership, they often invoke one of several sources of authority, as suggested in sidebar 4.4.

Because the roles of local clergy are often prescribed by denominational polity, pastors in various faith groups have vastly different degrees of formal authority. Catholic priests, for example, traditionally are the treasurers of parish funds, while Protestant clergy rarely assume such duties. At the same time, in congregational polity, the local church contract may specifically define the clergy's responsibilities. Because not all the possible role contingencies can be included in denominational polity or congregational contract, local traditions often influence the wide margin of undefined clergy roles and authority. For example, local customs may determine whether the clergy are welcome at the business meetings of some groups or whether church groups have the freedom to maintain separate bank accounts. Tacit role expectations reflect the practices that participants assume, often unaware that these may be in conflict with other sources of authority.

Frequently confusion and disagreement surround tasks, styles, and authority when new participants carry into a congregation ways they have operated in another situation that conflict with the expectations of older

members who claim the congregation has maintained a particular practice "for as long as I can remember." Sometimes role expectations and decision-making authority are borrowed and buttressed by the secular culture. For example, gender roles in some business or commercial situations have given more authority to women, which may clash with the limited latitude afforded women in the traditional (often official) structures of some churches.

You may also discover that your congregation turns to people with varied gifts and influence for different kinds of tasks. Some members are leaders because they are well-informed and communicate effectively with others. Still others are given authority because they have the particular skills that are needed, while others have authority because they are well-liked or have essential information. They know where the fuse box is, how to coax the photocopy machine into working, which plumber can be trusted to come in a

---

Sidebar 4.5
LEADERSHIP STYLES

Type 1: Received. Decision makers remain outside to guide the group to achieve an acceptable goal. Although members may be advisers and share in developing general goals, they receive and implement specific tasks as defined by others.

Type 2: Autonomous. In autonomous decision-making, group members function separately with their own independent spheres of responsibility. Areas of accountability are clearly defined and meetings are focused on turf distinctions.

Type 3: Assertive. Assertive decision-making is characterized by frequent and intensive interaction between members as a vehicle for conducting business and developing supportive relationships. Feelings are considered a natural and legitimate element in human interaction.

Type 4: Integrative. In this least common style, every decision is referred to the team, which establishes goals and shares together in the results. A fully integrative approach has no individual achievements, only team failure or success.

See Celia Allison Hahn, *Growing in Authority; Relinquishing Control* (Bethesda, Md.: Alban Institute, 1994).

hurry, and where the extra keys are hidden.

In unspoken ways, power may also flow to individuals who have accumulated additional influence because they are more active, more pious, more trusted, or larger contributors. Official committee chairs may come and go, but most congregations can point to a core of dedicated members whose long history of involvement makes them key players whenever the congregation faces a major decision.[9] They are the people who are called for advice and consent.

Because clarity about leadership roles is generally helpful and may be the key to resolving explosive situations, congregations may utilize an assessment instrument such as the one developed by Rusbuldt, Gladden, and Green,[10] which describes fifty activities that might be appropriately undertaken by either clergy or laity, or both. Congregations can use such an exercise to expose their assumptions about role assignment and task priorities, that is, Who should do what jobs? and How important are these jobs to us?

A simple, nonsexist index of leadership styles has been developed by Celia Allison Hahn[11] (see sidebar 4.5). Each style has its strengths and limitations, its advocates and critics, and its best application and its inappropriate imposition—and participants may rate them differently as a result of their experience and position in the congregation.

Looking at planning through the lens of process, we note the complex variety of interpersonal dynamics involved. Task, role, and authority are broad categories that help us better understand how a religious group decides what needs to be done and who will do it.

Building Community

Basic to community building is the recognition and maintenance of a boundary between those who are inside and those who are not. Assimilating new members into your congregation requires that those who already belong define that boundary for those who enter. You may recognize in the following example a boundary that is defined by an emphasis on children, common in numerous mainline congregations. Note in the example another aspect of the boundary defining process—the subsequent conflict around parenting roles:

On first arriving Mr. and Mrs. Jones are shown the toddlers' room for child care. As worshipers they are given a bulletin to guide them through the worship service. After the service they are invited to the coffee hour, where they discover a few friends and meet many people who share their interests.

A few days later the Jones family receives a letter from the pastor with a brochure describing various programs of the church. After they participate a few weeks, the pastor talks with them about their experiences in the church and the procedure to officially join the congregation. With other prospective members, they join a membership or confirmation class, where they meet church officers and share their faith stories. Here they receive new member literature from the denominational office and talk with the pastor about the faith of the church. After meeting with the church board, they are received as members in Sunday worship and are warmly welcomed by new and old friends.

Because of her involvement in a previous congregation, Mrs. Jones is appointed to the community ministry committee and is given materials that explain the work her congregation supports. Mr. Jones, known for his business acumen, is asked to serve on the annual stewardship campaign and is provided a planning kit from the denominational office. But when Mr. Jones was invited to work for a month (four Sundays) in the toddler's room "to show that dads care too," he said that he was not ready for that yet.

Assimilation includes an array of informal and formal processes that facilitate the Joneses' transition. The toddler program, worship, membership class, and committees are structured programs, while the bulletin, brochure, and planning kit are documents that enable the Joneses to belong. With the process lens, we see more clearly the sequence of events and the importance of relationships. How were the Joneses invited? When were faith stories shared? and How effectively did the pastor communicate? In the process of the Jones family joining church, we examine the value of friends at the coffee hour and of associates in the board meeting.

The lens of process makes us sensitive to the fact that Mr. Jones is surprised by the invitation to help in the toddler's room. Through process thinking we become aware that our communication, both the formal literature and the friendship network, failed to prepare Mr. Jones. We also recognize that the Jones family brings its own expectations to the church, and the tensions of this situation must be negotiated. Typically the arena for these adjustments is the informal associations, such as on-the-job training for board responsibilities, socializing over coffee, or the intimacy of a small study group.

You can begin your own study of process simply by reviewing the entry process with recent members. This exercise is mutually helpful because it allows new members to tell about their surprises and established leaders to discover what assumptions they have been making.

Process analysis looks at documents, personal interviews, and group discussions, asking people in every part of the church's life what helped them "learn the ropes." Based on feedback about how they are doing in the social fabric of the group, members develop invisible social antennas by which they sense what the group considers good behavior. By the signals members send, congregations establish the boundaries between acceptable and offensive activities within the group.

Maintaining Internal Boundaries. To maintain their standards, for example, when a vacancy occurs on a board or committee, the nominating committee may recommend a candidate based more on the person's modeling of social practices than on theological beliefs. The congregational council may reward outstanding members by naming them as delegates to the annual denominational convention because they represent the ideal. On the same basis, youth groups decide who is qualified to go on special trips, and budget committees decide which programs "represent our commitments" and get funded.

Thus congregations develop standards that are taught more by behavior than by explana-

tion. As with the wind, we are more apt to see their effect than to hear them spoken clearly. Gordon Lippit warns and advises:

> To act contrary to the norms may bring severe censorship or even total rejection by the group. Some norms are functional in getting the organization's task done; others may be incidental and nonproductive. Standards may rest on tradition as well as on changes produced by new experiences and requirements. Because norms and values sometimes persist beyond the point where they are functional, some groups and organizations find it useful ... to periodically make their operative norms explicit. They ask, "Is this the way we really want to behave? What purpose is served by this norm?"[12]

A review of your congregation's patterns of inclusion and nurture may be forced upon you when existing habits are challenged unwittingly, especially when a potential member is unwilling to conform. As they stumble over unwritten understandings about congregational life, these "outsiders" are themselves frustrated—and the norm is momentarily exposed for others to see. New pastors, for example, are sometimes unpleasantly surprised to find that they have offended, even alienated, some members of the congregation because each was operating from different premises about appropriate behavior for the parish.

You can see the difference between entrenched practices and random behavior in the way the congregation responds to maintain and enforce its unspoken practices. Pastors may remain in the board meeting when their salary is discussed, only later to be offended when challenged for what a board member considered boorish behavior. Sometimes newcomers find themselves in difficulty when they are "too pushy" in expressing a desire to serve on a committee. In one congregation a member was criticized for being "enthusiastic" and was informed, "That's not our kind of religion." In another, a newcomer was chastised by a careful but firm delegation of deacons who said that it was inappropriate for him to bring his children to the adult worship. Each of these congregations chose to defend actively the way they were already doing things rather than bring those norms into question. Such moments of stress provide invaluable information about the congregation's definition of itself and its membership—opportunities for intentional reflection and possible change.

Participants in the life of a congregation develop a variety of informal means to evaluate relationships. Sometimes the comments of oth-ers are forthcoming and affirming. Sometimes participants quietly observe the posture and attentiveness of people and note whether most of their responses are negative or positive. Participants are also attentive to what third parties say about their reception into the congregation. Sometimes they even ask others their perceptions about their participation,

especially about a performance or public presentation.

Congregations and their constituent committees also have various ways of checking out the fit between individual and congregational expectations. They can be attentive to the number of participants in various activities, the frequency with which particular people attend, the comments they make after the meeting, and the degree of enthusiasm expressed for what has happened. Such informal means of assessment, however, are not always accurate or complete indicators of individual or congregational satisfaction. A scowling face may be the result of unmet expectations or an upset stomach. We rarely know all the contributing factors, but we can examine carefully the level of satisfaction experienced by individual participants.

Exercise: Listening to Board Members. Some congregations use entry review as a foundational step in leadership development. An exercise to assist in listening to the review of a person's entry experience is contained in sidebar 4.6. Note that you learn most by talking to those who have recently been incorporated or elevated in congregational life. "Experience is the best teacher"—but only when it is carefully reviewed and openly shared.

The effectiveness of group building can be measured by listening to the ways information is provided, the degree to which members share in the goals of the group, and the extent to which initiatives are being communicated to everyone affected. You can also observe human relations issues: Is trust high, and do people feel included? In addition, you can look for the political dynamics, asking whether effective leaders have been found to rally the congregation and whether those with a stake in potential changes have been adequately consulted.

Getting things done in a congregation almost never involves only one decision-making body. It always involves communication among various official groups and informal communication among members. A look at routine lines of communication is often a helpful part of a process assessment. For example, a board may

---

Sidebar 4.6
NEW BOARD MEMBER REVIEW

Each new board person is interviewed for about an hour within the first months of taking a leadership position. After establishing the reason for the interview and discussing what will be done with what is learned, the interviewer follows a schedule of questions similar to these:

- Tell me about your experiences before the first board meeting. Did anyone talk to you about what the board did, when it met, how it was structured, or your responsibilities outside of the meetings?

- Had you heard about what goes on at board meetings from any of your friends in the congregation? Had you had experience on other boards? If so, were there orientation or training sessions for new board members?

- How did you learn what the ground rules are for speaking at meetings and making decisions? How did you learn about the group goals and how these are discussed and amended?

- Were you given material to read about this board: the constitution, the book of order, past minutes, or budgets?

- What is your reaction to joining the board? What knowledge do you think it would be important to share with others who will have an experience similar to yours?

want to assess the formal reports and informal feedback that are its way of knowing what other committees and program groups are doing. You can do this by asking someone to keep track of all the communications among those groups. A more thoroughgoing assessment would involve observing several meetings of both the board and the groups being assessed. Leaders in each would be interviewed to learn their perceptions about what the group was trying to accomplish, the quality of the communication, and support (or absence of support) provided by others in this effort.

Groups can also assess their own feedback and communication process. Philip Anderson has developed a Post Meeting Reaction form (PMR) to measure what he calls Christian Group Life[13] (see page 129 at the end of this chapter). By using this form regularly at the end of every meeting, members raise consciousness and learn to evaluate the meeting as it progresses—and perhaps to change their behavior accordingly.

Looking throughout the congregation at "the way things get done around here" can be valuable. In addition to governing boards, you may want to take a look at the selection and training of teachers, how budgets are prepared, how a new ministry or program was launched, how new members are brought into the choir, how worship is planned and improved, even how the kitchen is used and by whom. By making use of process insights and examining how your congregation listens and makes commitments, you can discover how the energy flows—or is blocked—in your community.

Attending to Personal Needs. In addition to assimilating individuals, effective group building depends on finding ways to celebrate and utilize the diversity of individual gifts over time. A wide variety of process related instruments have been introduced from disciplines allied with pastoral care, such as psychology and personal counseling. Although the scores of individuals who take these instruments are sometimes added together to develop a personality profile of the congregation, such a procedure is problematic. The frames of congregational study, taken separately and together,

suggest that communities of faith develop character and sustain a culture that is significantly different from the total of individuals. That is, the whole is greater than—or at least different from—the sum of the participants.

You may take a conversational approach with members by using some adaptation of the interpersonal needs assessment scale from a United Church of Christ manual on volunteers (see page 131 at the end of this chapter).[14] This nonthreatening instrument invites individuals to identify their own satisfactions as a

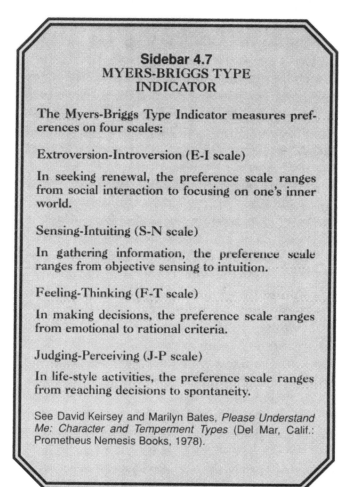

Sidebar 4.7
MYERS-BRIGGS TYPE INDICATOR

The Myers-Briggs Type Indicator measures preferences on four scales:

Extroversion-Introversion (E-I scale)

In seeking renewal, the preference scale ranges from social interaction to focusing on one's inner world.

Sensing-Intuiting (S-N scale)

In gathering information, the preference scale ranges from objective sensing to intuition.

Feeling-Thinking (F-T scale)

In making decisions, the preference scale ranges from emotional to rational criteria.

Judging-Perceiving (J-P scale)

In life-style activities, the preference scale ranges from reaching decisions to spontaneity.

See David Keirsey and Marilyn Bates, *Please Understand Me: Character and Temperment Types* (Del Mar, Calif.: Prometheus Nemesis Books, 1978).

basis for participating in congregational ministries.

A more complex, but still popular, personality analysis, the Myers-Briggs Type Indicator (MBTI), identifies differences based on distinctive ways of processing information. It has provided such significant insights into the social dynamics of congregations that a small library of MBTI resources is available for churches.[15] Although we cannot examine this scale in detail, you may be familiar with the four dimensions that can be initially elicited by a brief questionnaire (see sidebar 4.7).

These scales, taken together, produce sixteen types of individuals who have similar preferences in the ways that they respond to situations. (For example, a person with the type ENTJ is more likely be an organizer; an ISFP, to be a helper; and so forth.) Although this form of analysis was initially developed for individuals, Myers-Briggs analysis has also been applied to groups and even entire congregations, denominations, and Catholic orders. (For example, SJ seems more Ignatian; NF, more Augustinian; and so on.) In the same way, it has also been applied to explain the characteristics of managers, teachers, artists, politicians, and other professionals. Although procedures that use cumulative scores to characterize groups are problematic, sharing personal scores in a group often helps individuals to appreciate their "gifts differing" and to make the most of their diversity in management, education, planning, and personal relationships. An excellent survey of MBTI insights for congregations is provided in a book with the comprehensive title, *How We Belong, Fight, and Pray: The MBTI as a Key to Congregational Dynamics.*[16]

Congregational studies on personal needs and interpersonal dynamics provide a special ethical issue for religious leaders. Because informal process is often hidden and unexamined, using these instruments to expose such dynamics can be threatening to people. You should gather such information only when participants know and agree to the process by which information is shared—ideally, in an atmosphere of mutual trust and common purpose.

Congregational Size and Life Cycle. Most members recognize that the experience of belonging feels different in congregations of various sizes. Despite all other distinguishing characteristics (such as theology, polity, or social location), smaller congregations typically function more like extended families, while larger congregations assume more corporate

characteristics. In smaller congregations, the leaders are more relational, decision-making is more grounded in personal bonds, communication is more likely to be word of mouth, and conflicts are more personal.[17] In larger congregations, the leaders are more often chosen for their skills, the decisions are reached through structured procedures, the communication is more formal, and leaders seek to manage their conflicts within institutional procedures.

In *Sizing up a Congregation for New Member Ministry*, Arlin Rothauge identifies differences in member assimilation and community building among the *family* church (up to 50 active members), *pastoral* church (50-150), *program* church (150-350), and *corporate* church

---

Sidebar 4.8
CONGREGATIONAL LIFE CYCLE

Birth: Imaginative vision, few but enthusiastic members

Infancy: High energy and inclusive membership

Adolescence: Busy building a place and new activities

Prime: Creative conflict with members, staff, and program

Maturity: Well-established staff, program, and procedures

Aristocracy: Efficient but entrenched institutional life

Bureaucracy: Ineffective, but sustained by good memories

Death: Disillusioned hopes and institutional disintegration

See Martin F. Saarinen, *The Life Cycle of a Congregation* (Washington, D.C.: The Alban Institute, 1986).

(350+).[18] Lyle Schaller catches the spirit of these differences as he identifies seven personalities that Protestant churches assume based on their size: churches can be expected to exhibit the independence of a *cat* (less than 35 average weekly worship attendance), warmth of a *collie* (35-100), effort required of a *garden* (100-175), struggles of being *between-size* (175-225), grace of a *mansion* (225-450), comfort of abundant *resources* (450-700 weekly), and the autonomy of a *nation* (700.+).[19] Because members seem attracted and committed to congregations of a size that satisfies them, efforts (by new pastors and "other outsiders") to change the congregation's comfortable size are often met with rational ambivalence and emotional resistance.

The life cycle of a congregation also influences the sense of belonging and dynamics of leadership. Martin Saarinen, for example, has traced the energy levels and social dynamics for eight phases of congregational growth and decline (see sidebar 4.8).[20] He reminds us of the intimate interplay between social process and congregational history, between the rhythmic forces of membership growth and decline. Robert Dale, although accepting the ebb and flow of congregational energy in its life cycle, invites congregational leaders to help the church, as he says, *To Dream Again.*[21] To reenergize congregations, he identifies the contributions of leaders essential to every phase: for energetic dreaming at birth, we need visionaries; for the convictional faith in infancy, we need theologians; for the high goals of adolescence, directors; for the structures at institutional prime, organizers; for the ministry of maturity, activists; for the nostalgia of an established aristocracy, traditionalists; and so on, to the death of the church. From the perspective of the life cycle metaphor, the strength in one generation may be barrier to adaptation in the next. Throughout our discussion of the community building process, change is essential for survival. But, as the life cycle underscores, change implies discomfort and usually involves some level of conflict. In conflict, process is more charged with emotion.

Congregational Conflict

Conflict can provide a useful lens into many aspects of congregational life, including culture, leadership, and process. Congregations react to conflict differently. Some congregations ignore or suppress conflict; some embrace routine conflict as a positive good, viewing it as a sign of vitality; and some experience severe conflict that is difficult to resolve and that debilitates the congregation. Sociologist Georg Simmel[22] pointed out that the opposite of conflict is not peace but indifference. Conflict only arises when people care about and are committed to each other and the congregation. Consequently, even when conflict is too painful for easy discussion, such episodes can provide valuable learning experiences when participants are willing to work at deciphering the messages that appear in the chaos. What people are willing to fight about may put in bold relief the functional priorities of faith and practice of a congregation.

At the simplest level, congregational conflict indicates that the established, routine ways for making decisions have failed to resolve the differences. When they remain at the manageable level, such conflicts may help a congregation to define the goals, clear the air, reaffirm membership commitment, and get on with the life of the group. In process dynamics, analyzing conflict always requires the integration of the informal and formal dimension of congregational life. Formal procedures are often invoked to protect the minority voice while permitting the legitimate authority to act. Sometimes formal procedures are vested in a constitution or book of order, and in other congregations the bishop, whose decision "will be determinative," must be consulted.

But real conflict is never that simple. If the issues are rooted in informal dynamics involving personal relations or power allocations within the congregation, the imposition of formal solutions may leave the church members angry and alienated. Within the congregation, conflict always has a mixture of causes—sometimes embedded and hidden from view. When diagnosing conflict, look for multidimensional causes: Structurally, what formal procedure for resolution is possible? Relationally, who is involved, and how are these people related to one another within and apart from the formal procedures? Politically, where is the power, and what are the likely rewards in various potential courses of action? Culturally, what assumptions and beliefs do people bring to the conflict and use to frame the meaning of the conflict issues?

One hopeful place to begin is with the acceptance of conflict as a natural and potentially healthy experience. In every congregation tensions inevitably exist between change and stability, between conformity and individuality, between centralized authority and broad participation, and the like. Sidebar 4.9 shows the way Speed B. Leas and George Parsons identify these as creative tensions.[23] Rather than assuming that conflict is destructive, Parsons and

---

Sidebar 4.9
CREATIVE TENSIONS IN CONGREGATIONAL LIFE

Between the stability of planning and the spontaneous energy of discovery.

Between efficiently concentrated power and the broad base of dispersed authority.

Between the clarity of mandatory rules and the individuality of discretionary process.

Between the continuity of structured management and the adjustments of transforming leadership.

Between the solidarity of collegial belonging and the authenticity of individual participation.

Between the comfort of known continuity and the creativity of constant change.

According to Speed B. Leas and George Parsons, *Understanding Your Congregation as a System* (Washington, D.C.: Alban Institute, 1993).

Leas argue that constructive tensions form the basis for dynamic ministry. With respect to the pressures that are familiar and often productive in every congregation, they define six existing and essential tensions and show that these can be assets to ministry. With their approach you can begin with the assumption that this natural condition can strengthen your ministry. Conflict management is like planning under pressure. Leaders must listen to various perceptions of

the problem, then develop creative options, and ultimately help the congregation to act.

Unfortunately, open conflict is often so threatening that it is suppressed, sometimes effectively but sometimes disastrously. If you or your leaders are uncomfortable with emotional stress, you are likely to delay looking at causes until the crisis, like wildfire, is almost out of control. When leaders restrict information and suppress dissent, the sources of information may be mislabeled and the voices of conscience are often made to suffer.

Conspiracies of Silence. Conflict is escalated when trust is betrayed but information is denied. This can happen when a trusted treasurer embezzles church money, or when a lay leader is discovered in an unethical situation, or when a venerated pastor is guilty of sexual misconduct. Rather than confront difficult situations, congregations often respond by denying the evidence and punishing those who present it.

Marie Fortune captures this conspiracy of denial and punishment in her description of a congregational meeting convened to report charges that members had raised concerning their pastor.

> I weighed the costs and benefits of taking the floor and delineating the charges. I wanted members of First Church to have the information I believed they needed, and I wanted them to feel some empathy for the women. But, in the midst of this heightened hostility, I feared that listing the charges against Donovan—which included rape—would only serve to increase their rage against the women.... Knowing what I know now, I would take the chance of being misheard and misunderstood, because I believe it is wrong for victims to be silenced as these women were.[24]

The leader who reported this experience felt the "heightened hostility" that prevented her from speaking. Members of the congregation, who had come to be informed about the case, felt frustrated by the lack of specific detail. Without this information, they blamed denominational officials for their intervention, and they also blamed the women who brought the charges. Even after the details were later published and the charges vindicated, congregational denial took the form of alienation, hostility, and verbal abuse toward the several women who had been courageous enough to testify against the pastor. Most members of the congregation simply did not want to hear information that would destroy their image of their trusted and beloved pastor.

Process review may challenge the intentional silences that shield practices, the exposure of which may require a change of worldview or a radical reconstruction of the ways members view their leaders and themselves. Under pressure of the Civil Rights movement in the 1960s, as the nation changed many of its public policies toward racial segregation, most all-White churches were ambivalent about their commitments. A White church might deny that its members were prejudiced and at the same time block its doors to African Americans who wished to attend. When openly exposed, their behavior was in conflict with their stated values. At such moments, simple honesty threatens congregational unity. Although we must be sensitive to the power of a conspiracy of silence, process review seeks to expose what is being silenced in ways that strengthen healthy religious commitments by calling forth integrity in personal and social practices.

Exercise: Listening in Conflict. In a typical situation, as tension begins to build in a congregation, your vestry, board, or session may find that officers report talking to "certain individuals" (who remain nameless) who are very upset. When the messages come anonymously, other board members have no way of assessing the real extent of dissatisfaction in the congregation. This insider information seems to push board members apart from one another and chokes off their ability to talk openly among themselves or throughout the congregation. In this mind-set, the board itself can become a "secret" committee (not sharing what it has discussed or its decisions

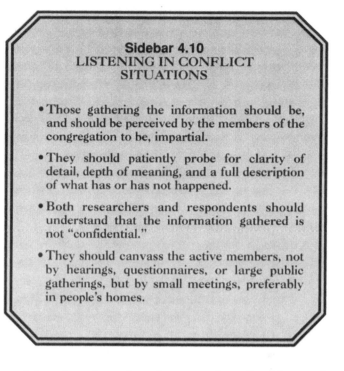

Sidebar 4.10
LISTENING IN CONFLICT SITUATIONS

- Those gathering the information should be, and should be perceived by the members of the congregation to be, impartial.

- They should patiently probe for clarity of detail, depth of meaning, and a full description of what has or has not happened.

- Both researchers and respondents should understand that the information gathered is not "confidential."

- They should canvass the active members, not by hearings, questionnaires, or large public gatherings, but by small meetings, preferably in people's homes.

with others) and make emotionally charged decisions based on information that may be partial and slanted. We are fortunate to live in a time when the lenses of gender, race, class, and other charaxteristics are more openly discussed.[25] You should consider several precautions before attempting to gather information in conflict situations.

At the most basic level, those gathering the information should be, and should be perceived by the members of the congregation to be, impartial (see sidebar 4.10). If they have something at stake in the conflict, their judgment is likely to be skewed, and other members are not likely to be candid with them. These people should be skilled (or trained) in the art of listening and in the skills of patiently probing for clear details, deep meaning, and a full description of what has or has not happened. In conflict settings, gathered data must include information about the presenting cause or issue; the various individuals and groups involved; the structural guidelines for change; and the power, values, and vested interests of those involved. Those who are angry, frightened, upset, or have an axe to grind often find it difficult to assess facts and meanings in a balanced fashion.

If the information is to be discussed in settings beyond the information gathering interview, respondents must understand that it is not "confidential" and may be shared with all the parties involved (perhaps in a composite report to protect vulnerable sources). One reason for sharing information is so everyone has an opportunity to hear and appreciate the views of others and the depth of those concerns. Trust, built on open process, is essential in order for informants to take the risk of sharing. Three typical procedures that are dangerous and often counterproductive should be avoided.

Although questionnaires can be helpful to learn the views of members on relatively objective issues, they are rarely appropriate for conflict situations because the issues are more sensitive than the instruments can measure. Questionnaires can score attitudes, but they fail to express the complex values and experiences behind these attitudes. Further, questionnaire responses are often misunderstood as a vote, affecting a decision before the various parties have opportunity for discussion and problem solving together. To get in-depth data, you must talk with people personally to clarify what they are thinking and feeling.

In such explosive situations, public meetings (as in Marie Fortune's report above) are typically nonproductive and frequently abusive because participants are rarely able to speak fully about their perceptions and concerns, and sometimes the atmosphere of the meeting raises rather than lowers the negative emotions of all involved. These feelings often lead people to exaggerate and distort, resulting in notions that participants would reject under less threatening conditions.

When working on emotional conflicts, you will find that hearings are also a dangerous and divisive method for gathering data. There are three problems with hearings: (1) they are adversarial by definition; (2) they attract those who have the strongest views (often an axe to grind); and (3) they put the decision-making power in the hands of those who gather and report the information.

Whatever method you use to gather data, focus clearly on discovering who needs to talk with whom and mediate the conversation so that the parties involved can actively work to resolve their own conflict.

Internal Conflict Diagnoses. To accumulate information when dealing with emotionally charged conflict that leaders think they can manage, you should gather the participants into small groups in homes or in the congregation's facilities. Because a climate of trust is essential, these conversations are more successful when groups consist of people who would otherwise feel comfortable talking in one another's presence. Although exchanges between strangers or people whose views are radically different may be essential, some people are intimidated by such encounters, and the conversations are unlikely to be fruitful unless the emotional safety of all participants is assured.

On newsprint or on individual sheets, facilitate conversation by beginning with these sorts of questions:

- What is your name, your age, and the length of time you have been a member of this congregation?

- What programs, committees, and activities do you most enjoy?

- What do you like best about this congregation?

- What problems are you aware of in this congregation?

- What would you change, if you personally could change anything in this congregation?

- What internal problems or community challenges should the congregation address?

The age and activity level provide an introduction to the discussion and offer an opportunity to see whether the congregation seems divided along generational lines or over programmatic preferences. Discussions about strengths, problems, and priorities for change provide clues about the "glue" that holds people in the congregation. In some congregations, the glue is strong family ties; in others, positive relationships that go back many years, the fact that the congregation is near their home, or the particular faith stance of that congregation. Some motives are not strong enough to hold members through intense conflict, while others will help members endure and even mature as they journey through unresolved conflict.

From the trenches of a split congregation, you can see and hear the divisions. When describing a crucial committee in a divided church, Steven Warner caught the spirit of polarization:

A pastor nominating committee was elected in October. . . . They began their work by dividing into two subcommittees, one to produce a survey of the state of the church, its membership, and community (the "church information form," or CIF), and the other to compose a statement of goals of the congregation (a "mission study"). But it soon became evident that the nominating committee was deeply divided along theological party lines that coincided roughly with the subcommittees—liberals on the CIF group and evangelicals on the mission group—and the weekly meetings became unpleasant. Participants report that when they recessed for lunch, half the members would sit at one table and the other half at another, and members of one faction would refer to those of the other as "they" and "them." Behind their backs, they reviled each other respectively as "churchmen" and "cultists."[26]

In higher levels of conflict, participants tend to see themselves as substantially benevolent in their motives and their opponents as essentially malevolent. They tend to see issues dichotomously, as either/or, right or wrong. They tend to believe they know the true motives of the opposition's behavior, and they tend to greatly exaggerate both the level of threat and the consequences of action that has been taken or might be taken. The higher the distortion, the more difficult and frightening the conflict will be to those experiencing it.

Not all conflict is so polarized. A process view of conflict begins by assessing its level of intensity. In *Moving Your Church through Conflict*,[27] Speed Leas has identified five levels of conflict (see sidebar 4.11) that can be seen in congregations (and other social groups, from street gangs to international political circles). He sees these as

steps in a process of escalating conflict. However, he does not believe that one level of conflict inevitably leads to another, although he does note that conflict climbs the steps one at a time and is disarmed one step at a time. In *"The Way We Do Things Here"* Penny Edgell Becker[28] makes the useful distinction between conflict in which the parties are within a particular level and conflict in which members are at different levels. She has found that when members agree that they are on the same level (especially levels

---

Sidebar 4.11
LEVELS OF CONFLICT

1. Solving Problems
Language is reasonable, clear, and specific to the issues. Issues are seen as problems to be solved, and participants are fluid in their views and commitments.

2. Disagreement
Language is less clear and forthcoming and may include barbed humor. Issues may mix personalities and causes. There may be some distrust of the motives of other groups.

3. Contest
Language may distort information in order to "make points." Issues are clouded by distrust, and there are strong factions divided by clear barriers.

4. Fight/Flight
Language is cold, fixed, and self-righteous. Issues are stated in great principles that go beyond the present battles. Opposing camps seek to hurt each other.

5. Intractable
Language is that of propaganda, seeking to mobilize allies to destroy the enemy. Issues are vast, and participants are united to remove "them" or die trying.

Summarized from Speed Leas, *Moving Your Church Through Conflict* (Washington D.C.: Alban Institute, 1985).

---

1 through 3), resolution is relatively easy and swift. When members seem to be at different levels, the conflict is more likely to escalate, become bitter, and have a lower possibility of simple resolution. That is, when you help everyone to play by the same rules (agree on

the level of conflict), solutions come more easily.

Through home interviews or other proven procedures, you should have ample information to determine the intensity of feelings and the focus of the conflict. Although Becker found that congregational conflict is often aroused in program areas like liturgy and social advocacy, the conflicts themselves centered around questions of leadership and authority (53 percent), faith and theology (35 percent), and finances and facilities (12 percent). With this distinction you can begin to help the congregation separate the presenting issue from more systemic causes.

Personal Feelings. Naming the conflicts rarely explains why members invest such energy and seem willing to pay such an emotional price.[29] You can also help members to name how and why they care because that determines the social dynamics of their participation. A conflict over whether to sell the parsonage may be to the pastor a simple matter of using resources efficiently, while long-term members may see this issue in terms of preserving their congregation's tradition and maintaining their status and presence in the community. A proposal to use inclusive language in liturgy may be seen as the loss of aesthetic beauty and traditional meaning for one group, while another sees the issue as inclusion or exclusion with respect to full membership in the religious community. Because all these perceptions are real, they must be recognized before resolution can occur without lingering bitterness.

To explore and utilize this human dimension of conflict, Peter L. Steinke[30] has summarized current studies in family systems applied to church conflict, leadership, and decision-making. Steinke asks questions that illumine the personal and emotional side of conflict:

- What are the emotional stakes and how high are they?

- What will happen if one group loses? What will be the effect on them? on the whole congregation?

- Is this an emergency? Or is it possible to explore at length the concerns that people are raising, thereby lowering the anxiety levels?

Family system theory interprets conflict through the dynamics of personal relationships, such as levels of anxiety, intimacy, stability, clarity, and compassion. Using this approach, you can help the members to identify the feelings they may have imported from beyond the immediate conflict, feelings that may influence, if not dominate, efforts at resolution.

In addition to appreciating different perspectives, you should anticipate specific triggering events, especially sudden changes, that may spark conflict. These may include the arrival of a new pastor, the election of new lay leaders, or the introduction of a new constituency into the membership as the community undergoes racial or economic change. These transitions may lead to conflict by disrupting relationships and introducing dissonant assumptions that bump up against each other in informal interaction. Anticipating events that trigger conflict can help a congregation prepare in advance. Also, tracing conflict to specific triggering events may make it seem less pervasive, mysterious, and unmanageable, giving participants confidence that a solution is possible.

Explosive Issues Versus Rational Process. In a time when emotionally charged conflicts—over issues such as abortion rights, sexual misconduct, and the ordination or marriage of homosexuals—have undermined the rational process of congregational and denominational meetings, Hugh F. Halverstadt offers procedures that may be helpful even if they challenge common wisdom. Halverstadt[31] distinguishes between what he calls "issues," which can be negotiated through open, democratic procedures, and "broken relationships," which must be mediated in a more carefully contained environment. To distinguish between them, he asks:

- What is the arena? Is this a structural or personal battle?

• What sorts of communication exist? Where has the conflict been discussed—in meetings at church, or in private conversations in people's homes?

• What is the scope and centrality? Who is involved? How many? Is it just one person or the whole congregation?

• Of those who care, are they more concerned with ideology or with feelings?

Based on this sort of information, Halverstadt says that leaders have a responsibility to determine when the open inquiry characteristic of democratic procedures can be effective and when the diplomacy of quiet negotiation is more appropriate. His views challenge leaders to consider carefully their approach to listening in conflict situations and their method of determining when therapeutic rather than democratic procedures are more appropriate. His approach is supported by other studies in cross-cultural communication and civic negotiation that suggest the open democratic process is not always preferable, and may be counterproductive in some situations.[32]

Halverstadt also raises questions about clergy and congregational leadership roles in times of conflict. When defining and resolving congregational conflict, he says that three functions are essential: partisan advocates, impartial moderators, and stabilizing members. He urges advocates to champion their causes, moderators to keep the conflict within the rules (fair fight), and members to maintain their commitment to the survival of the congregation. In his experience, these roles become confused when clergy try to be both partisan advocates and impartial moderators of the process. In these situations religious leaders lose their credibility for some portion of the participants, and the process is undermined. In his view, clergy can be strong advocates for particular views, as long as others (lay leaders, church officials, outside consultants) will moderate the process to keep "a fair fight."

Within congregations, issues and personalities (causes and feelings) get so easily intertwined that when a congregation is extensively and emotionally involved in conflict, outside professional assistance is often required for constructive, lasting solution. On the bright side, a positive resolution of conflict will build a congregation's self-confidence and release new energy, unity, and commitment. The challenge, as Michael and Deborah Bradshaw Jinkins remind us, is to move from impassioned situations in which emotions have "power *over*" the congregation to liberating conditions that give "power *to*" move forward into ministry, from internal conflict to constructive action.[33]

Engaging the World. Conflicts are sometimes reflected in the ways congregations engage the larger world. Engagement can take a variety of forms—from evangelistic outreach that invites others to join the congregation to advocacy for public programs and policies that reflect religious convictions. Congregations also engage the world through service to those in need and in promoting public policies consistent with their cultural values and moral theology.[34] Although with other lenses we examine the rationale of these positions, through process thinking we note the impact of this engagement both within and beyond the congregation. When challenging social order, for example, religious groups have engaged in public controversy around such causes as abolition of slavery, child labor laws, prohibition, and civil rights. Because these are controversial issues, the congregations that engage in these campaigns often develop passionately committed members through the activity of opposing an even greater enemy beyond themselves.

In the Civil Rights movement, Dr. Martin Luther King, Jr., responded to those establishment leaders who asked why his movement seemed so disruptive: "I am not afraid of the words 'crisis' and 'tension.' I deeply oppose violence, but constructive crisis and tension are necessary for growth. Innate in all life and growth is tension."[35] Never condoning hatred for a person (see sidebar 4.12), Dr. King nevertheless used the name of Eugene "Bull" Connor, Birmingham's Commissioner of Public Safety, as the living symbol of oppressive

Sidebar 4.12
FROM "LETTER FROM THE
BIRMINGHAM JAIL"

"I confess that I am not afraid of tension. I have earnestly worked and preached against violent tension, but there is a type of constructive tension that is essential for growth...

Whenever the early Christians entered a town, the people in power became disturbed and immediately sought to condemn the Christians for being 'disturbers of the peace' and 'outside agitators.' But the Christians pressed on in the conviction that they were a 'colony of heaven' called to obey God rather than man."

See Martin Luther King, Jr., *Why We Can't Wait* (New York: American Book Library, 1963).

racism, the enemy against which he mobilized countless congregations across the country. King's naming of the enemy caused then President John F. Kennedy to observe, "The Civil Rights movement owes Bull Connor as much as it owes Abraham Lincoln."[36]
The strength to challenge the culture with a religious vision for the greater good is a lesson that can be learned from the Black church tradition, as described by Robert Michael Franklin:

The liberating culture that developed within black congregations empowered ordinary people to resist dehumanization, to struggle for social change and justice, and to celebrate the presence of God in their midst, even when they sometimes felt abandoned. Every song, prayer, sermon, and gesture reflected some awareness both of hard times in this world and of the certainty that God was on their side. But black congregations were not content merely to survive the horrors of the past; they also made claims upon the nation's identity, conscience, and moral obligation to practice fairness and mercy toward its most disfranchised citizens. Their public mission was to compel America to become America for everyone. Hence the African-American religious narrative may offer clues to all sorts of congregations about how to renew hope and energize ministries that can positively transform society.[37]

Although the cause may reflect a broad vision, the particular social location of the participants will shape the process by which these conflicts are understood and undertaken. Social dimensions—such as class, race, gender, and other forms of access to (or alienation from) power—define a congregation's perspective on engaging in social action. Jack Rothman defines three approaches to organizing for community action: those who have equal access to power and information gather in an open, democratic procedure to make their own decision—*an inclusive process*; those who agree that technical information and professional guidance are required allocate their decision to a specialist—*a client process*; those who see themselves denied information or access to power seek to block the decision until they are included—*a protest process*.[38] These socially shaped perspectives of engagement in community decisions are so compelling that, as Rothman points out, each of these three perspectives sees the other two as offensive and often dangerous.

Conflict, along with planning and group building, is a natural and basic expression of the process that weaves congregational members together and sustains them over time. The unique dynamics of each congregation are more than just procedures that can be taught from a seminary classroom; they must be appropriated by experience and shared with respect.

Uniting Faith with Action

Two admonitions may help in your congregational study. First, the social dynamics of process defy any single approach or simple description. The voices of experience free us from the burden of claiming too much too soon. James D. Anderson and Ezra Earl Jones suggest three perspectives on congregational life that can help you sort out the complexity of the problems you face when interpreting congregational process.[39]

1. *You have a mess:* When people talk about "the problem we are having," they usually

mean "the mess we are experiencing." Avoid looking for *the* problem, and instead work to *unpack the mess* into a set of defined, workable problems. Look for tools that help you understand these problems.

2. *You need workable solutions:* A workable solution is the bridge between *what is happening* and what the leaders have agreed *ought to happen.* To know where to go, you need to understand both the undesired past and the hoped for future.

3. *When stuck, recycle:* Count on things going wrong, mistakes happening, and people becoming upset. Such mistakes are opportunities for increased communication, the improvement of our capacities to solve problems, and the clarification of our management gifts.

Second, you can do it yourself, with practice. Edgar Schein, for example, provides a practical procedure to help a group listen to its own deliberations by appointing one of its members as a process consultant.

At a couple of times during the meeting and at the end of the meeting the consultant will give "feedback" on observations and direct the group in an analysis of the process. For example, with information from the process consultant, the members might well agree that the chair did railroad the decision, but they feel that this was appropriate because they were short of time, and needed to get on with more important things.[40]

Schein's process consulting entails both research and intervention, analysis and action. It can be done by a third party from within the congregation or by designated members from within the group. Eventually the congregation can become its own consultant by identifying the elements of the process that frustrate and those that facilitate the power of the group to act in faith.

By looking at your congregation through the lens of process, you have been able to see sources of stability and potential for change. For windows into process thinking, we used planning for the future, building community, and dealing with conflict. These dynamics are foundational to belonging, deciding, and leading congregations. By understanding process, you can see yourself more clearly and shape the kind of congregation you believe yours should become.

NOTES

1. Penny Edgell Becker and Speed B. Leas also made substantial contributions to the development of this chapter.

2. An excellent and widely used approach to process is provided by Lee G. Bolman and Terrance E. Deal, *Reframing Organizations* (San Francisco: Jossey-Bass, 1991). Of the four frames they introduce, three are particularly relevant for this discussion of process: the *structural frame* looks primarily at the formal or official lines of authority and communication; the *human relations frame* emphasizes the relationships and emotional bonds of the organization; and the *political frame* focuses on priorities of power and clusters of interests. For similar divisions in organizational theory, see George W. Litwin and Robert A. Stringer, *Motivation and Organizational Climate* (Boston: Harvard, 1968); James D. Anderson and Ezra Earl Jones, *The Management of Ministry* (San Francisco: Harper & Row, 1978); Marlene Wilson, *How to Mobilize Church Volunteers* (Minneapolis: Augsburg Publishing House, 1983); and Tex Sample, *U.S. Lifestyles and Mainline Churches* (Louisville: Westminster/John Knox, 1990). Based on their broad acceptance, we make reference to these three frames throughout the discussion of process.

3. Samuel G. Freedman, *Upon This Rock: The Miracles of a Black Church* (New York: HarperCollins, 1993), 91-93.

4. For a more extended discussion of process in settled and unsettled times, see Ann Swidler, "Culture in Action: Symbols and Strategies," *American Sociological Review* 51 (1986): 273-86.

5. These two concepts, task and role, have been the cornerstones of the work of Lyle E. Schaller, one of the best known consultants in congregational dynamics for three decades. Since his early writing, for example, *Parish Planning: How to Get Things Done in Your Church* (Nashville: Abingdon, 1971), Schaller has shown the importance of helping church leaders to identify specific tasks and accept the responsibilities to see that the work is done.

6. For an extensive discussion, see Penny Edgell Becker, *"The Way We Do Things Here": Culture and Conflict in Local Congregations* (Cambridge: Cambridge University Press, 1997). Chapters 1 and 8 provide an overview, while chapters 3-6 cover examples of congregations with different core tasks or mission.

7. Kennon L. Callahan, *Twelve Keys to an Effective Church* (San Francisco: Harper & Row, 1983), has been particularly helpful in moving churches to action by identifying priority tasks.

8. Edgar H. Schein, *Process Consultation: Its Role in Organization Development* (Reading, Pa.: Addison-Wesley, 1969), 11. The same kind of complexity inspired the widely used Managerial Grid of Concern for People and Concern for Production developed by Robert R. Blake and Jane Srygley Mouton, in *Building a Dynamic Organization Through Grid Organization Development* (Reading, Pa.: Addison-Wesley, 1969).

9. For further discussion of the sources of power that might be evident in congregations as social organizations, see Amitai Etzioni, *A Comparative Analysis of Complex Organizations* (New York: Free Press, 1961), who theorized that power could be based on coercion (rarely in voluntary organizations), remuneration (positive rewards of all sorts), or, more likely, community norms such as prestige, esteem, and solidarity. John French and Bertram Raven expand the options to five bases for power: reward, coercion, legitimation, referent (identification), and expertise (John R. P. French, Jr. and Bertram Raven, "The Bases of Social Power," in *Group Dynamics*, 3rd ed., ed. Dorwin Cartwright and Alvin Zander [New York: Harper & Row, 1968], 259-69), while Jeffrey Pfeffer distinguishes between personal sources of power (sensitivity, popularity, and the like) and structural sources that come from both legitimate authority and being in a strategic location for communication and brokering (*Managing with Power: Politics and Influence in Organizations* [Boston: Harvard Business School Press, 1992]).

10. Richard E. Rusbuldt, Richard K. Gladden, and Norman M. Green, Jr., *Local Church Planning Manual* (Valley Forge, Pa.: Judson Press, 1977), 235-39.

11. Celia Allison Hahn, *Growing in Authority; Relinquishing Control* (Bethesda, Md.: Alban Institute, 1994). For an expanded and more intentionally theological discussion of leadership and authority, see the final chapter. Also see Jackson W. Carroll, *As One with Authority: Reflective Leadership in Ministry* (Louisville: Westminster/John Knox, 1991).

12. Gordon L. Lippit, *Organizational Renewal* (New York: Appleton Century-Crofts, 1969), 49.

13. Philip Anderson, *Church Meetings that Matter* (Philadelphia: United Church Press, 1965), 50-52.

14. *The Ministry of Volunteers: A Guidebook for Churches* (St. Louis: Office of Church Life and Leadership, United Church of Christ, 1979).

15. For a basic introduction, see David Keirsey and Marilyn Bates, *Please Understand Me: Character and Temperament Types* (Del Mar, Calif.: Prometheus Nemesis Books, 1978); and Isabel Briggs Myers and Peter B. Myers, *Gifts Differing* (Palo Alto, Calif.: Consulting Psychologists Press, 1980). For application to education, see Gordon Lawrence, *People Types and Tiger Stripes* (Gainesville, Fla.: Center for Applications of Psychological Type, Inc., 1979). And for application in religious settings, see Chester P. Michael and Marie C. Norrisey, *Prayer and Temperament* (Charlottesville, Va.: The Open Door, 1984).

16. Lloyd Edwards, *How We Belong, Fight, and Pray: The MBTI as a Key to Congregational Dynamics* (Washington, D.C.: Alban Institute, 1993). In addition to his excellent but brief work, Edwards includes a bibliography of selected publications for further study.

17. See Carl S. Dudley, *Making the Small Church Effective* (Nashville: Abingdon Press, 1978); see also publications by Steve Burt, Anthony Pappas, David Ray, Lyle Schaller, and Douglas A. Walrath.

18. Arlin J. Rothauge, *Sizing Up the Congregation for New Member Ministry* (New York: The Episcopal Church Center, 1983). Also see Roy Oswald, *How to Minister Effectively in Family, Pastoral, Program and Corporate Size Churches* (Washington, D.C.: Alban Institute, 1991).

19. Lyle E. Schaller, *Looking in a Mirror* (Nashville: Abingdon, 1985).

20. Martin F. Saarinen, *The Life Cycle of a Congregation* (Washington, D.C.: Alban Institute, 1986).

21. Robert Dale, *To Dream Again* (Nashville: Broadman, 1981).

22. For basic work, see Georg Simmel, *Conflict: The Web of Group Affiliations*, trans. Kurt H. Wolff (Glencoe, Ill.: Free Press, 1955). For research and application of his concepts, see Lewis Coser, *The Functions of Social Conflict* (Glencoe, Ill.: Free Press, 1964).

23. Speed B. Leas and George Parsons, *Understanding Your Congregation as a System* (Washington, D.C.: Alban Institute, 1993).

24. Marie M. Fortune, *Is Nothing Sacred?* (San Francisco: HarperSanFrancisco, 1992), 85.

25. For increasing sensitivity, see Mary Field Belenky, et al., *Women's Ways of Knowing: The Development of Self, Voice and Mind* (New York: Basic Books, 1986); and Thomas Kochman, *Black and White Styles in Conflict* (Chicago: University of Chicago Press, 1981).

26. R. Stephen Warner, "Mirror for American Protestants: Mendocino Presbyterian Church in the Sixties and Seventies," in *The Mainstream Protestant "Decline": The Presbyterian Pattern*, ed. Milton J. Coalter, John M. Mulder, and Louis B. Weeks (Louisville: Westminster/John Knox, 1990), 215.

27. Speed Leas, *Moving Your Church Through Conflict* (Washington, D.C.: Alban Institute, 1985), offers concepts helpful for understanding the social dynamics of congregational process.

28. See Becker, *"The Way We Do Things Here."* Also see Penny Edgell Becker, "Straining the Tie that Binds: Congregational Conflict in the 1980s," *Review of Religious Research* 34, no. 3 (1993) 193-209.

29. Penny Edgell Becker, "Congregational Models and Con-

flict," in *Sacred Companies,* ed. Jay Demerath, Peter Dobkin Hall, Terry Schmitt, and Rhys Williams (New York: Oxford University Press, 1997).

30. In *How Your Church Family Works: Understanding Congregations as Emotional Systems* (Washington, D.C.: Alban Institute, 1993), Peter L. Steinke explains and applies the pioneering contributions of Edwin H. Friedman, *Generation to Generation: Family Process in Church and Synagogue* (New York: Gilford Press, 1985).

31. Hugh F. Halverstadt, *Managing Church Conflict* (Louisville: Westminster/John Knox, 1991).

32. See, for example, David W. Augsburger, *Conflict Mediation Across Cultures: Pathways and Patterns* (Louisville: Westminster/John Knox, 1992); and Robert Fisher and William Ury, *Getting to YES: Negotiating Agreement Without Giving In* (Boston: Houghton Mifflin, 1981).

33. For a willingness to address creatively the sensitive subject of power in the church, see Michael and Deborah Bradshaw Jinkins, *Power and Change in Parish Ministry* (Washington, D.C.: Alban Institute, 1991).

34. For four models of engagement, see David A. Roozen, William McKinney, and Jackson W. Carroll, *Varieties of Religious Preference* (New York: Pilgrim Press, 1984). For comparison of constructive and destructive conflict in congregations in changing communities, see Nancy Tatom Ammerman, *Congregation and Community* (New Brunswick, N.J.: Rutgers University Press, 1997), 334-35, 344-45.

35. Quoted from John Anstro, *Martin Luther King, Jr.: The Making of a Mind* (Maryknoll, N.Y.: Orbis Books, 1982), 241. For "Letter from the Birmingham Jail," see Martin Luther King, Jr., *Why We Can't Wait* (New York: American Book Library, 1963).

36. *Martin Luther King, Jr.: A Documentary,* ed. Flip Shuke (New York: W. W. Norton & Co., 1976), 71.

37. Robert Michael Franklin, "The Safest Place on Earth: The Culture of Black Congregations," *American Congregations,* vol. 2, *New Perspectives in the Study of Congregations,* ed. James P. Wind and James W. Lewis (Chicago: University of Chicago Press, 1994).

38. Jack Rothman, "Three Models of Community Organization Practice," in *Strategies for Community Organization* (Itasca, Ill.: Peacock Publishers, 1979), 25-44.

39. Anderson and Jones, *The Management of Ministry.*

40. Schein, *Process Consultation,* 55.

APPENDIX 4.1

Post Meeting Reaction Form

From Philip Anderson, *Church Meetings that Matter* (Philadelphia: United Church Press, 1965), 50-52.

This is a checklist to help you evaluate your meeting and to increase sensitivity to some of the relationships in the life of the Christian community of faith. Check the number on the rating scale that corresponds with your evaluation of the meeting in each of the following categories. For example, if you feel that responsible participation was lacking, check 1; if you feel that responsible participation was present, check 7; if you feel that the responsible participation of the group was somewhere in between, check an appropriate number on the scale.

A. RESPONSIBLE PARTICIPATION 1 2 3 4 5 6 7 **A. RESPONSIBLE PARTICIPATION**

was lacking. We served our own needs. We watched from outside the group. We were "grinding our own axes."

was present. We were sensitive to the needs of the group. Everyone was "on the inside" participating.

B. LEADERSHIP 1 2 3 4 5 6 7 **B. LEADERSHIP**

was dominated by one person.

was shared among the members according to their abilities and insights.

C. COMMUNICATION OF IDEAS 1 2 3 4 5 6 7 **C. COMMUNICATION OF IDEAS**

was poor; we did not listen. We did not understand. Ideas were ignored. vigorously presented and acknowledged.

was good. We listened and understood one another's ideas. Ideas were

D. COMMUNICATION OF FEELINGS 1 2 3 4 5 6 7 **D. COMMUNICATION OF FEELINGS**

was poor. We did not listen and did not understand feelings. No one cared about feelings.

was good. We listened and unerstood and recognized feelings. Feelings were shared and accepted.

E. AUTHENTICITY 1 2 3 4 5 6 7 **E. AUTHENTICITY**

was missing. We were wearing masks. We were being phony and acting parts. We were hiding our real selves.

was present. We were revealing our honest selves. We were engaged in authentic self-revelation.

F. ACCEPTANCE OF PERSONS 1 2 3 4 5 6 7 **F. ACCEPTANCE OF PERSONS**

was missing. Persons were rejected, ignored, or criticized.

was an active part of our give-and-take. We "received one another in Christ," recognizing and respecting the uniqueness of each person.

G. FREEDOM OF PERSONS 1 2 3 4 5 6 7 **G. FREEDOM OF PERSONS**

was stifled. Conformity was explicitly or implicitly fostered. Persons were not free to express their individuality. They were manipulated.

was enhanced and encouraged. The creativity and indivdiuality of persons was respected

H. CLIMATE OF RELATIONSHIP 1 2 3 4 5 6 7 **H. CLIMATE OF RELATIONSHIP**

was one of hostility or suspicion or politeness or fear or anxiety or superficiality.

was one of mutual trust in which evidence of love for one another was apparent. The atmosphere was friendly and relaxed.

I. PRODUCTIVITY 1 2 3 4 5 6 7 **I. PRODUCTIVITY**

was low. We were proud, and happy, just coasting along. Our meeting was irrelevant; there was no apparent agreement.

was high. We were digging hard and were earnestly at work on a task. We created and achieved something.

APPENDIX 4.2

Personal Preferences

From "Volunteers and Volunteer Ministries," a booklet from *The Ministry of Volunteers: A Guidebook for Churches,* copyright 1979 the Office of Church Life and Leadership, United Church of Christ.

The following chart asks you to express your preferences in relation to two choices. You are asked to mark on the line (a continuum) to indicate which of the two choices is your preference and how strong that preference is.

Example: When asked to become a volunteer in the church or community, I prefer

To be a leader _____ _X_ to be a follower

This person has a relatively strong preference for being a follower and, therefore, probably would prefer being a member of a committee rather and the chairperson of the committee.

If you are attracted to both choices equally, then mark the line in the middle. Please note that not all choices are opposites. You are asked to place only one mark on each line.

When asked to become a volunteer in the church or community I prefer:

to be a leader	_____	_____	to be a follower
simple, routine tasks	_____	_____	challenging, new projects
an informal fellowship	_____	_____	a task group with a clear assignment
to do whatever is needed	_____	_____	to do a job that is important and respected
to work with people I know well	_____	_____	an opportunity meet and get to know new people
much responsibility	_____	_____	little responsibility
to be known as skillful and intelligent	_____	_____	to be known as friendly and caring
to be liked by others	_____	_____	to achieve something significant
a job that doesn't require much preparation	_____	_____	a job I can prepare for by reading and doing homework
to see concrete results	_____	_____	to maintain smooth and harmonious relationships
to work on a small task or problem	_____	_____	to tackle large problems facing the community
a job where I can witness to my faith	_____	_____	a job that will be appreciated by my closest friends
a job that will strengthen the church	_____	_____	a job that will make my community a better place for the poor and disadvantaged
to know what is expected of me	_____	_____	to try new things and redesign the job to fit me

Chapter 5
Resources

WILLIAM MCKINNEY
WITH ANTHONY T. RUGER, DIANE
COHEN, AND ROBERT JEAGER

This chapter treats a congregation as a collection of elements drawn out of a wider social and religious context that together have the capacity or the potential to accomplish social and religious goals. This frame for understanding congregations has as its focus all the raw materials of congregational life—human, economic and capital, spiritual, and reputational. Resources are sometimes hard and countable (money, people, staff, and buildings), but they are also sometimes soft and relational (shared experiences of coming through difficult times, connections to other institutions, and the strength of members' commitment to the congregation). These soft social resources may be difficult for the outsider to see, but they are no less real than the money in the bank.[1]

Focusing on resources is misleading when we yield to the temptation to pay attention only to that which is easily measurable. Often we hear large or wealthy or prestigious congregations referred to as "resource-rich" and small or less prestigious congregations as "resource-poor." Such judgments fail to distinguish, however, between *resources* and *capacities*. For example, a large congregation may have more access to money, people, staff, and influence than a small congregation, but it may lack the ability of the smaller congregation to mobilize those resources toward its ends. To use a resource frame well, then, you will want to be sensitive to the congregational culture and process that give resources their meaning and put them to work, as well as to the wider ecological setting from which most resources come. Your study of resources should take place alongside examination of the congregation from other perspectives.

Melvin Williams provides a powerful example of our distinction between resources and capacities in his anthropological study of Zion, a Black Pentecostal congregation in Pittsburgh. Despite meager resources, he says:

> As long as they serve the church physically and financially (often public assistance is a source of their giving), they have a place in the design, a node in the social network. This place gives meaning, expectation and reward to the lives of those whom mainstream ideals seldom penetrate unless reinforced through the Zion subculture.[2]

Williams's study captures several important insights about the ways raw materials brought into the congregation from outside (money, life experiences of members, and social status) become sources of strength for the congregation. In Zion's case, members are poor and struggling. Its measurable resources are very limited. Williams points out, however, that the congregation's culture is sufficiently strong to transform limited resources into considerable capacity.

Sidebar 5.1
MONEY, BUILDINGS, AND IDENTITY AT
FIRST CHURCH, WINDSOR

In truth, dry rot and demographic trends convinced people of the need to raise money. The enthusiasms of Van [the church's senior minister], Henry and Janet Filer only served to promote the plan. Van actually had little interest in the project initially. He never wanted to be remembered as curator of a living museum along Palisado Avenue, and he had no desire to raise money for the sake of historic preservation. In fact, he would say as much out loud. Once, during a meeting with the property committee, when the discussion about church architecture started to sound like a high-toned missive, he fired off his own blunt opinion: "We're a church, dammit, not a historical society."

But not everyone agreed. In fact, some people thought Van deserved the blame for letting their fine old buildings decay. Just two years before, an analysis by engineers and architects had detected so much neglect at the church's two-hundred-year-old meetinghouse and parsonage that the congregation felt forced to call a special committee to assess the needs.

For years, surface inspections on Sunday mornings must have been sufficient to satisfy the property committee, known formally as the Prudential Board. Their reports regularly gave the buildings and grounds passing marks. Until the professional engineer's tour, the Prudential Board had somehow failed to see lead paint peelings in the children's playgrounds, dim lighting in hallways, distressed stairways, strangely pocked ground around grave sites and rickety foundations. Occasionally, someone commented on bits of brittle shingle from Van's roof found scattered around the sidewalks on Sunday mornings, but no one recognized that Van's own dining room had become uninhabitable—termed "hazardous" in the professional report. Rotting joists and decayed beams lay beneath the floor. It should not have taken a trained engineer to discover a foundation wall caved in underneath the sanctuary. Evidence that the leaching field for raw sewage had backed up into the church's 360-year-old cemetery was unthinkable, but there it was, as clear as daylight on Easter morning—an explosive matter, for sure, should certain families' ancestors come washing up.

With fresh demographic figures in hand, a new property committee sounded a note of prophecy. Their reports would begin, "In light of the coming millennium ... ," and go on to remark about the need to "hold market share" of Windsor's churchgoers, and predict a "potential downsizing of pledges." They needed money to repair the property, more members to raise money, more money to meet the needs of new members. Suddenly, everybody was feverish about growth. A case of millennial fever struck in Windsor, and the congregation startled awake, seeing its future suddenly in doubt.

And so it was that the pressure of prudent capitalization, not God, finally caused Van to accept the one job he had avoided throughout his ministry. The time had come, at last, for a major fund drive, and though Van was not pleased by the thought, he offered to work alongside Henry Holcombe and Janet Filer, as a good sport, to wheedle and cajole for the cause.

A second example of careful attention to congregational resources is the book *Congregation* by journalist Gary Dorsey. Dorsey spent more than a year with a United Church of Christ congregation (First Church of Christ) in Windsor, Connecticut, and his book is an account of his experience and observations. Note in sidebar 5.1 his account of the congregation's ambivalence about money and buildings, yet those very material sides of existence evoked their sense of history, loyalty, mission, and identity. By carefully examining first a capital campaign to renovate the church's aging building and, later, a dispute over a church's outreach funding, Dorsey uses questions about resources as a window on the life of the congregation itself. Later in this chapter we will return several times to Dorsey's First Church for illustrative material.

Whether congregations are large or small, rich or poor, they cannot be fully understood without a look at the materials with which they do their work and the commitments and expectations that turn those raw materials into resources. Congregations are certainly more than the sums of their parts, but the unique parts from which each congregation fashions its presence and work in the world deserve your attention.

Membership Resources

A simple song popular in many Christian churches makes both a sociological and a theological point:

> I am the church.
> You are the church.
> We are the church together.[3]

Perhaps more in North America than in other parts of the world, individuals in congregations have the strong sense that they *are* the church. This sense is affirmed more in some traditions than others, but even in religious bodies where connections are officially prescribed, there is resistance to "external" authority imposing its will on local communities of faithful people.[4] Congregations often want to tailor their own services and ministries to the particular people who make up the membership. In turn, those particular people provide the resources of time, energy, money, and skill that will make any given effort possible. Understanding the resources of a congregation begins with an inventory of the resources its members supply—both by who they are and by their more tangible assets—and that assessment often begins with a demographic profile.

When we describe the age, gender, marital status, ethnicity, or socioeconomic characteristics of a congregation, we are compiling a demographic picture of the congregation. Such a picture can help us understand the congregation's culture and often throws light on its relationship to the ecological context. Who your members are is partly a function of who is available in your community to become members. Other frames of analysis also may begin with a demographic profile, but for our purposes, the characteristics of the members are being studied for what they can tell us about the skill, energy, connections, and money individuals may have at their disposal.

We are assessing what resources are available for nurturing and sustaining the congregation's tradition, faith, and vision.

Who we are as individuals and in the aggregate as faith communities is a complex combination of characteristics and the meanings attributed to them—some characteristics inherited at birth and some gained through the choices we have made. Consider, for example: a thirty-six-year-old, single woman, the daughter of Italian immigrants, with a college education and a middle-management job in an insurance company. These characteristics by no means exhaust her identity, but they constitute important ingredients of the meanings she and others attribute to her. By recognizing these characteristics, you honor what she brings and become sensitive to what she may expect in your congregational life. The same is true for congregations, whose demographic composition tells us a good deal about their inheritance and their choices. Many of those characteristics, in turn, have consequences for what the congregation is able to do.

Gathering Information About Resources

With a questionnaire, you can quickly and simply gather demographic information that is easily summarized (although throughout this book we are fairly cautious in recommending questionnaire surveys). Often, the decision to conduct a congregational study is followed too quickly by constructing a list of questions or searching for a ready-made survey instrument. Questionnaires are, however, helpful in studying membership and commitment resources. They are especially helpful when comparative data are available on similar or neighboring congregations. As you begin, think about what sorts of information on individual characteristics might be useful in your planning and decision making. Age may tell you something about resources of experience and energy, for instance; employment status may tell you about available time; and average commutes may tell you whether people can easily attend meetings. In each case, you will be interested both in averages and in the distribution. You want to know both what is "typical" and just what the range of difference is in your congregation.

The chapter on methods contains a detailed list of items you might want to ask, along with hints about how to construct a questionnaire. Also, included in appendix A is the Parish Profile Inventory developed by Hartford Seminary's Center for Social and Religious Research.[5] This instrument has been used in hundreds of congregations in the United States and Canada and comparative data are available from the center. As always, remember that you should limit your questionnaire items to those that will be most useful to you, rather than asking every possible question because other congregations have asked it. You may also need to add items. For distinguishing cultural traditions, for instance, you might want to know what proportion of your congregation is native-born African American and what proportion is from the West Indies or other Caribbean islands. Just as congregations benefit from more detailed ancestry or ethnic data, you might want to know members' previous denominational affiliation.

From a resource perspective and for planning purposes, information on the socioeconomic status of members can be particularly helpful. You will almost certainly want to include questions about social class. We are referring, of course, to indicators of people's education, occupational status, and income, all of which have strong influences on religious participation. As indicators of social class, they affect people's choice of a congregation, their preferences for worship styles, their theological and pedagogical assumptions, and even their beliefs about the congregation's mission in the world. In addition, the skills people have gained through education are resources a congregation can utilize; their occupations place them in networks that may be useful for the congregation's work in the community; and of course, their income levels determine how possible it is for them to be generous in providing financial resources to the congregation. Coupling income data with age and occupational data may also tell a congregation something

about its likely future resources. Knowing, for example, that a high proportion of the congregation's annual income comes from members on fixed income or approaching retirement can be a spur to initiate planned giving programs and to restructuring stewardship programming to focus on younger supporters.

Survey questionnaires are a cost-effective and nonintrusive way of accumulating this sort of demographic and socioeconomic data on members. For a smaller congregation, much of the same data can be assembled by a small task force of knowledgeable people who simply work through the congregation's rolls. While some data may be estimated, this method can be remarkably accurate. What such a task force cannot do, however, is to assemble data on individuals' attitudes and commitments.

When summarizing the distribution of demographic characteristics, it is usually most helpful to convert findings into percentages. This will not only indicate the proportion of members in each category (thus showing the homogeneity/heterogeneity of the congregation) but will also reveal the typical or modal member. Constructing an age-sex pyramid[6] is another simple and revealing way of portraying the age and gender composition of the congregation. Tables and simple graphics can enable you to present a picture of your congregation's members that will help everyone to see the wide range of potential they represent.

Commitment Resources

Member resources remain *potential* resources until they are mobilized by people's willingness to use them on behalf of the congregation and its work in the world. The spark that makes that work possible is commitment. What does it mean to be a committed member of a congregation? of your congregation? Commitment is difficult to measure, but you can see the evidence in numerous activities and behaviors.

Worship attendance and member giving are widely used as indicators of congregational commitment because attending services of

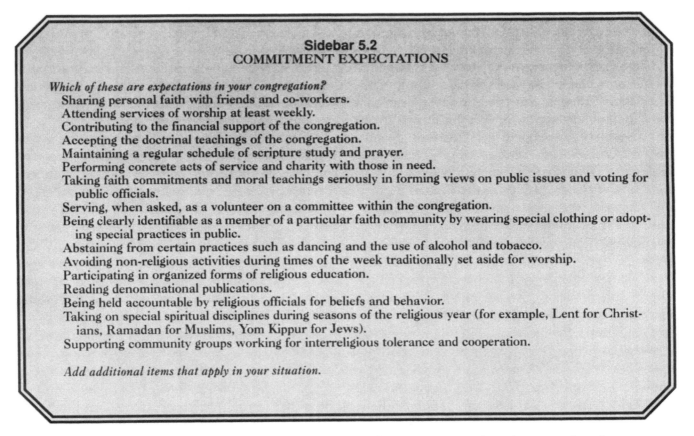

Sidebar 5.2
COMMITMENT EXPECTATIONS

Which of these are expectations in your congregation?
Sharing personal faith with friends and co-workers.
Attending services of worship at least weekly.
Contributing to the financial support of the congregation.
Accepting the doctrinal teachings of the congregation.
Maintaining a regular schedule of scripture study and prayer.
Performing concrete acts of service and charity with those in need.
Taking faith commitments and moral teachings seriously in forming views on public issues and voting for public officials.
Serving, when asked, as a volunteer on a committee within the congregation.
Being clearly identifiable as a member of a particular faith community by wearing special clothing or adopting special practices in public.
Abstaining from certain practices such as dancing and the use of alcohol and tobacco.
Avoiding non-religious activities during times of the week traditionally set aside for worship.
Participating in organized forms of religious education.
Reading denominational publications.
Being held accountable by religious officials for beliefs and behavior.
Taking on special spiritual disciplines during seasons of the religious year (for example, Lent for Christians, Ramadan for Muslims, Yom Kippur for Jews).
Supporting community groups working for interreligious tolerance and cooperation.

Add additional items that apply in your situation.

worship and helping to support the congregation financially are expectations in most religious traditions and are relatively easy to measure. Without the basic materials of people in the pews and dollars in the bank, congregations would be hard-pressed even to survive.

These measures are also, however, incomplete and fail to recognize that member expectations vary across faith and denominational traditions and among congregations within the same denomination. For example, some traditions expect that a member in good standing will adhere to church doctrines and teachings on fundamental moral behavior. In other traditions, the individual, and the individual alone, is the final authority on matters of faith and morals. In some traditions family rituals and participation in festivals or communal celebration of the high holy days are of equal or greater importance than weekly community worship. Serving the poor and participating in public life is a religious duty that receives high priority in some congregations, less in others. Before you can ask *how much* commitment is present in your congregation, you need to assess the com-

mitment *expectations* in your local congregation.

One way to approach this task is to assemble a focus group (see the methods chapter for hints on how to do this). Using a list like the one in sidebar 5.2, invite members to indicate what sort of expectations your congregation ought to have of its members. Ask each participant to list in order of priority the ten most important expectations. Then, on newsprint, list each item and record the rank order given by each member. Remember that some of these activities will seem foreign to many congregations. Practices that are central for members of some faith communities (sharing faith for most evangelicals, advocating interreligious tolerance for Unitarian Universalists and Jews, and adopting distinctive forms of dress for Amish and some Mennonites) will be strongly resisted in others. The question for discussion is, What does *your* congregation expect of its members?

Once you have a sense of your congregation's key expectations, you may want to include questions about those commitments on a survey questionnaire. For each activity,

TABLE 5.1

Comparison of Carmel and Berean Churches

Activity	Percent Highly Involved		Percent Not Involved*	
	Carmel	Berean	Carmel	Berean
Private prayer and meditation	76	83	15	12
Worship services (or liturgies)	65	86	1	5
Sunday school or Bible study groups	14	54	76	38
Church fellowship activities	5	27	74	53
Church building upkeep	3	14	94	73
Seeking converts and new members	2	16	93	76
Choirs or other music groups	18	13	78	71
Community/social ministries	8	13	76	78
Civic, school, professional or other community groups	34	21	33	61

*Highly involved = daily or weekly participation; not involved = never or a few times per year. Remaining members (not shown) were involved at least monthly, but less than weekly.

you can ask whether and how often the person participates, whether they have a leadership role, and the like. For each matter of doctrinal or moral commitment, you might ask whether the person agrees or disagrees and how strongly. Summarizing the responses to these questions can provide a valuable picture of the degree and range of commitment present in the congregation. Sorting out the responses based on age, length of membership, gender, and other such factors can further help you to see where investment in the congregation is deep and where it is lagging.

In her study of congregations in changing communities, Nancy Ammerman made use of a survey questionnaire that asked members about participation in a variety of church and community activities. Table 5.1 shows results for two of her congregations.[7] Carmel United Methodist Church is a large congregation located in the growing northern suburbs of Indianapolis, Indiana. Berean Seventh-Day Adventist Church is a mostly African American congregation in South Central Los Angeles, California. What you can see in the table are very different participation patterns. Although members of both churches participate regularly in acts of prayer and public worship, in other ways Berean members are much more active in congregational life, especially Sunday school, Bible study, and church fellowship activities. Berean members are also more likely to participate in evangelism efforts. Carmel members, on the other hand, more often mention involvements in civic, political, professional, and other community groups.

Whether these findings are positive or negative for Berean or Carmel depends on each congregation's understanding of its expectations of members. Some congregations would be surprised to find—as with Carmel—93 percent of their members were not involved in seeking converts or new members. Others would marvel at the high participation of Carmel's members in civic and professional activities. Similarly, some would celebrate Berean's high levels of religious education activity, but others would wonder why so few members of either congregation say they are active in community ministries.

Membership Change over Time

Your study of your congregation's commitment resources would not be complete without attention to the basic question of membership growth and decline. The most basic level of commitment, after all, is the decision to join and to remain a member. To undertake such an assessment will require that you locate and organize whatever membership records you have. Congregations and denominations vary in the amount of attention they give to statistics and membership records. Even in traditions where record keeping is of low priority, however, the creative leader can often recreate a statistical record of trends over

time. Harry S. Stout and Catherine Brekus have illustrated just how much one can learn by using old records. In their study of Center Church in New Haven, Connecticut, family connections in the congregation are traced back to 1639![8]

To illustrate the usefulness of official records in congregational studies, we turn to First Church of Christ in Windsor, Connecticut, the subject of Dorsey's book *Congregation*. Like most older congregations, First Church takes record keeping seriously. Annual reports to the congregation from its ministers, clerk, and other officers have been prepared with care and are maintained in the church's library. All of the data reported here are publicly available to First Church members. Most are also reported each year to the United Church of Christ, with which First Church is affiliated.

In figure 5.1, we trace the membership of First Church by five-year intervals from 1950 to 1985 and annually from 1986 to 1994. The figure also shows average church attendance for years in which this was collected and reported.[9] We see in the figure that membership in First Church has grown fairly steadily over the years,

Figure 5.1 Membership and Attendance Trends
First Church, Windsor

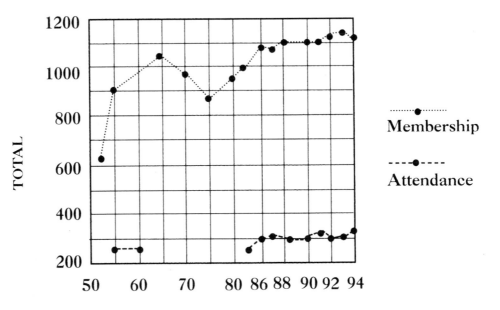

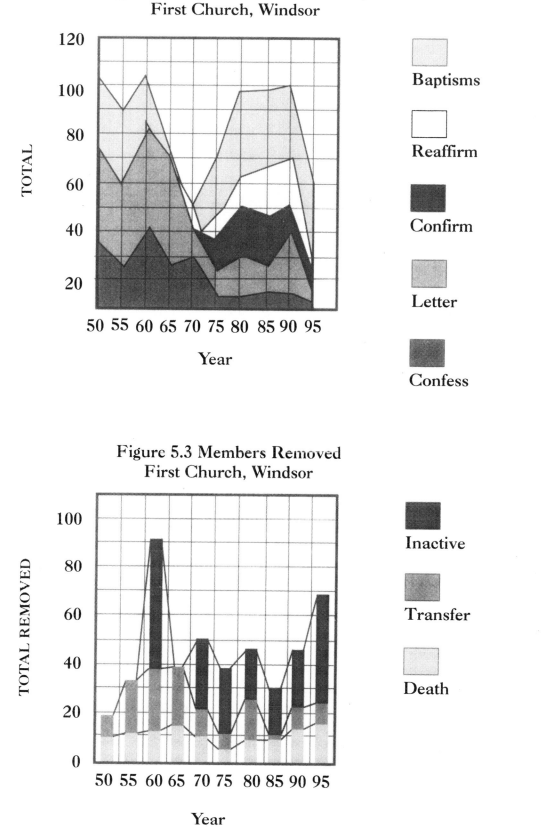

Figure 5.2 Additions to Membership
First Church, Windsor

Figure 5.3 Members Removed
First Church, Windsor

TABLE 5.2

Membership Change in First Church, Windsor: 1975–1995

	1975–1985	1986–1995	Change
Average Members Added Per Year			
Baptisms	21	26	+5
Transfers In	12	10	-2
Confession	23	18	-5
Average Members Removed Per Year			
Deaths	11	11	0
Transfers Out	17	21	+4
Dropouts	25	33	+8
Ratio: baptisms to deaths	1.95	2.38	+.43
Ratio of transfers in to transfers out	.69	.50	-.19
Ratio of additions by confession to dropouts	.94	.55	-.39

reaching over one thousand members in 1965, dipping a bit in the 1970s, and again reaching one thousand in the 1980s. The church continued to grow slowly through the 1980s and 1990s. Worship attendance has increased from under 250 in the mid-eighties to 300-plus by the mid-nineties. On a typical Sunday, 29 percent of the members attend services. This graph provides, then, a picture of how First Church's membership resources (both absolute numbers and the number actively participating in worship) have changed over time.

It does not, however, tell us where those members have come from or where those who left have gone. In a formal sense people come into congregations in three ways, and they leave in three ways.[10] They may be born into it, they transfer in from another congregation, or they may enter a congregation from the ranks of the unaffiliated. They leave because they die, they transfer to another congregation, or they drop out into the ranks of the unaffiliated.

In reality, the picture is somewhat more complex. Religious traditions have very different understandings of membership or affiliation. For example, Islam teaches that all human beings are born Muslim; one does not "convert" to Islam but "returns" to the Islamic faith of his or her birth. In most Christian traditions one becomes a Christian at baptism but often is not considered a church member until he or she is confirmed. Traditionally, a Catholic remains a member of a parish until he or she moves to a new parish or is removed from the parish rolls.

Having determined your own most useful definitions of membership, you can benefit from looking at ways people enter and leave. Figures 5.2 and 5.3[11] plot additions and losses at First Church. In the first we see the number of people who became part of the congregation's life each year through baptism, reaffirmation of faith, confirmation, letter of transfer from another congregation of the United Church of Christ or another denomination, and confession of faith.[12] Baptisms have fluctuated a great deal over time, but currently number about twenty per year. Confirmations, recorded separately only since the early seventies, were higher through the 1970s than in the 1980s and 1990s. Transfer additions have decreased over time.

The number of members removed per year was fairly high in the early sixties, then declined to around forty in the seventies and eighties, and has risen to about sixty per year more recently. In the nineties, First Church has been receiving fewer new members per year than in earlier periods. The number of deaths per year has been quite stable over time. By contrast, the number of transfers to other congregations and of members moved to the inactive list or dropped has fluctuated a great deal.

In table 5.2, we look at the same information in a different way. We have averaged the total number of additions and removals per year for two periods: 1975-1985 and 1986-1995. The table shows us several things about the changing shape of First Church's membership:

- Baptisms are up an average of five people per year, and new members received by confession of faith are down. Members received by transfer are also down, though by a smaller proportion. In recent years First Church's growth has come more from within than from the outside.

- The church's ratio of baptisms to deaths is improving. In the earlier decade the church reported 1.9 baptisms for each death; in the later period there were 2.4 baptisms for each death.

- The ratio of transfers in to transfers out is not improving: in the earlier period the church received sixty-nine members from other congregations for each one hundred it lost, but in more recent years it received fifty for each hundred lost.

- Similarly, the church loses a higher proportion of its members to inactivity than it gains by confession of faith: ninety-four confessions per one hundred dropouts in the earlier decade, fifty-five per one hundred dropouts in the past decade.

Such statistical analysis does not mandate specific programs, but it can help you identify the source of potential problems. For a con-gregation to grow over time, its additions to membership must exceed its removals from membership. In other words, the congregation's births, additions by transfer, and additions by confession must be larger than its removals due to deaths, transfers, and inactivity. A congregation may have relatively little control over deaths and births. In highly transient communities, congregations must aggressively seek replacements for the members they are losing, and special communities, such as vacation areas or college towns, create unique problems for congregations that want to grow. For most congregations, including First Church, the ratio of new members by confession or reaffirmation of faith to dropouts is the key indicator of long-term growth prospects.

More than simply plotting charts and graphs, you need to listen carefully to the insights and energy of members as they comment on these changes over time. "Oh, that was the year of the dreadful interim minister who couldn't preach. Nobody joined that year." "In 1974 the deacons reviewed the rolls and dropped off all the dead-wood." "Remember the Sunday the entire Miller family got baptized? That's why the number of baptisms looks so high in 1993." You will also benefit by inviting members to think about what these membership numbers say about the congregation's future needs and its ability to accomplish its goals. Membership numbers are important indicators of the raw material with which a congregation can work, but they have their real meaning only within the context of that congregation's sense of identity and mission.

Financial Resources

As spiritual organizations, North American religious groups are often ambivalent about money. Although giving money is a primary index of commitment, many congregations have generally avoided disciplined treatment of financial resources. This chapter tries to meet this void with careful procedures that you can employ to organize and interpret the foundational resource of wealth in your congregation.

One of your first tasks in assessing the financial resources of your congregation will be to think about the basic categories and format that will guide your work. One of the reasons so little is known about congregational finance is that local communities of faith use hundreds of different methods to keep their books. Nonreligious institutions usually must use standardized, generally accepted accounting methods and reports, especially when communicating with the government or the investing and donating public. Congregations, however, are exempt from such regulations and use reporting formats as varied as the congregations themselves. Both for your work in studying the congregation's resources and for the long-term good of the congregation itself, it will be to your advantage to seek high standards in accounting and clarity in reporting.

Even struggling congregations may discover that keeping track of details and producing reports can be accomplished by the use of microcomputer-based spreadsheets. Not just professionals but volunteers in your congregation can enter your financial information into a spreadsheet that provides a flexible and efficient way to organize your analysis and provide you with a ready tool for producing graphic reports.

Looking at Budgets

Keeping track of money in an organized way is good stewardship all of the time, but it also helps when the congregation wants to assess whether its resources are being deployed in a manner consistent with the congregation's purposes and goals. Most congregations report the sources and uses of their money through budgets and regular financial reports that show actual revenue and expenses in relation to the budget.

A budget is simply an organized listing of the money coming into and out of the congregation. The money coming in is called *revenue*. The list of revenues includes payments on pledges; cash or "loose" offering collected during worship; special gifts such as memorials; funds contributed from other judicatories; rents paid by other organizations for use of the congregation's buildings; income from savings accounts or other investments; and the money collected from pancake breakfasts, golf outings, bingo games, rummage sales, can drives, bake sales, and so forth. A simple revenue budget is shown in sidebar 5.3.

You may find it useful for your records and your board's decision-making if you provide more detailed listings in each category. The nature of the details will vary widely from congregation to congregation. The details are especially important if the revenue is for a specified restricted purpose, or if the revenue category represents a significant amount of the congregation's revenue. In sidebar 5.4 we have added sample detailed categories.

Sidebar 5.3
SAMPLE REVENUES FOR A CONGREGATIONAL BUDGET:

Major Categories and Subcategories

Pledges, gifts, grants and other contributions
   Unrestricted from members and friends
   Restricted from members and friends
   Grants (excluding judicatory support)
Judicatory support
Payments and fees
Return from investments
Miscellaneous

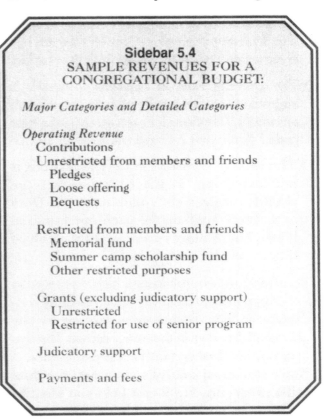

Sidebar 5.4
SAMPLE REVENUES FOR A CONGREGATIONAL BUDGET:

Major Categories and Detailed Categories

Operating Revenue
   Contributions
   Unrestricted from members and friends
      Pledges
      Loose offering
      Bequests

   Restricted from members and friends
      Memorial fund
      Summer camp scholarship fund
      Other restricted purposes

   Grants (excluding judicatory support)
      Unrestricted
      Restricted for use of senior program

   Judicatory support

   Payments and fees

The money flowing out of a congregation is called *expense* or *expenditure*.[13] One normally thinks of expense as a payment for goods or services, such as the purchase of books for the library or the payment of an electric bill. Expenses can also include the contributions of the church to the affiliated denomination or to missions conducted by agencies other than the congregation itself.

How you list your expenditures will depend on the way you will use this information. Some congregational budgets use "natural" expenditure classifications; that is, they group expenditures of a similar type. Using this method, all clergy and staff salaries would be grouped on a single line on the budget, all supplies shown on a single line, and so forth.[14] By contrast, some congregations use "functional" or "cost center" classifications. These congregations group their expenditures by the *purpose* of the expense, often dividing up single expenses like salaries to reflect the multiple functions served by a single item. For instance, you may wish to report all expenses associated with worship—organist and choirmaster compensation, flowers, candles, organ repair, purchase of music, printing of bulletins, dry cleaning of choir robes, perhaps even part of the pastor's salary and part of the building maintenance expense—as one "department" or purpose. Many congregations create separate budget categories for program functions such as facilities maintenance, administration, education, particular mission projects, contributions to mission, community service, and the like. Examples of the two approaches appear in sidebar 5.5.

If you are interested in how specific goals are being addressed, functional accounting may help you learn what you need to know. If you are most interested in looking at fixed expenses in comparison to revenue flow, natural expense classifications may be most helpful. Both types of accounting help you to assess how the congregation's money is being used.

You may also want to distinguish between operating budgets and capital budgets. *Operating budgets* report normal, annually recurring revenues and expenses. For instance,

members and friends normally make annual pledges for the ongoing work of the congregation. Pastoral compensation, staff salaries, materials, electricity, and many other expenses are regularly paid by the congregation throughout the year to keep normal operations going. All of these recurring revenues and expenditures for the continuing programs and commitments of the congregation can be considered the "operating" budget.

Sidebar 5.5
SAMPLE CONGREGATIONAL EXPENSE BUDGET CLASSIFICATIONS

Classified by type	*Classified by purpose*
Clergy salaries	Pastoral services
Clergy benefits	Worship
Staff salaries	Sunday school
Staff benefits	Adult education
Insurance	Soup kitchen
Heat, light, power	Denominational mission
Repairs	Administration
Office supplies	Facilities maintenance
Educational materials	Manse maintenance
Contributions	

From time to time, however, special revenues or expenditures come along that are not likely to recur every year unless the congregation is quite large or exceptionally well organized. For instance, a sanctuary roof probably needs resurfacing or replacing every couple of decades. Or a congregation may receive a bequest to its endowment from a member's estate. *Capital budgets* report special types of revenues and expenditures that are associated with the capital assets (endowment and buildings) of the congregation and are not part of its normal operating expenses. These may contain categories for anticipated repairs and for special fund-raising projects. Suppose, for example, an old roof will need to be replaced in two years. A capital budget allows the congregation to keep track of the specially donated funds and progress in fund-raising to ensure that gifts to the roof fund are not confused with normal pledges. Some congregations, on the other hand, include major building repairs in annual operating budgets. The variety of approaches simply means that congregations design their own unique systems for constructing budgets and keeping track of special funds.

To make your job easier when looking for the congregation's financial strengths and weaknesses, we suggest developing a simple format for organizing all budget data. You can

Figure 5.4 Sample Congregation Surplus (Deficit)

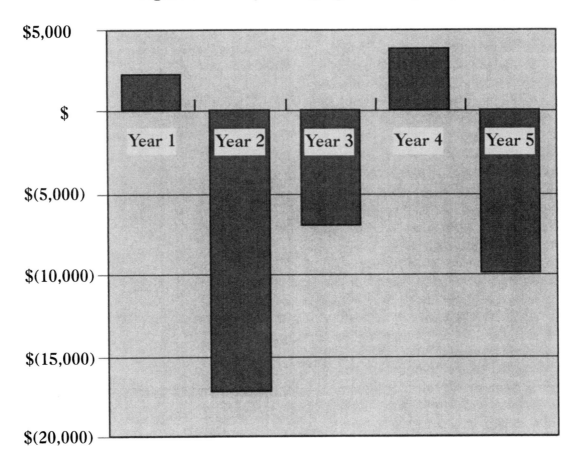

TABLE 5.3
Sample Congregation
Results of Operations (in thousands)

	Revenues	Expenditures	Surplus (Deficit)
Year 1	$95	$94	$1
Year 2	99	107	(8)
Year 3	102	104	(2)
Year 4	110	108	2
Year 5	107	112	(5)

TABLE 5.4
Actual Versus Budget
First Church, Windsor, Connecticut
Year Ending December 31, 1994

	Actual	*Budget*	*Variance*
Revenue	$443,485	$453,930	($10,445)
Expenditures	442,726	453,930	(11,204)
Surplus (Deficit)	759	—	759

TABLE 5.5
Sample Congregation
Sources of Revenue

	Year 1	Year 2	Year 3	Year 4	Year 5
Contributions	$72,500	$73,500	$75,500	$83,500	$79,000
Fees	8,000	8,500	9,000	9,000	8,500
Investment return	15,000	16,500	17,000	17,500	20,000

TABLE 5.6
Sample Congregation
Analysis of Contributions by Type and Purpose

	Year 1	Year 2	Year 3	Year 4	Year 5
Unrestricted pledges	$55,500	$51,000	$53,500	$51,000	$54,000
Loose offering	11,000	8,000	9,000	12,000	$10,000
Restricted—operating and mission causes	5,000	5,000	5,500	5,500	$ 6,000
Restricted—capital purposes	1,000	9,500	7,500	$15,000	9,000

modify this by adding categories, but keep in mind (1) the importance of achieving comparability across years and (2) the need to take careful notes so others can know what budget lines have been grouped in what ways.

Analyzing Financial Results and Trends

When you have organized your financial books, you can see your current situation and project trends. Analyzing trends requires that you compile several years of data, because any single year may not be representative. Although the form of financial reports will vary from congregation to congregation, it is important that the year-to-year data be consistent and comparable. If, for instance, you wish to know the trend in annual pledged giving, you should be careful to exclude capital gifts, special gifts, or other non-pledge income from the revenue figures for any of the years studied.

The reports of annual operations are of enormous interest to the congregation's governing board, which is responsible for maintaining or enhancing financial resources. This analysis of congregational finance, once all the numbers are compiled, should begin with an overview of annual operations. If revenues exceed expenditures, the operations are said to produce a surplus, be in balance, or be "in the black." If expenditures exceed revenues, the congregation shows a deficit, or a net loss for the year. Deficits, of course, weaken the congregation's financial base. A simple statement of total revenues, expenditures, and the surplus or deficit is a good place to begin. It is always a good idea to graph the results, as this will help in spotting trends.

We see in table 5.3, for instance, that Sample Congregation tends to run deficits that are larger than the occasional surplus. In table 5.4, we return to First Church in Windsor to see what can happen when revenues fall short. By adding a comparison to the budget, we can see that they avoided a deficit by keeping expenses below budget, as well.

The analysis should not stop there, though. Even churches with no apparent deficit should look further to assess the strengths and weaknesses of their financial resources. It is possible, for instance, that the budget was balanced by moving money in ways that portend long-term dire consequences. Some danger signs to look for include:

- transfers from reserves or funds functioning as endowment to cover a shortfall in pledges;

- relying on a bequest—which obviously will not recur; to balance the budget;

- achieving a balanced budget by postponing necessary maintenance projects

- cutting benevolence to cover local expenses;

- providing only cost-of-living increases to employees who deserve larger increases due to exceptional performance;

- decreasing the overall financial reserves of the congregation.

As you analyze your resources, just as important as these basic financial considerations are your own program and mission concerns. When someone asks, What kind of year was it? certainly part of the answer should be to report whether or not the congregation had an operating surplus or deficit. But a more comprehensive response would also answer questions such as these:

- Were the congregation's programs and services conducted with adequate quality and quantity?

- Were the gifts to others maintained or increased?

- Were the facilities kept in good, up-to-date condition that enhanced our ability to do programming?

In other words, did the congregation sustain or expand its mission, service, and commitments while maintaining its physical and financial resources for the future?

Having examined the basic flow of money in and out of the treasury, you may want to look more carefully at some of the components of that story. If you want to look more carefully at your revenue, for instance, you can begin by compiling a simple table showing major sources of revenue over time, something we have done for Sample Congregation in table 5.5. From this table we next construct two graphs (figure 5.6). The first graph shows the dollar amount of each type of revenue. Examination of the graph helps us see whether each source of revenue is growing or declining, and whether total revenues are growing or declining. The second graph shows the percentage contribution from each source. This type of graph does not tell us whether total revenues are growing or declining, but it does show increasing or decreasing dependence on various types of revenue. In Sample Congregation, for instance, the relative dependence on investment is growing. If the proportions of types of revenue sources do not change much from year to year, you might want to show simply the most recent year's revenue as a pie chart. Such charts often convey proportions more clearly than do the stacked bars used in figure 5.4. For instance, the pie chart in figure 5.5 shows that

Figure 5.5 Sample Congregation Proportion of Revenue, Year 5

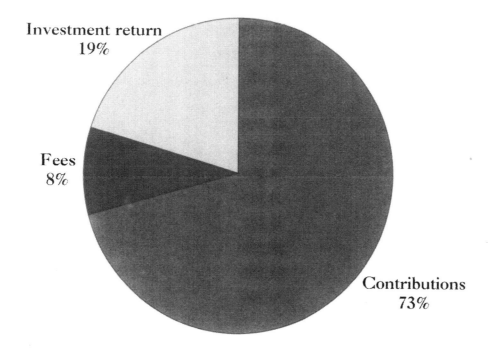

Investment return
19%

Fees
8%

Contributions
73%

the Windsor congregation relies on pledges, loose offerings, and designated gifts for 83 percent of its activities.

You can learn more about trends in giving once you have separated out the various sources of your congregation's revenue. Look at changes (and projected changes) in various sources of income in the context of your local economy and the demographics of the congregation. In Sample Congregation we see a steady increase in contributions, with an unusual or anomalous increase in year 4. Often a member will know the reasons for annual fluctuations; if not, you should look further into the records to determine the cause. Investment (or endowment) return has also increased in this congregation over the five years. This too should be examined to see if this was caused by new gifts to the endowment, excellent investment results, or some other factor.

Give special attention to the relationship between regular operating revenue and special capital fund drives or bequests and grants— items that do not recur regularly but may have short-term impacts on other sources of income and on total revenue. As we saw in table 5.5,

for instance, Sample Congregation's overall gift revenue grew, but as table 5.6 shows, unrestricted pledging is generally not growing. Indeed, the best year for pledged and loose offering income occurred five years ago. The growth in overall giving came in response to special appeals for capital purposes.

Some people fear that special appeals divert money from or compete with annual pledges. Sometimes donors simply redesignate their annual pledge or forgo increasing their annual pledge in order to respond to special appeals. At the same time, because a well-organized special appeal focuses the attention of members and friends on the congregation's potential and its needs, overall commitment, including regular pledges, is likely to increase.

Analyzing Member Giving

Beyond the overall picture of income and expense over time, you will want to take a special look at the income that comes from member

TABLE 5.7
Pledges Arranged in Descending Order of Amount Pledged
First Church, Windsor

Pledge Number	Pledge Amount	Cumulative Amount	Percent of Pledges	Percent of total Pledged
1	9,100	9,100	0	4
2	8,520	17,620	1	8
3	7,280	24,900	1	11
4	5,250	30,150	2	13
5	5,200	35,350	2	15
6	5,200	40,550	2	18
7	5,000	45,550	3	20
8	4,680	50,230	3	22
9	4,160	54,390	4	24
10	3,900	58,290	4	25
....				
243	35	229,166	97	100
244	30	229,196	99	100
245	25	229,221	99	100
246	25	229,246	100	100

TABLE 5.8
Analysis of Pledge Income
First Church, Windsor

Pledges by Quintile	Amount Pledged	Percent of Total
Top Quintile	139,054	61
2nd Quintile ($600-1,300)	45,569	20
3d Quintile ($361-600)	24,788	11
4th Quintile ($200-361)	13,667	6
Bottom Quintile (Under $360)	6,188	3

giving. In fund-raising circles, one frequently hears reference to the "80-20 rule," a formula that suggests that in most organizations 80 percent of the revenue comes from 20 percent of the members. Professional fund raisers developed that rule—along with others—as a tool to project the number and size of gifts needed to obtain a specified campaign goal. Although it may be accurate for large campaigns, such as capital drives for universities, most local congregations

Figure 5.6a Contributions by Type and Purpose

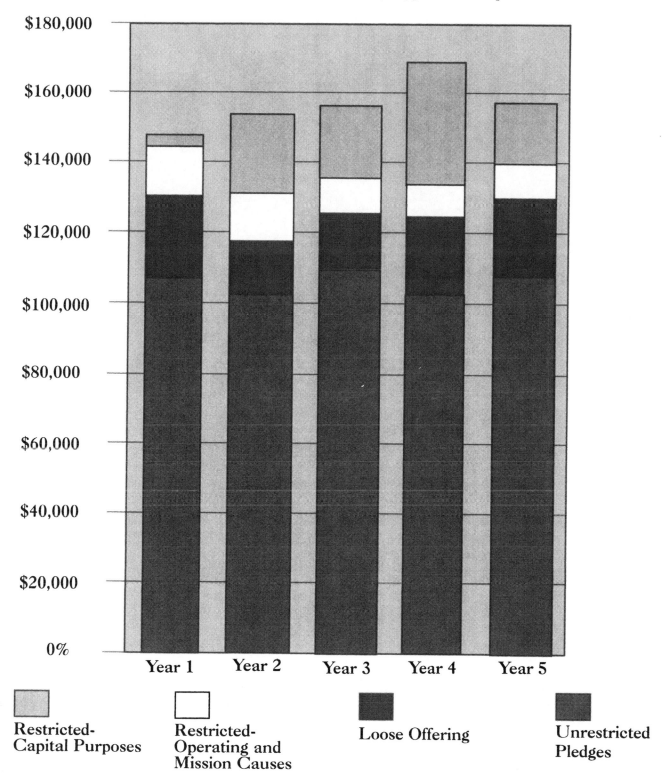

Restricted-
Capital Purposes

Restricted-
Operating and
Mission Causes

Loose Offering

Unrestricted
Pledges

Figure 5.6b Revenue Proportions

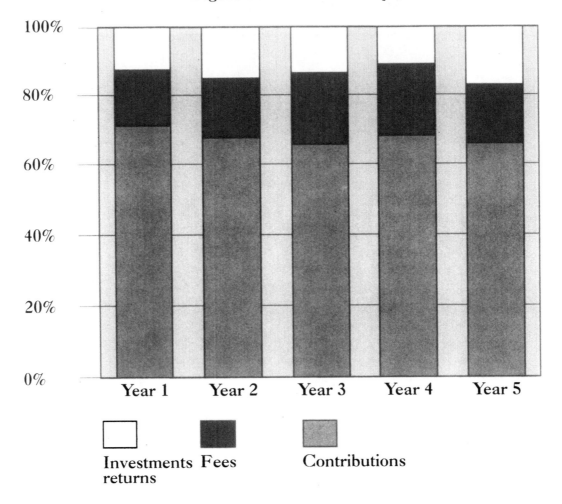

work with a smaller number of potential donors and a narrower distribution of wealth.

Although the precise distribution of gifts projected by the rule may not match the experience of your congregation, you may learn a great deal by analyzing what proportion of gifts comes from various portions of the congregation.[15] One New England congregation, following such an exercise, realized that two members over age 100 were accounting for close to 20 percent of annual pledged income!

To show the distribution of giving, list all pledges from the largest to the smallest, adding each one to the previous total to calculate a running total. The second step is to divide that running total by the grand total of pledges to find the percent of all pledges accounted for at

each step. In the example of First Church Windsor, shown in table 5.7, the largest pledge ($9,100) is 0.4 percent of the number of pledges but 4 percent of the total amount raised. Examining the table further shows that the ten largest pledges (representing 4 percent of the pledging units) provide more than a quarter of the total amount pledged. These data may be graphed as shown in figure 5.7. A steep initial slope indicates that a few pledges contribute a large portion of the total. These major gifts are obviously essential to the success of any fundraising effort.

In addition to examining the actual pattern of member giving in your congregation, you may want to gather information that will help you think about potential giving. Tithing, or setting aside a fixed percentage (often 10 percent) of

Figure 5.7 First Church of Christ, Windsor, Cumulative Pledge Total

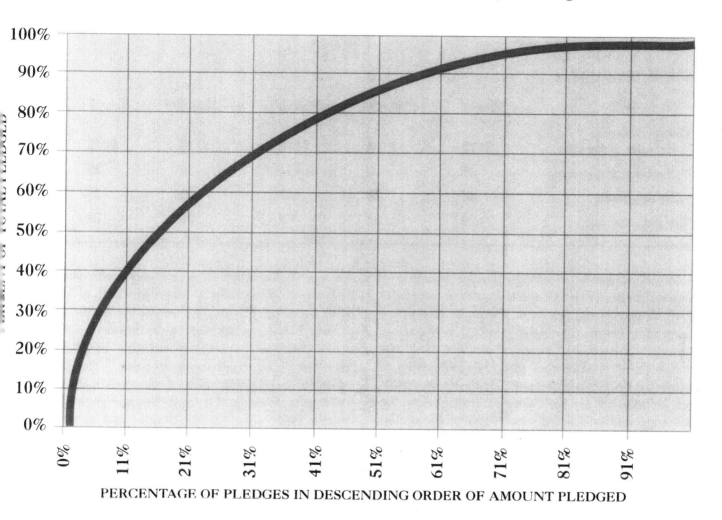

PERCENTAGE OF PLEDGES IN DESCENDING ORDER OF AMOUNT PLEDGED

one's income, has traditionally received strong emphasis in evangelical Christian and Mormon congregations. In recent years the concept of proportionate giving and the "half-tithe" have become a fixture in old-line Protestant and Roman Catholic circles, as well. If you use a survey questionnaire, you may want to include questions about income and giving to learn about your congregation's patterns. You will, of course, want to assure your members of the anonymity of their responses to such questions, but information about the financial resources of the households in your congregation can be invaluable in assessing your realistic potential.

In the absence of detailed information gained through a questionnaire, some congregations can use census data to approximate potential congregational revenue. In the town of Windsor, for example, the per capita income is approximately $84,000. To the extent that church members' incomes parallel the community average, one might project a 10-percent pledge as $8,400; a half-tithe, $4,200. First Church's average pledge (based on a combination of individual and household contributions) is $2,266, which suggests that if member incomes are indeed comparable to those in the community, households are contributing 2.7 percent to the congregation.

Analyzing Expenditures

Just as a detailed look at trends in income can help you to understand the congregation's actual and

TABLE 5.9

Expenditures (in thousands)

Sample Congregation

	Year 1	Year 2	Year 3	Year 4	Year 5
Congregational: Salaries & benefits	$120	$125	$130	$135	$140
Supplies & services	39	40	42	36	35
Gifts to others	30	30	30	25	25
Capital expenses	0	20	5	20	20

potential resources, so an examination of trends in expenditures can reveal much about the congregation's demands and priorities. Expenditure proportions may be tabulated and graphed in the same manner as revenues, including graphing both the dollar amount expended and the proportion of expenditures for various categories from your budget. In table 5.9, we see Sample Congregation, for instance, cutting back gifts to others as the persistent costs of salaries and benefits rise and capital costs are incurred. In figure 5.8, we return to First Church, Windsor, for a look at 1994 revenues and expenditures. Pie charts, though they do not reveal trends, may communicate proportions more clearly than a stacked bar chart.

Such charts and tables can help you to assess whether your expenditures are coinciding with your stated mission and programming goals. Some congregations, for instance, as a matter of policy, budget funds for others in proportion to the funds spent for congregational purposes, perhaps even matching every dollar spent on congregational activities and maintenance with a dollar for mission outside the congregation. Others are not able to be so generous, but both careful planning and careful examination of financial records can help each congregation to make good decisions about how to allocate scarce dollars in ways that reflect their own goals.

Capital Resources

The *capital resources* of a congregation include both its financial and physical assets. What is an asset? An asset, in a financial and accounting sense, is usually a tangible thing of value that you own. If you own your own home, even if you have a mortgage, your home is one of your assets. The original painting by Picasso hanging in your hallway is an asset. Your great-grandmother's collection of nineteenth-century stamps is an asset. The cash in your pocket and in the bank, your stocks, bonds, gold bars, and jewelry are all assets. Not everything you own would be called an asset, however. One of last month's newspapers has value only as a recyclable, so it would not usually be considered an asset. While we have argued that your members and their commitment are "assets" to the congregation, here we turn our attention to the sorts of tangible assets an accountant can list. Financial assets include cash and investments owned by the congregation. Physical assets include all the congregation's buildings and land, plus all the equipment and furniture it owns.

You will want to know your liabilities as well as your assets. A liability is an amount you owe. Any loan, like a mortgage, is a liability, as it represents an amount you have to pay back. Put another way, liabilities constitute a claim on the future financial resources of the congregation. The most common long-term liability is a building loan or mortgage. Short-term liabilities or debt include accounts payable (bills that are due) and any short-term loans or lines of credit. Long-term debt includes mortgages,

Figure 5.8 Proportions of 1994Expenditure,
First Church of Christ, Windsor, CT

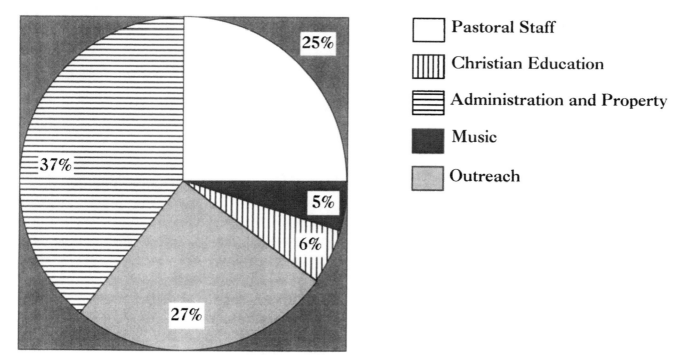

Pastoral Staff

Christian Education

Administration and Property

Music

Outreach

Figure 5.8a Proportions of 1994 Revenue, First Church of Christ, Windsor, CT

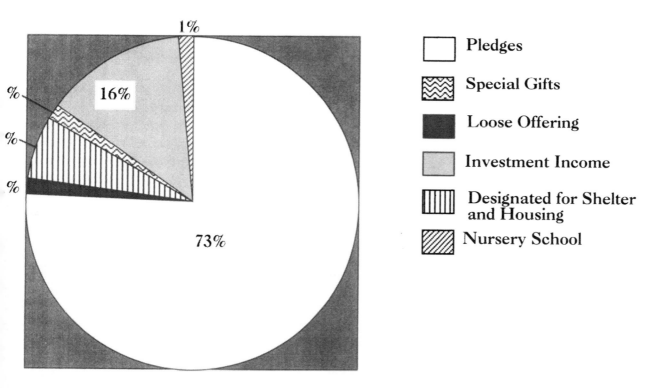

Pledges

Special Gifts

Loose Offering

Investment Income

Designated for Shelter
and Housing

Nursery School

TABLE 5.10
Sample Congregation
Congregational Debt

	Year 1	Year 2	Year 3	Year 4	Year 5
Short-term	$2,000	$3,000	$4,500	$5,000	$7,000
Long-term	25,000	24,000	23,000	22,000	21,000

loans from the denomination, and any other financial obligation requiring the congregation to make structured repayment over several years.

Assessing long-term assets and liabilities provides a picture of the ability of a congregation to sustain itself over time. Constructing a table or graph that summarizes long- and short-term debt over the recent past can often reveal areas deserving careful attention in planning. In the example shown in table 5.10, the long-term debt of the congregation is being steadily reduced, but the short-term debt is rising. The reason for increases in short-term debt may be deficit operations or reductions in revenue that necessitate borrowing to meet obligations.

Beyond looking at the regular flow of operating money in and out of your congregation's budget, a full understanding of your financial resources requires, then, a look at these capital assets and liabilities. As with operating budgets, there may be several types of items in a capital budget. There may be a line for a drive to create a new endowment or another for a fund to replace the roof. There may be lines showing gifts and bequests—some of which may be restricted by the donor for use for buildings, furniture, equipment, renovations, endowment, or other purposes. Capital budgets also list the uses of the funds, whether they are to be expended (as in the case of building additions or renovations) or invested (as in the case of endowment). Capital budgets should be viewed and analyzed using all the tools we have already discussed.

For most congregations, buildings constitute the largest category of assets. We will return to the importance of these physical assets in the section on sacred places, but we first turn to another kind of capital asset—endowments. For some readers, a discussion of endowments is irrelevant, but we are convinced that endowments will become even more important in congregational finance in future years, becoming part of the budgets of groups in more and more parts of the United States. Where possible, we have used several extended endnotes to cover some of the more detailed issues surrounding endowments, but we want to suggest here some of the sorts of questions you might ask when examining the endowment resources of a congregation.

Endowment and Funds Functioning as Endowment[16]

An endowment is an amount of money donated to an organization with the restriction that the principal of the endowment be held in perpetuity. The principal is the amount of money originally given. This kind of gift is intended to last forever—that is, the principal is to be invested and not spent, ever. Some endowments have lasted for centuries. Indeed, it was the church in the Middle Ages that invented endowments, as landowners willed their property to the local cathedral to help pay for upkeep. Endowments are created by donations of various sorts, including capital fund drives, wills, and bequests. Only a donor can create a true, permanently restricted endowment, provided that the organization accepts the gift.[17] In addition, the governing board of the congrega-

TABLE 5.11
Sample Congregation
Spending Rate of Endowment

	Market Value	Amount Consumed	Percentage Consumed
Year 1	$652,000	$59,332	9.1%
Year 2	684,600	60,245	8.8%
Year 3	753,060	56,480	7.5%
Year 4	737,999	50,922	6.9%
Year 5	752,759	48,929	6.5%

tion may add unrestricted funds to an endowment. To be precise, such board-designated additions are *functioning* as endowment but are not donor-restricted endowment because the governing board in the future is free to reverse the designation of unrestricted funds.

Endowments and funds functioning as endowments are generally invested in stocks, bonds, mutual funds (made up of stocks and bonds), and other kinds of financial assets. The financial benefit from investments is known as the *total return*. The total return comes to the investor as income and appreciation. Income is generally thought of as interest and dividends paid to the investor, while appreciation (and depreciation) refer to the value of the stock or bond itself.

You may want to address two key issues in examining your endowment: *asset allocation* and the *spending and reinvestment rate*. Asset allocation is the decision regarding how much of an endowment should be invested in different kinds of assets—stocks of large companies, small company stocks, international stocks, fixed income securities, real estate, venture capital, and so on. Different kinds of assets carry different risks and different long- and short-term rates of return.[18] Most congregations invest in a diversity of asset classes to reduce the variability of returns.[19] A report showing the asset allocations of your congregation's endowment should be regularly provided by the bank, brokerage, or investment

adviser with custody of the investments. The governing board will want this information to make sure that the long-term investment policy of the congregation is sound and that the policy is being followed by the investment manager. Good decisions about asset allocation can have a profound impact on the future financial health of the congregation and its mission.[20]

The other key piece of information you should examine is the spending and reinvest-

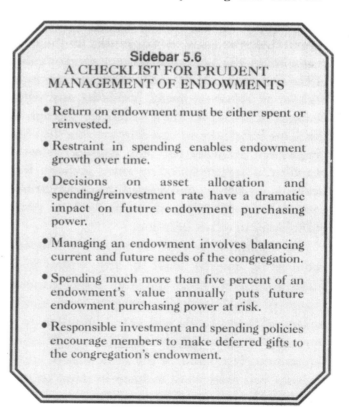

Sidebar 5.6
A CHECKLIST FOR PRUDENT MANAGEMENT OF ENDOWMENTS

- Return on endowment must be either spent or reinvested.

- Restraint in spending enables endowment growth over time.

- Decisions on asset allocation and spending/reinvestment rate have a dramatic impact on future endowment purchasing power.

- Managing an endowment involves balancing current and future needs of the congregation.

- Spending much more than five percent of an endowment's value annually puts future endowment purchasing power at risk.

- Responsible investment and spending policies encourage members to make deferred gifts to the congregation's endowment.

ment rate. The people who created endowments intended them to be used to meet the needs of future generations. Congregational leaders face the challenge of deciding how much of an endowment to use to meet current needs and how much to reinvest for the future. The endowment's dividends, interest, and capital appreciation are revenues that can be either spent or reinvested. The amount reinvested for the future helps the investment grow and thus provides more return in the future. On the other hand, current needs of the congregation provide pressure to spend more in the present. You will want to look at how endowment income has been used (spending and reinvestment rates) in recent years.[21] When you do, you should not forget to factor in inflation rates. Even if the principal in an endowment fund is not touched and spending rates remain steady, the income it produces is worth less when inflation takes its toll. Many congregations regularly reinvest some of the endowment's income to keep future income growing at least on pace with inflation.[22]

Table 5.11 shows Sample Congregation's consumption rate, expressed as a percentage of the endowment's market value. To obtain this ratio, simply divide the amount of endowment return that was spent or consumed by the congregation by the beginning-of-year market value of the endowment and similar funds. Be sure to include all amounts spent, including any withdrawals of principal. Such a table (or a graph of the same information) can demonstrate the congregation's progress (or lack thereof) toward reaching a target spending rate, perhaps five percent—a figure considered an equilibrium norm that will allow the principal to grow sufficiently to offset inflation.

An examination of financial resources requires a careful look at any endowment funds that a congregation may have. Assessments of the long-term strengths and weaknesses of those funds will entail attention to a variety of details of their management. Sidebar 5.6 summarizes some of the principles of stewardship you may want to keep in mind as you consider the information you collect.

Physical and Space Resources

Imagine you are a traveler entering a strange town or neighborhood. You are interested in Trinity Episcopal Church and ask about it. You are told that Trinity Church is on a prominent corner in town, that it has an unmistakable and magnificent tower or dome, that it is a beautiful (and possibly old) place, and that you must go inside and see it for yourself!

In reality, of course, Trinity is a community of faith, a group of people bound together by a common set of beliefs, values, and commitments. It is by no means defined or contained by its building. Furthermore, a congregation's property is only one of an array of spiritual, human, and temporal resources that are available to promote the life and welfare of its faith community and often the community at large.

And yet, sacred places do have enormous presence and power. They can enable and enrich a congregation's life and help to define its identity. Almost always they embody its history, having housed a lively mix of activities. Some activities, like ghosts, are remembered from years ago, while others are very real, serving people in the here and now. Understandably, therefore, a person might equate a congregation with its building; after all, the sacred place is the most visible and symbolic link between a congregation and the greater community.

In the hearts of members, sacred places have special qualities that distinguish them from other congregational resources. You might say that property is the "elephant you can't ignore." Its size, its demands on financial and human resources, and its centrality in the life of the congregation all urge that it be well cared for and managed, and that calls for a careful inventory of physical space. On the positive side, the intermingling between people and place can be a very powerful dynamic that profoundly advances and strengthens a congregation's life and outreach. On the other hand, the loyalties and passions inspired by a building can lead to conflict and dissension, especially when hard choices have to be made about its care or use in the face of declining resources and changing needs. To develop a comprehensive understanding of congregational dynamics, you can inventory the powerful role sacred places play in congregational and community life.

Sacred Places and Congregational Life

One way to recognize the spiritual power and symbolic meaning of your religious building is to note the parallels between a family home and a sacred place. Like a home, a sacred place powerfully evokes and "remembers" the life of its "family" or community of faith. Just as a well-used kitchen in an old house makes the viewer almost lose himself or herself in memories of countless family meals and conversations, so too your worship space and social hall have the ability to link people to previous experiences of celebration, learning, fellowship, and inspiration. Similarly, the layers of physical change and the signs of aging and renewal in family homes parallel those of sacred places. The wearing away of steps and hallways or the addition of improvements and artistic touches that embellish and enrich the building make the growth and change of "family" very tangible and real.

Sacred places, however, are more than the dwellings of particular groups of people. They also symbolize larger relationships. They embody the congregation's relationship with a divine being that does not reside there alone. Furthermore, they are places where the concept of "family" often extends to the entire community—where everyone in need is encouraged to take part and be served.

You can see how congregational property profoundly influences the ways a congregation sees itself, and how, in turn, the community sees the congregation. James P. Wind has written of the "gossamer threads" that connect people to sacred places, those elusive, remembered senses of belonging and personal significance that "maintain contact with the deepest parts of the human spirit."[23] These connections or threads may have been woven by special moments that symbolize the turning points in human life, such as weddings, christenings, bar mitzvahs or bat mitzvahs, and funerals. On the other hand, these connections may have been made over the course of countless, repeated experiences such as weekly worship services, daily drop-offs of children for day care, or Sunday concerts and recitals.

In times of enormous economic change, social upheaval, increasing needs, and constrained resources, sacred places have taken on a symbolic meaning that is valued by members and nonmembers alike. For example, sacred places:

- stand for stability and continuity.

- bring to life—through many layers of building additions, embellishments, and enrichments—the generations of people who have passed through before.

- help define the self-image and identity of the congregations that own them.[24]

- provide a visual and social point of identity for the communities that surround them.[25]

Given these many messages and meanings, religious leaders working to change and strengthen congregational life must endeavor to understand, honor, and work with the loyalties, affections, associations, and memories of congregants and others. Your congregation is challenged to bind together these "gossamer threads" to provide energy and direction for new initiatives and programs, balancing the imperative to be good stewards of existing resources with the need to create programs that inevitably put new demands on those resources. Making those judgments will depend on a solid assessment of the strengths and liabilities of the congregation's current physical spaces. This assessment will need to be undertaken alongside an understanding of the cultural and process dynamics of the congregation; attention to such concrete elements as parking spaces and electrical systems adds a dimension to cultural and process dynamics.

Sacred Spaces and Congregational Mission

You can assess the mixture of feelings associated with your building. Sometimes sacred places seem to have a powerful hold over the members of a congregation and its neighbors in the greater community. At times it may seem that the property is serving its purposes very well and is beloved by all. At other times it may seem to be getting in the way of important opportunities for growth, change, and new outreach. The care of property may seem to absorb a disproportionate amount of the congregation's energy and financial resources, or the building's appearance, for many members, may take precedence over its use for outreach. Sometimes the building's history will seem to mean more to lay leaders than its future potential for congregational life and outreach.

As with other resource inventories, your accounting of building resources should be done with the specific programs and goals of the congregation in mind. Thus, it is essential for you to understand how the property is viewed and valued by members, and to ask hard questions about mission and priorities. An inventory of sacred space can become an important ingredient in reimagining what is possible, as well as a reminder of what is necessary for sustaining the work to which the congregation is committed.

Your efforts to develop thoughtful, deliberate property evaluation is accentuated by the fact that many congregations are passive managers of their properties, reacting to needs and problems instead of anticipating and planning for them on a regular basis. Whether a congregation is responding to a building-related crisis, exploring space alternatives for new ministries and community programs, or contemplating a full-fledged renovation campaign, you should begin with a comprehensive understanding of a property's physical needs and repair priorities. In the absence of a building crisis or major expansion, your need for this kind of physical planning may not be very obvious in the day to day life of a congregation. The practice of anticipating and addressing property needs on a regular basis, however, will make you a more effective manager of your building *and* other resources.

Every use of the building makes demands on the congregation's resources. The rental of space for Twelve Step programs or neighborhood meetings will, for example, call on the energy of clergy, the time of paid staff and volunteers, and the resources of the congregation to keep spaces clean, orderly, and in good repair. Program decisions are more responsibly made when property resource questions can be knowledgeably addressed.

You must also assess the shifting needs of your congregation and community to better understanding the new demands on your congregation's building resources. Dramatic changes within a congregation's membership ranks, clergy and staff, or liturgy and worship practices—as well as changes in the larger community—can compel many institutions to reassess both their spiritual and programmatic objectives. This self-study or assessment process, which is an essential part of a congregation's long-term planning, may reveal that buildings are not always fully or effectively utilized for meeting pressing human service and ministry needs.

By thoroughly understanding your building resources, you can create a responsible plan for their use that responds to your identity and mission and to the needs of your community. Good facilities planning leads to timely repairs and renovations that keep properties functional. Sound property management will ensure that buildings are efficiently and safely used. Creative financial management and fund-raising can develop new sources of revenue and conserve limited resources. Finally, collaboration and communication between a congregation and its wider community will build alliances for stewardship and outreach, helping to maintain a healthy balance between the care of a building and its full and active use. But all of that begins with knowing what you have.

Creating an Inventory of Sacred Spaces

Your assessment of your physical space can begin with a walk through your buildings. For each separate space, note its size and general appearance. Record who uses the space, for what, and during what hours each week. Include in your list a *conditions survey*. The most basic survey examines each exterior and interior component of a building, describes existing conditions, identifies immediate repair problems, and notes areas that are in need of further investigation. Also include in your list the things that make each room or space especially attractive and useable. Because sacred spaces are not just functional, include as well the places where historical items, works of art, and sacred objects evoke a divine presence and special memories.

As you list spaces, include both the obvious public rooms like sanctuaries and classrooms and the less obvious spaces like entryways and halls. Restrooms are essential, so make sure they are on the list as well. And be sure to take your walk around the entrances and grounds, too. In each place, try to imagine how the space might look to a newcomer, to someone with difficulty walking, or to a child. Think about what sort of activity each space invites or limits.

When you have finished with this preliminary inventory, you should be able to compile summaries that include such items as the number and size of rooms suitable for public gatherings, the number and size of rooms suitable for children's education, the presence and distribution of special equipment (pianos, electronic equipment, and the like), and the location of spaces with special historic and aesthetic significance.

In-Depth Assessment. Although it is critical to begin with a visual inventory, you should also assess the parts of your building that you may not be able to see. Many congregations find that they need to undertake a more in-depth planning and investigative process, particularly if a property is going to be used more intensively or it has been some time since a comprehensive assessment was undertaken. To achieve this in-depth investigation, you may wish to develop a master plan. Going beyond the basic conditions survey, a master plan looks at mechanical systems (heating, cooling, electrical, plumbing, fire and life safety—such as exit signs and emergency lights), the way space is currently used and its potential for more intensive use, and possibilities for mak-

ing a building accessible for those with disabilities. Your master plan will provide the basis for prioritizing needed work, will describe specifically how repair and renovation work should be carried out, and will help you develop a timetable for its execution. Assessing your property's condition and potential will take time. A basic conditions survey may take only a couple of weeks for an architect to prepare, but a more extensive master plan may take anywhere from one to six months to complete. The latter will depend on the size and complexity of the building, the range of repair problems to be addressed, and any plans for the redesign and more intensive use of space.

Few congregations have among their members the expertise needed to determine the more detailed and structural conditions of the buildings. Most will need to look for an outside expert to conduct an accurate and thorough assessment. This outside expert will usually be an architect who brings a general understanding of the way buildings function, and who can call in structural engineers, mechanical systems experts, liturgical designers, historians and conservationists (for older properties), stained-glass studios, and other specialists to supplement his or her expertise as needed.[26]

Keep in mind, however, that a congregation is a special kind of property owner. Understanding your congregation's mission and internal decision-making process is an important part of a successful consulting relationship with an architect. In addition to the architect, you should find someone who is not only qualified to assess building problems but is sensitive to your congregation and the way it operates as a religious (and largely volunteer) institution. The people who assist you should have experience working with religious buildings and recognize typical problems; understand how to renovate space to accommodate new and existing congregational and community programs; be familiar with current repair technologies, especially when working with older buildings; and be prepared to help a congregation establish a long-term maintenance program for ongoing repairs and seasonal work.

As a religious congregation, you need to monitor a variety of problems that are typical of all buildings, and you need to keep in mind that some problems are particular to religious properties. The complex roof line of a church or synagogue, for example, is often punctuated by towers, steeples, dormers, or domes (especially characteristic of older properties), making regular inspection, maintenance, and repair a formidable challenge. Stained-glass windows present their own challenges. Protective glazing for stained-glass windows—usually installed to prevent vandalism—can often do more harm than good if not installed with the right materials and adequate ventilation. Many congregations are also working to alter their properties to make them accessible and welcoming to people with disabilities. Other items you will want to look for as you inspect your property are listed in sidebar 5.7. In addition to checking for items that need immediate attention, you will want to gather the information you need for developing a regular schedule of long-term maintenance.[27]

You can prevent small, inexpensive repairs from getting out of hand (and help manage major expenses over time) by developing a strategic plan for regularly assessing your building's condition. Good property management requires careful planning and constant oversight on the part of a congregation's governing body, which is guided and informed by a property committee with responsibility for building care and upkeep. This committee should, in turn, designate to individuals responsibility for key tasks, such as monitoring energy consumption and undertaking seasonal maintenance inspections.

Planning repair, envisioning changes, and raising money will take time. Because repair and renovation work may require more money than a congregation can raise over a two or three-year time period, this kind of project is often planned in phases over a longer period of five to ten years. Project phasing enables a congregation to move forward with the most urgent repairs at the same time that it plans and implements a sound fund-raising campaign.

Involving the Community in Property Analysis

Underutilized space can serve as a significant impetus for rethinking how a congregation might better manage its property on behalf of a wide array of congregational and community

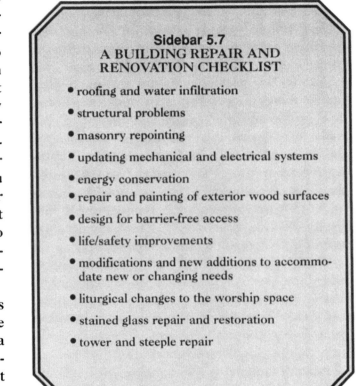

Sidebar 5.7
A BUILDING REPAIR AND RENOVATION CHECKLIST

- roofing and water infiltration
- structural problems
- masonry repointing
- updating mechanical and electrical systems
- energy conservation
- repair and painting of exterior wood surfaces
- design for barrier-free access
- life/safety improvements
- modifications and new additions to accommodate new or changing needs
- liturgical changes to the worship space
- stained glass repair and restoration
- tower and steeple repair

purposes. Because the buildings you own may be among the most visible and accessible public spaces in your community, one aspect of assessing your property resources is to find and match the needs and potential partners in the larger community.

After deliberating about their own needs, priorities, and resources, some congregations may decide they have the ability to support a combination of new uses of their property, and perhaps even to provide the funding, as well as staff and congregational volunteers, to develop and administer those uses. Other congregations, however, may choose to go beyond their own members to seek help from the greater community both to identify needs and develop new programs and partnerships that might share space in your properties.

Sidebar 5.8
SPACE PLANNING AUDIT

Planning Considerations

Begin with an inventory of each individual room or space throughout the property, recording how and when it is used and by whom.

- Consider how certain activities might be consolidated to increase the efficiency of current space usage and identify the spaces available for sharing.

- Assess the physical condition of each space and the need for improvements or renovations to accommodate new users or programs (this may require the assistance of an experienced architect).

- In instances where the improvements needed are of a more substantial nature and a single user is involved (such as a day care center), consider asking the user for help in covering renovation costs.

- Make certain any repair or improvement project complies with building codes and life safety requirements.

Legal and Tax Implications

- Become familiar with zoning laws which govern the kind of uses that can take place in a particular area or neighborhood.

- Consult an attorney to make sure that prospective space sharing arrangements, along with any additional revenue, will not jeopardize a congregation's tax exempt status.

Property Management Issues

- Consider what, if any, additional security measures need to be put in place.

- Determine parking needs and capacity.

- Make sure the congregation and those organizations invited to share space carry adequate liability and property insurance.

- Decide what fees or rents may be charged for certain spaces and uses.

- Develop rental and lease agreements.

- Establish guidelines and policies that govern space use and the relationships of one space sharer to another, *and put these procedures in writing!*

You can collect this information in a variety of ways: A simple survey mailed or hand delivered to neighborhood residents might ask about basic matters such as gender, age, and home ownership, what kind of services a neighborhood church or synagogue might offer, and what community needs and priorities exist. (Trinity Memorial Church in Philadelphia used such a door-to-door survey successfully and expanded its outreach services for the homeless based on response and support from its neighborhood.)

Alternatively, a day-long community forum might be the arena to invite input and participation by neighborhood residents, along with key civic and business leaders, representatives from nonprofit and governmental organizations involved in human services, community development representatives, and people interested in historic preservation and the arts. A professional facilitator might help plan and implement this kind of forum. You might also use the leadership of a volunteer from the congregation (or a local nonprofit organization) who has experience in human resources, community, or social service planning. This person can help both the congregation and community members to articulate their respective needs, goals, and resources, and to reach consensus about the best ways to use the building.

After a survey, forum, or other information gathering effort, you may need additional research to determine whether needs or services identified are being met by other nearby congregations or organizations. This may point to new avenues of cooperation that can strengthen existing programs. Congregations may also discover new partnership opportunities with established service providers and neighboring religious institutions.

Other identified needs may inspire a congregation to start any number of programs from scratch, for example, to bring certain services like child care closer to home or to provide space for a fledgling arts organization. Whatever course is taken, you will want to focus on services or programs that are in keeping with your own newly defined strategy for ministry and community outreach. The dialogue begun with the community can become an integral part of your ongoing assessment process and refinement of your mission to members and neighbors.

Building Congregational Life and Community Partnerships

Creative thinking and strong leadership can transform even difficult buildings into valuable resources. All too often, congregations feel overwhelmed by their building and worry that the building's physical condition or empty spaces will compel them to give up and move on. Including the community in your congregation's property assessment process invites the possibility that others who use the building will share the cost of maintenance as well. As with every other material resource, space can be mobilized and transformed by the imagination and commitment of a congregation's members and its partners in the community.

Indeed, the availability of affordable, welcoming, flexible, and well-located space can make possible a myriad of ministries that serve the greater community. A recent public policy research project sponsored by Partners for Sacred Places has indicated that 70 percent of the outreach or service programs supported or assisted by congregations take place in their buildings.[28] By sharing space with partners in the community, you can draw in the resources and energies of a wide range of leaders and interest groups, including municipal officials, performing arts organizations, neighborhood leaders, historic preservationists, and human service groups. These partners can do much to lighten the burden of property upkeep by sharing the costs of repairs, contributing materials for renovations and repairs, and connecting your congregation to larger circles of potential donors and supporters.

Common Fears About Sharing Space

Before you develop such new partnerships, you may need to undertake a process that draws out the fears and misconceptions held by staff and members. Some congregation members, for example, worry that they are losing control over their place of worship, especially if they feel no connection to the purpose or programs of groups that are likely to be sharing space. As in other aspects of congregational dynamics and planning, building consensus among members is key for making new space arrangements. You need to work diligently to keep members abreast of the different organizations and programs that might find a home in your property.

Like most congregations, you may have already acquired some space sharers and tenants on an unplanned, ad hoc basis over a period of years. This ad hoc arrangement works well when the need for shared space is relatively modest—perhaps an hour or two each night for different weekly meetings. But this approach must be modified if your congregation wants to share space in your building more creatively and intensively.

Letting Go of Sacred Places

What does a congregation do when its membership becomes so small that the management, care, and use of its property becomes an impossible task? Or when a major and unavoidable repair project looms ahead, and the congregation's resources will clearly not be up to the task? Having assessed the repair needs of a building and the resources of the congregation, the inescapable conclusion is sometimes that radical solutions are called for. Sound planning and stewardship practices may provide creative options when your congregation is stretched beyond its capacity. When property care and management demands become chronically distracting and unmanageable, some congregations have sold their property and merged with others or relocated in a more modest facility. In decisions to reconfigure your property use or ownership, careful planning and consultation with professionals in a variety of fields such as community development, architectural design, and real estate law will be essential.

Even when situations look desperate, however, alternative solutions may still be possible. National patterns have shown that even small congregations with constrained resources can maintain a long-term presence in large, old properties by reconfiguring property uses and responsibilities in dramatic new ways. A number of options are available, including the following:

- Arranging for a nonprofit organization—perhaps a major user of the congregation's property—to assume responsibility for managing the building's uses and raising funds for its care. If space has been shared with another congregation, day care center, or performing arts groups in the past, it may be possible for one or more of those groups to take on more responsibility for the property.

- Create a new nonprofit organization that is chartered to work closely with the congregation to create a new, mixed-use center serving the community. For example, the First Unitarian Church in Oakland, California, has signed a long-term lease with the Center for Urban Family Life, which is now responsible for funding the repair of the church building and managing a wide range of programs. In a case

like this, the congregation can retain its normal use of the property while shedding the day-to-day headaches of administration and fund-raising.

- Undertaking a major, collaborative fund-raising campaign that explicitly invites the larger community to share in the responsibility for the care of the property. An increasing number of small congregations with large buildings have retained their ministries and presence in older properties by broadening the base of support for their properties in this way. For example, the Rittenhouse Coalition for the Restoration of Sacred Places in Philadelphia has successfully brought together Baptist, Episcopal, and Unitarian Universalist churches in a joint effort to raise funds from sources that would not have supported any of them individually. Several hundred thousand dollars have been raised, effectively doubling what the congregations could raise from their own members.

- "Spinning off" portions of the congregation's property to others who can use and support them. St. Vincent de Paul Church in Albany, New York, for example, entered into a careful and innovative study of the current and potential use of its thirteen buildings. Ultimately, the parish decided to sell several of its properties, lease several others, and retain several more.

Even the most creative and open process, however, may lead to the conclusion that a congregation simply needs to start afresh in a new and more manageable space. A careful, deliberate planning effort will help to ease the congregation's transition from one property to another. The following steps can be invaluable:

- Maintain open and continuing communications about the decision-making process and its findings with members and neighbors alike. Dissension and disagreement are inevitable, and critics need opportunities to be heard and a serious chance to explore and present alternatives. In the end, the information and criteria that are used to make a decision to leave the property should be clear and compelling to all.

• Support and encourage a "mourning process" for the congregation. Old and new members alike will need opportunities to remember, document, and celebrate their history and heritage, and should be encouraged to find connections and continuities between what the congregation used to be and what it will become.

• Be aware of and responsive to the community's welfare. Efforts can be made, for example, to ease the transition for programs and ministries that will be dislocated when a property changes hands. Given that religious properties are integral to the fabric of communities, it is also important to give the community every opportunity to continue sharing and enjoying the building in its new capacity. Every effort should be made to discourage the dismantling of properties (for example, removing windows, fixed altars, and other built-in elements that are integral to a building's integrity); otherwise, a compromised building can damage community morale and hinder certain new uses. Careful planning will also be necessary to find a responsible buyer for the property; otherwise, there will be a temptation to sell to an early bidder who is not capable of maintaining the property in the future.

• Find opportunities to create and preserve symbols in the new property that link the congregation to its heritage in the old property. Scriptures, vestments, and liturgical items of enormous significance to the congregation will naturally find a home in the new property, but portable furnishings that are central to worship and congregational life, such as a pulpit or communion table, can also help keep ties to congregational heritage.

• Begin a new cycle of sound resource management in the new facility. Whether the congregation has moved into a smaller, tra-ditional worship place, a former residence, or a commercial building, the congregation should commit to assembling the resources that will make good stewardship possible. Those resources should include a strong maintenance plan, annual budget allocations for long-term repairs, space planning for current and prospective programs, and training for staff and volunteers to help them guide and oversee the care of the property.[29]

Your congregation's sacred places—its buildings, furnishings, and grounds—are among its most tangible and powerful resources. Careful inspection and imaginative inventories of their potential are an essential component of caring for the resources. Whether planning a long-term maintenance schedule or seeking new community partnerships, your knowledge of your spaces and their condition are the necessary starting point. Whatever your creative alternative, a thorough understanding of a building's current and potential use is fundamentally good stewardship of your resources.

Conclusion

We began this chapter by distinguishing between resources and capacities. We argued that the raw materials of congregational life are drawn from the wider social and religious context and can be mobilized by the congregation's culture and processes to accomplish religious and social purposes.

You may want to close your study of congregational resources by reflecting on the ways your congregation's resources have been mobilized in the past. When, for example, have members shown extraordinary commitment to a special project? Have there been moments when your buildings met a special congregational or community need? Has a special mission gift made possible life-changing events that members remember years later? Reflecting on ways resources have become capacities can provide the clues to latent possibilities in your congregation's present and future.

NOTES

1. The previous *Handbook* dealt with resources in several chapters, most specifically in terms of the demographic dimension of identity. Some critics, reviewing the previous edition, asked whether we ought to give more attention to the people who make up the congregation. Others cited the need for more explicit attention to issues of buildings, finance, and volunteers. Still others felt the *Handbook* underplayed the role of religious faith itself as a dimension of congregational life. This chapter represents a response to many of those observations.

2. Melvin D. Williams, *Community in a Black Pentecostal Church* (Pittsburgh: University of Pittsburgh Press, 1974).

3. Richard K. Avery and Donald S. Marsh, "I Am the Church" (Hope, Mich.: Hope Publishing, 1972).

4. For an excellent discussion of this point, see Robert J. Schreiter, *Constructing Local Theologies* (Maryknoll, N.Y.: Orbis, 1985), chapter 6.

5. Center for Social and Religious Research, Hartford Seminary, 7 Sherman St., Hartford, CT 06105.

6. For instructions on constructing an age-sex pyramid, see Murray H. Leiffer, *The Effective City Church* (Nashville: Abingdon, 1961), 150ff.

7. Table 5.1 contains data collected for the "Congregational Communities Project." These two congregations are described in Nancy Tatom Ammerman, *Congregation and Community* (New Brunswick, N.J.: Rutgers University Press, 1977).

8. James P. Wind and James W. Lewis, eds., *American Congregations*, vol. 1 (Chicago: University of Chicago Press, 1994), chapter 1.

9. Greater detail might have been available with further research in First Church's records. Such detail is usually not necessary for obtaining a sense of trends over time.

10. See also William McKinney, "The Role of National Religious Institutions in Congregational Affiliation and Growth," in *Church and Synagogue Affiliation: Theory, Research and Practice*, ed. Amy L. Sales and Gary Tobin (Westport, Conn.: Greenwood, 1995).

11. The three figures illustrate different ways of presenting membership data for congregational use. The first simply plots total membership and church attendance. Its value lies in its simplicity. One need not be a statistician to understand that years are plotted along the horizontal axis and total people on the vertical axis. It is helpful to see one trend (membership) alongside another (attendance). We might have plotted other data (for example, church school enrollment) in the same graph, but presenting much more data runs the risk of clutter. Figure 2 is more complex. We wanted to look at overall additions to membership and their components. We chose an area graph. The data in figure 3 are similar but are shown in a "stacked bar comparison."

12. Baptism may be as a child or an adult. Practices vary widely by tradition and even by congregation. In Roman Catholicism and many Protestant and Anglican traditions, this takes place shortly after birth, but for Baptist, Pentecostal, and other religious communities, baptism is a rite for adults. At First Church, the vast majority of baptisms are of young children. Confirmation is usually a rite of passage for teenagers in which the individual reaffirms his or her baptism. In the figures presented here, many of those listed as additions by confirmation will also have been counted in earlier years as additions by baptism. First Church began reporting confirmations in 1971. Most congregations' records do not distinguish between confirmands baptized in the congregation and those baptized elsewhere. Confession of faith usually implies baptism but often not confirmation; reaffirmation of faith suggests a baptized (and perhaps confirmed) individual making an adult decision to identify as a member of the religious community.

13. Certain kinds of outflows are called *losses*, but it is unusual to budget these.

14. The congregation's treasurer or accountant will, of course, wish to keep detailed records of each employee's compensation, but for budgeting and reporting purposes the expenditures may be combined.

15. Patterns of fund raising and giving vary greatly by faith tradition. For example, most Jewish congregations are supported through a dues structure.

16. We recognize that endowments are uncommon in many religious traditions. Some readers will not find this section helpful. For congregations who depend on endowment income, issues raised here are of considerable importance.

17. On rare occasions, organizations are offered endowments or other gifts that they do not accept. The usual reason for turning down an endowment gift is that the gift carries a restriction that is incompatible with the core purposes of the organization.

18. From 1926 to 1992 stocks were the best performing asset class in 84 percent of rolling ten-year holding periods (Ibbotson Associates, as quoted by Scudder, Stevens & Clark, Inc., *At the Helm*, Fall 1993.)

19. Studies of college and university endowments show great variability in asset allocations. One sees equity allocation as high as 85 percent for some schools (1986 NACUBO endowment study). More typical of the "better" performing institutions is an equity allocation of 68 percent (Association of Governing Boards of Colleges and Universities, *Improving Endowment Management*, 1985.) A common recommendation for long-term asset allocation is 60 percent equities.

20. Imagine that in 1926 the treasurers of two neighboring churches in a particular city were in the habit of eating lunch together from time to time. They enjoyed the meetings, as it gave them an opportunity to discuss the church-related issues of the day, compare notes on their churches and pastors, swap ideas about investments, and cement their friendship.

During the course of one of their lunches in 1926 the two treasurers discovered that each church had an endowment of $100,000 and that each governing board allowed three percent of the market value of the endowment to be spent annually. The only difference, they discovered, was that First Bond Church invested the endowment entirely in corporate bonds while the First Equity Church its entire endowment in the stock market.

Little did they know what was to come. The stock market crashed in 1929, ushering in the Great Depression. The turbulence in the world and nation continued as the Second World War, the cold war, the Civil Rights movement, the Vietnam conflict, the energy crisis, and unprecedented inflation followed in the next several decades.

Throughout this uncertain century the treasurers of the two churches continued to meet for lunch. In 1991, as their predecessors had, they compared notes on their endowments. Each governing board had firmly held to the investment and spending policies of 1926. First Bond Church's endowment had nearly a fourfold gain, growing to over $467,000. That endowment provided Bond Church with $14,000 in annual budgeted income. By contrast, the First Equity Church endowment, invested in stocks, had a sixtyfold increase in value and was now worth $6,000,000. Those assets provided an income of $180,000. While the two churches remained similar in outlook, First Equity Church, by virtue of its larger endowment, was more able to support programs, maintain its facilities, and contribute to missions.

What accounts for this difference? Not luck, or the acquisition of new gifts, because in this parable we assumed no new additions to the endowments. The growth occurred because of the long-term compounding effect of investment returns. The difference in investment return of stocks and bonds over the period of 1926 to 1991 was about 4 percent. That seemingly small difference compounded over 65 years produces a startling contrast.

The First Equity Church did not even have a lucky or smart money manager selecting stocks: In the parable First Equity Church simply invested in a broad index of stocks in the market—in companies that went belly-up as well as those that became immense successes.

21. State laws provide guidelines for the use of endowment return and should be consulted.

22. A well-designed spending and reinvestment policy accomplishes many things beyond determining the amount to be spent. Such a policy theoretically (1) allows the governing board and investment managers to invest the assets for the best long-term total return for the church, rather than for short-term cash flow needs; (2) provides a stable and predictable source of revenue for operations; and (3) allows all unspent total return to be reinvested to protect the investment principal from erosion by inflation. Such policies are common in colleges, universities, and theological schools, with a spending rate of 5 percent of a three-year average of the endowment market value functioning as a norm, if not a standard formula. J. Peter Williamson, *Funds for the Future: College Endowment Management for the 1990s* (Westport, Conn.: The Common Fund, 1993), 5-111. Elaborations of this simple formula attempt to smooth the revenue stream and restrain spending, while remaining responsive to long-term market trends. See Samuel H. Ballam III and Robert T. Forrester, "Endowment Spending Rates," *Higher Education Management Newsletter* (May 1988).

23. James P. Wind, Address to Sacred Trusts XI, Salt Lake City, Utah, Spring, 1993.

24. Stained-glass memorials to early leaders, for example, say much about the congregation's heritage, just as liturgical arrangements or painted scriptural quotations on sanctuary walls give evidence of the congregation's theology, both past and present. The use of spaces for child care, recreation, or music says a great deal about the congregation's commitment to ministry and service (although this reality, all too often, is poorly advertised!), and the care of its building(s) and grounds almost always communicates something about how the congregation practices the stewardship of its resources.

25. John T. McGreevy, *Parish Boundaries: The Catholic Encounter with Race in the Twentieth-Century Urban North* (Chicago: University of Chicago Press, 1996).

26. Congregations frequently express frustration about finding experienced and qualified architects. One source of referrals are other congregations involved in similar repair and renovation efforts. For congregations with older buildings, the network of local and statewide historic preservation and planning organizations often maintains information on architects, as well as other building-related consultants and contractors. Once your congregation has several leads to architects, proceed by checking credentials and work experience, talk with other clients of the architects, ask to see samples of written reports, and take a look at comparable repair and renovation projects the architect has completed.

The congregation's building committee—which should include laity familiar with the property—should plan to meet with at least two or three architects with whom it feels comfortable. Tour the property with each architect and discuss the problems identified before taking the next step and soliciting proposals from them for planning and designing repair and renovation work.

27. Several excellent publications are available to guide congregations in the regular inspection and ongoing care of their properties. These publications include everything from seasonal checklists to descriptions of typical conditions to look for as part of an ongoing maintenance plan.

28. Robert Wineburg, of the University of North Carolina at Greensboro, has found, in addition, that the availability and flexibility of religious properties was the single most important catalyst motivating human service groups to work with congregations in Greensboro.

29. For further information and assistance, contact Partners for Sacred Places, a national, nonprofit, nonsectarian organization dedicated to assisting congregations and their communities with the stewardship of religious properties. Partners can be reached at 1616 Walnut Street, Suite 2310, Philadelphia, PA 19103. Phone (215) 546-1288.

Chapter 6

Leadership and the Study of the Congregation

JACKSON W. CARROLL

Consider the following scenario: An actor is offered a lead role in an ongoing drama. What makes the drama unique is that it is open-ended and at least partly improvisational. It has an ongoing story with a cast of characters who have been playing their parts for some time, but the script is not fixed. It is constrained only by the story that has unfolded thus far, the set and setting, and the capacities of the actors who take part in the drama. The lead actor's role is to interact with others of the cast in shaping the unfolding story.

Is such a scenario fanciful? Perhaps. But it provides a partial and useful analogy for what happens in congregations, especially when a new pastor comes into a congregation as its primary leader or when new lay leaders take office. The leader assumes a role in a setting where there is an ongoing narrative and a cast of characters who have helped to shape the congregation's story over the years. That story is their own, shaped by them as they take part in the play, but it is also part of a larger narrative about God's dealing with God's people throughout history. What has gone before, both in the congregation's local story and in its participation in the larger story of its religious tradition, sets limits on the congregation's unfolding story, but it does not determine the story or seal it off from new possibilities, new

twists and turns in the story. The pastor's and lay leaders' roles as lead actors are to interact with the others in the congregation's cast, leading them as they build on what has gone before to shape this particular congregation's unfolding story in its particular time and place.

What must the leaders do to carry out this task? The purpose of this chapter is to answer this question in some detail. We do not attempt to offer a general discussion of congregational leadership. Rather, our focus is primarily on leadership as it relates to congregational study, that is, on leadership tasks involved in understanding, becoming part of, and helping to shape a congregation's unfolding story. Let us set the stage for this discussion by considering leadership in relation to the frames we have discussed in preceding chapters.

Before those exercising leadership can play any significant part in shaping the next act of the congregation's narrative, they must become acquainted with the set and setting—the congregation's social context and its place in it. What resources, opportunities, and constraints do the congregation's buildings, location, and role in the larger community offer to the congregation as it engages in its ministry and mission? How are its facilities and their location in the larger community an asset or liability? What is the setting like? What are the issues that face those who live there? Do these issues have any significance for the unfolding story of the congregation? Does the congregation's story suggest ways of being involved in the setting? How are those who live in the setting like or different from the actors already involved in the congregational drama? How might the congregation recruit these neighbors to become actors in the narrative that the congregation embodies? Which of the larger communities the congregation belongs to have a bearing on its story?

Another key task for leadership is learning the congregation's particular story. How can a pastor or lay leaders lead a congregation's unfolding drama if they are not aware of the story or stories of which the congregation is a part? The pastor may know the larger story of the religious tradition(s) in which the congregation participates and may also have experience in other congregational dramas that seem similar to this one. But the pastor must also learn the unique story of this particular congregation if he or she is to be a helpful and effective leader. What are the implications of this story for the unfolding narrative? What important twists and turns has it taken in the past? Who are the keepers of the story? In what ways is the story enacted in rituals and expressed symbolically in language or material forms? How does the congregation's particular narrative embody the larger narrative of its religious tradition(s)? What is its character? Is it pessimistic or hopeful? Is it exclusive or inclusive? Is the narrative held in such a way as to seal off change, or does it open the congregation to new directions?

Those who are asked to lead the unfolding congregational drama also must learn how things are done in the congregation—how things happen. Which actors do what? Are there informal as well as formal stage directions? Do the actors plan together what to do next, or do they really improvise? How are decisions made about what the congregation does? Who makes such decisions and by what authority? How widely among the congregational actors is decision-making shared? What happens when conflicts arise over how to do things or what the next act should be? What should be done when one of the lead actors cannot act or uses the trust that his or her position carries to take advantage of one of the others in the cast? Are the conflicts dealt with openly and directly, or are they hushed up and smoothed over without really being addressed? How does this congregation assess what it is doing? How are new actors incorporated in the drama? How are the congregation's actors prepared for new roles they must play? Are there expectations or norms about how congregational actors are to participate in the story? Are there sanctions for those who fail to live up to expectations or play their roles adequately?

Yet another set of key questions centers around resources available to the congregation for enacting its drama. What about the set and its props—the physical facilities available? How adequate are they? How well maintained? What about financial resources? Most congregations, unlike some theaters, have no outside "financial angels" (though they may have endowments). The actors must themselves generate the necessary financial support to carry on the story. How well is this understood and the responsibility shared? Are the financial resources sufficient for the tasks at hand? And what of people resources? Who are the actors? How did they join the company? What gifts do they bring to the drama—gifts of faith and faithfulness and talents to be used in shaping the unfolding story? How well are they supported and encouraged in the use of these gifts?

Although we placed the chapter on theology first in this book as a reminder that doing congregational studies is at heart a practical theological task, we place it last here in this list of leadership tasks as a further reminder that as congregational leaders reflect on the congregation's set and setting, its story thus far, its ways of doing things, and its resources, they must also always be asking, Where is God present in this congregation's unfolding story? Where is God present in its setting? What constitutes faithfulness for this congregation in this time and place and with the particular resources that are available to it? What is God calling it to be and do in the next act? What theological questions are raised by issues and decisions that the congregation faces? What resources are present in its own story and in the larger religious traditions of which it is a part that can help it to answer these questions?[1]

The multifaceted approach to leadership that these various tasks imply is similar to what Barbara Wheeler has called a "voluntary" or "open systems" approach. In a helpful analysis of three approaches to congregational studies, she draws out the different implications for leadership in each approach.[2] What she calls the "wineskin" or "contextual" approach views the congregation as primarily the creation of its context. The congregation has little dynamism in its own right but gets its identity as it adapts to external challenges. The task of leadership in this adaptive process is to bring new life, new meaning, and direction to the congregation.

An almost opposite view is what she calls the "cultural" approach to congregations, which understands congregations as rich repositories of meaning that precede a particular leader's or group of leaders' involvement in the congregation and last beyond their tenure. Leaders are more likely to be incorporated into the local culture than to transform it. Their task is to "harvest the local knowledge," bring it to consciousness, and give it shape.

Her third perspective, the "voluntary" or "open systems" approach, understands congregations as a complex interplay of external and internal factors. Contextual forces act on congregations and call for adaptive responses, and internal meanings and capacities within congregations enable them to *choose* to shape their own lives and *act on* rather than always *be acted upon* by their environment. In this view, the leadership task is that of goading "the whole community into action, assisting them in remaking old symbols in appropriate contemporary form." Wheeler maintains that to some extent one's theological convictions will influence one's choice among the three approaches to congregations and leadership. Although proponents of each approach will find help in this handbook for exercising the task of leadership, our perspective, as noted, is nearest to that of the voluntary approach.

In summary, when you assume a lead role in a congregation's drama, whether as clergy or layperson, you assume a demanding and difficult task. You must work hard, be willing to learn, have the ability to improvise, place considerable trust in the other actors in the situation, and be open to the leading of God's Spirit. It is more a matter of artistry than technical expertise. To be sure, some of the issues that congregations and their leaders face are relatively routine, and the responses to them are generally uncomplicated. These are not our primary concern. Many congregational issues, however, are complex, have multiple dimensions, and do not lend themselves to simple or "tried-and-true" answers. As Russell Ackoff once wrote:

> Managers are not confronted with problems that are independent of each other, but with dynamic situations that consist of complex systems of changing problems that interact with each other. I call such situations *messes.* Problems are abstractions extracted from messes by analysis. Managers do not solve problems; they manage messes.[3]

Issues that qualify as "messes" demand learning and innovation on your part as congregational leaders. What we have presented in the preceding chapters provides perspectives, methods, and techniques for addressing many of the learning tasks that will help you understand the congregation, confront its "messes," and find ways of leading the congregation through them. Doing congregational study will not in itself provide the answers to the messes. Rather, it provides the knowledge that you can draw on—sometimes tacitly, sometimes explicitly—as you determine the particular moves you will make. The issue at hand may be deciding what kind of stewardship program to use, calling a new pastor, hiring a new staff member, determining whether to begin an alternative worship service, establishing budget priorities, or debating whether to engage in a program of church growth. It may involve painful decisions as diverse as whether to sell one's historic but inadequate building and relocate, or how to deal with a problem of sexual abuse in the congregation. In every case, you will find the information gained from asking questions as part of a congregational study essential for responding faithfully and effectively to the issue. Such study will rarely tell you how to respond; it will, however, provide invaluable direction in shaping an appropriate and faithful response.

A Perspective on Leadership[4]

Many definitions and discussions of leadership exist. Some try to specify traits or characteristics of good leaders; others focus on the various roles leaders play or on differing leadership styles. Still others consider leadership in terms of situational dynamics, based on the belief that what a particular leader does is contingent upon the dynamics of the situation. And still others try to synthesize these various perspectives.

Although our approach to leadership draws from several of these perspectives, it is not our purpose to review this broader literature here.[5] Instead, we focus on leadership in congregations, primarily in relation to congregational study. In doing so, we agree with those who view leadership not as a set of traits that a "good" leader must have, but as an *activity* that can be exercised by various people within a congregation or other organization.[6] As an activity, leadership in relation to congregational study involves assisting a congregation's members in several key tasks: *(1) helping the congregation gain a realistic understanding of its particular situation and circumstances; (2) assisting members to develop a vision for their corporate life that is faithful to their best understanding of God and God's purposes for the congregation in this time and place; and (3) helping them embody that vision in the congregation's corporate life.* The last task also includes solving problems, resolving issues that threaten to "sidetrack" or hinder the pursuit of the vision.

Specific and more traditional roles of ordained and lay leaders—for example, preaching, teaching, liturgical leadership and other priestly roles, ordering the congregation's life, developing necessary resources, providing systems of congregational care and nurture, evangelism, and engaging in acts of service and prophetic witness in the community—are among the particular ways leaders undertake the three key tasks. Different religious traditions will understand these leadership activities, and how they are carried out, somewhat differently. African American congregations, for example, expect the pastor to take a preeminent leadership role. They often place less emphasis on shared leadership of clergy and laity. Traditions with a distinct liturgical emphasis will view the leadership tasks through the lens of priestly understandings of religious leadership.

In addition to differences in religious tradition, congregational size also makes a difference in leadership expectations. As we will emphasize at several points in what follows, small congregations often value leadership styles that are different from the styles preferred by large congregations. Such differences notwithstanding, we believe that for the good of your congregation, leaders (lay and ordained) must engage in one way or another in the three leadership tasks we consider here. Later in this chapter, we explore in some depth what these tasks mean in relation to congregational study—how congregational study enriches your capacity to accomplish these tasks—and we suggest other methods and techniques of congregational study that can facilitate leadership.

Authority to Lead

Before doing so, however, we consider an important resource that those entrusted with leadership in congregations bring to their tasks: their authority as leaders. Authority is legitimate power. It is the capacity to direct, influence, coordinate, or otherwise guide the thought and behavior of others in ways they acknowledge as right or legitimate. The leadership of those who have authority is accepted as being consistent with the beliefs and values of the congregation and its religious tradition and as contributing to the congregation's mission.[7] Because of this, the authority to lead is an important resource for leadership.

Authority is not, however, synonymous with leadership. Some who have authority to lead do not provide leadership regarding the tasks noted above. They may be unwilling or unable to use their authority to lead. In contrast, an individual or a group can engage in leadership as we have described it without having the authority (legitimacy) to do so—for example, individuals or groups who are impatient with the lack of leadership from those who have authority, or those who disagree with the direction an organization is taking, may challenge the organization's direction on the basis of its espoused values. While Martin Luther King, Jr., and his colleagues in the Civil Rights movement had authority within the Black church and Civil Rights organizations, they had no authority in the larger society outside these organizations to challenge racial segregation. Still, they exercised leadership in the society in a striking and effective manner. In his book *Leadership Without Easy Answers*, Ronald Heifetz describes those who lead without authority or beyond their authority as providing "creative deviance on the frontline"; that is, they often deviate from authorized norms for doing things and are also frequently closer to the experiences of those who are stakeholders in the situation than are those who hold formal authority to lead.[8]

Leading without authority also occurs within congregations. As many congregational leaders know, members who have no authority within the congregation nevertheless raise important questions and challenges to the congregation's formal leaders about aspects of the congregation's life and work. Such challenges, often based on a different vision of what it means for the church to be faithful, may lead the congregation to re-vision and reorient the way it goes about its mission. At other times challenges by those without authority come because the formal leaders are (or are perceived to be) ineffective or misguided. Or they may be believed to be engaging in inappropriate or wrong behavior—

for example, sexual abuse or mishandling of funds. Sometimes, of course, challenges may come from those in the congregation who may have no authority but have power—Mr. or Ms. "Big Bucks," for example—and who use it to get their way, despite the wishes of others. They may engage in "deviance on the frontline," but their challenges may not always be creative as far as the congregation is concerned.

Whatever the reason for the challenges, they often lead to conflict. Although it is tempting to assume conflicts are always damaging and should be avoided at all costs, this is a mistake too many congregations make. To be sure, conflicts are painful, and some are damaging. If, however, they are faced directly and openly, most can lead to greater congregational health. For example, conflicts that reflect different visions for a congregation or different strategies for reaching a commonly held vision can be healthy in helping the congregation to clarify its vision and find ways to give it expression. Likewise conflicts over ineffective formal leadership or improper behavior by formal leaders can lead to corrective measures that are essential for restoring both member morale and congregational integrity. (See chapter 4 on process for a discussion of congregational conflict.)

In summary, it is important to avoid equating authority and leadership. Some who emerge as leaders in a congregation have no authority to lead but make critical contributions to its life. At the same time, however, the authority to lead is a resource that may be used (or misused) in important ways.

When we think especially (though not exclusively) about clergy, two aspects of their authority are particularly important: These include differences in the *sources of clergy authority* and in *ways in which authority is granted*.[9] Some clergy have authority because they claim a special calling from God or because their ordination sets them apart and defines them as having a unique relationship to God or the sacred tradition. They have authority because *they represent God or the sacred* in a distinctive way. Other clergy have authority on the basis of *particular competence*—specialized knowledge and skills—

for leading a congregation. Neither of these two sources of authority excludes the other, though different religious traditions and different Christian denominations have often given more emphasis to one or the other of them.[10]

Also important are the ways in which authority is granted or earned. Here the distinction is between *formal* or *office authority* and *informal* or *personal authority*. While both are forms of legitimate power, formal or office authority is the authorization to lead that a clergyperson receives, for example, through ordination. The denomination or congregation—depending on the religious tradition— sets the person apart and acknowledges that he or she has the necessary calling from God and/or the special competence (the requisite gifts and graces) needed to perform certain representative roles central to the group's religious tradition—for example, preaching, teaching, liturgical leadership, and, in some traditions, ordering the life of the congregation. Lay leaders receive office authority through election to an office, which may be acknowledged in some traditions in a commissioning service. Informal or personal authority, in contrast, is earned by the pastor or lay person on the basis of his or her personal qualities. Although such qualities may be no more than that the leader is a likable person, personal authority is usually given and sustained on much more solid grounds. It comes from a recognition of the leader as a competent, authentic, and trustworthy person. It is what John Fletcher came to call "religious authenticity" as he listened to laity talk about what was important to them about pastoral leadership.[11] A pastor who exhibits religious authenticity is one who is trusted— and granted personal authority—because he or she has "head and heart" together; that is, he or she is trusted as both being competent and exhibiting spiritual depth. Being granted personal authority by a congregation will not be acknowledged in a formal ceremony, but when it is given, it is not unlike experiencing a second ordination.

Calling and competence, office and personal authority are not mutually exclusive. Both are important for leadership, and they reinforce each other. Office authority often opens the door for pastors or laity to exercise leadership, signaling in effect that these people are authorized (either by their denomination or the congregation) to lead. Personal authority, however, is a particularly important resource when a congregation (or an individual) is facing a complex problem for which there are no clear-cut or easy answers. Having personal authority makes a leader more likely to establish what Ronald Heifetz calls a "holding environment" in which she or he *has the power to hold the attention of another party and facilitate adaptive work.*"[12] Adaptive work is the kind of work needed to frame or reframe a congregation's vision for ministry and explore ways of giving expression to the vision in the face of the particular challenge the congregation is facing. Using an extended case of a physician and a family in which the husband-father was ill with a terminal cancer, Heifetz describes how the physician's personal authority allowed her to help the family work through the various issues the cancer had created for them. Her personal authority not only established the holding environment in which they could face the issue and contain the stresses that the illness created for them, but it also established her right to command and direct their attention, to diagnose their problem, and to help them develop a plan for addressing it. Further, it established a situation in which they could gather and share information necessary to face the issue and in which she could sequence the flow of information about the process of the illness and eventual death based on her assumptions about the family's resilience. And because she had their trust and access to the necessary information, she could also frame and reframe the issues, helping the family to face the consequences of various ways of approaching the future and to deal with conflicting points of view. Finally, Heifetz notes, her authority gave her the power to choose the kind of decision-making process that she and they would follow—for example, whether it would be consultative, consensual, autocratic, or of some other type.

The process Heifetz describes is equally applicable to congregational leadership. Your authority to lead—especially your personal authority, whether as pastor or lay leader—provides a holding environment in which you can lead the congregation as it faces difficult problems in its corporate life (or as individual members face difficult personal problems).[13] In the holding environment you can help them face up to their problem and contain the stresses the problem creates for them. You can assist them in gathering and examining needed information for understanding and responding to their problem. You can help them to frame and reframe the problem in light of the information at hand—and to frame and reframe their vision for ministry as it illumines the particular problem they are facing. Your authority as leader also permits you to help the congregation face and deal with conflicts the situation produces. And your authority also allows you to choose, within limits of congregational polity and culture, what kind of decision-making process will be followed: Should you, as leader, function primarily as a consultant and let the congregation decide? Should you and the congregation seek a consensus? Or should you simply tell the congregation what it should do?

To summarize, although individuals and groups can exercise leadership without authority, having authority is an important resource for leading congregations. The leader's relationship to God or the sacred and her or his knowledge and skills are important grounds for granting authority for leadership. As these grounds are recognized formally and especially informally, pastors and lay leaders are accorded the trust that is necessary for facing and responding with faithfulness to difficult and often "messy" issues that congregations confront.

Leadership Tasks and Congregational Study

Earlier, we indicated our belief that leadership is best considered as an activity that can be exercised by various people within a congregation or other organization. We further suggested that, as an activity, it involves several key tasks: (1) helping the congregation gain a realistic understanding of its particular situation and circumstances; (2) assisting members to develop a vision for their corporate life that is faithful to their best understanding of God and God's purposes for the congregation in this time and place; and (3) helping them embody that vision in the congregation's corporate life while attempting to address various challenges that arise. What, more specifically, do these three tasks involve in relation to congregational study?

Gaining a Realistic Picture of the Congregation and Its Situation

A crucial task for leaders and a key first step in practical theological thinking is helping a congregation gain a realistic picture of itself, its situation, and its possibilities in the present and immediate future. Practical theologian Don Browning calls this activity "descriptive theology" and emphasizes that understanding the concrete situation of ministry in all its particularity is not simply preparation for the "real" work of theological reflection but is an important theological task in its own right and part of an overall process that he calls "strategic practical theology."[14]

In a general planning process, when you work to gain a realistic picture of the congregation and its situation, your task involves achieving a holistic perspective that incorporates the several frames that we have considered in preceding chapters. Those doing the planning need to understand their congregation as an organization in relation to a larger context, as a culture, as a set of processes or ways of doing things, and as a collection of resources that can be mobilized in behalf of its mission. When addressing more specific issues—for example, making changes in the congregation's worship life, planning a stewardship campaign, or addressing a conflict over the use of space—less comprehensive (but no less realistic and accurate) assessments are needed. Without such realistic assessments, whether general or specific, planners often experience frustration. Either they fail to see new possibilities for the congregation because of an inadequate grasp of the situation, or they find that their dreams for the congregation do not fit the realities of the situation. They are blocked by "mental models"—images or assumptions, often untested, about the ways things are—that do not fit the situation. As Peter Senge has written, "Our 'mental models' determine not only how we make sense of the world, but how we take action."[15] Consider the following examples:

- When vestry members of a small, urban Episcopal congregation were asked about their number one priority for their parish, without hesitation they said attracting young families with children. They had once had a number of young families as members and a strong children's Sunday school. Now, however, not only were there no young families in the community surrounding the congregation, the average age of the congregation's members was almost seventy, and the youngest member was fifty-three! Vestry members were operating with an image or "mental model" of the congregation that reflected that earlier period but was totally out of touch with present realities.

- A rural congregation, also small, had almost the opposite experience. It was growing significantly because young families were moving into its community. Its educational facilities, however, were woefully inadequate to handle the growth. A proposal to build a new church school building was met with immediate resistance from older members who made up the core leadership group. They had grown up during the depression years and remembered their parents' struggle to pay off the debt on the present facilities. Despite the large influx of reasonably well-off new members, the older leaders could not imagine being able to raise the funds needed for a new building, much less going into debt

for such a project. Like the urban congregation, they were also operating with a mental model of the congregation that was out of touch with their present circumstances.

- The pastor of a mainline Protestant, suburban congregation decided to change the worship service of his congregation by incorporating elements from so-called seeker worship services modeled after Willow Creek Community Church in suburban Chicago. Younger members of the congregation, including later baby boomers and Generation X members, were enthusiastic about the innovations, especially the use of praise choruses and other popular Christian music in the service. The music director, a classically trained musician, was livid, as were many older members of the congregation, who preferred traditional hymns and the more formal liturgical patterns and language to which they were accustomed. Here too we see the clash of mental models, two powerful visions that reflect both differences in the experiences of older and younger generations and theological assumptions about what constitutes appropriate Christian worship.

Many such examples could be identified, not only from congregations but from all sorts of organizations, large and small. The point is that our mental models often hold us captive to old ways of thinking and acting that have no relevance to the present circumstances—like the woman who cut the wings off the chicken before putting it in the roasting pan without ever asking why (see Johnny Ray Youngblood's story in the introduction). Or one group's models may be in conflict with another's. In some instances, the models may reflect untested assumptions about the culture—for example, that we're an inclusive congregation; or about the context—for example, the vestry members who assumed that there were still many young families in their community; or about process—for example, that the congregation has an open decision-making process; or about resources—for example, that we could not possibly afford to build new educational facilities.

Often, too, our mental models reflect what are called "cohort" or generational differences in perspectives, perspectives shaped by experiences during the years in which a generation came of age.[16] The music and "worship wars" referred to previously are examples. A problem with mental models, as Senge has noted, is that they are often tacit. They exist below the level of awarenes. Thus, if, you as leaders are to help a congregation make a realistic assessment of its situation, you will need to help members become aware of their models, their assumptions about the way things are. This involves both *inquiry*—surfacing relevant data regarding the issue under consideration—and *reflection*—asking how the data confirms or challenges and corrects existing mental models. There are several ways of doing this; we begin with more comprehensive or complex ways.

Needs Assessment. As congregations engage in planning for current and future ministries, one way of examining and challenging existing mental models is to undertake a "needs assessment" process. Such a process involves gathering the information necessary for identifying the needs and priorities for ministry of individuals and groups who are already participants in the congregation and also of those in the larger community who are not members. Gathering data about the needs and concerns of these two groups is an important strategy of inquiry for planning based on reasonably accurate information rather than untested assumptions.

Some may object to a congregation engaging in needs assessment because they equate the process with consumer demand analysis. To them, needs assessment suggests a reactive response that reflects the lack of a clear sense of the church's purpose, a kind of "knee-jerk" approach to ministry and mission. Such criticism should not be taken lightly. Congregations are not called to be chameleons, uncritically adapting their coloration to the circumstances. To change the metaphor, con-

gregations are not called to "scratch every itch" identified as a need. To use needs assessment strategies in an uncritical way is to grossly misuse them. If, however, we think of needs assessment as enabling a congregation to understand more fully how it can legitimately meet the spiritual and material needs for ministry—of its members or of those outside the church—then needs assessment is not simply a means of market analysis. It is a positive tool for a more faithful and effective ministry.

One of the best known recent examples of needs assessment is that of Willow Creek Community Church in South Barrington, Illinois. Willow Creek, the prototypical megachurch, has pioneered "seeker ministry" using what it learned from its efforts to understand composite "seekers," whom the staff named "Unchurched Harry" and "Unchurched Mary." Using a variety of needs assessment methods—for example, discussions, surveys, and door-to-door canvassing—Willow Creek's then mostly volunteer leadership team led by Bill Hybels, now senior pastor, developed a strategy for moving Unchurched Harry and Unchurched Mary out of their easy chairs in front of the television to the point of Christian maturity. Willow Creek's research suggested five reasons that such people were indifferent to the church: (1) churches were always asking for money, while often nothing significant seemed to be done with the money; (2) church services were boring and lifeless; (3) church services were predictable; (4) sermons were irrelevant to daily life in the real world; and (5) the pastor made people feel guilty and ignorant, so they left church feeling worse than when they entered.[17] The reasons Unchurched Harry and Unchurched Mary gave for avoiding involvement in the church became the basis for many of the innovative strategies that Willow Creek has pioneered for attracting seekers and leading them to mature faith. Some have criticized Willow Creek's seeker strategy for its heavy market focus; however, the effectiveness of needs assessment in helping Willow Creek leaders shape a distinctive ministry provides a clear testimony to its usefulness for them and other congregations with different understandings of ministry. A less dramatic but nonetheless effective example of using needs assessment is described in sidebar 6.1. In this instance, a pastor sent to a dying congregation undertook a needs assessment that played a key role in helping him and his lay leaders redevelop their congregation.

Sidebar 6.1
NEEDS ASSESSMENT AT GOOD SHEPHERD LUTHERAN

Located in Oak Park, Illinois, an integrated community, Good Shepherd had lost about half of its members to white flight. By 1981, the membership had dropped to 50. The remaining members voted to keep the congregation open and to work to revitalize it. The denomination assisted them by sending in Pastor Jack Finney, designating them as a mission redevelopment congregation, and giving them modest financial support. "The key to surviving," according to Jack Finney, "is to put down roots in the local community." He got census data and discovered that the most common household type in south Oak Park was the two-parent couple with children. Nationally, it was this type of family that was returning to the church in droves, looking for spiritual nurture for the adults and a Christian education for the children. Jack Finney advertised and went out visiting. People started to come in. One woman remembers the change this way: "One spring there were six people in the choir, and in the fall there were 25." [At the time of this writing] average attendance stands at 185, with just under 400 baptized members.

From Nancy Tatom Ammerman, *Congregation and Community* (New Brunswick, N.J.: Rutgers University Press, 1996).

In what follows, we suggest several methods of needs assessment that involve a variety of congregational members. At times, however, as in the example in sidebar 6.1, the pastor may be the key person doing the needs assessment.

Several strategies are available for undertaking needs assessment of existing congregational members. An existing general-purpose questionnaire, the Church Planning Inventory (see appendix A), contains a number of items that can help a study team create a profile of member needs and interests. Or the team may decide to design a questionnaire of its own, following the guidelines discussed in chapter 7, to ask about concerns specific to the congregation. As is noted there, a major limitation of questionnaires is that they generally offer fixed questions and responses. The needs and program possibilities asked about are limited to those conceived of by the designers of the questionnaire, and the survey may not capture other possibilities and concerns that a face-to-face interview, for example, may turn up. Often a small number of face-to-face interviews with a representative group of members will help to expand the possibilities included in the final questionnaire. Allowing for open-ended, write-in responses is another way of getting additional information, but many people do not make the effort to complete them. Despite these limitations, carefully constructed questionnaires are an important way for you to conduct a needs assessment of existing members.

As an alternative to questionnaires and individual face-to-face interviews, focus groups are an important tool for doing needs assessment. They allow for group interaction about needs and program possibilities while also taking less time than conducting interviews with individuals. These too are discussed in chapter 7. How the groups' participants are chosen is especially important when creating focus groups for needs assessment. In some cases it is helpful for each group to reflect a cross section of the congregation, so that, for example, every group contains older, middle-aged, and younger generations, or is made up of more active and less active members. In other cases, and particularly in doing needs assessment, it may be more helpful to construct the groups so that each represents a particular age group and includes both more active and less active members. In either case, when you construct the groups, you should attempt to ensure that participants represent the congregation's membership or the particular group you are trying to represent.

When engaging in needs assessment for planning ministries to those outside the congregation's membership, you will find that many of the methods and techniques suggested in chapter 2 on context and further elaborated in chapter 7 on methods are appropriate. A primary strategy of inquiry is careful examination of United States Census data—especially the detailed census data about social and economic characteristics of community residents. One group of congregations in North Carolina discovered from a newspaper report of census data that their county was among the top ten in the United States in the number of unwed pregnancies. The report was a catalyst for further inquiry and reflection, leading not only to a challenge of existing mental models about their community but also to cooperative action by members of the congregations to address the issue.

Offering a perspective on religious preferences, values, and life-styles of residents in particular areas of a community, several census data providers have constructed profiles based on a combination of United States Census survey data. In the following chapter, we discuss some of the limitations of these profiles; however, used with care, such data can be useful in giving a congregation insights into the characteristics and needs of people in their "ministry" area. Although we believe that it would be a misuse of life-style data to decide, for example, to limit ministry only to people who are "like us" in life-styles and values, life-style data can help congregational leaders make a realistic assessment of who lives in the area and what their interests and needs for ministry are likely to be.

The use of life-style data raises an important point for all efforts at needs assessment. If questionnaires, focus groups, analysis of census data, and other techniques of data gathering are not simply to lead to the kind of reactive, market approach that we criticized earlier, all such inquiry must include reflection. The aim of such data gathering is to challenge existing mental models about what the congregation is or is not, what it can or cannot do. The data also can suggest new possibilities for ministry and mission. But alternative mental models and alternative possibilities for ministry and mission need to be tested from the perspective of the congregation's core convictions about God and God's purposes, as we suggested in the chapter on theology.

Other Strategies for Inquiry and Reflection. Although needs assessment strategies are most appropriate when you seek a more comprehensive picture of the congregation or its community to inform planning and to challenge existing mental models, a variety of other tools and strategies are helpful in dealing with more specific issues. All of them involve what some have called "slowing down the action" as a form of "reflective practice."[18] They are tools and strategies for stopping to reflect on an issue in the midst of deciding on a particular course of action or strategy: reflection-*in*-action. They are also useful for learning by reflecting on one's practices after the fact: reflection-*on*-action. In either case, whether you stop to reflect in the midst of trying to decide how to act or reflect on an action already taken, what you aim at is to slow down the action and to think explicitly about what you are doing or have done, not simply in terms of the particular strategies used to resolve the issue, but, more importantly, in terms of the mental models that you have used concerning the issue. What assumptions are you making about the issue? On what information are you basing your decision? If we only examine our strategies of action without considering our assumptions, we engage in what some have called "single loop" learning. "Double loop" learning, in contrast, examines not only the strategies used but the assumptions that governed our choice of strategies. Were those assumptions accurate?[19]

Various techniques are useful for slowing down the action as you consider a particular issue. We suggest three here that in no way exhaust the possibilities.

The Ladder of Inference. If you take action on the basis of your assumptions, and if, as we have suggested, these assumptions are often tacit or implicit, then one way of slowing down the action is to make public and explicit the process of reasoning that has led an individual or a committee to propose a particular (often contested) action strategy, or the process that led to the choice of a less than satisfactory strategy. What was the "ladder of inference" that you "climbed" to reach a particular conclusion? What information—observable data—did you use to interpret the situation and make your decision to use a particular strategy? Does everyone agree that the information was correct? How did you interpret the information? What assumptions did you make that led to your conclusions? How do aspects of your personal experience shape your assumptions and interpretations—for example, what difference does your particular role in the congregation make? Your gender? Your race? Your age? How do your assumptions and interpretations reflect your basic beliefs about God and God's purposes for your congregation? Slowing down the action by asking these various questions will help your group to make public and explicit the inferential process that your members used (or are using) to arrive at a particular conclusion.

Frame Experiments. Frame experiments are another way of slowing down the action. To repeat what we have emphasized throughout, the frame through which you look at any issue, like the frame through which you look at a landscape, significantly affects what you see. As Bolman and Deal put it, "Frames are both windows on the world and lenses that bring the world into focus. Frames filter out some things while allowing others to pass through easily. Frames help us to order experience and decide what action to take."[20] A frame experiment, simply put, involves stopping a discussion about an issue and asking, What would the issue look like if we considered it from a different perspective? How would our action be different if we adopted a different frame? In the categories of this handbook, this would involve reframing the issue in terms of context, culture, processes, or resources, much as we have suggested above. What new information does each of these frames require when thinking about your issue? In what ways does each frame add new information? What new strategies of action

are suggested? Which way of framing the issue is most in line with your basic theological convictions? In the case of the example about contemporary worship and music, a frame experiment may also involve considering the matter in terms of the way different generational cohorts (or other relevant groups in the congregation) frame the issue. As we noted, the perspective of an older generation may differ significantly from that of, for example, young members of Generation X. Conducting frame experiments offers a way of challenging existing mental models that may be constraining your thinking and action about an issue. The more frames you consider, the more options you discover for effective action.

Scenarios. A more difficult but often helpful way of slowing down the action involves developing alternative scenarios about a particular course of action you are considering for the congregation. Scenarios are imaginative leaps into the future. They are more extended frame experiments that involve creating a picture (or alternative pictures) of what your congregation might look like if it followed a particular course of action.

Consider this example: A Protestant church with a congregational polity is faced with inadequate facilities to meet the needs of its growing congregation. It is located near the heart of the town and is quite accessible, but its lot is relatively small and there is no possibility for acquiring more property for expansion. Some members propose that the existing building be renovated and expanded within the limits of the existing lot, because the church is in such a choice location in the town. Another group proposes buying a larger church building in another part of town that a very large Roman Catholic parish wishes to sell because it has outgrown its space and is itself relocating. The Catholic parish's facilities, however, would be more than adequate for the Protestant congregation. Yet another group in the congregation proposes buying an available tract of land, also in a different, rapidly growing part of the town, and starting afresh with new facilities. A straw vote shows the congregation to be almost evenly divided among the three options.

The congregation's executive committee and board of deacons decide to hold a retreat to consider the matter. Before the retreat, the committee appoints three groups of six to eight people. Each group is assigned one of the three options and instructed to develop scenarios for that option. The scenarios will be shared and discussed at the retreat.

To develop a scenario,[21] each group must first of all clarify its focus—its sense of the congregation's basic purpose or vision (a task that we will consider more fully in the next section). Second, the group must get information as accurate as possible about the likely future—in this case, the next five to ten years. What things are generally certain about this future if current trends—for example, population demographics, land use patterns, and so forth—remain constant? And what are key uncertainties—for example, the economy, the loss of key members, a change of pastors, and so forth—about which they must nonetheless make assumptions? A third step involves creating several stories that depict alternative futures that might plausibly happen to the congregation as it tries to realize its purposes, taking into account the various certain and uncertain factors identified in the previous step. At this step, thinking in terms of frames may prove helpful in creating the different stories. The group is not primarily concerned with how likely or unlikely each story may be; rather, it cares about how each story illumines group members' understanding about the congregation's future. Finally, the group must consider what strategies would need to be followed if the congregation is to realize the most positive of its possible futures and minimize the negative ones. Which strategies will likely be effective no matter which scenario comes to pass?

In the example we are using, the stories each group creates will depend on the particular group's assignment with reference to the congregation's building issue. Each group will then gather to share its scenarios with the others, indicating which one it believes is most likely to happen and what the consequences for the congregation will be. The groups will try to make their reasoning as clear as possible. Although the scenario exercise alone may

not resolve the conflict between the three building options, it will help each group gain much greater clarity about the strengths and weaknesses of its own and the other options facing the congregation. It will also help make explicit the assumptions that lie behind each possibility. Finally, it will have provided the members with more adequate information about the congregation and its context.

A Caution About Assessment Strategies. In this section we have emphasized the importance of critical reflection in gaining a realistic assessment of your ministry situation. To some of you, such methods may seem too cognitive, leaving too little room for intuition and other nonrational (not irrational!) ways of knowing. Sometimes members of congregations will resist such processes as foreign to their way of doing things. We acknowledge the cognitive emphasis in the methods we have proposed, and we encourage their use as one of the ways that God's Spirit guides us. We prefer to think of these strategies as a form of critical theological reflection, and we would like you to cultivate intentional use of such reflection as a matter of course in your ministry practices. In no way, however, do we wish to discount intuition or other ways of gaining insight into a situation. Jack Finney, whom we met in sidebar 6.1, exhibited considerable skills, including cognitive ones, in his efforts at redeveloping Good Shepherd Lutheran, but he is also described as having "an uncanny ability to make connections—to see a need and imagine who and what could meet that need."[22] In the final analysis, it is making these connections that is important. We believe that the kinds of reflective methods we have suggested are important aids in the process.

Developing a Vision for Ministry. A second leadership task is helping your congregation develop a vision for its ministry that is faithful to its understanding of God and God's purpose for it in this particular time and place and that is commensurate with its size and resources. Some writers distinguish between vision and mission. Lovett Weems, Jr., suggests, "mission

[is] 'what we exist to do'—for example, to worship God and bear witness to God's purposes for humankind—and a vision is 'what God is calling us to do in the immediate future in this particular place (next year, next three years, or some other time period).' "[23] In other words, the mission statement defines a general purpose for the congregation while the vision statement translates that general purpose into a more specific statement of direction. This is a helpful distinction: Broader purpose statements do need translation into more specific and immediate visions if they are to become realities in your congregation's life.

Visions Versus Vision Statements. It often is helpful for you to express your vision in writing so that it can be discussed, shared, and referred to by various groups across the congregation. We will suggest below a process for developing a formal vision statement. Before doing so, however, we want to emphasize that *having a vision for your congregation's ministry does not require having it in writing.* What is important is that you have a vision (which may include multiple complementary visions) for your congregation's ministry and that the vision becomes embodied in your congregation's practices. If it is embodied in practices, whether it is expressed in a written vision statement is beside the point. We know some small congregations that would find writing a vision statement too "bureaucratic" and alien to their informal style. They nevertheless have a vision of their congregation's ministry that they act out—for example, members understand themselves to be a family of care and support, and they express this vision both in their life together and in reaching out to needy folk within their community. They *do* their vision rather than write it out in a vision statement.

In some cases, leaders have helped a congregation come to own a vision for its ministry that its members could not have imagined because they did not believe they had the resources to realize it or because they were reluctant to try. These leaders have done this by building the vision into practices that helped their congregations discover resources or overcome their reluctance to own the vision.

In the first instance, when members doubt their capacities to achieve a vision, a leader can help a congregation take small first steps to build confidence for envisioning and pursuing some larger goal. From success in winning small victories, members discover capacities and a vision for ministry they had not previously recognized or considered. Samuel Freedman describes how members of St. Paul's Community Baptist Church joined other Brooklyn congregations to form the East Brooklyn Congregations (EBC) to work for community renewal. Earlier EBC's efforts at organizing had met seemingly insurmountable problems—especially recalcitrant city government—that had left member congregations demoralized and questioning whether they had the resources to make any difference. New leaders, determined to revitalize the group, involved congregations in activities aimed at achieving small victories which built their confidence and emboldened them to undertake more demanding projects. Out of these small victories they gained a new vision for their work and a new confidence in their resources to pursue the vision.[24]

In other instances, when a congregation has the resources to pursue a vision for ministry but is reluctant to do so, a similar strategy of building a nascent vision into congregational practices until the vision becomes widely shared may often be successful. Several lay leaders of a United Church of Christ congregation in Long Beach, California, were aware that their congregation was beginning to attract some of the large number of gay and lesbian people in the Long Beach community. They wondered if it was not time for their congregation to declare itself an "Open and Affirming" congregation (the denomination's official designation for congregations that have covenanted to be open and supportive of gay and lesbian members and their concerns). Not sure that the members would support such a vision, these lay leaders subtly included the issue as one to be considered by a search committee seeking a new pastor. The new pastor, the Reverend Mary Ellen Kilsby, had already led one congregation through the process of becoming Open and Affirming. In her early months at the Long Beach church, she developed a series of informal discussion groups to get to know the congregation. Although the groups were primarily for the purpose of helping her become acquainted with the congregation, she also designed each group intentionally to include both gay and straight people. In these meetings, members of the two communities had opportunity to hear one another's stories and struggles and answer one another's hard questions. Although not all members were convinced that the congregation should become Open and Affirming—a few left the church along the way—the small group process helped to build a near consensus to become Open and Affirming. The final vote convinced even the dissidents that, in the small group process, they had been heard and were still respected.[25] The vision came to be accepted because it had been built into congregational practices.

Although it is not necessary that your congregation's vision for ministry be captured in a written statement, it often is helpful to have such a statement to refer to as you assess where you are headed or how particular program proposals fit into the congregation's overall sense of purpose. We suggest below a process for developing a written vision statement. As we do so, we also enter this warning: For some organizations, including congregations, vision statements are just so much window dressing. Like earlier ventures into management by objectives and strategic planning, formulating vision statements can function primarily as a ritual—a rather empty one—that a congregation engages in because other organizations and congregations are doing it, or because a denomination requires it, or because the congregation's leaders think it might be a good idea. It gives them a sense of legitimacy. We know congregations whose vision statements now gather dust on a shelf in the pastor's study, and we know other congregations that have vision statements but have

not altered their way of operating in any significant way as a consequence. We offer this warning not to be cynical about formal vision statements or to discourage their development, but because we want to encourage congregations to be realistic about the statement's limitations as well as their usefulness.

Having entered our warning, we continue to believe that formal vision statements can serve more than a symbolic function in a congregation's life, that they can make a difference. An old Chinese proverb, cited by organizational consultant Burt Nanus, says, "unless you change direction, you are likely to arrive at where you are headed."[26] A congregation may or may not be headed in the right direction at this time and place in its life, but it may not know that unless it is willing to take a look at itself and its current direction and to make whatever adjustments are indicated. Who are we? Where are we now? What do we really care about as a congregation? What is our reason for being? Gaining some clarity regarding these questions is important, whether one drafts a formal vision statement or not. Becoming clear about what we really care about as a congregation can help to lower anxiety, reduce backbiting, and heighten morale. In Hartford Seminary's Church Planning Inventory (appendix A) there are two questions that analysts have learned to turn to before looking at anything else in a congregation's profile. One asks about members' current morale; the other asks whether respondents agree that "there is a sense of excitement among members about our church's future." The two are highly correlated. High morale and a positive sense of the future almost always go together. One way of developing a positive sense of the future is to become clear about what we really care about and what our reason for being as a church is. Thus we come back to consider what it means to help a congregation clarify its vision in a meaningful way.

Shared Vision or Multiple Visions. Although most congregations can develop general mission statements that are broadly shared in the congregation, that broad sharing may not be possible when you attempt to express more specific visions for ministry. Very often members differ in what they really care about in a congregation's life. Multiple visions express the ways various individual members or groups interpret what your congregation should be about in its gathered and scattered life. Sometimes the multiple visions are complementary or at least not conflicting. Some members see the church's ministry primarily in terms of meaningful corporate worship, yet others want to emphasize community ministries. As long as these ministries are not seen as monopolistic or exclusive, a congregation should be able to develop a statement that encompasses these multiple visions—as in the example in sidebar 6.2 of the Lutheran congregation we encountered above. In the example, we can see how several different visions find expression.

Difficulties arise, however, when the multiple visions are not so compatible or are in open conflict. One group wants the church to be open to and supportive of gays and lesbians and to welcome them into church membership. Others insist that this is contrary to Scripture and cannot be permitted. A Southern Baptist congregation is divided as to whether its vision for ministry lies with the fundamentalist leadership of the Southern Baptist Convention or with the more moderate Cooperative Baptist Fellowship. A rural church in North Carolina is split over conflicting visions regarding their church's responsibility in the community. Should the congregation openly oppose the neighboring corporate hog farm that is polluting the area with waste spillage and foul odors? One faction says yes; another resists involvement, arguing that such issues are outside the church's primary area of responsibility, which they define as leading people to new life in Christ. A Catholic parish that has long had a parochial school is told by the diocese and the pastor that it will need to close the school, for it is no longer financially possible to sustain it. Many in the congregation, however, see the school as not only serving its members but as an important part of its mission to serve the community. Jewish congregations are often conflicted over how to respond to converts or to children with Jewish fathers and Gentile mothers.

It is not surprising that multiple visions exist. In an unpublished lecture, Rabbi Edwin Friedman, who has written helpfully on congregational leadership,[27] told of his experience when his first congregation set out to build a new building. Everybody was coming up with plans for the building, so Friedman imagined a cartoon for the synagogue newsletter. He would draw the synagogue differently from the viewpoint of the various affiliates: The sisterhood's vision would have an enormous building, which would be the kitchen. Next to it would be a small sanctuary. The brotherhood might have a gymnasium in their vision, while the religious school director's vision would center on a huge school. Although he did not actually draw the cartoon, he said:

> What I had realized at that point was that I was the only person involved in this who

---

Sidebar 6.2
MISSION STATEMENT OF GOOD SHEPHERD LUTHERAN CHURCH

GOOD SHEPHERD LUTHERAN CHURCH, a diverse congregation, welcomes in the spirit of Christ all men, women, and children without regard to race, nationality, marital status, family composition, sexual orientation, or socioeconomic status, inviting all to participate fully in the life and ministry of our parish. We encounter Christ in each person and therefore treat one another with trust, love, care, and respect.

GOOD SHEPHERD LUTHERAN CHURCH responds to the Gospel through dynamic corporate worship. We proclaim the Word and celebrate the Sacraments with vitality, openness, and joy through a variety of prayers, songs, and liturgies.

GOOD SHEPHERD LUTHERAN CHURCH ministers with the poor by sharing with them, learning from them, and empowering them.

GOOD SHEPHERD LUTHERAN CHURCH nurtures spiritual growth and encourages, teaches, and supports its members as they witness to the world and each other following Christ's example.

GOOD SHEPHERD LUTHERAN CHURCH members express their gratitude to God by committing themselves to a high level of worship attendance, financial support, and talent sharing.

could see the whole congregation. Only the minister can see the whole thing. You can never count on any member of the congregation to see it all. Not even the senior warden [the chief lay officer in Episcopal parishes].[28]

We do not agree with Friedman that clergy are less vulnerable to partial visions than laity. (We would not be surprised if the pastor were to draw a study, or more likely the pulpit, out of proportion to all the rest!) We do agree, however, that as a primary leader in the congregation the pastor has a special responsibility to try to envision the whole on behalf of the congregation. Although other members of the body have their own distinctive leadership roles to play, the clergyperson must try to function as the "eyes" of the congregation. In addition to attempting to build the vision into the practices of the congregation in ways we noted above, the pastor may also find it important to articulate the vision to the congregation in what Friedman calls an "I Have a Dream" speech. Such self-definition, in which the leader differentiates himself or herself from the congregation's anxiety and states his or her vision for the congregation, is not aimed at securing agreement around the leader's vision. What it does instead is to help others in the congregation define and clarify their own visions. Some will hold visions that agree with the leader's, some will not. But because of the clergyperson's self-definition, those who disagree are, in Friedman's experience, more likely to want dialogue than a fight. Out of the dialogue, further clarification may be forged which leads to agreement on a vision for the congregation that incorporates or transcends the differences. Or, failing that, members may continue to disagree, and in some cases, the disagreements may lead dissenters (or the clergyperson) to leave the congregation. At least those who disagree would have made an effort to find common ground rather than refusing to talk or, equally as problematic, attempting to "paper over" differences.

We can connect Friedman's helpful perspective with what we said earlier regarding the "holding environment" that the pastor's authority creates and that makes "space" for doing the hard work of visioning. In this environment, to borrow the family systems language that Friedman uses, the pastor functions as a "nonanxious presence." We would add that, in the holding environment, the pastor must not only define her or his vision for the congregation and help them clarify their own, the pastor must also be willing to help members face the contradictions between the core values they espouse as a congregation and the realities of their present life. Finally, he or she can help them explore realistic options for the future and to reflect on the theological implications of the options. This is a particularly important instance of the pastor's exercise of the teaching office. Some of the most effective pastoral teaching will happen not in formal classrooms or in the pulpit but when the pastor functions within the holding environment as we have just described it.

In the envisioning process, then, the pastor is often something of an "inside-outsider" who has enough critical distance from the congregation to be able to see it whole, to see its "warts" and its possibilities, and to define his or her dream for the congregation. Yet, if the resulting vision is to be the congregation's vision and not simply that of the pastor, it will need to be a shared one, owned as broadly as possible by members of the congregation.

Characteristics of a "Good" Vision Statement. Having acknowledged that visions rarely come easily, is it possible to say what constitutes a "good" vision statement? We put "good" in quotation marks to emphasize that there is no one vision that is good and right for every congregation; nonetheless, we can emphasize several criteria against which a congregation's vision may be tested.

- The vision is *faithful to the congregation's best understanding of its religious heritage.* In the Christian tradition, this implies faithfulness to God's purposes as found in Scripture and in church traditions, as well as openness to the ongoing leading of God's Spirit.

- The vision statement is *oriented to the future.* Rather than affirming only who we are in the present, the vision provides a statement of a desired future for the congregation that its members are committed to bring into being.

• The vision is *appropriate to this congregation.* It takes into account the congregation's history, its core commitments, its size and resources, its unique capacities, and what its members care about deeply. A congregation's vision for its future need not be bound by its past or present, but neither can a congregation ignore them. As we will emphasize below, unless it builds significantly on the core values in the congregation's culture, the vision is highly unlikely to be accepted.

• The vision statement is *realistic* in terms of the congregation's social context. It is based on the best possible information about present realities and likely trends.

• The vision statement *contains both judgment and promise,* good news and bad news. It makes judgments on some aspects of the past and present, including, where necessary, core values and practices, while envisioning a more desirable future for the congregation.

• The vision is, in so far as is possible, *a shared image of the desired future.* Although the pastor may initially take the lead in stating the vision, the vision grows out of a process of dialogue that fosters broad ownership of it.

• The vision statement is *specific enough to provide direction for the congregation's life* but *broad enough to encompass multiple but complementary visions* important to groups within the congregation.

Sidebar 6.3 provides an example of the preamble to a congregational covenant that expresses the vision of Oakhurst Baptist Church, Decatur, Georgia. The congregation, located in the midst of considerable transition and racial change, chose to stay and become a multiracial Christian fellowship. We believe that it meets the criteria of a "good" vision

statement outlined above, and we encourage you to test it against the criteria.

Sidebar 6.3
OAKHURST BAPTIST CHURCH COVENANT (PREAMBLE)

We are together to be the church of God in Christ. We are not here by chance, but God through His grace is making of us a fellowship to embody and to express the Spirit of Christ.

In this fellowship, "we are no longer Jews or Greeks or slaves or free men or even merely men or women, but we are all the same—we are Christians; we are one in Christ Jesus" (Galatians 3:28, *Living Bible*). Therefore we reject any status in this fellowship in terms of church office, wealth, race, age, sex, education, or other distinctions.

[The covenant continues with a list of specific commitments that each member is called to make.]

Congregational Study and the Visioning Process. How can congregational study be of help in the visioning process, especially when the aim is to write a statement that captures the vision that the majority of the congregation shares? The kind of information that study of the congregation's ecology, culture, processes, and resources offers is essential for gaining a realistic understanding of the congregation's (and its setting's) past, present, and likely future. Likewise, several of the methods for gathering information that we described in the preceding section are relevant—for example, needs assessment strategies and the development of scenarios. See also chapter 7. Theological reflection, as described in chapter 1, is especially critical as the congregation develops its vision and tests its faithfulness to God's purposes.

There is no single method for bringing this information together to develop the vision statement. Here are some suggestions, however, for one way of going about it.

First, the relevant congregational leadership body—vestry, session, administrative board, or the like—gives its blessing to the development of a vision statement and commissions a committee or task force, including the pastor(s), to undertake the process. Although the task force is responsible for putting together the final vision statement, it is charged to do so by involving as many of the congregation as possible in the various phases of its work.

Second, the task force gathers or asks others to assist it in gathering the relevant information about the congregation's ecology, culture, processes, and resources. The task force may carry out a parish survey or engage members of the congregation in focus group discussions about the church's desired future. Other task force members may analyze budget and membership trends over the past decade. Still others may gather demographic data about the community along with projected trends. These findings will be the most helpful if they are summarized succinctly and widely shared with the congregation as a whole.

Third, the task force will attempt to involve congregational members in discussion of what they genuinely care about in this congregation and what they desire for its future. This might be done in the context of a potluck meal by breaking the larger group into small discussion groups, each with a leader and recorder. Or it might be done in a series of discussion meetings in homes of members, again with leaders and recorders. Use of the time-line exercise, described in a previous chapter, might be one strategy for helping members to articulate their beliefs about the congregation's core values. The exercise helps surface what is both changing and enduring in a congregation's life and culture. In addition, assuming that members have had some access to the data gathered about the congregation and community and that they also have their own personal impressions, each might be asked to imagine that it is five years from now and they have been able to bring into being the congregation that they most desire theirs to be. How would they describe it in a sentence or two? Sharing these individual visions should trigger further lively discussion, both about the visions and the likelihood of their realization.

Fourth, armed with both the congregational

study information and the summaries of the group discussions, the task force begins the hard work of developing a proposed vision statement. A retreat setting may provide the needed distance from normal routines to enhance the process. An initial step at the retreat might be to ask each person, including especially the pastor (recall Friedman's point about the pastor's role), to describe his or her envisioned congregation five years hence, just as the broader membership did. The task force might also attempt to develop scenarios, using the methods suggested earlier. Because the task force has more time for discussion than did the members in their small groups, the task force may discuss different visions for the congregation using such questions as the following:

• What is currently so central to our congregation's life that it must continue if we are to be faithful as a congregation? What does it mean for us to be a church or synagogue? Asking participants to frame their core assumptions in terms of biblical passages is a way of helping them define what is central to their understanding of their congregation's mission and to develop more specific visions for ministry. Sidebar 6.4 gives several examples of how biblical passages can be woven into reflections on congregational outreach as study teams seek to define how they will be involved in community ministries.

• Who are the groups of people, inside and outside the congregation, who will most likely be the beneficiaries of this congregation's ministries five years from now?

• What would we as a congregation need to be doing to meet their needs, assuming these activities are in keeping with our core theology and values?

• Assuming that all the various groups of people and their needs are important, can we nevertheless put them in any order of priority?

• Considering myself as a member of one of these groups that will participate in and benefit from the congregation's ministries, what is it that I personally and passionately want our congregation to be and do five years from now?

Sidebar 6.4
BIBLICAL REFLECTION AND VISION

By our Baptism we have been called to be disciples and to go and preach the Good News of Jesus. How better to do this than by actions that prove our love for the brokenhearted, the downtrodden and the rejected! (Luke 4:18-19).
—ST. MARY'S CATHOLIC CHURCH, INDIANAPOLIS

"Do nothing from selfishness or conceit, but in humility count others better than yourselves. Let each of you look not only to his own interests, but also the interests of others" (Philippians 2:3-4). . . . Our members recognize that the desire for personal salvation without social redemption is not only selfish but impossible. . . . We have conservative and progressive members enabling our churches to live in a "dynamic middle" rather than a "dead center."
—MERIDIAN HEIGHTS PRESBYTERIAN CHURCH

God's great compassion, or the Kingdom, has three aspects: inner, beyond, and historical. . . . Our understanding of the call to social ministry is founded on this perception of the Kingdom, where the operating dynamic is love, and the character is peace and justice. The church is attempting to give its community a glimpse of this Kingdom.
—EDWIN RAY UNITED METHODIST CHURCH.

Adapted from Carl S. Dudley, *Basic Steps in Community Ministry* (Washington, D.C.: The Alban Institute, 1991), 46ff.

Having answered questions such as these about the future, the task force can attempt a first cut at stating a vision for the congregation. It may then want to return to its data about past and current realities in the congregation's life and social context and ask:

- What factors in our current situation and projected trends (congregational and contextual) are most likely to facilitate the realization of our emerging congregational vision?

- What factors in our current situation and projected trends are most likely to hinder or block its realization?

These two questions involve undertaking what is sometimes called a "force field" analysis. In this kind of analysis, you begin by drawing a line down the middle of a chalkboard or newsprint. On one side you list the facilitating forces. On the other, you list the blocking forces. This allows you to weigh whether facilitating forces will be stronger or weaker than blocking forces in the realization of your vision.

On the basis of this discussion, the task force will make any necessary revisions to its vision statement, which it will take back to the governing board and to the congregation for discussion and approval. Assuming acceptance by the board and congregation, the leaders of the congregation now have before them an additional set of leadership tasks if the vision is to be implemented in the congregation's life and not become mere window dressing. These texts are the subject of the final section in this chapter.

Some Concluding Observations About Developing a Vision Statement. First, as we emphasized above, the process we outlined is only one process among many that you might choose to follow. It is, moreover, probably too cumbersome and involved for many small congregations, which usually do things in a much more informal and spontaneous fashion. We believe that small churches can and must (if they are to be faithful and effective in their ministries) have a vision for their work, whether it is written in a formal statement or not. If you are a leader of a small congregation, you will need to adapt the suggestions that we have offered to help you in this task. You can find other helpful suggestions in books specifically devoted to small church leadership.[29]

Whether your congregation is small, mid-size, or large, the visioning process will also likely be different (or at least have a different feel to it) depending on where your congregation is developmentally. New or young churches will likely approach visioning differently from ones in stable situations. Both are in a different place than congregations experiencing declining memberships and resources. Every congregation, in fact, will need to adapt the process to meet its particular circumstances—circumstances that can be illumined by congregational study.

Second, the process that we have outlined may appear overly rational, but it need not and should not be so in actuality. While envisioning is hard work, it can nevertheless be fun, involving all the creative energy and imagination that you can muster. Envisioning is much more an art than a science or technical process.

Third, as we also noted previously, developing a vision that is faithful to your congregation's understanding of God's purposes for it in this time and place may involve conflict, as members disagree over alternative visions or as the vision for what it means to be faithful challenges some of your current practices. Painful though such conflict often is, facing and working through it can be healthy in the long run as you find ways of reconciling individual visions and bringing them in line with assumptions about God's purposes. As we said, there may well be times when no agreement is forthcoming, when some members may agree to disagree or decide that they can no longer be part of the congregation.

Embodying the Vision

The final task of leadership we hold up here is that of embodying or institutionalizing the vision in the life of your congregation—in its structure, processes, and programs. To paraphrase the prologue of John's Gospel, the vision must become flesh in the congregation's life, full (we hope) of grace and truth. Most "window dressing" vision statements—those that end up on the shelf unused—typically have failed either because they did not really express central values and beliefs of a majority of the members, or because, even if they did, the congregation failed to embody the vision in the "stuff" of day-to-day congregational life. In a classic book on leadership, sociologist Philip Selznick described the core meaning of institutionalization as "infusing with value."[30] *When we institutionalize a vision for ministry in the life of the congregation, we infuse with value the vision and the structures that embody it.*

Members begin to value the congregation and its ministries in new ways as a source of personal growth and satisfaction. To be sure, this can have its liabilities; members may attach so much value to particular expressions of congregational life that they resist new challenges. To put it biblically, they become "at ease in Zion." We return to this problem below. Now, however, our concern is ways that you may embody the vision so that it does become infused with value for your congregation's members. We assume that a congregation's vision for ministry both affirms valued elements in the congregation's current life and that it calls for some new ways of expressing its ministry and mission. How can you build ownership for and embody the vision?

One important strategy is liturgical and educational. We have known congregations that have made their vision statement a regular or at least occasional part of their worship life. For example, the pastor may include regular references to elements of the vision statement in sermons or perhaps preach an entire sermon that interprets the statement in light of Scripture and some current issue. Some vision statements also lend themselves to use in litanies or congregational affirmations of purpose. Some congregations rehearse their vision or church covenant every time they observe the Lord's Supper or celebrate a baptism. Such liturgical use sets the vision quite squarely in the congregation's central encounter with God in worship—an important way of infusing the vision with value. In addition to using it as a part of worship, others have used the vision statement as a shared reading at a board, session, or vestry meeting, sometimes coupled with a brief discussion of what it might mean in terms of a specific issue on the board's agenda. Your congregation's vision statement might also be an occasional discussion topic for a religious education class, which explores the statement's implications for particular issues current in your congregation's life or social context. Occasionally printing the vision statement in bulletins or newsletters is also a way of rehearsing and celebrating the vision. Framers of the vision statement need to keep in mind its possible liturgical and wider symbolic use and to pay careful attention to the language in which they express it.

Beyond celebrating the vision statement in liturgies and using it educationally, a more difficult task involves translating your vision into congregational reality, developing more specific objectives and strategies for bringing the vision into being and embodying it in the congregation's structures and practices. There is a large corpus of literature on planning that we will not review here. Some of it is written especially for church leaders.[31] Our general advice is as follows:

- Keep planning tied to your vision of what is genuinely valued in the congregation.

- Keep it based on what you have learned through congregational study.

- Assign responsibilities and accountability for implementation to appropriate existing groups, creating new structures if existing ones are not appropriate.

- Keep personnel and resource issues before you. (Who will do the jobs and with what resources?)

- Don't plan too far ahead. (Although you may have programs that are projected to continue for several years, thinking in terms of what you can accomplish in one year or less will help you keep the planning more manageable and make it less likely the plan will be scrapped as too complex.)

- Continue efforts to discern God's will in the particular ways you plan to implement the vision.

- Keep it simple! Elaborate planning documents may appear impressive, but, like vision statements, they are prime candidates for gathering dust on someone's shelf.

Your planning process will no doubt lead to some desired changes in the ways the congregation will do things. Some changes will be small; others will be major; still others will fall somewhere in between. Some will involve only the pastor and a few key leaders, but others are likely to affect significant numbers of congregational members. As ways of giving expression to the vision statement, these too need to be institutionalized.

Over the years, students of organizations, including congregations, have developed a number of generalizations about factors that can help or hinder the adoption and embodiment of visions in the congregation's life. We summarize several of these generalizations—many of which reflect simple common sense—which we believe are especially pertinent to congregational studies as we have encouraged it in this volume. The generalizations come from a variety of sources, and we will not try to trace their "pedigrees." Although they may repeat some of the things we have said before in this and other chapters, they bear repetition for emphasis. We state them with the caution that they hold "other things being equal"—a reminder that congregations are complex systems that do not fit simple generalizations. The generalizations focus on change, because embodying a vision generally involves making changes in established ways of doing things.

Some Generalizations about Embodying Change.

- The more a congregation's members are able to name their core values and claim positively their identity, the more likely they are to be open to change that affirms rather than threatens their core values and identity.

- Change is more easily accepted when it is seen as giving organizational and programmatic expression to aspects of the congregation's core values and identity, or when it is seen as realizing lost elements of these values and identity.

- Change is more easily accepted when it is seen as adding value to a congregation's life and does not require the loss of other valued elements, a bit of "having one's cake and eating it too" that is often difficult to achieve!

- The more leaders can highlight the contradictions between what members really value in the congregation and current realities in the congregation's life, the more likely they are to mobilize the congregation to accept a proposed change.

• Changes that are functionally incompatible with existing organizational arrangements will have low probability of acceptance unless the organizational arrangements are altered to accommodate the change.

• The greater the scope and pervasiveness of the change, the more slowly it will be accepted.

• Congregational change will be more readily accepted when it has the support of the congregation's informal leaders: "gatekeepers," "matriarchs," or "patriarchs."

• Change will be more readily accepted when it has the support and endorsement of the top formal leaders in the congregation, especially the pastor.

• Change will be more readily accepted when there are visible examples of other similar change efforts that have proved successful and provide models for other congregations.

• Change will be more likely to persist when an organization establishes positions whose holders are accountable for implementing the change and when necessary resources are allocated for the task.

• Change that involves addressing issues in the congregation's social context is more likely to be accepted and undertaken when such action is viewed as consistent with the congregation's core values and identity.

• When proposed community change efforts based on the congregation's vision for ministry come into conflict or tension with members' interests in other non- or extra-congregational settings, members will resist the change efforts or seek to restrict congregational responses to educational programs rather than direct action.

• Change efforts in the community will more likely be successfully accomplished when the congregation joins efforts with allies in the context (other congregations and religious organizations, community organization, social welfare agencies, and so forth).

• Change that involves the congregation (or members of it) in social ministry within its context will more likely be accepted when leaders are perceived as giving equal attention to internal congregational needs, including member pastoral care. (One congregation that we have worked with called these "out house" and "in house" ministries!)

• The more any change is perceived to be open and amenable to revision as experience dictates, the more likely it is to be accepted.

• The more conflicts over change efforts are managed constructively—openly and with full discussion—the more likely the change will be accepted.

Other generalizations like these could certainly be put forward. We have not exhausted the list. Perhaps, however, these will prove helpful in their own right and also serve to remind you that visions and the changes they imply do not fall full blown into congregational life. They require the hard work of infusing the vision with value and building it into the congregation's life. That is an ongoing key task of leadership.

Problem Solving: Attending to the "Little Foxes that Spoil the Vine." In the chapter on congregational processes, we addressed the issue of problem solving. Although we need not repeat what we said there, we want to acknowledge that problem solving is a key leadership activity in efforts to embody and sustain a vision for ministry. Some of the problems that arise may subvert the dream or at least divert significant time and energy from pursuing it. They are, to use a biblical metaphor, "the little foxes that spoil the vine" (Song of Solomon 2:15). A personnel conflict, a sexual abuse charge against a staff member or layperson in the congregation, a discovery of misappropriation of the congregation's funds by an officer, a conflict over spending, or a dispute over who is in charge of the congregation's kitchen—these are examples of the numerous problems that can undermine pursuit of a vision.

In other instances, the problem that must be solved has to do with some blockage within the congregation's life that must be removed or a lack of resources that must be addressed before the vision can be embodied. For example, Grace Baptist Church in Anderson, Indiana, had fallen on difficult times as the city experienced a deep recession in the late 1970s and early 1980s. Expenses (especially for its school) exceeded its mostly working-class members' ability to give as many members experienced layoffs from their jobs. Debts mounted and needed repairs to facilities were deferred. A new pastor, eager to move the church forward in its ministries, realized that this could not happen until finances were brought under control. He informed the members of the extent of their fiscal problems, asked them to pray and fast about it, held a special offering for debt reduction, and involved the congregation in a decision-making process about its future. (The previous pastor had made most decisions and had kept the congregation uninformed about financial matters.) Through various measures that were put into place, the church not only survived its crisis, it paid off its debts and made necessary repairs on its buildings. "I've been trying to reteach them," the pastor, the Reverend Leigh Crockett said, "that if God wants us to have something, why can't he give us the faith to believe we can put it into the bank and then go buy it? And that's what we've done." In short, the pastor and the congregation not only solved a pressing problem that blocked their vision, they also learned new ways of behavior that will serve them well in the future.[32]

Evaluation. Implied in what we have said above about program implementation and embodiment is the need for periodic assessments of how you are doing in your efforts to realize and implement your vision(s). As is the case with literature on planning, a number of resources address the mechanics of program evaluation.[33] We will restrict our discussion here to a few key points.

Informal evaluation goes on all the time in the congregation. Members in casual conversation evaluate the pastor's sermons, the choir's anthems, or the food at last week's potluck. Much evaluation of this sort occurs in the parking lot after meetings. Informal evaluations like these are often based on very limited, subjective judgments; although they may be accurate, they may also be considerably biased and destructive. At best, they are relatively limited in scope. Thus, evaluation efforts of a more formal sort are also needed. Although they, too, will mostly involve the subjective judgments of congregational participants, care in selecting sufficiently large, representative groups of individuals to provide responses will help to give a more holistic and objective picture of the program or activity one wishes to evaluate.

Many kinds of evaluation strategies exist, some using very elaborate experimental designs and others as simple as holding a brief discussion following a meeting to give participants opportunity to give feedback to a few questions about the program. Many other strategies fall along a continuum between these two extremes.

One major distinction in the evaluation literature especially pertinent to periodic congregational evaluations is between *formative* and *summative* evaluations.[34] Formative evaluations are undertaken to get feedback and improve new or existing programs. Summative evaluations are done for the purpose of making basic decisions about whether an existing program should be continued or terminated. You will find both kinds of evaluation useful at times in congregational life, but we suspect it is more likely that you will use formative evaluation to improve existing programs. In some cases, however, we suspect that you would be better served using summative evaluation as a means of terminating no longer effective programs that have survived by dint of inertia! A relatively simple evaluation strategy that combines elements

---

Sidebar 6.5
A MODEL FOR PROGRAM
PLANNING AND EVALUATION

1. CONTEXT

What congregational characteristics—for example, congregational identity, context—are relevant to the program?

What are the relevant characteristics of members or other participants in the program (age, gender, needs, wants, and so forth)?

What are the relevant characteristics of the physical setting?

Is/was the program appropriate to the congregation and its context? To member/participants?

What in the situation or setting may have facilitated or blocked the program's objectives?

2. INPUTS

What are the appropriate strategies—for example, teaching, training, preaching, group action, and so forth—for accomplishing program goals?

What resources—for example, books and materials, educational and training designs, sermons, action strategies, and so forth—are needed?

What "people" resources—for example, consultants, evaluators, and the like—will we need?

How appropriate and helpful were each of the above in achieving program objectives?

3. PROCESS

How well do/did participants understand the program?

How effective was the communication?

Is/was the space, physical setting appropriate/adequate?

What were the interpersonal dynamics between participants? Did they help/hinder program objectives?

Pacing of the program? Too fast? Too slow?

Other relevant processes and their contribution to the program?

4. PRODUCTS

What do/did we expect to happen? Have we stated these expectations clearly so that they can be evaluated?

Were these expectations realized? What facilitated/blocked their realization?

Were there unintended consequences, positive or negative?

How might we reframe and redesign the program for the future?

Do the results lead me/us to reframe my/our basic assumptions?

Adapted from E. Guba and D. Stuffelbeam, *Evaluation: The Process of Stimulating, Aiding and Abetting Insightful Action* (Bloomington: Indiana University Press, 1970).

---

of both formative and summative evaluation and connects them with planning is known as CIPP (Context, Inputs, Process, and Product). Although the categories of the strategy are slightly different from our lenses or frames, the categories are sufficiently similar that they are easily usable in congregational study. The CIPP model (with suggestions as to how it relates to our congregational studies framework) is outlined in sidebar 6.5.

Increased understanding of the benefits and techniques of formative evaluation can lead congregations to see the value of year-round evaluative processes. Consider this example: An urban United Methodist congregation decided, as a way of giving flesh to its vision, to begin a meals program for elderly residents in the nearby community. They would start with two nights a week and expand as demand and resources permitted. They chose the evening meal because they assumed that it would be easier to get volunteers to assist in the preparation.

An earlier needs assessment indicated that at least one hundred elderly people lived within easy walking distance of the church and would benefit from the meals program. Most had low incomes and many had only limited access to easy grocery shopping. The meals program began with high expectations. Yet during early weeks, the number participating in the program was only one-third of what the members had projected. They asked those who were coming—one kind of formative evaluation—what was behind the lack of participation. And several members visited in the surrounding community to ask those who were not participating why this was so. They discovered a flaw in the initial program design: Many of the elderly people who would have liked to come to the meals were fearful of doing so because it required them to travel to and from their homes after dark. The dinner hour was the problem, not the program. With this new information, planners shifted to the noon hour, necessitating, however, that they recruit a different set of volunteers for whom a midday commitment was no problem. They found a pool of volunteers among active retired members.

The example illustrates the significance of formative evaluation, especially early in a new program's life. Rather than scrapping the program as unsuccessful, the planners were able to make midcourse corrections that helped them reshape it into a successful venture.

The kind of data you collect for evaluations and the techniques you use to get them obviously depend on the kind of program or issue you are evaluating. For some issues, especially when there is considerable conflict, face-to-face interviews conducted by someone from outside your congregation are appropriate. Sometimes focus groups are useful to gain insight and feedback about a particular program or issue. Sometimes a questionnaire mailed to all or a random sample of members will suffice. Many times, however, the formative evaluation may be no more than a brief set of questions that a leader distributes at the end of an early session of a study group or workshop eliciting feedback about how the group and leader might function better in future sessions.

Evaluation can be a significant tool for helping to institutionalize the programs that give expression to your congregation's vision for ministry. Leaders can encourage regular evaluation by modeling it in their own practices.

Some Concluding Observations

In this chapter, we have explored three major tasks that we believe the activity of leadership involves. To repeat, leadership involves: *(1) helping your congregation gain a realistic understanding of its particular situation and circumstances; (2) assisting members to develop a vision for their corporate life that is faithful to their best understanding of God and God's purposes for this congregation in this time and place; and (3) helping them embody that vision in their congregation's corporate life.* Though the pastor, rabbi, priest, imam, or other central religious leader may have primary responsibility for major aspects of these tasks, they are not hers or his alone but are appropriately shared with other leaders in the congregation. Clergy leaders in particular have multiple demands—priestly, pastoral, educational, and administrative—laid on them in the congregation. The demands are often more than any one clergyperson can handle. Thus we reiterate the importance of shared leadership throughout the congregation's life and especially in the three tasks that we have highlighted in this chapter.

One further word about these three tasks: They are, in fact, ongoing. You are not finished when you have analyzed the situation, articulated a vision, and worked at embodying that vision in the congregation's life. Continual monitoring of the situation in and outside the congregation; ongoing questioning of the congregation's vision in terms of its breadth, appropriateness, and faithfulness to God's purposes; and regular assessment of how well the vision(s) is embodied—these require that you continually "stir the congregational pot" and (changing metaphors) keep the congregation moving on its journey as a pilgrim people for whom God has prepared yet new challenges.

NOTES

1. To reiterate what we have said, these various learning tasks do not refer to discrete elements in a congregation's life that exist independently of each other. Rather, they offer different frames for understanding the same congregational drama. The congregation does not change as one reframes his or her view; rather, the perspective from which one views it changes, and one is helped to see different aspects of the one congregation and, often, different possibilities for responding to the issue at hand.

2. Barbara G. Wheeler, "Uncharted Territory: Congregational Identity and Mainline Protestantism," in *The Presbyterian Predicament: Six Perspectives*, ed. Milton J. Coalter, John M. Mulder, and Louis B. Weeks (Louisville: Westminster/John Knox, 1990), 67-89.

3. Russell Ackoff, "The Future of Operational Research Is Past," *Journal of Operational Research Society* 30, no. 2 (1979): 90-100, cited in Donald A. Schöen, *The Reflective Practitioner* (New York: Basic Books, 1982), 16.

4. Our perspective on congregational leadership, especially that of clergy, gives primary attention to matters of *organizational leadership* rather than, for example, to priestly or sacramental roles. We do not by any means assume that these or other "slighted" leadership roles, or some adaptation of them, are not important leadership roles. Issues of organizational leadership, however, have increasingly occupied religious leaders as they have tried to lead congregations in the United States. Such demands, in part the result of the voluntary associational character of religious groups in the United States, were initially most keenly felt by Protestant leaders, but they are also increasingly being experienced by Catholics, Jews, and Muslim leaders as all religious traditions in the United States move towards what R. Stephen Warner has called "de facto congregationalism." See Warner, "The Place of the Congregation in the American Religious Configuration," in *American Congregations*, vol. 2, ed. James P. Wind and James W. Lewis (Chicago: University of Chicago Press, 1994), 54-99.

5. For those wishing to review the various perspectives, see Robert J. House and Mary L. Baetz, "Leadership: Some Empirical Generalizations and New Research Directions," in *Research in Organizational Behavior*, vol. 1, ed. Barry M. Staw (Greenwich, Conn.: JAI Press, 1979), 341-423. See also Ronald A. Heifetz, *Leadership Without Easy Answers* (Cambridge, Mass.: The Belknap Press of Harvard University Press, 1994), 13-27.

6. Heifetz, *Leadership Without Easy Answers*, 29.

7. See Jackson W. Carroll, *As One With Authority: Reflective Leadership in Ministry* (Louisville: Westminster/John Knox, 1991), 36ff.

8. See Heifetz, *Leadership Without Easy Answers*, 183 ff., for a discussion of leadership without authority.

9. For a more complete discussion of these differences, see Carroll, *As One With Authority*, 34-60.

10. See David S. Schuller, Milo L. Brekke, and Merton P. Strommen, *Ministry in America* (San Francisco: Harper & Row, 1980) for examples of the how different denominational families give weight to different aspects of ministry and grant their clergy authority based on these different values.

11. John Fletcher, *Religious Authenticity in the Clergy* (Washington, D.C.: The Alban Institute, 1975).

12. Heifetz, *Leadership Without Easy Answers*, 103 ff. (Emphasis in the original.)

13. It is important to acknowledge that the "holding environment" can be abused when the leader uses his or her power illegitimately to exploit a person or congregation. Most sexual abuse cases involving clergy and a parishioner occur when the clergyperson takes advantage of the other in the holding environment that his or her authority has established.

14. Don S. Browning, *A Fundamental Practical Theology* (Minneapolis: Fortress, 1991).

15. Peter Senge, *The Art and Practice of the Learning Organization* (Garden City, N.Y.: Doubleday Currency Books, 1990), 175. Senge's book, while focusing especially on business organizations, provides a helpful perspective on various tasks of leadership in building what Senge calls "learning organizations," organizations whose members engage regularly in reflection about what they are doing and why. An accompanying manual (Peter M. Senge, et al., *The Fifth Discipline Fieldbook* [Garden City, N.Y.: Doubleday Currency, 1994]) offers helpful strategies and tools.

16. See, for example, William Strauss and Neil Howe, *Generations: The History of America's Future, 1584-2069* (New York: William Morrow, 1991). For discussions of the baby boom generation with reference to religion, see Wade Clark Roof, *A Generation of Seekers* (San Francisco: HarperSanFrancisco, 1993), and Dean R. Hoge, et al., *Vanishing Boundaries: The Religion of Mainline Protestant Baby Boomers* (Louisville: Westminster/John Knox, 1994).

17. See James Mellado, "Willow Creek Community Church," Harvard Business School Case Study # 9-691-102, 1991.

18. See, for example, Chris Argyris, et al., *Action Science* (San Francisco: Jossey-Bass, 1978); Schoen, *The Reflective Practitioner*; and Carroll, *As One With Authority*. Several of the examples of slowing down the action presented here are drawn from these sources and also from Senge, et al., *The Fifth Discipline Fieldbook*.

19. See Argyris, et al., *Action Science*, for a discussion of single and double loop learning.

20. Lee G. Bolman and Terrence E. Deal, *Reframing Organizations* (San Francisco: Jossey-Bass, 1991), 11.

21. For a more complete description of this process, see Senge, et al., *The Fifth Discipline Fieldbook*, 275ff. See also Bolman and Deal, *Reframing Organizations*, 343ff.; and Peter Schwartz, *The Art of the Long View* (New York: Currency Doubleday, 1991) for discussions of scenario planning.

22. Nancy Tatom Ammerman, *Congregation and Community* (New Brunswick, N.J.: Rutgers University Press, 1997).

23. Lovett Weems, Jr., *Church Leadership* (Nashville: Abingdon, 1993), 42.

24. Samuel G. Freedman, *Upon This Rock: The Miracles of a Black Church* (New York: HarperCollins, 1993), 307ff.

25. Ammerman, *Congregation and Community*, 174-85.

26. Burt Nanus, *Visionary Leadership* (San Francisco: Jossey-Bass, 1992), 3.

27. See Edwin H. Friedman, *Generation to Generation* (New York: Guilford Press, 1985).

28. The lecture was to a group of Episcopal clergy. The transcript of the lecture contains no date or place information.

29. See, for example, Carl S. Dudley, *Making the Small Church Effective* (Nashville: Abingdon Press, 1967); Steve Burt, *Activating Leadership in the Small Church* (Valley Forge, Pa.: Judson Press, 1988); Douglas A. Walrath, "Leading From Within," in *Carriers of Faith*, ed. Carl S. Dudley, Jackson W. Carroll, and James P. Wind (Louisville: Westminster/John Knox Press, 1991), 141-55; and Lyle E. Schaller, *The Small Membership Church: Scenarios for Tomorrow* (Nashville: Abingdon Press, 1994).

30. Philip Selznick, *Leadership in Administration* (New York: Harper & Row, 1957), 17.

31. See, for example, Douglas Walrath, *Planning for Your Church* (Philadelphia: Westminster Press, 1984), and Richard E. Rusbuldt, Richard Gladden, and Norman Green, *Local Church Planning Manual* (Valley Forge, Pa.: Judson Press, 1977). For strategies for developing ministries in the congregation's community, see Carl S. Dudley, *Basic Steps in Community Ministry* (Washington, D.C.: The Alban Institute, 1991).

32. From a case study in Ammerman, *Congregation and Community.*

33. See, for example, Walrath, *Planning for Your Church,* and Rusbuldt, Gladden, and Green, *Local Church Planning Manual,* for discussions of how evaluation relates to planning. In the previous *Handbook for Congregational Studies* (Nashville: Abingdon, 1986), we included an extensive section on evaluation in the chapter on program.

34. See Michael Q. Patton, *Qualitative Evaluation Methods* (Beverly Hills, Calif.: Sage Publications, 1980), 22.

Chapter 7
Methods for Congregational Study

SCOTT L. THUMMA

Every congregational member or leader has probably "researched" some facet of congregational life. Almost unconsciously we gather information, reflect on what we have found, and share our conclusions, sometimes pointedly, with others. Yet this informal, casual, and experiential investigation seldom gets at the root of an issue. This chapter specifically addresses the various methods used in a disciplined study of congregational life. Earlier chapters have introduced specific ways of gathering and analyzing the information you might need for understanding a congregation through a particular frame. This chapter takes up the more general work of research.

Often the impetus for examining a congregation is rooted in a specific issue or problem. What sort of issue might become the focus for a study? Imagine yourself, for instance, as a disgruntled hymn singer in the midst of a worship service. "Why are we singing this old tired hymn again this week?" you ponder. You begin to count how often you have had to sing it in the last few months. Perhaps you begin systematically to list off names and character flaws of worship committee members in an effort to understand why this selection appears in the service every few weeks. After that fruitless exercise, you gaze around the sanctuary to observe how many other wor-shipers also look bored or irritated at the hymn selection. In one corner a vocal group of elderly women sings robustly, although at a slightly slower tempo. Other members seem as distracted as you. They shuffle their feet, dig in their purses for mints, flip through the hymnal, and participate minimally in the singing. Toward the back of the sanctuary many young couples, some with disruptive toddlers crawling between their legs, appear to be enjoying the hymn. You silently conclude, "This hymn must be Pastor Bob's attempt to appease those young families he wants to fill the church with."

Now suppose you express your concerns to the pastor and worship committee in such a strenuous manner that a study of hymn selection is ordered. A committee consisting of the worship chairperson, the organist, and a few other interested members is formed. Using the methods described in this chapter, this committee begins their study by analyzing bulletin records to see exactly which hymns have been used over the previous year. They also construct and distribute a simple questionnaire asking people to rate their impressions of the present hymn selections and to suggest possible alternative songs. In addition, several members of this committee visit the weekly worship committee planning session to observe the process used to create the order of worship. They further hold a group interview (focus group) one Sunday evening to discuss this issue. Their discussion focuses on current music in the church and what it communicates to its members and to first-time visitors. This focus group then proposes an alternative hymn format that might better reflect the stated identity and purpose of the congregation, as well as complement the church's current evangelistic efforts. The committee reconvenes and analyzes all its findings. Finally, the committee offers its report to the congregation during a short meeting following a Sunday morning service. A fruitful discussion takes place and a unanimous decision is reached to adopt the changes to the hymn selection process suggested by the committee. As the formerly unhappy worshiper, you leave the meeting quite satisfied. You even got elected to the worship planning committee!

No matter what issue has brought you to this study, your focus for investigation should shape both the methods used and the forms those methods take. As noted in the introduction to this book, the necessary first step of a congregational self-study is to define and clarify the precise problem to be addressed. You must decide what information is needed, why you want it, who will undertake the study, and how the gathered information will be used. A second and equally essential activity will be to adopt the appropriate methods of investigation. These tools will enable you, your committee, or your congregation to step out of its everyday, taken-for-granted perceptions and reflect on key issues in a more systematic, precise, and analytic manner.

Certainly one need not tackle every congregational issue with the vigor and multiple tools used by this hypothetical hymn committee. At the same time this example demonstrates the possible avenues of study available to a congregation. This chapter focuses directly on when and how to use the methods most commonly adopted in the study of congregations.[1] We will discuss participant observation, interviewing, conducting a time-line exercise, archival and census analysis, and the use of questionnaires. In addition, this chapter con-tains a brief section on data storage, interpretation, and presentation format. This chapter intentionally does not provide a detailed theoretical portrayal of these methods. Bibliographic endnotes accompany each of the chapter's subsections and offer references for the interested reader who wants to consult more scholarly and thorough discussions of these methods.

This introduction to research methods assumes that the congregational study will take place within the interaction of a congregation's life. Whether the researcher is an outside consultant or student or an inside research team, information about the congregation should be collected and presented in a sensitive and ethical manner that maintains trust and integrity between members. Before beginning to collect information on a congregation, remember that informed consent and the permission of all parties involved should be obtained by the primary researcher. Doctor of Ministry candidates and other students should be aware that many schools require a research design to be approved by a "human subjects" committee prior to beginning. The goal of ethical investigation is to explore the congregation, not to destroy the congregation's dynamics. Sensitive and careful use of these methods both enhances the acceptance of the report and contributes to understanding of the issue that prompted the study in the first place.

A Disciplined Perspective

A person does not need to be a psychiatrist to reflect on his or her emotional states, a CPA to rectify personal debt, or a physiologist to improve health and fitness. Neither must you be a social scientist to investigate your congregation's dynamics, well-being, and vitality. What is required, however, is to follow a discipline of investigation, an ordered system of examination and exercises that can lead to insight and self-understanding. This methodological section describes just such a regimen—a plan for formulating research questions and focused tasks to aid in uncovering the patterns and systems inherent within your congregation. Such an effort requires a self-conscious determination to follow formal means of information collection, from both majority and minority voices, to uncover patterns and structures of congregational life that may contribute to its current situation. It does not require, however, the embrace of the rigid objectivity of an experimental scientific approach involving hypothesis testing and theory-driven research. Rather, what is needed are exercises in gaining distance on a well-known reality and a willingness to deal with whatever uncomfortable issues may be unearthed in the process.

Following this disciplined approach entails *the adoption of a different perspective,* in other words, viewing the old situation with new lenses. A novel view of a familiar subject helps the observer become constructively reflective, critical, and analytical. The various frames introduced in this book offer such new perspectives, but the first task of re-framing is gathering the information you need.

One of the best ways to gain this perspective is to disrupt your "taken-for-granted" perception of the congregation. Attempt to view the congregation, its local environment, the worship service, and members' interactions in a unique manner. Envision yourself as a first-timer, a newcomer, a visitor to the church, synagogue, or mosque. Imagine yourself in the role of someone who has special physical needs or who is of a different race, socioeconomic class, region of the country, or faith tradition. If a research committee is responsible for the study, choose people who represent distinctive subgroups within the congregation, such as new members and old-timers, singles and families, teenagers and retirees, or people of racial, ethnic, and economic minorities. Over several weeks during Sunday worship, sit in different locations in the sanctuary. Drive to the building using different routes or enter using different doors. You may even wish to ask several nonmember friends to visit the congregation and relate their impressions to you. Each of these simple efforts may open those who are responsible for the study to new visions of the mundane patterns so often overlooked in your congregation. Once you have begun to see your congregation differently, you will be ready to think more creatively about what questions deserve your focus and what methods you should choose for addressing them.

Each method described below is applicable to any number of different research questions and frames of interpretation. These methods do not remedy congregational problems by themselves. They are, however, tools by which information can be collected to address a certain organizational "mess." The particular method and its content will in large part be determined by the task at hand. It is, therefore, crucial at the outset of the self-study to consider the study's specific focus. For instance, the self-study might be undertaken as a generalized examination of the entire congregation. This approach would be particularly relevant if you were exploring the culture of a community, writing a congregational history, constructing a vision statement, or if you were a pastor or rabbi assessing the character of a congregation you were just beginning to serve. On the other hand, a specific process or needs assessment issue might prompt you to examine a particular facet of the congregation's organization. In either case, you may want to begin the study with relatively unfocused observations and interviews and then later attend to more specific investigations. By initially being open to many factors, you may find new relationships or influences that you did not know existed.

This chapter describes numerous methods that can be used to study a congregation. Some are better suited for certain issues than others, and most can be used in a variety of situations. It is strongly recommended that a study team employ several or all of these methods, because a multiple-method approach can overcome the limits of a single method. In addition, the information collected by one research method can be used to clarify or correct material gathered by another. This strategy, called triangulation, allows for a more accurate, broader, and more nuanced portrayal of the congregation than if one chose a single research method.[2]

Direct Observation

The first and perhaps most potent method available to a congregational study team is its members' own powers of direct observation. Disciplined observation is just that: the intentional and systematic investigation and description of what takes place in a social setting.[3] It is the conscious perceiving, recording, reflecting on, and analyzing all that happens at a congregational event, whether it is a worship service, a committee meeting, a church school class, or a coffee hour.

This research activity may be the most comfortable and readily embraced method in the book. After all, this is a tool each member has used since joining the congregation. Nevertheless, being an insider has its disadvantages. Besides the imaginative distancing exercises we have already mentioned, inside observers may want to read some congregational studies mentioned throughout this book to become familiar with groups very different from the one under study. You might actually become an outsider by visiting a place of worship radically different from your own.[4] Having encountered something unfamiliar, you may be better able to imagine how an outsider might perceive your own familiar congregation.

At the same time, you should also call upon your knowledge as an insider to guide your investigation. You *do* know something about what things mean in this congregation. That knowledge will help you to know what to observe and how to interpret what you see. Insiders know enough to ask key questions. Outsiders, on the other hand, sometimes provoke a clarity of insight by their very naivete, but they may also miss the import of a story or gesture because they do not know enough to "read between the lines." Insiders, however, can sometimes miss just as much because they do not notice the things they take for granted. Your challenge is to realize the strengths and weakness of being an inside observer, maintain a distanced perspective, and use your familiarity with the setting to your advantage. Your observations can often be enhanced by inviting new members, nonmembers, or independent consultants to be part of the study.

How and What to Observe

Generally, the task of observation involves allowing yourself to see as many details as possible. Pay attention to all the particulars of your setting, such as the people who are there and what they do. Think about how you would describe the worship service or other event you are observing to someone who had never experienced anything like it. Many observers, for instance, attend events and *play the role of reporter*—taking copious notes on who, what, when, where, and how.

The observation protocol shown in sidebar 7.1 is a checklist of categories to examine and specific questions to ask yourself while trying to understand the general dynamics of your congregation's worship service. You may not be interested in all these items, but this list should help you begin to become accustomed to what you want to look for. Obviously, if the event to be studied is a committee meeting or informal social gathering, the specific actions noted would be different, but the observational categories remain the same. Remember that much of what happens in social interaction takes place as nonverbal communication. Pay attention to symbolic gestures, unspoken physical cues, emotional expressions, and what is not verbalized, in addition to spoken comments. If you need quotations from the minister's sermon, you may be able to get a transcript or audio tape, or (with permission) tape it yourself. Interactions, gestures, and the emotional tone of meetings, however, rarely show up on tape.

You may also want to sketch a picture of the seating patterns you observe during the services over a period of several weeks. These drawings need not be "to scale" or in great detail but should focus on where specific members or groups sit, who has access to the "sacred spaces," and the patterns of movement within the service. Note on your sketch where the young families with children, the teenagers, and the older adults cluster. Are there "choice" pews or seats for honored members, key lay leaders, and big givers? What are the routes of entry and exit for those people who habitually come late

Sidebar 7.1
OBSERVATION PROTOCOL

1. Demographics

• What is the social composition of those you are observing—their age, sex, race, ethnicity, apparent family composition, and social class?

• How do ordinary members compare demographically to the clergy? to others within the congregation's local community?

• Are there significant minority groups within a larger membership majority? Are there well-defined sub-groups, sitting apart from the whole, such as parents with babies, teens, or older adults?

• What is the dress of the participants? Are the members formally or informally attired? How does their dress compare to the leaders' dress? Are there special costumes for the clergy? Are the laity expected to wear a prescribed "uniform" or particular articles of clothing?

• What can be deduced about their social, moral, and economic commitments based on their attire; the type of vehicles they drive; bumper stickers; and the bike, gun, or ski racks?

2. Physical Setting

• What do the church grounds look like? Is the landscaping similar to or different from the surrounding community? Is the church visible to passersby? Is a sign evident and readable from the road? What is the parking area like? Is it paved, well kept, lighted, patrolled, and marked with special handicapped and visitor parking spaces?

• Describe the exterior of the building(s). What is the church architecture like? How does it compare to neighboring buildings? Does the building connote anything about what takes place inside? Is the primary entryway clearly marked and evident to visitors? What does the entryway and greeting foyer imply about the welcoming attitude of the church?

• Describe the interior of the building(s), the physical space. Is it plain or ornate, well-lit or dark, small or large, traditional or contemporary? Is the building "user-friendly," with ushers, informational signs, handicapped access, and visitors' stations?

• What is the arrangement of seating and standing space? Describe the seating: theater-style seats, bequeathed pews, folding chairs? How is the sacred space arranged, decorated, and set off from the other parts of the sanctuary?

• What props and equipment are used or displayed? Describe the altar, chairs, tables, railed areas, pulpit, musical instruments, choir lofts, audio and video devices, and sound system. What explicitly religious icons, symbols, or artifacts are evident, such as Bibles, candles, statuaries, scrolls, wall hangings, stained-glass windows, murals, baptistry, shrines, hymnals, or prayer books?

3. The Event

• What happens in the course of the worship event? What is the format, length in time, number and order of distinct segments, such as informal gathering time, announcements, testimonials, prayers, sermons, ritual celebrations, music, and singing. Describe what takes place during these activities and the roles of both the leaders and the congregation. Is there considerable bodily movement? Are these activities formal or informal, highly ritualized or seemingly spontaneous?

• Who participates in each segment of the service: many people or a few; only ordained leaders or also lay people; only one demographic group of the membership or a diversity? Does the congregation participate in unison, in groups, or individually? What are the interactions like? Are they formal or informal, explained or dependent on insider knowledge?

• How is the event orchestrated: by the senior clergy person, by a worship leader, by a written source like a bulletin or prayer book, by unspoken traditions and habits? What programs or worship guides are announced or published?

• What other events take place at the church throughout the week? Who presides over these? Who attends and participates? What do these say about the concerns of the congregation?

4. Interactional Patterns

• Who interacts with whom? Prior to the service, where do people gather? Is there a subtle segregation by sex, class, race, or cliques in these gatherings? Are all equally incorporated into the interactional patterns? Who is left out? Are the membership interactions stiff and formal or casual and informal?

• Are the congregational members highly focused and engaged in what is taking place, or are they minimally involved and easily distracted? Do they follow along in the sacred texts and hymnals and participate in the ritual motions? Are they actively recording sermon and announcement notes or doodling on the bulletin? Are any members asleep, flirting, or disciplining children? During the service, do disruptive interactions take place? How are these kept to a minimum? Are there pockets of rebellious or unruly participants, and how are they treated?

• From the interactions within the service, can you tell anything about the governing structures or power hierarchy of the church? Who seems to be in charge? Who seems to be respected and honored? Who are those without power? Does congregational authority seem highly concentrated or diffused?

• What is the nature of interactions following the event? Do the members have access to the leaders, formally or informally? Is the tone or mood of the members light, serious, fired up, sleepy, relaxed, or hurried as they leave? Are there other events following the service to encourage lingering or increased participation, such as meetings, lunches, trips, and recreational activities?

5. Verbal and Written Content

• Listen carefully to what is being said by the members in the pews, halls, classrooms, and parking lots. Record jokes and gossip, complaints and grumbling that are shared with you. Do not eavesdrop, however. You have no right to information you overheard if the speaker did not know you were a researcher or that you were listening. Are there common greetings, "buzzwords," or concerns voiced. Is there a difference between what is said officially and what is heard informally?

• Read carefully everything passed out or available on racks, tables, or in the pews. What groups or causes are sponsored or supported by the church? What does this literature report about the concerns of the church?

• Notice the words of the hymns. Do members seem to be paying attention to these words? Record the prayers but also listen for the emotional content. What is being said and why? Are these hymns and prayers addressed to a deity or to each other? Do they evoke a distant or close, warm or cold, formal or familiar relationship with the sacred or within the community?

• Carefully pay attention to the words of the preacher and other lay leaders. What is the style, tone, and language of speaking?

• Has this message changed recently with a new pastor, a new contextual situation, or a new ministry direction? Is there a call by the leaders or others to change direction? What future hopes and visions are members offered?

6. Meaning

• Rather than focusing specifically on what is said, pay attention to the meaning conveyed in the message, especially concerning who the people are as a social, moral, and spiritual community. How is members' involvement with the world described? Are members instructed to care primarily for their own, for local needs, or for global issues? Are ethical codes and behavioral norms rigid and absolute or flexible and relative? What is the character and content of the theology being espoused?

• What is the overall message: one of challenge, comfort, criticism, exposition, invigoration? What is the character of the service? How does it seem to relate to the lives of the membership? What does salvation mean to these people? What implications can you draw about the faith of the members and its role and importance in their everyday lives?

but insist on sitting on the front row? Are there set paths and routine maneuvers within the sacred areas of the church? These and other such items should be recorded on your map.[5]

The primary discipline of learning about a congregation entails both the observing and the recording of what you see and hear. Once you have learned to be a careful observer, your precise observations need to be entrusted to something more reliable than your memory. If you have selected a specific event for observation because you think it will tell you something important about the congregation's dynamics, take notes while you observe. Occasionally, note taking will be too obtrusive and awkward, but most often nobody will mind. Jot down what you notice about the scene and the actors, as well as key phrases from the conversation or sermon or ritual. Write down just enough to jog your memory later. Then, when you have a chance after the event, go back to your notes. Ideally, you should type a complete (and legible) version of what you observed, preferably into a word processing program. If time and energy are limited, you may instead jot in the margins of the notes you have already taken any additional observations and ideas needed to fill out your account of the event. Once you have your notes in a form that you can use in the future (and this does not at all require polished prose), file them along with other notes you are keeping in your efforts to understand the congregation. These files, in turn, should be organized around the key questions you are asking. More will be said below on the organization and storage of data.

Sometimes note taking on the scene is more difficult—especially if you are a primary actor, like the clergyperson. In those cases, the regular discipline of keeping a research journal may work. When you have in mind a clear set of questions about the congregation, you can mark off sections in a journal or files in a computer system. Then, whenever you sit at your desk after a meeting, worship service, or pastoral call, you can ask yourself what you have observed that helps you answer those questions. This is a particularly profitable strategy when what you need to know are the dynamics that happen in the normal course of your work. Another valuable way of capturing your observations and thoughts immediately after an event where you could not take notes is to dictate them into a tape recorder. The use of a recorder is especially helpful while traveling between interviews or events, but you must be diligent about transcribing the audio tapes promptly.

Keeping the Focus

You are engaged in a congregational study for a reason, guided by the quest for answers to a question or problem. As the earlier example of a congregation's analysis of hymn selection showed, the reason for the study shapes what you will look at. As this example suggests, part of the task of observation is deciding what you need to observe in order to address the specific concern that prompted the congregational study in the first place. Think about what aspects of the congregation's life most correspond to the issue under investigation. If, for instance, you want to know the place of children in the congregation and new ways to serve them, you could begin by observing the dynamics of the existing classes and programs. You would examine the demographics both of those participating and of those teaching. You would also observe the physical setting of the areas used for the youth. You might pay attention to what is being formally and informally said to children by the adults. How do the adults and children interact? What is the role, if any, of the youth in the worship service? You might even want to sit in the diminutive chairs of the preschool class or lay on the floor in the nursery to envision what a child's perspective of the space would be.

A similar research plan could be designed for any area of investigation. If your study's agenda is to examine the congregation's context with the idea of improving community ministries, then perhaps observation of the neighborhood parks, businesses, after-school hangouts, and malls might be in order. See, for instance, the walk around Evanston described in chapter 2. If the goal of the study is to improve clergy and laity relations, then observation of worship services, committee meetings, and informal gatherings may yield the most applicable information. You would want to observe prayer times, Bible study groups, healing services, and retreat gatherings in addition to worship services if your interest is in assessing the spiritual life of the congregation. Chapter 3 points to several ways observation can be used to assess a congregation's culture. A study of the congregation's resources, on the other hand, may entail only a cursory investigation of social gatherings, simply to gauge participation.

The key to the effective use of direct observation is to find the times and places in your congregation that most appropriately address your research question. Once you find these, open your eyes and play reporter. Gather the facts about who is doing what, with whom, when, where, and how often. What you observe will eventually become a vital piece of the congregational portrait you draw from your research.

Strengths and Weaknesses

Direct observation can be a powerful tool for understanding congregational dynamics. This method allows you to detect and participate firsthand in subtle nonverbal patterns of interaction, symbolic rituals, and power relations. By gaining some distance on the phenomenon, you can experience with renewed senses what is taking place in your congregation. Other research methods such as interviewing or surveying rely on verbal and cognitive categories. Observation, on the other hand, brings you "in touch" with all of what it means to be a part of the congregation—its smells, physical impressions, sounds, sights, and emotional sensations. These tell much about the essence of a community of believers. Indeed, a group's theology is in large part embodied and enacted in these practices and interactions. Participant observation provides an empirical rendering of the "works" and "fruits" evidence of the con-

gregation's life of faith. When what you need to know is embedded in the interaction of the congregation's members, observation is an important method to use.

The strength of direct observation likewise is its weakness. Observation is an individual experience; thus, the resulting data can be subjective, impressionistic, and skewed. Each person has "blind spots" or favored perceptions. If the congregation is very large, one set of eyes cannot view all the activities. Likewise, you can never know from observation alone if what you think is going on is actually how others perceive or attribute meaning to an event. Therefore, a single observation should never be used alone to understand a problem. At the least, multiple observations by several team members should be evaluated. In addition, it is a good idea to use other research methods to substantiate or correct observation findings.

Interviewing

One of the best ways to correct for the inadequacies of observation is to talk with those whom you have been watching. In its own right, however, the interview is also an effective method of information collection. The stories, criticisms, and explanations given by members provide valuable insight into individual impressions and attitudes regarding the congregation. Interviewing methods are quite diverse, ranging from informal conversations over coffee and gossip at the water fountain to highly structured verbal surveys and well-planned focus group discussions. Whether formal or informal, interviewing is not just talking. Rather, it involves a disciplined search for responses to your research issues. As with participant observation, who you interview, which method you use, and what you ask are shaped by your reasons for doing the study.[6]

Unlike observation, which can often be done unobtrusively, interviewing involves personal, one-to-one interaction. More than any other research method, the interview event is a com-

Sidebar 7.2
HINTS FOR INTERVIEWING

1. Schedule your interview well ahead of the meeting date. Confirm the time with the interviewee the day before you are to meet. Do not schedule an interview for longer than two hours. Arrive on time.

2. Allow the person being interviewed to select a place that would be most comfortable for him or her. Encourage the person to choose a location with as few distractions as possible; restaurants are seldom good for formal interviews.

3. If you use a tape recorder, check your tape, batteries, and sound levels before you start.

4. Be prepared with a list of issues you want to cover and an opening question. Otherwise, allow the direction of the conversation to be determined as you go along. Even if you use a tape recorder, make notes during the interview about what you have covered and those issues to which you wish to return.

5. Begin your meeting with informal and casual small talk. Wait for a lull, a question, or another verbal bridge into the formal interviewing. Describe the reason for the study, define your participation, and detail your use and protection of any recorded material. Then begin with your predetermined opening question.

6. Use photos and other concrete objects on occasion, if necessary, as stimulants to conversation.

7. Focus on events or specific experiences that have led this person to his or her beliefs or opinions. Rather than pushing the interviewee by using *why* or *what do you mean* questions, ask for *examples* or *for instances,* especially when trying to flesh out ideological issues or abstract ideas.

8. Listen, listen, listen. Do not give advice or argue, and interrupt only to clarify. Encourage the person with nods and smiles. Pay attention, be warm and personable, and do not overplay the researcher role.

9. Beware of asking questions that could only be answered by damaging either the interviewee's or other congregational member's esteem or social standing. Do not encourage gossip, but record it if it arises. Do not push sensitive issues if you perceive discomfort by the interviewee. Remember, this person is part of your congregation.

10. Use interviews to check out the information provided by others, but do not break confidences by relating what took place in other interviews. Let the person know what you already know, and ask him or her to tell you more, to fill in details only he or she can provide, or to correct misinformation.

11. Pay attention to what happens and what you see in the surroundings during the interview. For instance, note how the person responds to family members, whether he or she prays before meals, the prominence of religious symbols or literature in the home, and so forth. Likewise, record the interviewee's response to the interview process: Was the person outgoing or reserved, forthright or reticent with opinions? These characteristics may tell you much of the person's place and role in the life of the congregation.

12. If you are less familiar with those you will be interviewing, it is good to record a set of brief demographic facts (age, race, gender, occupation, approximate socioeconomic level, years of membership, and depth of involvement in church life) about each person you talk to. Often this information, once tallied, will help you check to see if those you interviewed adequately represent the congregation as a whole.

13. You will want to test your questions on a spouse, friend, or other study members prior to conducting the interviews. Your questions may need to be refined further as you begin the interview process.

plex social encounter. As in all interpersonal situations, those participating in the interview will assess each other's social standing, group influence, and trustworthiness. What is said will be colored by how an interviewer and interviewee present themselves and how they wish to be seen by the other. For that reason, it is often better if interviewers are not the senior leaders of the congregation. It is also important that the interviewer restrain any tendency to dominate and influence the stories being told. He or she should be neither the detached reporter/researcher nor the emotionally involved participant, but a little of both. Be yourself, but stick to your agenda, ask questions, and then listen uncritically and with encouragement. This is especially important when you know the person you are interviewing.

Whom and How to Interview

Choosing the people you interview is a crucial task in a congregational study. Every faith community has several members who are most vocal about their opinions but whose views may not accurately represent the entire group. There are also segments of a congregation that may know little about issues affecting other segments. You might not want to interview only the members of the young couple's group, for instance, in your effort to understand the life of the whole congregation. You might want this group as your interview pool, however, if the study was aimed at determining how better to serve the needs of young couples. Exactly who is chosen to be interviewed should be shaped both by the focus of the study and the diversity within the congregation. If the self-study is an effort to explore the reasons visitors never stay long enough to join, you would want to interview defected members and estranged visitors. On the other hand, if the reason for the study is to form a mission or vision statement, a representative group of active members might be in order.

Those chosen to be interviewed should adequately reflect the distinctive subgroups within a congregation. If the membership has well-defined groupings along age, gender, class, or racial lines, you would want to talk with people representing the diversity of these subgroups. Those interviewed should be drawn not only from the list of highly involved insiders but also from more marginal participants. In addition, both old-timers and newcomers should be selected for interviewing. Newcomers are often surprisingly perceptive about the unique folkways of the congregation, especially to what is different or attractive. In a gener-

alized study of the congregation, remember that you want to hear from as many diverse points of view as possible. In a specific issue-oriented study, you instead need those with the more pertinent data, keeping in mind the possible diversity of opinions within this group.

Any self-study should begin with interviews of the congregation's most knowledgeable insiders. Talk with those people who are seen as the "wise ones," the "oral historians," or the "custodians" of the community's stories. These people can be invaluable when you are getting a feel for the history, traditions, and norms of the congregation. Seeking out such guides is crucial. You may want to conduct a formal interview with one such person in which you ask broad questions about the history and customs of the congregation. Develop a relationship with this person as one who can be "on call" for you throughout the study. Perhaps he or she can even become a study team member. When you need advice on whom to ask, what something means, or why everyone is so upset about the new pulpit furniture, your key informant is the person to consult.

A good congregational study will rely on a key informant or two, but drawing the full picture will require a much broader base of interviews. Once you have a general idea of the research questions and the congregational dynamics, you are ready to do the additional interviewing. How many should you do? In a small congregation, five to ten interviews may be plenty. In a very large congregation, it may take thirty or forty interviews to give you a full picture. This task should not be left to one person but rather should be undertaken by several members of the study team.

What do you do in an interview? The hints listed in sidebar 7.2 are some good starting points for a semistructured interview. You should come to the interview with an outline of the topics or issues you wish to cover. Occasionally, you will want to write out exact questions, but in most instances you can let the conversation itself dictate how you ask the questions and in what order. Do think specifically, however, about where you want to start. Opening with a broad orienting question (such as allowing your informants to sketch out a story about their own life, their faith journey, the history of the congregation, or what they think is most important about a given program or ministry) is often helpful. It is also a good idea to ask about more routine issues prior to sensitive ones. Think about the interview as a process of building rapport, even with someone you know well, which opens the door for you to ask the more difficult questions.

Throughout the interview you can ask follow-up questions that let you cover most of your predetermined topics. In addition, comments such as "Earlier in the interview you said . . . " and "Could you follow up on what you said before . . . " create a sense of continuity to the interview that deepens trust and disclosure. Along the way, do not hesitate to ask for clarification. You should not assume you know exactly what someone means. Try to be an active listener, encouraging them with nods and the invitation to "say more." Remember that you are there to learn what they have to say, not to be their teacher, preacher, or counselor.

You will want to remember what your interviewee says, and that will require either good notes or a tape recorder—preferably both. If you use a tape recorder, make it clear to the person how the tape will be used. If you promise confidentiality, be sure that you are the only one with access to the tape, and do not quote from the interview without the person's permission. When possible, review your tape or notes shortly after the interview. Jot down any additional thoughts that will help you to recall the topics covered and the nonverbal dynamics of the interview. Then you can file these notes along with everything else you are collecting for your study.

Asking Questions in Interviews

The format of an interview can vary considerably. At one end of the scale is the *unstructured, ethnographic interview.* Here questions are quite general, allowing for open-ended responses. The issues to discuss may be predetermined, but the exact questions are seldom developed in advance. Begin a conversation with the interviewee, and then allow the discussion to flow on its own. The interviewer may occasionally press for more detail and depth or interject a specific question if an area of interest has not been addressed. The idea with this type of interview is to start with a broad question about faith or about the person's experience in the congregation and then to let the discussion take whatever direction the interviewee sees fit. This format often uncovers rich stories about personal lives and the significance of the congregation to that person. It may also uncover "forbidden" stories from the underside of the congregation.

If the focus of the study, however, is a needs assessment or problem analysis, then most interview questions would specifically address that issue. These questions would be more specific and direct in order to obtain more precise and detailed answers. The format for asking questions of this sort often takes a *structured form,* with each question planned, written in advance, and asked in exactly that form during each interview. These set questions may ask for a simple yes or no answer or a choice between predetermined options, or they may be open-ended, thus allowing for expansive and nuanced responses. They do not vary, however, once their form is established.

You might even opt for a *schedule-structured interview* that is essentially a verbal questionnaire asking set items with a choice of a few fixed responses. Many phone surveys and opinion polls use this format. This structured form is valuable if you have a large number of issues to examine or if many people within your congregation have difficulty reading or responding to written material. It also works well if you intend to do an exact comparison of responses across all those interviewed.

Somewhere between these types of interview formats is the *semistructured interview.* It allows for planned questions around specific issues and general items but also employs the freedom of an unstructured approach. The people being interviewed are permitted to respond to questions in the language and format most meaningful to them. If you conduct many such interviews, you have the freedom to allow people to deviate from the predetermined subjects, knowing that you can learn the specifics from others. You never know where one member's verbal wanderings may lead or what significant facts will be uncovered by a flexible interview.

Focus Group Interviews

Sometimes gathering five to fifteen people together for a group discussion or "focus group" interview is possible or necessary.[7] These gatherings can range from an informal chat with a Sunday school class to a randomly selected group intentionally called together to address a specific research issue. Although conducted similarly to a regular interview, the dynamics and the content of these interviews are different from those with a single person. Group interviewing entails a merging of several research methods. As in an individual interview, you will ask questions, either structured and focused (such as, "Given our present budget constraints, which of these three options should we pursue in the renovation of the sanctuary?") or open-ended and generalized ("Let's talk about what first attracted you to the church"). At the same time, the participants will also be interacting and creating an "event." You can treat this gathering as another moment in which to observe directly the group dynamics. You might even employ a questionnaire or focused exercise such as a "time line" or a "space tour," both of which are described below and in earlier chapters, to stimulate discussion and collect yet another form of information. Other exercises that can both generate discussion and increase what you learn from congregational members include role-playing and examination of a case study or other written material. In all, group interviewing can be a complex but profitable research method.

Group interview material, unlike the responses of a single interviewee, is the product of a collective effort. Each person's response will nudge the memories of others, and the perceptions of one participant will be modified by the opinions of others. For that reason, you might get a broader and deeper reflection on certain aspects of the congregation; however, you seldom get intimate or sensitive personal reflections. What you hear may not necessarily reflect the "objective reality" some outside observer might have recorded. Nevertheless, a focus group will produce the story that group is willing to live with, a story that by itself has profound formative power. It can be a central part of the information you are gathering about the congregation, no matter what your research agenda.

Given the interactive nature of the event, you may have to act as a firm moderator, perhaps steering the conversation from a volatile topic, checking the participation of one dominant member, encouraging the silent spectator, or shifting the entire focus if it has gotten off the specific issue to be discussed. These group interactions can often be emotionally significant events for the participants. Congregational members seldom have adequate opportunities in their lives together to "tell their stories" to each other. Spontaneous prayers, confessions, tears, hugs, or earnest renewal of commitments are not unusual in group interviews.

Prepare for group interviews much as you would an individual interview (see the list in sidebar 7.2). Plan your topics of discussion, perhaps write out several key questions and especially your opening question. You may want to have participants initially fill out a small data sheet to keep track of the demographic characteristics of people you interviewed. Prepare your tape recorder ahead of time, and assign an assistant to be in charge of it. Allow each person to introduce himself or herself to the group after you have explained who you are, the purpose of the gathering, and your policy regarding the data and tape recording. Depending on the setting, an opening or closing prayer may be appropriate.

Keeping the Focus

As with each of these methods, what you will ask should be guided by your research interest.

If your intent is to get a generalized understanding of the congregation, such as for a study of its culture, its vision, or its traditions and history, then a wide range of questions, probably relatively unstructured, would be asked of a diverse sample of the membership. Both the questions and responses would be open-ended, impressionistic, and often narrative in form. The responses might be difficult to interpret or compare, but such broad-based conversations are necessary for a general study. Where specific policy issues are your concern, more focused and structured questions are appropriate. The discussion about using interviews in chapter 4 illustrates this method's potential for uncovering process dynamics. That chapter also highlights the use of the group interview in the midst of conflictual situations.

Recall the earlier example of the hymn investigation. Using a structured interview approach, a study team might interview a percentage of the congregation and ask them to rate their fondness for a list of five hymns, offer their five favorite ones, and discuss their impressions of the current worship format. Those interviewing with an unstructured approach might avoid the issue of specific songs and instead explore the nature of worship in the congregation, what it says about their theology or priorities, and whether this musical impression matches the actual or imagined identity of the congregation. The set of answers from each of these interview procedures would yield a perception of the congregation's music. One approach might yield quite specific guidelines for the future, while the other may help to uncover assumptions about worship from which guidelines can eventually be deduced.

Strengths and Weaknesses

One of the most obvious strengths of interviewing is that it allows the researcher or study team to hear individual stories, diverse perspectives, and minority voices they might not encounter otherwise. Interviewing allows access to unobservables, such as attitudes, personal feelings, and individual interpretations. These conversations also allow investigators to test their ideas, assessments, and observational impressions. Group interviewing provides an opportunity for additional observation of interactional dynamics. The interview process, whether group or individual, also furnishes the chance to strengthen bonds between interviewers and their subjects, strengthening the community in the midst of the study process. The process can create ownership of a study and encourage increased participation in the task of uncovering the layers of the congregation.

On the other hand, interviewing must not be understood as hearing the "objective truth" about the congregation. Each interview contains personal perspectives, opinions, points of view, and often unfounded speculation. Interviewing may encourage confession or gossip. Any information gained in a single interview should be checked and substantiated, regardless of the source. For that and other reasons, multiple interviews are an absolute necessity. With each interview, another piece of the puzzle is added to the complete picture of the congregation. Nevertheless, remember that even a collection of interviews is only as good as the questions asked and the process of selecting those who will respond. The interview must focus on the research issues at hand but also be mindful of the unspoken biases of those being interviewed and how representative they are of the group being studied.

Sometimes the way a story is told to an interviewer is constrained considerably by other stories that lie beneath the surface. Such is often the case when scandals have rocked a congregation. These unspoken parts of the story may be expressed subtly in interviews. As the observer gets to know a congregation, the knowing looks, the hesitations and evasions, the non sequiturs may begin to add up. When sufficient trust exists, these other stories may be told. Also remember that a congregation is never described by only one story. There are always more stories to be heard and layers of experience that have not yet have been uncovered.

A Congregational Time Line

One form of focused group interview that is very helpful in gaining a general understanding of the congregation is the time-line exercise. This time line is exactly what it says—a historical rendering of the life of the congregation as recalled by its members. The goal of this exercise is to understand how congregational members situate both themselves within that history and their congregation within a broader context—local, denominational, national, and global. The time line offers an opportunity for a collective effort at history telling. It is a tool for uncovering links between external demographic, cultural, and organizational shifts and the internal stresses and strains historically experienced by the congregation. The basic exercise, however, can be shaped in a number of ways to suit the particular focus of your study.

A good way to undertake this exercise is to invite a cross section of congregational members to spend an evening or an afternoon in this structured, collective reflection on the past. As in group interviewing, consider bringing together ten to thirty people of diverse backgrounds, including those with different duties and levels of involvement in your congregation. This exercise can be quite fun and often works well when combined with a potluck or other initial fellowship time.

Prepare for the event by gathering the necessary materials, including markers of different colors, sheets of legal paper, and twenty-five to fifty feet of three-foot-wide butcher paper. Tape the paper up on a wall of the fellowship hall or other more public area, running the length of the room and high enough for all to see. On this paper draw a horizontal line from one end to the other, about half way from the paper's top. With this line as a scale, mark off years appropriate to your congregation's history and study's purpose. You might begin numbering the line with the date the congregation was founded, marking off increments of decades until more recent times, when you might switch to yearly intervals. Use whatever system fits your circumstance. (An example of

a time line can be found in chapter 2.) As you begin the exercise, one or two study group members will record above the line facts about the congregation suggested by participants, and they will write below the line facts external to the congregation around the appropriate years. You could use different colored pens to mark further distinctions. You may also want to tape-record this event or have one of the study team members take notes. If the group is larger than ten to fifteen, you might ask groups of three to five people to construct their own smaller versions of the time line on sheets of legal paper. This would allow more participation by each person as well as prime the discussion and provide additional detail that may not get recorded on the large time line.

Once the participating members have gathered, explain the exercise and how it fits into the current self-study. To begin the exercise itself, encourage participants to identify when they (or their families) joined or to recall their earliest memories of the congregation. You might start by having each person initial the appropriate point on the time line for their entry into the congregation's history. They should be invited to relate important events in the congregation's past—when new clergy came, when building additions were made, when ministry directions changed, or when controversies happened. They should also be encouraged to reflect on and offer one or two of significant moments in their lives as members of the congregation—when they sought aid after a loss, when a couples with new children class began, or when they accompanied the youth group on a mission trip to Honduras. Title these events and write them on the paper in line with their respective dates, above the line. Because you have marked off time segments, you can write down the events in whatever order people offer them. This historical brainstorm does not have to proceed in chronological order.

Also ask those gathered to reflect on the significant events in the community, the region, the nation, the world, and their denomination. You may want to note political changes such as the elections of new leaders; assassinations; wars; natural disasters; shifts in the community's residents, landscape, or resources; times of difficulty, like factory closings, recessionary periods, race riots, or heated social debates. Spend the most time on local happenings, but do not neglect larger patterns or events. Record these items near their appropriate date below the time line.

Encourage participants in their attempts to recall, connect, and elaborate on the events noted. Much like the group interview, participants will jog each other's memories. In all likelihood certain historical "experts" will attempt and be allowed to speak for the group. Discourage this. Draw out observations from all those involved. This is where having earlier small group discussions might help considerably. Each person has a story to share; encourage them to express it.

Leave the time line up in this public space for a week or two, so that others can share in the exercise. You may wish to post instructions for others to add their memories of events. Save the time line for possible future use. Perhaps someone may later volunteer to construct a comprehensive congregational history based on this exercise. The study group might decide to distribute a scaled-down version of the time line in the congregation's newsletter or bulletin. In any case, the material collected will add to the knowledge of the congregation and its place in its social world.

The time-line exercise is an excellent method for developing an informal history in relation to contextual events. The exercise also provides another situation in which the social interactions of members can be observed. Finally, it allows congregational members an opportunity to tell their stories and become more involved in the study process. Several of the previous chapters describe other ways the information gained from this method can be interpreted and employed in a congregational study. It is important to bear in mind, however, that the goal of the time-line exercise is not to produce scholarly history but to construct or uncover the collective memory of the congregation on the basis of individual and group recollection.

Archival Document Analysis

Much more information exists about your congregation than just what is enacted or spoken. Think for a moment of the many forms of written and recorded materials produced by your congregation each week. These may include service audio and videotapes; sermon transcripts; church school literature; worship bulletins; newsletters; ministry booklets; evangelism tracts; church directories and photo albums; congregational constitutions and bylaws; attendance data and financial records; committee, denominational, diocese, or conference reports; and even newspaper stories or advertisements. Each of these artifacts offers a tangible record of a particular slice of the congregation's history, processes, and resources. These physical accounts can be extremely valuable, depending upon the focus of your research. Obviously, if your intent is to study the financial resources of the congregation, certain of these records are essential. The discussion in chapter 5 shows how a researcher can interpret and understand a congregation's resources using archival data. Written records, however, also contain a great deal of information about how decisions are made, what vision is held by the members, and their sense of culture and identity, as the discussion of artifacts in chapter 3 demonstrates.

The question is, How do you turn this mass of archival documents into a meaningful source of information? One initial method might be to select a single source of material—old newsletters, for instance—and rather thoroughly read it through, simply absorbing the information and the story it tells. The knowledge gained from this process provides valuable insights into the culture, norms, and significant themes of the congregation. It is an especially helpful method when you are unfamiliar with the congregation, as a new minister or outside researcher, or do not know yet what facts you need for your study.

Another more systematic method by which gathered documents are managed is referred to as *content analysis*. Content analysis is the disciplined examination of written or recorded arti-

Sidebar 7.3
STEPS IN DOCUMENT CONTENT ANALYSIS

1. *Determine which types of documents would be the most valuable for your research question.* Would an analysis of sermon transcripts help understand the church or synagogue's character and identity? Do the financial records adequately describe the congregation's resources? Can an examination of church photo albums help uncover its present dysfunctional relationships?

2. *Identify which items are indicators of the themes and questions you are exploring.* Does the way the senior minister is addressed in worship services indicate how she is perceived by the church? Would counting the number of times a lay leader speaks or is present in front of the congregation define his power in the group? Can you compare records of membership, contributions, and participation in missions to determine the congregation's level of commitment? Do you need to look or listen for the exact words such as "love" and "family," or will you count how often a statement refers to these ideas without using the words explicitly?

3. *Decide how you will select the specific documents to be analyzed.* Will you look at every record, pamphlet, or newsletter issue? Should you randomly select a number of documents from each month or each year? Would it be best to examine only the committee notes from the groups most involved in the issue at hand? Think about what group of documents will give you a fair picture of the congregation, and be careful not to select in such a way as to skew your results (for instance, analyzing orders of worship only for first Sundays in a church that has Communion each first Sunday).

4. *Construct a set form, questionnaire, or code book to record the items you are tracking.* If you are looking for items that indicate a congregation's theology, for instance, you might want to start with a list of the major themes you recall. Then as you read or listen, you can add to your list. Each time you encounter a reference to a given theme, note what was said, what kind of reference it was (Bible verse, story, testimony, and so forth), when it occurred (date), in what context (Sunday morning, special occasion, and the like), and other information you think might be relevant. Your form may have a line for each occurrence, with columns for theme, date, type of reference, and so forth.

5. *Once the form is constructed, do a "test run" of your instrument on a document or tape to see how it works.* Does the form allow enough room for your written comments? Are there other key words or ideas you want to include on the form? Do you need to be more specific in what you are looking for? For instance, when examining how often a hymn appeared in old worship bulletins, would a simple yes/no checklist of the top forty favorite hymns identified by the congregation be adequate, or would you want to list every title?

6. *After you, or members of the study team, have examined a document, you may want to ask another person to perform the same task and then compare the results for greater accuracy.* Have you interpreted certain statements or figures as another person would? Are your criteria for coding and assigning a particular item to one category clear and well-defined, so others can duplicate your work? If there are differences, you may need to discuss and revise the criteria of your content analysis.

7. *Finally, construct a table of results to summarize your findings.* The goal will be to quantify, to count or give a number value, to the occurrences of various events, ideas, or themes related to your research interest. How many references to God's justice have you counted, for instance, and has that number increased or decreased over time? How many announcements of events for children are contained in the newsletters you analyzed, and did that number change over time? Hints for strategies of analysis are found later in this chapter.

ifacts of a congregation.[8] Within this methodology you may look at the more overt aspects of the document, such as the actual figures of a budget, the hymns sung last month, the specific ministries being advertised, or congregational attendance figures. Likewise, content analysis can be used to investigate other more latent characteristics of a document or recorded event, such as the ways a minister refers to God in sermons, gender stereotypes in Sunday school literature, how much time a particular subgroup has to speak at the annual meeting compared to the time granted other such factions, the implicit story of the congregation as told through the past dozen years of newsletter commentaries, or the identification of the major power players in the organization based on an analysis of the history of committee leadership. In addition, content analysis can also be used in a generalized manner to identify such things as prominent theological themes, aspects of culture, or missionary emphases.

Keeping the Focus

Content analysis requires both the disciplined selection of sources to analyze and careful formulation of questions to explore. You should begin with a focused examination of the available documentary resources, guided by clear collection methods and coding strategies. These steps are described in sidebar 7.3. You need to decide what you will look at, in what ways, and what research questions you will ask of this material. Your particular decisions about these issues must be carefully guided by your research rationale. Ask yourself what you are looking for in each report, transcript, or recording. Just as with interview questions, the form and content of questions asked of documents shapes and limits the information gained. You can make note of highly structured, specific information, or you can look for broad and general themes, but the choice of themes and sources will depend on the issues that are guiding your overall study.

Strengths and Weaknesses

Whether you are counting specific items or uncovering general patterns, the investigation of archival materials and a more specific analysis of its content may yield considerable hidden treasures. Analysis of these documents is usually inexpensive and relatively simple to do. It is an ideal task for members of a study team who are less outgoing or who are unable to commit hours away from their home. If the documents are portable, examination can be done anywhere. Analysis of documents may be the only way to get at certain information such as a congregation's income, budget, and attendance history. This is an ideal approach for examining changes that have taken place over time. It is often the only method for exploring events that happen too quickly or simultaneously and therefore cannot be fully observed as they occur.

A disciplined look at the documents of a congregation can sometimes correct and supplement perceptions gained through casual observation or interviewing. For instance, at South Meridian Church of God, one of the churches described in Ammerman's *Congregation and Community,* interviewees consistently claimed that the economic downturn in their community had no real effect on the congregation. A careful examination of budget records revealed, however, that there were indeed church cutbacks during the worst years of layoffs. Both the perceptions and the raw numbers were important to telling the story of that congregation's resources.

At the same time, when undertaking content analysis it must be remembered that the documents produced by a congregation were produced for a specific reason. They have a distinct agenda, whether to promote the group's identity, gloss over its troubles, or make a point to a dissident faction. It is also important to remember that a congregation's official documents may be intentionally shaped around a set party line. Worship attendance or ministry activity records destined for denominational headquarters may be crafted in such a way to gain the favor or respect of certain officials. It is also true that lists of congregational officers and committee leaders may not disclose the group's actual power structure. Perhaps those with the most power and influence manage to be exempt from such service.

Chances are quite good that not all the necessary information about a congregation can be found in its artifacts. Even questions about resources or budgets require an investigation of members' perceptions and willingness to give in the future. In addition, the information you seek might not have been collected in the form you need. You may

Sidebar 7.4
HINTS FOR USING
CENSUS DATA

1. Think carefully about the limits or scope of the area you want to examine. Do you need state, county, city, zip code, and census tract information? Do you want to look at the immediate neighborhood around the congregation, the area served by the congregation, a community of potential members, or those neighborhoods where the majority of members reside?

2. Many congregations have at least two constituent pools from which they draw or to whom they minister. The immediate neighborhood surrounding the buildings may have a distinctive population in comparison to the more spread-out "parish" in which a congregation's members live. It may be helpful to focus on both of these areas and later to compare the differences. Table 7.3 illustrates such differences between one zip code area in Anderson, Indiana, and the city as a whole.

3. Not everyone in your study team will be equally interested in demographic information. Identify those who have used such figures before, either in their work or in school. Ask one of these people to familiarize himself or herself with the types of information available and the key terms used by the Census Bureau. The most challenging thing in reading census information is remaining clear about the terms and categories being used. Refer to the definitions provided in census publications for terms such as "nonfamily household" or "foreign born."

4. Ideally the team member who gathers census information should have access to the Internet or a large library system.

5. Be creative with the presentation of census information. Nothing is more boring than a recitation of a long list of demographic statistics. Often charts or graphs, even pictures or videos, can convey the information more dramatically and with a greater lasting effect.

6. Be careful when attempting to predict future patterns from past trends. Historic patterns over time do offer clues to the future, but they do not guarantee that increases or declines will continue. Increased personal mobility, rapid shifts in housing patterns, and fluid social conditions can foil even the best trend data when it is based on a survey taken each decade.

want to know attendance but the records only indicate membership, or you only need total income and outlay but must wade through pages of detailed breakdowns of every minute expenditure and source of revenue. The most appropriate documents could be difficult to locate because they have been stored, for instance, in a dusty closet or a sound booth in an unused corner of the gymnasium. Finally, you can never be sure if what you have counted and interpreted to mean one thing really does carry that meaning. For instance, does the fact that a minister uses images of love and family twenty-five times a week in her sermon mean that it is important for her or for the congregation as a whole? Nevertheless, the investigation of archival records, whether by general examination or a more structured content analysis, is another effective method for gaining a window on the happenings of a congregation.

Census Data and Secondary Source Records

Students of congregations can also gain information from publicly available documents, external to the congregation itself. The most useful and obvious of these sources is the United States Census. For those who do not wish to deal with the complexities of census data, there are numerous privately packaged market research reports and computerized demographic programs. In addition, newspaper and historical records for your locale, denominational research reports, city and county publications of population growth and economic forecasts, and even real estate neighborhood assessments all can be sources of important contextual information. Each of these evaluations of the congregation's local setting can provide insights into the economic and social makeup of local residents, the expectation of a community's growth and development, or contextual factors that may affect the health, life, and mission of a congregation.

Every ten years the United States Census Bureau collects a considerable amount of information on the residents of the nation. The extent to which the Census Bureau actually compiles information on all residents, however, has been a matter of dispute for years. Officials of large cities and minority advocacy groups argue that undercounting of homeless people, minority males, and non-English speakers disadvantages both them and the jurisdictions within which they reside. Despite such possible undercounts, census figures remain the best estimates of population numbers, demographics, and social characteristics of people within a particular area. This diverse information is available to congregations in many forms. It is available in many public and college libraries in printed form. These published volumes contain information on all geographic areas of the country. With the assistance of the research or documents librarian, you should be able to narrow down your search to your county, city, or census tract, depending on the needs of your study. The information contained in these volumes includes hundreds of demographic categories and subcategories, such as age, sex, race, income, marital status, occupation, family type, household living arrangements, home values, residential mobility, and even the distances people drive to and from work. The most recent decennial figures can also be compared to the census data from previous decades to get a sense of the changes taking place in a community. There is a wealth of information on your community, both past and present, if you are willing to put the time into digging through the many printed tables. If you are looking at your congregation through an ecological frame, you will want to pay attention to such information on your community, and chapter 2 includes a number of sug-

Sidebar 7.5
CENSUS DATA ON THE WORLD WIDE WEB

Here are the steps for accessing census data from the World Wide Web:

1. Use your Web browser to reach http://www.census.gov. From the Census Bureau home page, choose "search."

2. In most cases you will want to choose "place search" from the next menu. You will then be offered the chance to type in a place name or a zip code. The two examples below illustrate those two options. The first is for the city of Anderson, Indiana; the second is for zip code 46012, which is part of Anderson.

3. When offered the option of looking up 1990 Census data, choose the "STF3A" option or the "STF3B". You will then be presented with a very long list of possible tables from which to choose. The data below came from P8 (race), P12 (Hispanic origin by race), and P19 (household type and presence and age of children). You can browse through this list and experiment with which tables give you the information you need. Once you have checked off all the tables you want, go back to the top of the list and click on "submit." You will probably also have to choose the format in which you want to view the tables. The "html" default usually works well.

4. Your requested tables will next appear on the screen. With most systems, you can then choose to print them. They will probably look something like what is displayed in table 7.1.

5. If you want information on a specific census tract, the process is a little more complicated. Choose the link on the "place search" page labeled "1990 Census Lookup." Select the "STF3A" option again. Then choose the "Level State-County" option, and select your state. On the next page select the "State-County-Census Tract" option, and choose which census tract number you are interested in. A map of the tract numbers can be found at your library's reference section. After choosing a tract, you will be asked to select the demographic tables you wish to see. This will also produce the appropriate tables for your census tract.

6. If you are interested in older census data or in other demographic, economic, or market information, check out these sites with links to a multitude of demographic data:
www.trinity.edu/~mkearl/data.html
or
www.psc.lsa.umich.edu/ssdan.

TABLE 7.1

1990 US Census Data
Database: C90STF3A
Summary Level: State—Place

Anderson city: FIPS.STATE=18,
FIPS.PLACE90=01468

RACE
Universe: Persons
White 50452
Black 8515
American Indian, Eskimo, or Aleut 184
Asian or Pacific Islander 184
Other race 114

HISPANIC ORIGIN BY RACE
Universe: Persons
Not of Hispanic origin:
  White 50295
  Black 8496
  American Indian, Eskimo, or Aleut 177
  Asian or Pacific Islander 176
  Other race 60
Hispanic origin:
  White 157
  Black 19
  American Indian, Eskimo, or Aleut 7
  Asian or Pacific Islander 8
  Other race 54

HOUSEHOLD TYPE AND PRESENCE AND
AGE OF CHILDREN
Universe: Households
Family households:
  Married-couple family:
    With own children under 18 years . . . 4909
    No own children under 18 years 6777
  Other family:
    Male householder, no wife present:
      With own children under 18 years . . 364
      No own children under 18 years 417
    Female householder, no husband present:
      With own children under 18 years . . 2196
      No own children under 18 years . . . 1367
Nonfamily households 8305

1990 US Census Data
Database: C90STF3B
Summary Level: ZIP Code

Madison County (pt.): ZIP=46012

RACE
Universe: Persons
White 20355
Black 503
American Indian, Eskimo, or Aleut 52
Asian or Pacific Islander 18
Other race 9

HISPANIC ORIGIN BY RACE
Universe: Persons
Not of Hispanic origin:
  White 20286
  Black 503
  American Indian, Eskimo, or Aleut 52
  Asian or Pacific Islander 18
  Other race 0
Hispanic origin:
  White 69
  Black 0
  American Indian, Eskimo, or Aleut 0
  Asian or Pacific Islander 0
  Other race 9

HOUSEHOLD TYPE AND PRESENCE AND
AGE OF CHILDREN
Universe: Households
Family households:
  Married-couple family:
    With own children under 18 years . . . 2069
    No own children under 18 years 2823
  Other family:
    Male householder, no wife present:
      With own children under 18 years . . 114
      No own children under 18 years 78
    Female householder, no husband present:
      With own children under 18 years . . 384
      No own children under 18 years 251
Nonfamily households 2210

gestions for how to interpret it. Also see the hints for using census data in sidebar 7.4.

In recent years, with the advent of personal computers, census information has been made even more accessible. The data are available on machine readable magnetic tape, on CD-ROM disks, and through the Internet. An index of Internet census materials can be found on the World Wide Web at http://www.census.gov. Access to the Internet has become quite convenient, with public libraries and schools offering free connections. If no adult in your congregation has private access, perhaps one of the teenage members could look up the information at school. Both the CD-ROM and Internet forms have specialized but very easy ways to ask only for the information you want (see sidebar 7.5). For example, on the United States Census Web site, you can type in the name of your state, county, town, zip code, or census tract, check off the categories for which information you want, and in a moment's time receive a printout of those figures. The results of one such search are shown in table 7.1.

Demographic information is often presented by zip code areas. This format is, however, less stable than governmental or census boundaries. Because zip codes are created for United States Postal Service convenience, boundaries may change at any time, making historical trend analysis difficult if not impossible. Still, if your study is unconcerned with comparisons to the past, zip code information may be both more familiar and more workable, because most congregations know the zip codes of their members.

The local library can also be a source for other excellent information about the community around your congregation. Libraries often house county or city reports on the area. These reports may summarize United States Census and other demographic information into an easily readable form. Libraries also usually contain histories written about your area, as well as newspaper archives with stories of historic, social, and economic changes in the neighborhood. Local real estate offices can also be a good source of impressionistic information about your area, because a realtor's livelihood partially depends on accurate perceptions of housing trends.

In addition, there are any number of private companies that employ census figures and other survey information to create explicit market oriented reports for variously defined geographic areas. For a fee ranging from $50 to $500 or more, these companies will compile a picture of your community for you, saving you the effort of digging up the material yourself.

Some of these data-sorting companies, (such as P. C. Demographics, Asynch, and Scan/US), work primarily with demographic analysis and offer their clients user-friendly ways to manipulate this information. Other companies, such as Claritas Corporation and Percept, attempt to combine market research and buying pattern information with census data to create neighborhood clusters of distinctive "life-style groupings." These findings must be used cautiously, however. Their claim that "where you live determines how you live" is often overstated. In fact, the process may be exactly the reverse, that how you live determines where you will live. Even if their assumption were accurate, many of us can think of numerous people in our communities who are radical exceptions to the norms of the neighborhood. In addition, because

they make life-style projections based on demographic summaries, their assumptions are occasionally wildly wrong. The large families and agricultural occupations of a county of Amish residents showed up in one instance as "struggling Hispanic workers"! Still, the market projections and demographic information these services put together can be quite helpful.

If your congregation belongs to a denomination, the national research or mission office may be able to provide census demographic and marketing summaries for you. They are often able to offer the information to affiliated congregations at no charge or for a nominal fee. If your congregation has a denominational connection, one of your first steps in your analysis of the local context should be to contact the research people at your denomination's headquarters.

Keeping the Focus

A disciplined analysis of the mass of information external to the congregation can be quite helpful, depending on your research interest. If you are focusing on issues of decision-making or adult education, you may at first think that census data are irrelevant, but even internal problems may be reflections of changes in the demographic makeup of the community. If your study is of the local context and your aim is to increase mission efforts, begin an evangelism program, or plant a new congregation, census and demographic material is essential. Likewise, such an analysis may shed light on problems of visitor retention, stagnant or declining membership, or a congregational identity that does not fit the new residents in an area. It may provide new ways to view and minister to the local community, or it could show, following an analysis of the zip codes of members, that the congregation ought to relocate. Therefore, one of the initial issues in doing this research is, again, determining what you need to know and how you will use what you find. You will want to use your study's interest to narrow or expand your focus on the contextual and demographic information. Do you need county information or just figures for your immediate neighborhood? Will zip code areas or the more standardized census divisions fit better with your study? Do you want to look at how the area has changed over time or its present situation? Are the relevant issues the economic ones or the realities of ethnicity or changes in family structure?

Strengths and Weaknesses

Often there are considerable advantages in examining a holistic picture of the congregation's locale. This bird's-eye view can help uncover hidden patterns and trends in the neighborhood, as well as identify invisible members of a community. You may discover a far higher number of single people in your community or more immigrants or a more sizeable group of economically disadvantaged people than you realized were there.

Even with its assets, census data and other external resources do take time to find and analyze. In addition, this material almost always describes past events. The findings are seldom current with the most immediate happenings. Nevertheless, there is no better way to gain an overall picture of the congregation's context and societal influences than to use these methods.

When using census information, an effort should be made to link it to what ordinary members actually see and experience in their daily lives. Use your observations of the area and drives through the neighborhood to flesh out the raw numbers of the census. Refer to the descriptions of several of these hands-on methods in chapter 2 for more detail. Encourage the study group members analyzing the information to try to translate the numbers into personally familiar terms and experiences that can be related to the congregation. For instance, to understand the census numbers on housing patterns, describe the physical characteristics of local apartments or ask a member who is a resident to talk about living there. To get in touch with the finding that 60 percent of local residents have moved in the previous five years, ask a member to describe what it was like to relocate. The volumes of information available through census and other demographic reports will make the most sense

when connected to experiences with which your congregation can identify.

Questionnaires and Surveys

Questionnaires are something with which we are all familiar. Because of our frequent exposure to them and the perceived power of survey statistics in our society, questionnaires often come to mind at the early stages of a congregational study. A questionnaire can be an effective tool in congregational research. If not carefully focused and interpreted, however, it could also be a meaningless exercise and a waste of time and energy. These paper-and-pencil instruments are a good shorthand way to find out about the demographic makeup of the congregation or to get a picture of various values, beliefs, and attitudes. The congregation can be profiled with a summary of items like educational levels, types of occupations, family income, ethnic heritage, and length of residence in the community—all facts easily discovered by a simple questionnaire.

Written surveys may be extensive or a single page, created from scratch or borrowed (or purchased) from a professional source, generalized to explore a congregation's identity, or specifically focused on one crisis issue. It must be remembered, however, that any questionnaire employed should be designed and used to measure specific issues, attitudes, and beliefs that are thought to be relevant to a particular research question. You should adopt a disciplined approach to a survey's design, content, distribution, and analysis, just as you have in using the other methods discussed above.[9]

It is quite possible for your congregational study team to construct its own survey form. Many of the mechanics of questionnaire design are similar to structuring interview questions or shaping a content analysis code book. A self-designed questionnaire can be very useful in addressing highly specific research issues. If the task seems intimidating, however, the team can use one of the countless commercial surveys and analysis services available from both denominations and private consultants. Many of these survey instruments address specific congregational issues, such as the Needs Assessment Checklist, Pastoral Search Inventory, Church Planning Inventory, and the Role Expectation Checklist. Several of these are described in chapter 4 and reproduced there and in the Appendices. If your congregational study is focused on one of these specific areas, then using a ready-made and well-tested form might be advantageous. Likewise, if you wish to compare your congregation's data to a larger body of information, the use of a preexisting form would allow for such comparison. Finally, if none of the study team wants to tackle constructing a questionnaire, or if your affiliate denomination provides the service free of charge if you use their set forms, then a standardized survey should be chosen. It is also possible to construct an original document by borrowing and combining questions from other sources to suit your specific needs.

Keeping the Focus

The most important step in using a questionnaire, whether self-made or purchased, is to bring your specific research interests to bear upon the form. You must tailor the method to your study's focus. What information are you interested in collecting? What are you going to ask and of whom? These and other questions should shape the use of a written survey, just as they did the interview process or your observations. Do you even need to use a questionnaire, or could you better obtain the information by using another method? Despite our frequent linkage of "research" to "surveying," not every study of a congregation needs to include a questionnaire.

Questionnaires can be used quite well to explore members' attitudes about programmatic or process changes. If you need responses from a large percent of the membership around specific needs or member interests, then a survey is an especially effective method of inquiry. On the other hand, if your focus is the dynamics of leadership, participation behaviors in worship, or the social and interpersonal relationships among members, a questionnaire might be less helpful than other methods. For

most general studies of a congregation, however, surveys are excellent tools to collect demographic and general behavioral information.

Once you have decided to use a questionnaire, the purpose of your study should guide what you will ask. It is important to ask *only* what you want to know about or what you would be willing to change. Often questions on a survey are interpreted by respondents as votes for an actual congregational agenda. Members may be quite upset when they learn that their opinions about what hymns they like do not translate into the actual song list for worship services. Also, do not ask what physical changes people would like to make in your building's classrooms unless your plans include acting on this information.

Every survey does not need to include every type of question. In a study of proposed recreational activities, much of the survey would focus on opinions about various events and sports, members' current involvement in similar activities in the community, and their expected level of support for each potential program, with demographic issues playing a secondary role. A measure of members' theological convictions or current religious practices would probably be unnecessary if recreational activities were your focus. Likewise, a study of the culture of a congregation might use a survey to analyze members' demographics, religious practices, and theological, moral, and social convictions, with little attention to evaluation of specific programs or leadership processes.

Whom to Survey

Your specific agenda also shapes who should receive the questionnaire. For instance, would the entire congregation need to be polled regarding young adult extracurricular social events? Do only the congregation's leaders need to be asked what the requirements of the next pastor should be? Is it necessary to ask for the opinions of the entire congregation, or just a subset of the membership, around an issue? Are you concerned with the behaviors of only those who attend worship or all those on the membership rolls? These dilemmas of survey distribution indicate the need for responsible and disciplined sampling of the congregation. The matter of who should be included, however, is not always straightforward. For example, questions about the style of worship might logically be addressed only to those who attend. Many of those who are unhappy with the present worship form, however, might identify the style as their reason for not attending worship. If you did not attempt to include them in the survey, you might never know this. Improper sampling, whether unintentional or purposeful, can misrepresent the opinions of the congregation and destroy trust in the study or its leaders.

If you decide you want to survey the entire congregation and the membership is 250 or fewer, you should distribute the form to each person. If the membership numbers over that figure, however, you might consider giving the survey to a select subgroup. If you choose to sample, or select out, only a portion of the entire congregation, or population, to receive the questionnaire, how would you go about choosing this group? To select a random sample is not to make haphazard choices. Rather, it means that each member theoretically has an equal chance of getting the form. For instance, you can begin with a membership list, flip a coin, or toss a die to select where you will begin, and then select every second, third, or fourth person on the list until you have reached the end and have the necessary number. Another possible method, referred to as a stratified sample, works well with a highly divided or diversified congregation. The congregation is subdivided into distinct groups (by age, race, tenure, and so forth), and then people are selected from each of these subgroups using a random method. Each of these methods decreases the chance of bias in the sample selection and improves the degree to which the study may be generalized to the whole group. None of these strategies guarantees unbiased and representative results, however.

One other frequent but highly problematic method of choosing a sample *should be avoided.* This method is called an accidental sample. It happens when one chooses whatever group happens to appear at a given place or time, say the next twenty people who walk out of the sanctuary, or everyone entering a certain door,

or those milling around the coffee pot. These clusters may seem random, but in fact they nearly always are distinct subgroups. There is no way of knowing whether those groups actually represent the whole. Were these people together because they just left a leadership meeting, or did the nursing home bus drop off riders by that door, or were those lingering around the coffee pot doing so to complain about the pastor? One can never be sure.

Of course, there may be times when you want to survey only a specific group, such as only those members with young children. Even then, however, you may get different results if you distribute surveys to parents as they pick up their children from Sunday school rather than mailing the questionnaire to all members with children. The bottom line is, if you want to be able to generalize your findings to an entire population group, you should follow one of the disciplined selection methods described above.

As the previous example illustrates, it also matters *how* you distribute your survey. Perhaps the most economical and efficient method is to hand it out when people are already gathered for meetings or services. This is even more effective if you allow time for them to complete the survey and provide an easy way to turn it in immediately. This avoids mailing costs and ensures that nearly everyone present will complete the form. The disadvantage, of course, is that those who attend are not a representative sample of the entire membership. Even the cumulative attendance over several weeks may not guarantee representation of all those who normally attend. For instance, at one of the churches described in Ammerman's *Congregation and Community,* the project survey was distributed two Sundays in a row in the midst of a period of severe winter weather. Many of the older attenders stayed home those weeks and therefore never had the opportunity to complete the questionnaire.

The other most common distribution method is mailing the questionnaire (and return envelope) to the whole or a select group of members. This method would more closely approximate a representative sample of the entire membership;

however, it is also more costly and less likely to generate a high response rate. The rate of survey responses should be greater than 50 percent. Anything less than this figure should be treated as somewhat suspect, because those who responded were a self-selected subgroup of the whole with their own biases and interests in the survey. Of course, mailing the form might be the only way to address certain research questions, especially if you are concerned with differences between frequent and very infrequent attenders.

Creating Good Questions

Although a congregational study group's focus shapes the content of a survey, the form your questions take should follow careful and systematic guidelines. How you ask a question can make a considerable difference in the response you get. That is one good reason for adopting, or borrowing, questions from an existing survey. It is assumed that such a survey is composed of well-written questions, although this is not always the case. As you choose question forms, ask yourself about the specificity of the information you need (exact numbers or broad ranges?), the limits of space on your form, the congregation's sensibilities (will they be offended by this form of asking?), and your own personal preferences. When considering the type of question for each item you want to ask, make sure it is simple, straightforward, and addresses your research interests.

The first broad type of question is the *closed-ended, structured question*. Much like the structured interview question, this type not only asks the question in a set fashion but provides a choice of predetermined answers. The simplest of these is the *yes/no question*. These are effective and easy to analyze, but they can also become tiresome to answer if used too frequently.

• Are you a member of this congregation? Yes [ ] No [ ]

• When you were 11 or 12 years old, did one or both of your parents . . .

	YES	NO
a. Usually light Shabbat candles?	[ ]	[ ]
b. Use separate dishes for meat and dairy?	[ ]	[ ]
c. Have their own Succah?	[ ]	[ ]
d. Refrain from eating meat in nonkosher restaurants?	[ ]	[ ]
e. Fast on Yom Kippur?	[ ]	[ ]

One version of the yes/no question commonly used is the *contingency question* ("if yes, then . . . "). This type of question is best set off by a box or an indentation. It is sometimes necessary to give explicit written instructions ("If no, skip to question 7 on the next page").

• Are you a member of this congregation?   Yes [ ] No [ ]

    IF YES, in what year did you join? _____
        How long did you attend prior to joining? _____

    IF NO, how long have you attended here? _____
        Are you a member of another congregation?   Yes [ ] No [ ]
        If so, what congregation? _____

Another form of structured question offers a *multiple choice* of possible answers. The respondents are asked to select the option that most closely reflects their views or situations.

• How long have you been a member of this local church?
  [ ] Not a member   [ ] 2–4 years   [ ] 10–19 years
  [ ] One year or less   [ ] 5–9 years   [ ] 20 or more years

• Which one of the following best expresses your view of the Bible?
  [ ]   The Bible is a valuable book because it was written by wise and good people, but I do not believe it is really God's Word.
  [ ]   The Bible is the record of many different people's response to God, and, because of this, people and churches today are forced to interpret for themselves the Bible's basic moral and religious teachings.
  [ ]   The Bible is the inspired Word of God and its basic moral and religious teachings are clear and true, even if it reflects some human error.
  [ ]   The Bible is the actual Word of God and is to be taken literally.

In using this multiple choice type of question, be sure to create categories that are discrete and not overlapping. For instance, income categories of $10,000–$20,000 and $20,000–$30,000 mean that the person who makes exactly $20,000 has two categories to decide between. Instead, define them as $10,000–19,999 and $20,000–$29,999. Also, make sure the possible answers will produce the information needed for the study. In a question about congregational membership, do not ask people during which five-year interval they joined when you need to examine differences between those who have come during the last three years and those who came before. Simply to ask exactly what year the members joined is better.

In addition, with this type of question, you need to think carefully about the full array of possible answers. Having six categories for incomes under $50,000 and one for everyone else is not very helpful if almost everyone has an income over $75,000. In addition, questions about beliefs pose special difficulties. The range of answers about the Bible in the question above might be helpful in sorting out differences in a liberal congregation, but it might be of little use in discerning the important fault lines within a more conservative congregation (all of whose members might choose the last response).

• Some people prefer a great deal of innovation and variety in worship experiences, something new all the time. Others prefer the consistency of traditional worship forms. Please put a mark on the scale below that best represents your position.

Tradition   1   2   3   4   5   6   7   Variety

• Listed below are several alternatives touching upon important dimensions of a church's identity. Using the seven-point scale between each set of alternatives, please circle the number that best describes where your congregation falls, 1 meaning most like the characteristic on the left, 7 meaning most like the characteristic on the right, 4 meaning an equal mix of both.

Our church is more influenced   Our church is more influenced
by history and tradition.   1 2 3 4 5 6 7   by contemporary ideas and trends.

• If you had to locate your political leanings on a scale from liberal to conservative, where would you fall?
Liberal   1   2   3   4   5   6   7   8   9   Conservative

The *scaled* or *continuum question* is another form of closed-ended question. Rather than giving many possible options, however, it offers only one set of end-points and a range between. Several versions of this type of question are possible. When designing these questions, be careful to construct the end-points as opposites, rather than just random ideas.

An often-used form of a scaled question provides four or five verbal options to measure a respondent's assessment of a particular statement. This type of question works well with attitudinal questions, program evaluations, and an assessment of congregational needs, as the discussion of questionnaires in the chapter on process shows.

You should guard against wording questions so that it becomes obvious that the "correct" answer to each one is "strongly agree." You may want to vary the wording of statements to make some sentences positive and others negative, so as not to establish a set pattern for marking answers.

A second general category of survey questions is *open-ended questions*. This type of question is written to allow the respondent to fill in the blank and create his or her own response. Open-ended questions are very useful when you want to know specific ages, incomes, or dates of birth. By asking these demographic questions in the most specific way possible, the information can later be regrouped into many different patterns. For instance, if age were asked in set groupings (under 30, 30-50, 51-70, and over 70) you would never know exactly what the average age of the congregation was, nor would you ever be able to recombine members' responses into an under-40 age grouping, for instance. Likewise, open-ended questions such as "What is your age?" often take up very little space on the survey form. These fill-in-the-blank questions are also helpful if the study team is not sure of the full range of possible responses. In such a case, they can be used to supplement a closed-ended question, inquiring into other possible responses not previously specified. (See the race category questions in appendix B, for instance). In addition, open-ended questions are often an excellent way to conclude a questionnaire, allowing the respondent to express any additional feeling or thought. These wide-ranging concluding remarks may hint at underlying currents or tensions that had been neither perceived nor asked about in other contexts.

	Strongly Agree	Agree	Neutral or Unsure	Disagree	Strongly Disagree
1. A person can be a good Christian without attending church.	[ ]	[ ]	[ ]	[ ]	[ ]
2. Scripture is very important to my spiritual life.	[ ]	[ ]	[ ]	[ ]	[ ]
3. There is very little sense of excitement among members about our church's future.	[ ]	[ ]	[ ]	[ ]	[ ]

	Very Satisfied	Generally Satisfied	Somewhat Dissatisfied	Very Dissatisfied
Overall, how satisfied or dissatisfied are you with the music during Sunday morning worship?	[ ]	[ ]	[ ]	[ ]
Overall, how satisfied or dissatisfied are you with the Sunday morning worship, other than the music?	[ ]	[ ]	[ ]	[ ]

A second form of the fill-in-the-blank question asks for a *brief response*, often more than one word. These questions can be valuable if the possible range of responses is unknown. They can, however, occasionally be difficult to quantify. At times, respondents will suggest several possible answers when you only ask for one. Other times, a few responses will be nonsensical or farfetched. In addition, it is possible that you could receive seventy-five entirely distinct answers that might tell you nothing about your research interest except that there is great diversity of opinion. Often these brief comments will need to be combined into a smaller number of categories once all the survey forms are examined. This process of creating several generalized categories to organize the diverse answers is discussed below.

• What aspect of the congregation was most instrumental in your decision to join?

_____

• What part of the retreat did you find most spiritually satisfying?

_____

A third type of this question format is the *broad open-ended question*. This form asks for generalized and possibly extensive comments by the respondent. It might ask for additional information about a program or the strengths and weaknesses of the congregation, allow for expression of complaints, or invite respondents to comment on the questionnaire and the study process in general. In each case, such questions should be followed by sufficient blank space to allow people to write their answers.

• Is there anything else you would like to tell us about the importance of the Sunday school program for your family?

• Are there any other comments that you would like to make about what the church has meant to you or how it has ministered to you?

• Is there anything that you would like to tell the self-study committee that we have not asked about?

The simplest form of the open-ended question is the *short-answer question*. These are both straightforward and economical of space. They do result in a much greater variety of answers than the closed-ended questions. At the same time, these questions allow for more flexibility in grouping and recategorizing the responses later in the analysis of information.

• How long have you been attending this congregation? _____

• What is your age? _____

• What is your zip code? _____

• Rate from 1 to 10 your interest in participating in each of the following proposed church activities (with 1 being the most interest and 10 being the least)
   1. Adult softball league _____
   2. Parenting class _____
   3. Yoga instruction _____

Sidebar 7.6
GENERAL SUGGESTIONS FOR WRITING QUESTIONNAIRES

1. The questionnaire format should be eye-catching and uncluttered, with plenty of white spaces. The zoom feature on many word processing programs works well to evaluate the aesthetics of a questionnaire.

2. Use a clear, readable font but vary the size of the font or use bold and *italics* type (sparingly) to guide the eye through the questions.

3. Briefly introduce the survey form with a short statement about who is sponsoring the survey, why it is being done, whether the information will be confidential or not, what will be done with the final results, and any special instructions about how to fill out the form. Include this statement even if a cover letter will be attached to the form.

The purpose of this questionnaire is to help our church think about its present life and plan for the future. Please take a few minutes to respond to these questions. In most cases, you can just mark (X) the response that fits you best (though perhaps not perfectly) or fill in a brief answer. Where you are asked for your belief or opinion, we really want to know what you think. There are no "right" answers. When you really cannot answer, just skip on to the next item. We guarantee that your individual answers will be anonymous and held in the strictest confidence. When you have completed the survey, deposit it in the special boxes by the exits as you leave. We hope you enjoy filling out the questionnaire. After the results are tallied and the self-study is completed, a special church meeting will be held to discuss the future of our congregation. Thank you for your assistance in helping us better understand ourselves as a congregation.

4. Use topic headings and perhaps a short descriptive sentence to introduce a new section of the survey.

First, a few questions about your participation in the congregation.

Beliefs and Values
Please respond to each statement with a check (✓), indicating whether you strongly agree, agree, are neutral or unsure, disagree, or strongly disagree.

Finally, some background information about yourself.

Thank you for time and thoughtfulness. If you have any further comments about the church or the self study please write them below in the space provided.

5. Use the same format to define the space where answers should be written for all your questions. Generally it is best to ask the respondent to make an X, rather than a check mark, in the space defined by a box or brackets [ ] or by parentheses ( ). For certain questions, a blank line can be used to define where respondents are to answer. Never just leave an open space, unless you are asking an extended, open-ended question. At times it is also acceptable to ask the people to circle a response, for example, to indicate which is the most important of the several items they identified. Remind people to mark only one answer.

6. When using several sections of questions with different foci, maintain a common format. For instance, if you use parentheses to indicate where an X should be made, use them throughout, and always put them on the same side of the question. If you offer a range of response choices, for example, from agree to disagree, keep them in the same order throughout the survey.

Responses to questions in this format are sometimes very interesting and revealing. The questionnaire may have sparked members to recall issues not discussed or asked about. Often highly supportive as well as quite disgruntled members use this format to voice their opinions. Because of the potentially far-reaching nature of such comments, they should be treated more like an interview response than like something that can be turned into a numerical code.

Question Types Best Avoided

There are a few question formats that should be avoided, either because they are difficult to answer or difficult to analyze. The first of these is the *multiple-task question*. This type of question requires the respondent to think and do one thing ("check all the committees of which you were a member"), then analyze the list another way ("circle those for which you were a leader"), and sometimes to assess it a third time ("and underline the one to which you were most committed"). This type of question is relatively complex and often may be answered incorrectly. Another type that should be avoided by the novice questionnaire designer is the *rank-order question*. This format entails a list of options the respondent is asked to rank in order of importance. This type of question is rather easy to answer (although respondents often reverse the order you asked them to use), but it is very time consuming for the respondent and challenging for the analyst. Finally, use sparingly the questions that contain *lists of items to be evaluated*. This format has merit when you really need to know about all the programs of a congregation, but it can take considerable time to answer. For instance, a question like "Which of the following reasons were influential in your joining? (check all that apply)" might include a list of thirty possible options, each of which respondents must consider individually. Likewise, each option must be treated as a separate question for later analysis. At that later point, it may be difficult to perceive any patterns of response among so many categories.

How to Write Questions

Once the format and categories of interest are decided upon for a questionnaire, the task of writing the questions remains. The first general guideline for doing this is to use your knowledge of the setting to shape the questions. Use the congregation's own language, idioms, and special phrases. Write the questions in their words. This is especially true if you borrow questions from other survey forms. Customize the questions. If God is referred to as "He" in your congregation, use the masculine pronoun; if not, do not use it. Use the name of the church, the pastor, or a specific committee rather than generic terms. Do not talk about the "Eucharist" if your church celebrates the "Lord's Supper." The same strategy should be used in constructing the fixed answers to closed-ended questions. Use your knowledge of the congregation to identify

and word the responses that represent the range of opinions, beliefs, and demographic categories in your situation. If you want to compare your questionnaire results with others, you will have to keep the questions exactly as asked previously. If this is not a consideration, however, tailor your questions to suit your congregation, your issues, and your research interests.

A second guideline is to be careful of the wording of your questions. Avoid emotionally charged words or words with double meanings. Synonyms and antonyms do not always have exactly the same connotation in common language. For instance, "forbid" and "allow" are roughly opposites, but they do not carry the same verbal weight. Questions should also be free of vague and imprecise language. Avoid using words like "community," "vision," and "mission and ministry" as much as possible unless you further clarify their meaning.

Caution should also be taken not to write leading questions. Both a question's wording and the responses offered may influence or lead the respondent. Examples of this problem could include, "Do you agree with the pastor that a two-hour worship service is too long?" or "The sin of homosexuality can be an acceptable Christian lifestyle, yes or no?" or "Should we move forward with the building plan that God has given us?" You do not want to make it clear to the respondent what the "right" answer should be.

Another general caveat in writing questions is to avoid constructing sentences with several objects. This error is occasionally seen where one is asked either to agree or disagree with a statement. Questions of this type include, "Do you favor longer Sunday school time and more in-depth teaching for the children?" and "The Bible is essential to my faith; I read it daily." Ask yourself for each question, Could I both agree and disagree with parts of this statement? If so, rewrite it. Likewise, be careful not to write comparative statements for which no adequate comparison is given, such as "The singles ministry is better now (agree or disagree?)." A respondent might ask, "Than when? Last year, when I first joined, or when the new singles minister took over?"

The self-study group should also refrain from writing questions that are too general. For instance, questions like "Abortion is wrong (agree or disagree?)" and "We must strengthen the church's outreach (agree or disagree?)" are so broad that almost everyone will both agree and disagree. Be more explicit and specific in wording the questions: "Abortion as a means of birth control is morally wrong" and "We must strengthen the church's outreach efforts to inner-city teenagers." In addition, some terms can also be misleading. For instance, the word "work" in a question designed to ask whether the person's parents were employed outside the home ("Did your mother work during your childhood?") could be misunderstood by or give offense to those who worked taking care of the home or were self-employed in the home. The best strategy about writing questions is to be explicit, be exact, and be brief.

Examining existing questionnaires is one way to guide your own writing. Copies of general national surveys, such as the National Opinion Research Center's *General Social Survey, The Gallup Poll,* The Roper Center Poll, surveys by Princeton University's Religion Research Center, and the *National Election Study* by the University of Michigan can be found either in most public library reference sections or on the Internet, respectively:

www.icpsr.umich.edu/gss/
www.gallup.com
www.ropercenter.uconn.edu
www.princeton.edu/~abelson/index.html
www.umich.edu~nes/

More specific congregational questionnaires can be obtained from various consulting groups, several of which are mentioned in the introduction of this book. In addition, certain general questions about religious belief and participation are commonly asked, and accepted forms have been developed. A selection of these items is included in Appendix B.

Finishing Touches

Having chosen the general topics, format, and wording of your questionnaire, you now must contemplate the order of the questions asked. Considerable research has shown that even the order in which questions are asked can affect the responses. Begin with interesting and engaging questions that will be inviting to the respondent. Be sure not to introduce highly sensitive issues too quickly. Save the more tedious and mundane demographic questions for later in the survey. Pay attention to which questions you ask immediately prior to which others. For instance, if you were interested in certain moral attitudes, you might separate questions about whether capital punishment is morally acceptable from those about how the respondent feels about abortion. You might, for example, also get different answers depending on which of the following two statements you put first: "Caring for the earth is essential to being a good Christian" and "Recycling should be a social priority for our church."

Once you have written your questions and decided in which order they ought to go, the last step in preparation is to pretest your work. You can recruit family and friends or a small group of congregational members to try answering your questions.

These people can point out the places where the questionnaire is not self-explanatory, where questions are not easily understood, and the like. They may even find a typographical error! A pretest is a crucial last step to the disciplined, systematic use of a questionnaire. Do not skip it just to meet a deadline.

After pretesting, you can fine-tune your questionnaire and prepare to print it. The questionnaire itself should look inviting and attractive. You may want to decorate the upper corner of the first page with the congregation's logo or a graphic. The survey should be printed on slightly heavier weight paper than normal. And it should be short! Do not ask too much. Ask only what is relevant to your research issue. *One to two pages and never more than four is best,* unless you have highly committed respondents, money to pay for their time, or a very important issue to address. If the survey is two pages long, print the survey on one sheet of paper, front and back. If three or four pages, the questionnaire can be printed landscape-style (sideways) on either 8½-by-14-inch or 11-by-17-inch stock and then folded into a booklet. Finally, you are ready to distribute the questionnaire.

Strengths and Weaknesses of Surveys

One of the clear advantages of questionnaires is that they are an inexpensive and quick method for assessing the attitudes and characteristics of a broad range of members. You can hear the opinions of many more people than it would be possible to interview. This method is essential if you are investigating a large or very diverse congregation. Surveys are also an effective means of gathering demographic information and of asking certain sensitive questions (for example, about income) people might not answer in a face-to-face situation.

The results of a statistical analysis of information gathered through a questionnaire, for good or ill, have considerable persuasive social power in American society. In addition, material that is quantifiable allows both internal analysis of membership subgroups and external comparisons with other congregations. At the same time, questionnaires must be seen for what they are: a written record of what people are willing to say they think and do. What people say they will do or believe, however, and what they actually do or believe may be two different things. A survey does not directly measure behavior.

You should also remember that surveys do not work well in eliciting responses from some groups in the congregation. Those who have difficulty with reading, sight, or abstract reasoning may not be able to respond. They, along with other nonrespondents, represent an unknown voice not included in survey statistics.

As we have noted throughout, a questionnaire is only as good as its questions, but it is also complicated by the ambiguity in the responses people give. Even the clearest question can elicit vague or contradictory responses. What are we to make, for instance, of people who respond to one question that the Bible is to be taken literally but respond to another that Genesis is more about God's involvement in creation than about precisely how and when the world came into being? How are we to understand what it means when the congregation's answers are spread evenly over three different categories having to do with belief or mission priority, for example? And what if the issues your study team has identified are not the crucial ones? Questionnaires can never provide all the information you will need, nor do they interpret themselves. They must be used alongside other methods if they are to be fully useful.

Data Storage

Each step of a congregational study, including planning for storing the information you collect, should be undertaken in a systematic and thoughtful manner. The information you laboriously compile—the interviews, the observational notes, the questionnaires, and the artifacts—will be of little use to you if not systematically filed and carefully maintained. This seems like such a trivial aspect of the entire project, but be assured there is nothing worse than misplacing a set of crucial observational notes, recording over an interview with the church historian because the tape was not labeled, or having to go back through census data again because you forgot to write on your notes which census tract you were describing. Whether you are fastidious or prefer ordered chaos, following a few simple rules can help avoid such disasters.

Storage Tips

The first basic rule is to imagine that someone else will have to be able to find and interpret every piece of information you gather. Each document and artifact, then, will be plainly labeled, identified, and filed. This minimal effort will greatly facilitate any later analysis.

A second general guideline is to keep all study materials in a secure place to assure very limited access to the information and to guard the confidentiality you have promised to those you have interviewed. Because several people may be working with the information, a sign-out sheet should be used to keep track of who borrows what. In some cases, you may want to allow use of materials only on the premises.

Beyond these general rules of thumb, several specific comments apply to different kinds of information.

Observational Records. Both field notes and the detailed accounts of your observations should be well-labeled and identified by the date, time, type of event, and person who did the observation. Each observational account should be stored in a file (computer or paper), perhaps with the date as the file name. Identifying information should be included on all copies (handwritten notes, as well as finished file records), and the paper file should include information about how to locate any computer records that have been created.

When you print out (or type) notes from observations, leave an extra wide margin on one side for later notes about the patterns you see emerging. Make sure to indicate clearly and in consistent fashion when you are recording an actual quote, when it is a paraphrase, and when you have noted your own comments as an observer.

Taped Interviews. Interview tapes should be kept together, perhaps in a box. Label each tape with the interview date, time, and name of interviewer. If you have promised confidentiality to the interviewees, do not write their name on the tape. Rather, create a list of those interviewed and a corresponding code number. Include this number on the tape and have a trustworthy person or two keep a copy of the names and code numbers. Use this code to identify the transcripts as well. If the interview content is of an extremely sensitive nature but must be transcribed, employ a person outside the congregation to transcribe the tape.

Archival Records, Census Data, and Historical Artifacts. Treat these objects with care, and store them carefully in a well-labeled box. Remember, most historical documents cannot be replaced. Photos, old records, and important objects are vital but often forgotten pieces of your congregation's story. Creating a record of what you have collected will serve future members who want to learn about the past. Consult the archivist at your local library about methods of storing documents that will maximize their useable life.

Content analysis records and other summaries of findings should be entered into labeled computer files, and a paper copy should be stored in a file folder. In addition, this information as well as the final report and the other collected data should be added to the archive for posterity and for future congregational studies. You might even want to create a display of this material to be shared with the entire congregation.[10]

Questionnaires. The survey forms should be collected and numbered as they are returned. The information on the forms should be turned into numerical codes (1=female; 2=male, for instance) and entered into a spreadsheet/data management system, such as QUATTRO PRO, EXCEL, or LOTUS 123. If someone on the study team is familiar with a statistical analysis program, such as SPSS, SAS, or MINITAB, one of these could be used instead. Even many word processing programs contain very elementary spreadsheet and graphics features, although these are not recommended because of their limited statistical capabilities. Each field (column) will represent a question on the survey. These columns should be labeled with names descriptive of the question, for instance "age," "gender," and the like. The information from each survey form (each case) should then be entered in a single spreadsheet row. This file should be kept both in the computer and on a separate storage disk. The actual questionnaire forms may be kept in a file folder or storage box.

Data Analysis and Interpretation

No matter how carefully gathered and stored, no information is overtly self-explanatory. If a study team observes that only males lead worship, hears interviewees say that they come only for the preaching, finds from census data that 70 percent of the neighborhood has moved in the last five years, or discovers in a questionnaire that 85 percent of respondents want a new youth program, each of these "facts" has some value. Only as it is interpreted and applied in a disciplined way to the congregational study's focusing questions, however, does the information become knowledge that can help to solve problems or provide insight.

The analysis of your well-stored volume of information can be an intimidating task, especially if it is your first study. How do you make sense of all this material? What does it say about the problem at hand? What data analysis entails—whether it is narrative, statistical, or graphic in nature—is essentially sorting out like items or events and looking for patterns or generalizations by which to summarize them. Once the information is defined by patterns, themes, or percentages of respondents, then the task of interpreting the findings can take place. You want to understand the relationship among the diverse pieces of the congregational puzzle in order to discover the picture that is implied. The process is first cumulative and then comparative. You uncover the key ideas and patterns of behavior, and then you weigh them against each other to discover their relationship to and influence upon each other. To continue with the puzzle imagery, you separate all those pieces having a straight edge or a certain color in common, and then you compare them to see which fit together and how that section relates to the picture as a whole.[11]

Organization as a Prelude to Analysis

The organization of your study material into analytical categories begins at the very inception of the research. The process of deciding your study's interests and objectives narrows your research focus and, in fact, shapes the analysis. It determines what you will look at, what tools you will use, and to some extent what categories you will use to classify your information. Therefore, while you are collecting and storing your material in the manner described above, you might also begin dividing up pieces of the information by specific topics. No doubt many of these topical file folders will be defined by your earliest interests.

For example, say your study was prompted by the rapid upper-middle class gentrification of your multiracial working-class neighborhood. The research goal was to determine what response your social-activist congregation should have. That focus might immediately suggest two separate file drawers or computer directories, one for information collected within the congregation and the other for material from the neighborhood. File dividers or computer subdirectories might then be formed around broad research areas such as demographic and economic trends, attitudes of residents toward the change, needs of new and old residents, demographics of the congregation, theological ideas about ministry, and evaluations of current or projected congregational programming. Therefore, in addition to storing your files according to date or event, you could also begin to collect records in an analytically organized fashion.

As you move toward drawing conclusions, you will need to have a clear picture of just what you know about each of the pieces of the puzzle. By putting all the similar pieces together, you will begin to get that clarity. If you want to be able to describe the range of perceived neighborhood needs, for instance, you need to have all the relevant material—census reports, interview quotes, survey results, and the like—organized and stored together.

Analysis as an Ongoing Process

Your predetermined issues and research topics are essential for focusing the study, but researching a congregation is also an *evolving process*. Throughout the information collection phase, the study team should remain open to important information about the congregation that might be outside the predetermined research interests. As you begin to organize what you are learning—even while you are still in the midst of collecting information—new questions will occur to you. Take time to read back through your files and hold reflection sessions with team members. Try to identify the key issues, the emerging patterns, and the recurring stories in what you are collecting. Make marginal notes on observation records and interview transcripts that will identify those themes. This ongoing analysis will allow you to refine your observations and interview questions as you proceed.

If you are using a computer to store your files, you can enter specific codes related to this preliminary analysis to identify sections that relate to a given topic. For instance, if an issue of race is beginning to seem significant within your examination of the changing social context, you may decide to assign the notation [RACE] to any sentence or paragraph dealing with the topic. You can then use the search feature of your word processing program to quickly move through many files to find that specific notation. These subsections can be temporarily recombined into a file containing just the relevant comments on that subject. In addition, you can create a new file folder labeled with the same notation and put paper copies of the information in it, so members of the study team without access to the computer can review the developing themes. The result of this reflective procedure is that the analysis of your material has become an ongoing process, not just one massive task saved until the end of the study.

A Statistical Aside

Both material collected on surveys and other material can be turned into numbers for statistical analysis. Such analysis can help you describe your congregation (85 percent White; 15 percent African American, for instance) and sort out the relationships among the various pieces of information you have (such as that

people who have been members fewer than five years are more satisfied with the preaching than those who have been members longer). Statistical analysis, however, can be a daunting task. This section is not meant to be an exhaustive statistical guide; rather, it is a *very elementary introduction*.[12] If a member of your study team is experienced in statistical analysis, you may want to use these tools extensively; otherwise it is best to avoid the more complex statistical operations. Nevertheless, you need to be familiar with some basic statistical concepts.

A *variable* is an aspect of social life that is composed of a logical grouping of characteristics or qualities and on which there can be variation. Gender or race can be variables, for instance, but so can theological orientation or congregational commitment. The dimensions along which a variable varies are called its *values* or *attributes*. Thus, the variable of gender has the values of male and female; that of church participation, perhaps high, moderate, and low; and theological orientation might have several categories neo-orthodox, liberationist, feminist, or (more simply) conservative and liberal.

With this understanding, one can describe the *range and distribution of the values* for any given variable. A range is defined by its possible endpoints ($5 and $5000, perhaps, on a question about pledges), and the distribution is how many people fall at each place along that range. "How many" can be reported either as raw numbers or as percentages. If you are working with fewer than thirty respondents, percentages can be misleading; just report the numbers. Note also that if a variable has only two values, you do not need to state both percentages (60 percent *and* 40 percent, for instance) because the second one is defined by the first.

It is also possible to discuss *the relationships among several variables*. In this case, you would compare two variables, say level of income and the desire to stay in a changing community, to see whether there is any correspondence between them. Of these two, the factor that is thought to influence the other variable is called the *independent variable*. That variable that has been influenced is described as the *dependent variable*. In this case, the income of the person

TABLE 7.2
"Our church should remain in this neighborhood."

Values	Frequency (Actual number)	Percent (Percent of the total)	Valid Percent (Percent of 97 responses)
1 Strongly Agree	50	50%	51.5%
2 Agree	20	20	20.6
3 Unsure, Neutral	5	5	5.2
4 Disagree	10	10	10.3
5 Strongly Disagree	12	12	12.4
Missing	3	3	xxx
Total	n=100	100%	100%

TABLE 7.3
Frequency of Attendance by Year Joined

	Joined before 1960	Joined 1960-1980	Joined after 1980
Attend once a week or more	30%	20%	50%
Attend 1-3 times per month	50%	50%	30%
Attend less than once a month	20%	30%	20%
Total	100%	100%	100%
Number of cases	40	30	80

(the independent variable) would be presumed to have a possible influence on a member's desire to move or stay (the dependent variable). If people with higher incomes are more enthusiastic about staying and those with lower incomes are less enthusiastic, you have some indication that the two things may be related to each other. Does that mean that one characteristic causes the other? Absolutely not! Many other factors could contribute to a person's feelings about the neighborhood—home ownership in the neighborhood, having school-age children, childhood experiences, and educational levels all may have a role in choosing to stay or move.

If you think a relationship you see between two factors is really a function of some third variable, you can check perceptions by *controlling* for it. Perhaps you think home ownership in the community might affect your comparison of income and desire to move. You can control for that by first separating your respondents into homeowners and nonhomeowners. Then within each group you can see whether there is still a relationship between income and desire to stay or move. While it is possible to do these sorts of simple checks (and computer programs can control multiple factors at once), it is important to remember that causation still cannot be proven. It is best to avoid the use of that word and to substitute terms like "relationship," "association," "link," "connection," or "affinity" to describe the ties between variables.

If you are using a computer program to analyze the relationships among various factors in your study, you will be offered a variety of statistical measures of association. Even if you do not use these statistical measures yourself, you are very likely to see them in reports. They will usually vary between -1 and +1 (for example, r = +.36). The two end points of that scale indicate "perfect" association—for every unit change in one variable, there is a unit change in the other. Everyone who has high income, for instance, is uniformly enthusiastic about staying in the neighborhood (and vice versa). If the direction is positive, the indication is that the two vary together (both high and both low). If the direction is negative, the statistic is telling you that they vary inversely (when one is higher, the other is lower). A value of zero indicates no association at all, meaning that how a person scores on one factor has nothing at all to do with how he or she scores on the other. Between zero and one, the closer to one (either plus or minus) the value is, the stronger the association, that is, the more cases where the pattern holds.

In addition, most statistics are accompanied by an indication of how likely it is that this result would have occurred by chance if there were really no association between the two in the population. This is often indicated by something like "p = .01," which indicates that there is 1 chance in 100 that a relationship of this magnitude would show up in your results when there really is no relationship at all. This is often referred to as the *level of significance.* To say something is "statistically significant" is not at all the same as saying that it is "significant" in the usual sense of that word. Because of this precise use of the statistical term "significant," it is good not to use the term in reports.

The important test for your use of statistics is whether they help make sense of and say something of substance about your research issue. These more complicated measures may be helpful, but simple descriptive measures may do just as well. A simple descriptive way that information can be condensed statistically is by *counting the frequency* of occurrences. Your computer program might give you results that look something like those contained in table 7.2 for the statement "Our church should remain in this neighborhood." The table shows the total number (n) of cases (survey responses) with which the computer is working (n=100) and the percent of people choosing each value—first in relation to the total number of those surveyed (percent) and then in relation only to those who responded to this question (the valid percent).

The next step may be to summarize those responses by calculating the *mean* or *average*—in the case of the data in table 7.2, 2.05, meaning that the average answer was around the "Agree" category. For some variables (such as age or income), in fact, a table of frequencies would not be helpful, since 60 of the 100 people might have different ages. You might not need to know how many forty-one-year-old people there are, but you may need to know the congregation's average age. The mean is calculated as a simple arithmetic average (sum of the frequency times the value, divided by the number of cases).

You might also want to know where the midpoint in the age distribution is. That is the *median*—the point below which half the cases fall. When you have a distribution with several very high or very low values and big gaps in between, the median may be a better indication of "central tendency" than the mean (or average), which may be skewed by these extreme values.

For items like age and income, years of education, or years of membership in the congregation, you may also want to group responses into a few categories that reflect significant dividing points (years of membership that correspond to various clergy leaders' tenure, for instance), reporting the percentage of the respondents that fall into each.

A third measure of central tendency is the *mode.* It is the answer or value that occurs most often. If you wanted to determine the most common, the most frequently mentioned zip code in your congregation, for instance, you would use the mode.

These measures of central tendency offer summaries only of the typical values. They say nothing about the distribution of responses across those values. One can obtain a mean of 2.0 for responses to whether the congregation should stay, for instance, if all the respondents answered "Agree," or if seventy-seven people answered "Strongly Agree" and twenty-five marked "Strongly Disagree." In the latter case the congregation seems highly divided, while in the former it is highly unified. It is advisable, therefore, to look at the patterns of response to see whether there are several distinct clusters, two distinct poles, or an even distribution across all the possible answers.

Thus far the discussion has focused on one variable, but what if it is necessary to compare two variables, to map their relationship? If, for instance, you asked members to rate from 1 to 7 their favorite church programs, you can calculate the mean for each program and *compare scores*. You can also compare means between different subgroups (Do young members rate the music higher than older ones, for instance?). If you want to compare how different subgroups respond, you can also construct a *cross-classification* or *cross-tabulation table*. A cross-tabulation table has a cell or box for each possible combination of two variables. Inside each box is the number of people who reported that combination of responses. For instance, in table 7.3, 30 percent of the forty people who joined before 1960 attend once a week or more. Although the raw number of respondents is not included in this table, those numbers can be calculated (30% of 40 = 12). Notice that the percentages are figured down the column but they are compared across the rows. You compare the 50 percent high attenders among those who have joined more recently with the lower percentages among earlier cohorts. To make this clear, always put the independent variable (the one thought to influence the other variable) across the top of the table. The dependent variable (the one being influenced) goes on the side.

The Concluding Analytical Task

Be forewarned: the information gathering process will never seem finished; there are always a few more people to talk to or meetings to observe. Nevertheless, institute a firm ending date or set a limit to the number of research tasks, and stick to it. Once the research is ended, the study team might want to hold a retreat or arrange for a series of extended meetings. Spend the time necessary to skim all the material col-

lected. With a disciplined reminder of the focus that sent you into this study, look again for patterns, themes, and key ideas that appear consistently in what people said in interviews, what you observed in meetings, what you found in survey responses, and how the congregation portrays itself in documents. The idea is to sort out, reorder, and reconstruct the information in a systematic and disciplined manner so that you will be able to draw generalizations, summaries, and comparisons from the material. Sidebar 7.7 outlines several possible strategies that are useful in reordering and analyzing your material.

Remember also to look for systematic differences. First, compare your findings from different research methods, looking both for similarities and discrepancies. But more importantly, look for the ways various groups in the congregation think and act differently and the ways in which members are different from people in the community. How are these affinity groups defined (age, race, education, theological predisposition, for instance), and what effects does group membership have? Remember that "group membership" does not necessarily mean participation in an organized body; what you are looking for here are the clusters of people who think and act alike because they share key common life experiences.

At this point, you can also use the various frames suggested in this book as a way to look at what you now know. Those frames may suggest key organizing categories.

Presentation of the Findings

Once you and the study team have concluded your investigation, the task of reporting the findings remains. Summarizing a research effort is not always the easiest duty. You will probably have a diversity of findings drawn from several research methods. You may have discovered outright conflicting results or at least several ambiguous findings. The congregation to whom you address the presentation might be divided and contentious. Certain members of the congregation are sure to have their own ideas and opinions, no matter what your study results show.

The first thing to remember about the final report is that the focus of your study will guide the presentation of your findings. You must directly address the research issue for the membership. The congregational report will need to explain clearly the relationships between your findings and the issues at stake. Anticipate and attempt to answer the questions on the minds of members: What did you find out? How? What brought about this situation? and How do we as a congregation see what is happening? At the same time, you will probably also want to propose possible paths of action or scenarios for moving forward, but for each possible direction you will also need to address such questions as, How do we feel about potential changes? What do we have the resources to do? What are the costs?

When constructing a final report, then, you will need to be both descriptive researcher and visionary theologian. You will have to combine information collected from various sources and by different methodological tools. You must identify the most significant findings that relate to your study's focus but also remain open to unexpected findings. Finally, you will have to present the results clearly and simply to communicate both the findings and recommendations for action. To illuminate how this reporting process might work, here is an example.

Imagine a 150-member, small-town church that has found itself in the middle of a process of suburbanization. This congregation has always prided itself on being responsive to the needs of all people in the local area. In turn, the church is seen by the town's longtime residents as their cornerstone and moral guardian. At the moment, however, changes are rapidly taking place all around. Several manufacturing plants have been built recently near a new major interstate. Middle-class residential communities are springing up within a few miles of the church. Quite a few of these new residents have begun to attend its services, but the modest sanctuary has little room for additional members. It was unanimously decided at the last annual business meeting to undertake a self-study to research how best to address this situation. How does the congregation see itself?

Does it want to change? And if so, in what directions? Ought it to build a larger sanctuary in anticipation of new members? Should it finance this construction by offering a portion of a very large, vacant piece of church property to an upscale home developer who has been pressuring the leaders to sell? What else ought the congregation do to respond to the needs of this recently transplanted constituency—as well as the bewildered townsfolk? Can the church function as the town's moral exemplar and spiritual stabilizer within this new context?

The study was led by a group of members, with the Sunday school president, a core lay leader, in charge. This group decided to use the methods of observation, group interviewing, the time-line exercise, a congregational survey, and an analysis of the church's and county's historical records. They have collected and analyzed their findings and now are faced with the final task of presenting what they found.

For this effort, they would want to create both an oral and written report. The oral report should be a succinct, narrative sketch of the key findings, whereas the written report, offered to the congregation or to specific committees, should be considerably more detailed. The information could be presented in several stages, including offering basic findings at a general congregational meeting and a more detailed report to leadership committees or even to small, informal gatherings of members.

Visual Reporting

The presentation to the congregation could begin with a graphic summary of the study's key findings. It should be straightforward, readable, and have visual appeal. Sidebar 7.8 shows a possible introductory graphic that the hypothetical self-study team might use for their presentation.

Using graphics to present data is useful for both oral and written reports. It is an effective way to summarize a large amount of information in an attractive and accessible manner. The construction and use of graphs, tables, and charts is discussed and illustrated extensively in chapter 5. The guiding principle for graphics is to portray the information in such a way that it illuminates the focus of your study. These images should clearly make a relevant point, be easy to read, and contain all the information needed to understand the categories and ideas being described.

Narrative Reporting

Another method by which this hypothetical study team could convey their findings is through the use of a narrative description. This method is particularly valuable for verbal presentations, but it can also be used in written reports. This is the method most of us use daily to describe the experiences of our lives. We do not detail the number of birthday party attendees, their race, gender, and marital status, or their reported opinions of our food and drink selections. Rather, the atmosphere and dynamics of the event is best captured and transmitted through our stories. These tales may not present "hard facts" of the event as accurately (so they may be less useful for issues of resources or needs analysis), but they are excellent ways to paint an image of an occasion or its essence (thus, making this a good method for describing a congregation's culture, its processes, or theology).[13]

With the narrative method, you might also use a pertinent sacred story to discuss your results. Or perhaps a stage image with plots, scripts, and characters might convey your findings of a congregation's culture. On the other hand, a map or geographic image may be useful. A contemporary image of the Internet to describe a network of committees could be employed. Even metaphorical references to games or specific sports might helpfully represent what you have found out about how this congregation functions.

In this narrative style the imaginary study team mentioned above would draw on an easily accessible story to describe and summarize the facts uncovered. Perhaps during the time-line exercises several older members reflected on the church's significant role fifty years ago when the area changed from a farming village to a county-seat town because of a new state road. These longtime members described the church as being the positive force for bringing together the farmers and the new townspeople. Once this historical event was recounted, the study team had reshaped its investigation and begun exploring local historical records and the church's archives, where they found material that verified and amplified the account of the church's role in this earlier shift in context. This story became a catalyst for further investigation using group interviews and a congregational survey. Considerable focus was put on the issue of the church's attitude toward and role in this current population shift.

When the time came to present its findings, the study group described this earlier event in an effort to show what they had found out about the church's historic presence in the community. Using the time-line reflections, archival information, and interview comments, they painted a picture of "who the congregation was" during its previous population shift. Picking up on one member's interview comment, "Our church might need to be the lone voice giving a good report in this crisis," the study presenters used the story of the Israelite spies returning from the promised land (Numbers 13-14) to make a symbolic point about their findings. Their findings showed that most of the membership thought the church should lead the community by bringing the positive report, as Joshua and Caleb did, that this was still the "promised land," even in the face of giant uncertainties. Interview, observation, and survey findings all confirmed this willingness to embrace the strangers and to encourage the rest of the town to do the same. This story, along with the presentation of the church's historical precedent, offered a narrative summary of both who they were as a congregation and who they should be in this new situation.

When using a narrative, it is necessary to present it in the congregation's language, ground it in members' experiences, and make sure to direct it to their concerns. Above all, be true to the data collected. A certain image may make a powerful statement about the findings, but be careful not use a story, analogy, or myth that

Sidebar 7.7
METHODS OF ANALYSIS

1. *Order and organize the information.* You might group your research materials by the predetermined topics of interest in your research. For example, in an investigation of the church's changing context, a division about internal opinions and external changes, or a controversy over the purchase of a new organ, you might group materials in three categories: opinions for, opinions against, or alternate positions. The standard categories of who, what, when, where, and how can also be used to order information. In addition, the material might be grouped by categories that arise in the study and seem crucial to the issue. Perhaps racial makeup and tenure in the congregation are found to play a part in a conflict over the style of worship; thus you could reorder material using those groups. One way to be aware of these unforseen internal categories is to be sensitive to what seems puzzling, surprising, or problematic as the study team undertakes its research. Such anomalies are often the key issues.

2. *Focus on the frame categories.* Your use of the study material might be shaped by your focus on one of the previously discussed frames of interpretation. In that case, the suggestions and perspectives within a particular chapter would give form to and guide your analysis, whether your focus is the process of leadership or the description of resources.

3. *Examine the causes and consequences.* You could use your material to assess how and why certain events or situations happen as they do. What are the patterns of events, the unfolding steps of a dynamic, the processes that take place leading to an incident, or the changes necessary to produce a conflict? You seldom can identify an exact cause, but the attempt to uncover a causal link from the collected facts can help in the analysis. For instance, what factors distinguish between those who merely visit and those who stay to become new members?

4. *Compare and contrast components.* Organize your research material around comparisons of subgroups in the congregation. These groups may include older and younger members, males and females, those attending the early and late Sunday services, and families living near and far from the church.

5. *Seek out the exceptions.* Another way to approach the analysis of collected material is to attempt to understand the information that does not fit. Look closely at the exceptions, the "deviants" in the membership or group. Examine the material from the silent minority. What keeps them quiet, and what do they have to say? Why and how do certain members not feel involved?

6. *Classify and typologize the whole.* You may be able to see overarching classifications or divisions within your material that help explain or make sense of the information. Are there types of participants, behaviors, or relationships that seem distinct and identifiable? For instance, can you identify types of people who are attracted to the congregation? Can you define levels of membership, and do they make a difference?

7. *Explore the themes.* Are there themes, myths, or significant historical stories that characterize the entire congregation? Can these key narratives be seen as formative or normative for understanding the congregation itself? For instance, if one family runs the church, does the congregation see itself as one big extended clan, and what are the implications of this? Did the historical event of choosing to remain in a Black neighborhood define the entire character and function of a congregation? How might the legacy of being the stalwart "old First Church" in a rapidly deteriorating urban setting explain its difficulties? Can you come up with an image or myth that metaphorically captures the congregational dynamics?

8. *Relate the case to a larger reality.* How does your group compare to other congregations, the larger community, the denomination, or national trends? How do your congregation's giving patterns or involvement levels compare with others in the same denomination? Is your internal culture at odds with or similar to the external cultural reality of your town? Think about the specific ways in which your congregation or group is alike or different from another.

Many of these categories of analysis are borrowed from or inspired by Warren Paap, "Analyzing Data in Short-Term Class Projects," *Teaching Society* 4 (July 1977): 333-55.

seems to misrepresent or cloud the study's issues. Often these narratives provide the congregation with an image that makes sense of their difficulty, connecting it to their lives. As chapter 6 describes, these visionary stories may provide a congregation with the spiritual resources to address its situation, whatever that might be.

Statistical Reporting

Another common method of presenting study findings is to use numerical summaries. This form of reporting is best kept to a minimum in oral presentations but can be an efficient approach for extensive written reports. It is crucial, however, that this material be carefully considered to identify exactly what are the most pertinent findings. It is not necessary to recount detailed information from each survey question used. The entire set of statistical findings can be made available, but they may also hinder effective communication of a study's results.

Our hypothetical study committee's report, for instance, contained several statistics that confirmed observational and narrative findings. The group found that a majority of the 100 questionnaire respondents (70 percent) were in favor of opening their congregation to the newcomers, with 20 percent wanting to remain as they were, and 10 percent undecided. Nearly 80 percent of those interviewed expressed a desire for the congregation to act as it had in the past, as a positive leader in this issue. It was also discovered that the opposition to inclusivity came predominantly from several young families who had recently joined and who commented on the questionnaire that they came specifically because the church was small and intimate. A final highly suggestive finding about the possible direction the church should take came from the results of the question, "Please suggest three concrete actions you think the church should take to address this present situation." The study group summarized these results in graphic form and passed out copies to those in attendance (see figure 7.1). The responses to this question offered considerable stimulation for a lively discussion during the presentation about the church's future mission to the community.

By combining different styles of reporting and methods of presentation, the hypothetical study group was able both to convey some of the pertinent information they collected and to spark useful discussion about who the church had been, how it saw itself at present, and what it wanted to be in the future. The study group had collected more information than this, but their goal in the oral presentation was to give a simplified, general overview. Their written report included many other components, examples, and analyses of their findings.

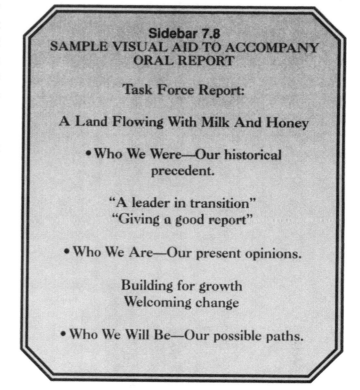

Whatever method of presentation is chosen, it is necessary to remember that a study group has the responsibility to involve the entire congregation. Make several copies of the final report available for inspection by the general membership. Invite comments and criticism. Encourage feedback on both the findings and the study process. By remaining open to feedback and comments, the study group shares with the entire membership the opportunity to shape the congregation's future direction. Even this late in the process, encourage the congregation to embrace the study and make it their own.

Conclusions

Throughout this discussion of methods for congregational studies, several themes have been emphasized. First, the study should have an explicit, well-defined focus. Second, the study from start to finish should be undertaken in a rigorous and disciplined manner. Third, the study should strive to be inclusive of the entire congregation. Once the study is completed, analyzed, and presented, these three requisites remain in effect. As a study team, you should continue to be responsible to the issue or problem that sparked the study and responsible for the continuing interpretation of the information you have gathered.

Congregational study is ultimately never "finished." The exploration of one facet of a congregation's life inevitability leads to the investigation, even informally, of other areas. These methods, we hope, provide you with a new and different way of seeing the congregation and its members. These study methods are a path into a reflective, disciplined examination that does not need to end.

Figure7.1 Proposed Actions

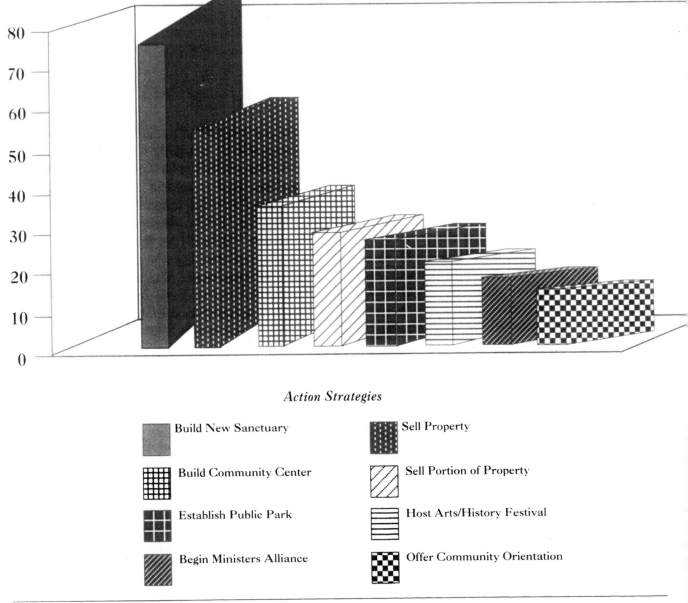

Action Strategies

Build New Sanctuary

Build Community Center

Establish Public Park

Begin Ministers Alliance

Sell Property

Sell Portion of Property

Host Arts/History Festival

Offer Community Orientation

NOTES

1. Methods specific to a single frame of analysis have been introduced in the preceding chapters. This chapter includes only those methods common to several of the chapters. Part of this discussion draws on material originally drafted by the authors of other chapters. I wish to thank both these authors and the Reverend Paul Wood, Dr. Thomas Frank, Dr. Joseph Reiff, and my spouse, Jennifer, for their comments and encouragement.

2. There are many fine general texts in research methodology. Books that address a wide range of methods include Earl R. Babbie, *The Practice of Social Research* (Belmont, Calif.: Wadsworth Publishing Co., 1995); David M. Fetterman, *Ethnology Step by Step* (Beverly Hills, Calif.: Sage Publications, 1989); Norman K. Denzin, ed., *Sociological Methods: A Sourcebook* (Chicago: Aldine Publishing Co., 1970); and Norman K. Denzin, *The Research Act: A Theoretical Introduction to Sociological Methods* (Englewood Cliffs, N.J.: Prentice-Hall, 1989).

In addition, several social scientific studies of congregations contain helpful methodological appendices. These studies include Nancy Ammerman, *Bible Believers: Fundamentalists in the Modern World* (New Brunswick, N.J.: Rutgers University Press, 1987); R. Stephen Warner, *New Wine in Old Wineskins: Evangelicals and Liberals in a Small Town Church* (Berkeley: University of California Press, 1988); R. Stephen Warner, "Oenology: The Making of *New Wine*," in *A Case for the Case Study*, ed. Joe R. Feagin, Anthony M. Orum, Gideon Sjoberg (Chapel Hill: University of North Carolina, 1991); and Samuel Heilman, *Synagogue Life* (Chicago: University of Chicago, 1973).

Several books specifically describe research on religious groups, including Richard E. Davies, *Handbook for Doctor of Ministry Projects: An Approach to Structured Observation of Ministry* (Lanham, Md.: University Press of America, 1984); Donald E. Miller and Barry Jay Seltzer, *Writing and Research in Religious Studies* (Englewood Cliffs, N.J.: Prentice-Hall, 1992); and Samuel Southard, *Religious Inquiry: An Introduction to the Why and How* (Nashville: Abingdon Press, 1976).

3. Books that specifically address the method of participant observation include John Lofland and Lynn H. Lofland, *Analyzing Social Settings: A Guide to Qualitative Observation and Analysis* (Belmont, Calif.: Wadsworth Publishing Company, 1984); William F. Whyte, *Learning from the Field: A Guide from Experience* (Beverly Hills, Calif.: Sage Publications, 1984); Danny L. Jorgenson, *Participant Observation: A Methodology for Human Studies*, Applied Social Research Methods Series, vol. 15 (Newbury Park, Calif.: Sage Publications, 1989); James P. Spradley, *Participant Observation* (New York: Holt, Rinehart and Winston, 1980); Norman K. Denzin and Yvonna S. Lincoln, eds., *Handbook of Qualitative Research* (Thousand Oaks, Calif.: Sage Publications, 1995); Catherine Marshall and Gretchen B. Rossman, *Designing Qualitative Research* (Thousand Oaks, Calif.: Sage Publications, 1995); and John Van Maanen, ed., *Qualitative Methodology* (Beverly Hills, Calif.: Sage Publications, 1984).

4. One guide on how to approach religious traditions with which you are unfamiliar is Arthur J. Magida, ed., *How to Be a Perfect Stranger: A Guide to Etiquette in Other People's Religious Ceremonies* (Woodstock, N.Y.: Jewish Lights Publications, 1996).

5. A superb example of one such sketch and its analysis can be found in Melvin Williams, *Community in a Black Pentecostal Church: An Anthropological Study* (Pittsburgh: University of Pittsburgh Press, 1974). Refer to chapter 3 for a reproduction of this drawing and a discussion of its use.

6. Sources that describe the method of interviewing in greater detail are Jack Douglas, *Creative Interviewing* (Beverly Hills, Calif.: Sage Publications, 1989); and Elliot G. Mishler, *Research Interviewing: Context and Narrative* (Cambridge, Mass.: Harvard University Press, 1986). Books on participant observation and qualitative methods, referenced above, also contain sections on interviewing.

7. One article that discusses the use of group interviewing in research is David L. Morgan and Margaret T. Spanish, "Focus Groups: A New Tool for Qualitative Research," *Qualitative Sociology* 7, no. 3 (Fall 1984): 253-70.

8. Books on the method of content analysis include Robert Philip Weber, *Basic Content Analysis: Quantitative Applications in the Social Sciences* (Beverly Hills, Calif.: Sage Publications, 1985); and Ole R. Holsti, *Content Analysis for the Social Sciences and Humanities* (Reading, Mass.: Addison-Wesley, 1969).

9. There are a large number of texts on survey research, questionnaire design and administration, and statistical analysis. These include Arlene Fink and Jacqueline Kosecoff, *How to Conduct Surveys: A Step-by-Step Guide* (Beverly Hills, Calif.: Sage Publications, 1985); Floyd J. Fowler, *Survey Research Methods* (Newbury Park, Calif.: Sage Publications, 1993); Earl R. Babbie, *Survey Research Methods* (Belmont, Calif.: Wadsworth Publishing, 1973); Donald C. Orlich, *Designing Sensible Surveys* (Pleasantville, N.Y.: Redgrave Publications, 1978); and Abraham Oppenheim, *Questionnaire Design and Attitude Measurement: Interviewing and Attitude Measurement* (New York: St. Martin's Press, 1992).

10. See James P. Wind, *Places of Worship* (Nashville: American Association for State and Local History, 1990) for additional suggestions on preserving historical records.

11. There are countless books on statistical data interpretation, several of which are mentioned elsewhere. A few books focus on qualitative or observational information, for example, Martha Feldman, *Strategies for Interpreting Qualitative Data* (Thousand Oaks, Calif.: Sage Publications, 1995); and Matthew B. Miles and A. Michael Huberman, *Qualitative Data Analysis* (Thousand Oaks, Calif.: Sage Publications, 1994).

12. There are many works describing statistical processes, analysis, and interpretation. Several of the more readable ones include Earl R. Babbie, *The Practice of Social Research* (Belmont, Calif.: Wadsworth Publishing, 1995); Richard M. Jaeger, *Statistics: A Spectator Sport* (Newbury Park, Calif.: Sage Publications, 1990); Lyman Ott, *Statistics: A Tool for the Social Sciences* (Boston: Duxbury Press, 1983); and John Hedderson, *SPSSX Made Simple* (Belmont, Calif.: Wadsworth, 1987).

13. See James Hopewell, *Congregation: Stories and Structures* (Philadelphia: Fortress Press, 1987) for a discussion of both how to go about helping a congregation construct its own story and the importance of that story for the congregation's self-understanding and empowerment. The discussion in chapter 6 regarding vision and purpose statements echoes this idea.

APPENDIX A

Parish Profile Inventory

Developed by Hartford Seminary Center for Social and Religious Research

The purpose of this questionnaire is to help your church think about its present life and plan for the future. Simply check the appropriate box or supply the required information as indicated. When answering questions with a limited number of choices, please choose the answer that comes closest to the right answer for you, even if it does not fit perfectly. Unanswered items reduce the usefulness of the inventory.

Please, do not sign your name on the questionnaire. We want to guarantee that your individual answers will be held in strictest confidence.

In some cases, more than one person in a household will receive an inventory. That is the way it is supposed to be, and it is important for each person to work independently and complete separate questionnaires. You will receive instructions from your congregation on how to return your inventory. If you misplace these instructions, you may use the address printed on the back cover.

Feel free to share any comments or concerns you have about the inventory. Space is provided on the back for that purpose, and for sharing any additional information about your church that you think would be helpful.

Thank you for your cooperation. We hope you enjoy filling out the questionnaire, and that in addition to assisting your church, you may find it a helpful means of reflecting on your faith and the meaning of your church experience.

Congregation Name: _____

APPENDIX A

I. TASKS OF THE CHURCH

A. Listed below are a number of tasks that a local church is likely to perform. Please respond to each item by indicating whether you are *generally satisfied* with your congregation's current performance of the task; or, whether you feel your congregation *needs to give it more emphasis* (that is, needs to do more of it or do it better); or, whether you feel the task currently *receives too much emphasis?*

	Needs to Give More Emphasis (1)	Generally Satisfied (2)	Receives Too Much Emphasis (3)
1. Providing worship that deepens members' experience of God and the Christian tradition	[ ]	[ ]	[ ]
2. Providing worship that expresses the Gospel in contemporary language and forms	[ ]	[ ]	[ ]
3. Providing Christian education for children and youth	[ ]	[ ]	[ ]
4. Providing Christian education programs for adults	[ ]	[ ]	[ ]
5. Helping members deepen their personal and spiritual relationship with God	[ ]	[ ]	[ ]
6. Sharing the good news of the Gospel with the unchurched	[ ]	[ ]	[ ]
7. Engaging in acts of charity and service for persons in need	[ ]	[ ]	[ ]
8. Encouraging members to act on the relationship of the Christian faith to social, political, and economic issues	[ ]	[ ]	[ ]
9. Providing a caring ministry for the sick, shut-ins, those in crisis, and the bereaved	[ ]	[ ]	[ ]
10. Providing pastoral counseling to help members deal with personal problems	[ ]	[ ]	[ ]
11. Providing fellowship opportunities for members	[ ]	[ ]	[ ]
12. Helping members understand their use of money, time and talents as expressions of Christian stewardship	[ ]	[ ]	[ ]
13. Supporting the world mission of the church through study and giving	[ ]	[ ]	[ ]
14. Helping members discover their own gifts for ministry and service	[ ]	[ ]	[ ]

B. Please read over the preceding list of 14 church tasks, and answer the following two questions by writing in the number of the appropriate task.

1. Overall, which one task does your congregation do best? _____

2. For the sake of *your own personal involvement* in your congregation, which one task would you most like to see strengthened? _____

II. ORGANIZATIONAL CHARACTERISTICS

In order to carry out its tasks, every church must deal with certain organizational issues, such as making decisions, sharing information, and developing resources. Listed below are a number of statements describing such issues. *To what extent do you agree or disagree that each statement describes your congregation?* A "Don't Know" (DK) response is provided, but please use it only when absolutely necessary.

Agreement That Statement Describes Congregation

	Strong (1)	Moderate (2)	Slight (3)	Disagree (4)	DK (5)
1. Members are well informed about what the various committees and groups in the congregation are doing	[ ]	[ ]	[ ]	[ ]	[ ]
2. The community around the church is well informed about the activities taking place in the congregation	[ ]	[ ]	[ ]	[ ]	[ ]
3. Study of the needs of the congregation and the community is regularly undertaken as the basis for church planning	[ ]	[ ]	[ ]	[ ]	[ ]
4. Members and groups get a lot of support and encouragement for trying something new in the congregation	[ ]	[ ]	[ ]	[ ]	[ ]
5. Members are encouraged to discover their particular gifts for ministry and service	[ ]	[ ]	[ ]	[ ]	[ ]
6. Lay leaders are provided the training they need for their committee and task assignments	[ ]	[ ]	[ ]	[ ]	[ ]
7. Every member who is capable and interested has an equal opportunity to hold key leadership positions	[ ]	[ ]	[ ]	[ ]	[ ]
8. The theological and biblical implications of important decisions are regularly discussed	[ ]	[ ]	[ ]	[ ]	[ ]
9. Important decisions about the life of the church are rarely made without open discussion by church leaders *and* members	[ ]	[ ]	[ ]	[ ]	[ ]
10. Disagreements and conflicts are dealt with openly rather than hushed up or hidden behind closed doors	[ ]	[ ]	[ ]	[ ]	[ ]

Agreement That Statement Describes Congregation

	Strong (1)	Moderate (2)	Slight (3)	Disagree (4)	DK (5)
11. It is easy to summarize for visitors and non-members how our congregation differs from other congregations in the area	[ ]	[ ]	[ ]	[ ]	[ ]
12. Members help each other out in times of trouble	[ ]	[ ]	[ ]	[ ]	[ ]
13. Cooperative projects and joint worship with churches of other denominations are highly valued in our congregation	[ ]	[ ]	[ ]	[ ]	[ ]
14. The *current* morale of our church members is high	[ ]	[ ]	[ ]	[ ]	[ ]
15. There is a sense of excitement among members about our church's *future*	[ ]	[ ]	[ ]	[ ]	[ ]
16. The congregation has an effective stewardship program	[ ]	[ ]	[ ]	[ ]	[ ]
17. The congregation has an effective program of new member recruitment	[ ]	[ ]	[ ]	[ ]	[ ]

III. CONGREGATIONAL IDENTITY

Listed below are several alternatives touching upon important dimensions of a church's identity. Using the seven point scale between each set of alternatives, please circle the number that best describes where your congregation falls, "1" meaning most like the characteristic on the left, "7" meaning most like the characteristic on the right, "4" meaning an equal mix of both.

1. Our church is more influenced by history and tradition.

   1 2 3 4 5 6 7

   Our church is more influenced by contemporary ideas and trends.

2. Members are similar in values and lifestyle to the people who live immediately around the church.

   1 2 3 4 5 6 7

   Members are very different in values and lifestyle from people who live immediately around the church.

3. Our church is very involved with the community around the church.

   1 2 3 4 5 6 7

   Our church is not at all involved with the community around the church.

4. Our church is primarily oriented to serving our members.

   1 2 3 4 5 6 7

   Our church is primarily oriented to serving the world beyond our membership.

5. Our congregation feels like one large family.

   1 2 3 4 5 6 7

   Our congregation feels like a loosely knit association of individuals and groups.

6. Our church is known as a prestigious one in the area.

   1 2 3 4 5 6 7

   Our strengths notwithstanding, our church is not considered one of the "status" churches in the area.

7. The church's approach to social issues is basically educational, leaving any action to individual conscience.

   1 2 3 4 5 6 7

   The church's approach to social issues is decidedly "activist." We have a proven history of taking a stand on social issues as a congregation.

8. The congregation's approach to individual salvation emphasizes education, nurture and gradual growth in the faith.

   1 2 3 4 5 6 7

   The congregation's approach to individual salvation stresses conversion and a born-again experience.

9. Our congregation gives strong expression to its denominational identity and heritage.

   1 2 3 4 5 6 7

   It would be difficult for a visitor to know to which denomination the congregation belongs.

APPENDIX A

IV. SIZE AND CONDITION OF FACILITIES

A. Please assess each of the following in terms of *size*.

	Excellent (1)	Adequate (2)	Needs Attention But Not Immediately (3)	Needs Immediate Attention (4)
1. Sanctuary	[ ]	[ ]	[ ]	[ ]
2. Educational Space	[ ]	[ ]	[ ]	[ ]
3. Fellowship Space	[ ]	[ ]	[ ]	[ ]
4. Parking	[ ]	[ ]	[ ]	[ ]

B. Please assess each of the following in terms of *general condition and aesthetic appeal*.

	Excellent (1)	Adequate (2)	Needs Attention But Not Immediately (3)	Needs Immediate Attention (4)
1. Sanctuary	[ ]	[ ]	[ ]	[ ]
2. Educational Space	[ ]	[ ]	[ ]	[ ]
3. Fellowship Space	[ ]	[ ]	[ ]	[ ]
4. Parking	[ ]	[ ]	[ ]	[ ]
5. Exterior and Grounds	[ ]	[ ]	[ ]	[ ]

V. ADULT EDUCATION AND FELLOWSHIP PROGRAMS

Which two of the following are the *best* times for you to attend adult programs? Which two are the *worst* times?

	Two Best Times	Two Worst Times
1. Weekend retreat	[ ]	[ ]
2. Saturday morning	[ ]	[ ]
3. Weekday evening	[ ]	[ ]
4. Weekday morning	[ ]	[ ]
5. Weekday afternoon	[ ]	[ ]
6. Sunday morning	[ ]	[ ]
7. Sunday evening	[ ]	[ ]

VI. TASKS OF THE PASTOR

In your judgement how high or low a priority would you like each of following tasks to be for the (senior) pastor of this church. It is worth remembering that every task can be highest priority, and that in reality, only 3 or 4 probably can be. You may want to read the entire list, then go back and make your priority rankings.

	Very High Priority (1)	High Priority (2)	Moderate Priority (3)	Low Priority (4)
1. Providing administrative leadership for the congregation's ministry	[ ]	[ ]	[ ]	[ ]
2. Actively and visibly supporting the church's stewardship program	[ ]	[ ]	[ ]	[ ]
3. Directly involving laity in the planning and leadership of church programs and events	[ ]	[ ]	[ ]	[ ]
4. Planning and leading a program of new member recruitment	[ ]	[ ]	[ ]	[ ]
5. Participating in local community activities, issues, and problems	[ ]	[ ]	[ ]	[ ]
6. Holding social justice issues before members	[ ]	[ ]	[ ]	[ ]
7. Planning and leading worship sensitive to the needs of the congregation	[ ]	[ ]	[ ]	[ ]
8. Attending to the spiritual development of members	[ ]	[ ]	[ ]	[ ]
9. Visiting the sick, shut-in, and bereaved	[ ]	[ ]	[ ]	[ ]
10. Visiting members at their home	[ ]	[ ]	[ ]	[ ]
11. Pastoral counseling of members having personal, family, and/or work related problems	[ ]	[ ]	[ ]	[ ]
12. Developing and supporting religious education program for children and youth	[ ]	[ ]	[ ]	[ ]
13. Developing and leading adult education programs	[ ]	[ ]	[ ]	[ ]
14. Supporting the world mission of the church	[ ]	[ ]	[ ]	[ ]
15. Participating in denominational activities beyond the local church, that is, at the regional or national level	[ ]	[ ]	[ ]	[ ]

VII. RELIGIOUS BELIEFS

1. Which one of the following best expresses your view of the Bible?

[   ] The Bible is a valuable book because it was written by wise and good people, but I do not believe it is really God's Word.

[   ] The Bible is the record of many different people's responses to God and because of this, people and churches today are forced to interpret for themselves the Bible's basic moral and religious teachings.

[   ] The Bible is the inspired Word of God and its basic moral and religious teachings are clear and true, even if it reflects some human error.

[   ] The Bible is the actual Word of God and is to be taken literally.

2. Which of the following best expresses your belief about sin and salvation?

[   ] Sin and salvation really don't have much meaning for me personally.

[   ] I believe all people are inherently good. To the extent sin and salvation have meaning at all, they have to do with people realizing their human potential for good.

[   ] All people are sinful, but have only to believe in Jesus Christ to be saved.

[   ] All people are sinful, but may receive salvation as meditated through the sacraments of the church.

[   ] All people are sinful, but only have to live morally responsible lives according to God's commandments and Christ's example, to earn salvation.

3. People sometimes descibe God as a "God of Justice" or a God who commands us to bring about justice. Which one of these statements best expresses your belief about what this means?

[   ] The church should work for justice and support groups that are working to end inequality and oppression.

[   ] I think of it at a more personal level. It means I should try to be just and fair in all my dealings.

[   ] Justice is actually a spiritual term that refers to God punishing evil, rather than activities of the church or individuals.

[   ] I'm really not sure what I believe about the meaning of God's justice.

[   ] Frankly, the concept of God's justice doesn't have much meaning to me personally.

VIII. YOUR CHURCH PARTICIPATION

1. How long have you been a member of this church?

   [　] Not a member   [　] 2–4 years   [　] 10–19 years
   [　] One year or less   [　] 5–9 years   [　] 20 or more years

2. How long does it usually take you to travel from home to church?

   [　] 5 minutes or less   [　] 11–15 minutes   [　] 31–44 minutes
   [　] 6–10 minutes   [　] 16–30 minutes   [　] 45 or more minutes

3. On the average, about how many times have you attended church services during the past year?

   [　] None   [　] About once a month
   [　] About once or twice a year   [　] About two or three times a month
   [　] Once or twice every three months [　] Four times a month or more

4. In how many church organizations, committees, and groups do you hold membership (not counting congregational membership itself)?

   [　] None   [　] One   [　] Two   [　] Three   [　] Four or more

5. Has your involvement in the congregation increased, decreased or remained about the same in the last few years?

   [　] Increased   [　] Remained the same   [　] Decreased

   5A. *If your participation has increased,* which of the following are reasons for that (check all that apply):

   [　] More time available   [　] Better health
   [　] Because of children   [　] Stronger faith
   [　] Accepted office or other responsibility in the church
   [　] More positive attitude toward the church

   5B. *If you participation has decreased,* which of the following are reasons for that (check all that apply):

   [　] Less time available   [　] Health problems
   [　] Because of children   [　] Decreased faith
   [　] Given up office or other responsibility in the church
   [　] More negative attitude toward the church

6. Approximately how much does your *family household* contribute to your church per year? (If single or widowed, you as an individual?)

   [　] Under $200   [　] $600–799   [　] $1,500–2,499
   [　] $200–399   [　] $800–999   [　] $2,500–3,499
   [　] $400–599   [　] $1,000–1,499   [　] Over $3,500

7. How many persons or families have you invited to visit or join your church in the past year?

   [　] None   [　] One   [　] Two–Four   [　] Five or more

8. In what denomination were you raised? If you were involved with more than one denomination when you were growing up, with which did you have the greatest identification?

   (1) [　] Baptist   (7) [　] United Church of Christ
   (2) [　] Disciples of Christ   (8) [　] Unitarian/Universalist
   (3) [　] Episcopal   (9) [　] Other Protestant: _____
   (4) [　] Lutheran   (10) [　] Roman Catholic
   (5) [　] Methodist   (11) [　] Other: _____
   (6) [　] Presbyterian   (12) [　] None

IX. BACKGROUND INFORMATION ABOUT YOURSELF

1. Gender?   [   ] Male   [   ] Female

2. Age?
   [   ] Under 20   [   ] 26–34   [   ] 45–54   [   ] 65–74
   [   ] 21–25   [   ] 35–44   [   ] 55–64   [   ] 75 or over

3. Race? [   ] White   [   ] Black   [   ] Hispanic   [   ] Other _____

4. Marital Status?
   [   ] Single, never married [   ] Widowed
   [   ] Separated or divorced [   ] Married

5. Do you have children in any of the following groups?
   a. Birth–4 years old   [   ] Yes   [   ] No
   b. Five–12 years old   [   ] Yes   [   ] No
   c. Thirteen–17 years old   [   ] Yes   [   ] No

6. What is your highest level of formal education?
   [   ] Less than high school graduate
   [   ] High school graduate
   [   ] Some college, trade, or vocational school
   [   ] College degree
   [   ] Post graduate work or degree

7. Are you (check one)?
   [   ] Retired   [   ] Employed part time
   [   ] Full time "houseperson" or student   [   ] Employed full time

   7A. *If currently employed or retired,* what is/was your occupation?
   (1) [   ] *Service worker:* policeperson, barbers, janitors, beauticians, porters, waiters, ushers, etc.
   (2) [   ] *Clerical worker:* bookkeepers, secretaries, mail carriers, telephone operators, shipping clerks, ticket agents, etc.
   (3) [   ] *Farmer*
   (4) [   ] *Operative or Laborer:* semi-skilled and unskilled workers in construction and manufacturing, apprentices, teamsters, stevedores, etc.
   (5) [   ] *Craftsmen, foremen:* tinsmiths, bakers, carpenters, masons, shoemakers, electricians, machinists, etc.
   (6) [   ] *Sales worker:* salesmen, insurance and real estate agents, brokers, stock and bond salesperson, etc.
   (7) [   ] *Proprietor, manager, or official:* public officials, credit officers, buyers, floor managers, etc.
   (8) [   ] *Professional, technical:* teachers, doctors, architects, accountants, artists, athletes, surveyors, etc.
   (9) [   ] *Other:* _____

   7B. *If married,* is your spouse employed?
   [   ] Yes, full time   [   ] Yes, part time   [   ] No

8. What is your household (family or single living alone) income range?
   [   ] Under $7,500   [   ] $15,000-24,999   [   ] $50,000-74,999
   [   ] $7,500-14,999   [   ] $25,000-34,999   [   ] $75,000 or more
                              [   ] $35,000-49,999

9. How many years have you lived in this general area?
   [   ] One year or less   [   ] 5–9 years   [   ] 20 or more
   [   ] 2–4 years   [   ] 10–19 years

10. How likely is it that you might move out of this general area within the next few years?
    [   ] Definitely will move   [   ] Probably will not move
    [   ] Probably will move   [   ] Very unlikely to move
    [   ] Might move (50/50 chance)

Comments are welcome.

APPENDIX B

Standard Demographic and Religious Involvement Variables: Examples for Alternative Styles of Question Construction

1. Age:
   Your age: ____

   What is your age? ____

   How old were you on your last birthday? ____

   Age? [ ] under 21   [ ]   26-34   [ ] 45-54   [ ] 65-74
        [ ] 21-25   [ ] 35-44   [ ] 55-64   [ ] 75 or over

2. Gender:
   Gender? [ ] Male   [ ] Female

   What is your gender? ____ man   ____ woman

3. Race and Ethnicity: [See the discussion about race and Hispanic origin in chapter 2.]
   Race? _____

   What is your race or ethnicity? _____

   Race? [ ] White   [ ] Black   [ ] Hispanic   [ ] Asian   [ ] Other _____

4. Marital Status:
   Marital Status? [ ] Single, never married   [ ] Widowed
                   [ ] Separated or divorced   [ ] Married

   What is you family status currently?
   ____ single, never married   ____ in a committed relationship (not legally married)
   ____ married (first marriage)   ____ widowed
   ____ divorced or legally separated ____ remarried after divorce
   ____ remarried after widowhood

   Are you married or single?   ____ single   ____ married
        If currently single, have you ever been married? ____ yes   ____ no

5. Income:
   What is your (total household) gross annual income? _____

   What is your annual household (family or single living alone) income range?
   [ ] Under $7,500   [ ] $15,000-24,999   [ ] $50,000-74,999
   [ ] $7,500-14,999   [ ] $25,000-34,999   [ ] $75,000 or more
                           [ ] $35,000-49,999

   Last year, your total family income was approximately:
   [ ] Under $30,000   [ ] $50,000-74,999   [ ] $100,000-150,000
   [ ] $30,000-49,000   [ ] $75,000-99,999   [ ] Over $150,000

6. Educational attainment:
   How many years of schooling have you had? _____

What is your highest level of formal education?

    ____ 1) high school graduation or less   OR   [ ] Less than high school graduate

    ____ 2) two-year college degree, some college,   [ ] High school graduate

         or a year of technical training   [ ] Some college, trade, or

    ____ 3) four-year college degree   vocational school

    ____ 4) some graduate education, but no degree   [ ] College degree

    ____ 5) master's degree   [ ] Post graduate work or degree

    ____ 6) doctoral degree

7. Occupation:

    What is your present occupation (or what was it before you retired)? _____

    If currently employed or retired, what is/was your occupation?

    [These are roughly the categories used by the United States Census.]

    [ ] *Service worker:* police person, barbers, janitors, beauticians, waiters, ushers, etc.

    [ ] *Clerical worker:* bookkeepers, secretaries, mail carriers, telephone operators, ticket agents, etc.

    [ ] *Farmer* or farm worker

    [ ] *Operative or Laborer:* semi-skilled & unskilled workers in construction, manufacturing and transportation, apprentices, teamsters, etc.

    [ ] *Craftsmen, foremen:* bakers, carpenters, masons, electricians, machinists, etc.

    [ ] *Sales worker:* salespersons, insurance & real estate agents, brokers, stock & bond sales, etc.

    [ ] *Proprietor, manager, or official:* public service, credit officers, buyers, floor managers, etc.

    [ ] *Professional, technical:* teachers, doctors, accountants, architects, artists, nurses, lawyers, etc.

    [ ] *Other:*_____

8. Employment status:

    [ ] Retired   [ ] Employed part time

    [ ] Full time "homemaker" or student   [ ] Employed full time

9. Number and ages of children:

    How many children do you have under the age of 22? ____ What are their ages? ____

    Do you have children in any of the following groups?

         a. Birth-4 years old   [ ] Yes   [ ] No   ____ Number

         b. 5-12 years old   [ ] Yes   [ ] No   ____ Number

         c. 13-17 years old   [ ] Yes   [ ] No   ____ Number

10. Number of years in the community:

    How many years have you lived in this community? _____

    How many years have you lived in this general area?

         [ ] One year or less   [ ] 5-9 years   [ ] 20 or more years

         [ ] 2-4 years   [ ] 10-19 years

11. Distance from home to work:

    How long does it take you to travel from your home to your job (one way)? _____

    How long does it take you to travel from your home to your job? _____

         [ ] 5 minutes or less   [ ] 11-15 minutes   [ ] 31-44 minutes

         [ ] 6-10 minutes   [ ] 16-30 minutes   [ ] 45 or more minutes

12. Length of membership in the congregation:

    How long have you been *attending* this congregation? _____ years

How long have you been a member of this local church?
[ ] Not a member   [ ] 2-4 years   [ ] 10-19 years
[ ] One year or less   [ ] 5-9 years   [ ] 20 or more years

13. Frequency of attendance:
About how many worship services do you attend at this parish during an average month?
About _____ services per month.

On the average, how many times have you attended worship services during the past year?
[ ] None   [ ] About once a month
[ ] About once or twice a year   [ ] About two or three times a month
[ ] Once or twice every three months   [ ] Four or more times a month

14. Congregational involvement:
Apart from worship services, about how many hours do you spend in committees, social events, educational and outreach programs of this church in an average month? _____ hours a month.

In how many church organizations, committees, and groups do you hold membership (not counting congregational membership itself)?
[ ] None   [ ] One   [ ] Two   [ ] Three   [ ] Four or more

Has your involvement in the church increased, decreased, or remained the same in recent years?
[ ] Increased   [ ] Remained the same   [ ] Decreased

15. Leadership roles in the congregation:
Within the last two years have you served on a parish committee or been on the Vestry?
[ ] _____ No   _____ Yes   _____ Number of committees

16. Congregational giving:
About how much does your household contribute to the congregation *each year*?
[ ] Less than $100   [ ] $600-$1199   [ ] $1800-$2399
[ ] $100-$599   [ ] $1200-$1799   [ ] $2400 or more

17. Distance from home to congregation:
How long does it take you travel from your home to the church? _____

How long does it take you to travel from your home to your congregation?
[ ] 5 minutes or less   [ ] 11-15 minutes   [ ] 31-44 minutes
[ ] 6-10 minutes   [ ] 16-30 minutes   [ ] 45 or more minutes

18. Congregational relation ties:
How many members of your household and extended family regularly attend here? _____

Think for a moment of your five closest friends (outside your family), how many are members of this church? _____

Among the people you consider your closest friends, how many would you say are members of your synagogue?
[ ] None   [ ] A few   [ ] Some   [ ] Most   [ ] All or almost all

19. Prior religious affiliation:
Have you ever belonged to a congregation of a different denomination? _____
yes _____ no
If yes, which denomination? _____

20. Importance or salience of religion:

How important would you say religion is in your own life?

[ ] Very important [ ] Somewhat important [ ] Somewhat unimportant [ ] Not important [ ] Unsure

21. Frequency of religious practices: (list any appropriate activity)

How often do you participate in or do the following activities:

	Daily	Weekly or more	2-3 times a month	Once a month	Few times a year	Never
Private prayer & meditation	( )	( )	( )	( )	( )	( )
Bible reading	( )	( )	( )	( )	( )	( )
Serve in church missions	( )	( )	( )	( )	( )	( )
Seek converts & new members	( )	( )	( )	( )	( )	( )

Index